# Just Enough CRM

ISBN 0-13-101017-4

Selected Titles from the
# YOURDON PRESS SERIES
Ed Yourdon, *Advisor*

## JUST ENOUGH SERIES
DUÉ  Mentoring Object Technology Projects
HAYES  Just Enough Wireless Computing
MOSLEY/POSEY  Software Test Automation
RUSSELL/FELDMAN  IT Leadership Alchemy
THOMSETT  Radical Project Management
TOURNIAIRE  Just Enough CRM
ULRICH  Legacy Systems: Transformation Strategies
YOURDON  Managing High-Intensity Internet Projects

## YOURDON PRESS COMPUTING SERIES
ANDREWS AND STALICK  Business Reengineering: The Survival Guide
BOULDIN  Agents of Change: Managing the Introduction of Automated Tools
COAD AND MAYFIELD with Kern  Java Design: Building Better Apps and Applets, Second Edition
COAD AND NICOLA  Object-Oriented Programming
COAD AND YOURDON  Object-Oriented Analysis, Second Edition
COAD AND YOURDON  Object-Oriented Design
COAD WITH NORTH AND MAYFIELD  Object Models, Strategies, Patterns, and Applications, Second Edition
CONNELL AND SHAFER  Object-Oriented Rapid Prototyping
CONSTANTINE  The Peopleware Papers: Notes on the Human Side of Software
CONSTANTINE AND YOURDON  Structure Design
DEGRACE AND STAHL  Wicked Problems, Righteous Solutions
DEMARCO  Controlling Software Projects
DEMARCO  Structured Analysis and System Specification
FOURNIER  A Methodology for Client/Server and Web Application Development
GARMUS AND HERRON  Measuring the Software Process: A Practical Guide to Functional Measurements
HAYES AND ULRICH  The Year 2000 Software Crisis: The Continuing Challenge
JONES  Assessment and Control of Software Risks
KING  Project Management Made Simple
PAGE-JONES  Practical Guide to Structured Systems Design, Second Edition
PUTNAM AND MEYERS  Measures for Excellence: Reliable Software on Time within Budget
RUBLE  Practical Analysis and Design for Client/Server and GUI Systems
SHLAER AND MELLOR  Object Lifecycles: Modeling the World in States
SHLAER AND MELLOR  Object-Oriented Systems Analysis: Modeling the World in Data
STARR  How to Build Shlaer-Mellor Object Models
THOMSETT  Third Wave Project Management
ULRICH AND HAYES  The Year 2000 Software Crisis: Challenge of the Century
YOURDON  Byte Wars: The Impact of September 11 on Information Technology
YOURDON  Death March: The Complete Software Developer's Guide to Surviving "Mission Impossible" Projects
YOURDON  Decline and Fall of the American Programmer
YOURDON  Modern Structured Analysis
YOURDON  Object-Oriented Systems Design
YOURDON  Rise and Resurrection of the American Programmer
YOURDON AND ARGILA  Case Studies in Object-Oriented Analysis and Design

# Just Enough CRM

Francoise Tourniaire

PRENTICE HALL PROFESSIONAL TECHNICAL REFERENCE
UPPER SADDLE RIVER, NJ 07458
WWW.PHPTR.COM

Editorial/production supervision: *Mary Sudul*
Composition: *FASTpages*
Acqusition Editor: *Paul Petralia*
Editorial Assistant: *Michelle Vincenti*
Marketing Manager: *Christopher Guzikowski*
Manufacturing Manager: *Alexis Heydt-Long*
Cover Design: *Nina Scuderi*
Cover Design Director: *Jerry Votta*
Art Director: *Gail Cocker-Bogusz*

 © 2003 Pearson Education
Prentice Hall Professional Technical Reference
Upper Saddle River, NJ 07458

All rights reserved. No part pf this book may be
reproduced, in any form or by any means, without
permission in writing from the publisher.

The publisher offers discounts on this book when ordered in bulk quantities.
For more information, contact
Corporate Sales Department,
Prentice Hall PTR
One Lake Street
Upper Saddle River, NJ 07458
Phone: 800-382-3419; FAX: 201-236-714
E-mail (Internet): corpsales@prenhall.com

Printed in the United States of America

10 9 8 7 6 5 4 3 2 1

ISBN 0-13-101017-4

Pearson Education LTD.
Pearson Education Australia PTY, Limited
Pearson Education Singapore, Pte. Ltd
Pearson Education North Asia Ltd
Pearson Education Canada, Ltd.
Pearson Educación de Mexico, S.A. de C.V.
Pearson Education — Japan
Pearson Education Malaysia, Pte. Ltd
Pearson Education, Upper Saddle River, New Jersey

*For Louise*

## ABOUT THE SERIES

In today's world of ever-improving technology—with computers that get faster, cheaper, smaller, and more powerful with each passing month—there is one commodity that we seem to have less and less of: time. IT professionals and managers are under constant pressure to deliver new systems more quickly than before; and one of the consequences of this pressure is that they're often thrown into situations for which they're not fully prepared. On Monday, they're given a new assignment in the area of testing, or risk management, or building a new application with the latest tools from IBM or Microsoft or Sun; and on Tuesday, they're expected to be productive and proficient. In many cases, they don't have time to attend a detailed training course; and they don't have time to read a thousand-page *War and Peace* tome that explains all the details of the technology.

Enter the Just Enough Series of books from Yourdon Press. Our mission is, quite literally, to provide just enough information for an experienced IT professional or manager to be able to assimilate the key aspects of a technology and begin putting it to productive use right away. Our objective is to provide pragmatic "how-to" information—supported, when possible, by checklists and guidelines and templates and wizards—that can be put to practical use right away. Of course, it's important to know that the refinements, exceptions, and extensions do exist; and the Just Enough books provide references, links to Web sites, and other resources for those who need it.

Over time, we intend to produce "just enough" books for every important aspect of IT systems development: from analysis and design, to coding and testing. Project management, risk management, process improvement, peopleware, and other issues are also covered while addressing several areas of new technology, from CRM to wireless technology, from enterprise application integration to Microsoft's .NET technology.

Perhaps one day life will slow down, and we'll be able to spend as much time as we want, learning everything there is to be learned about IT technologies. But until that day arrives, we only have time for "just enough" information. And the place to find that information is the Just Enough Series of computer books from Prentice Hall PTR/Yourdon Press.

## ABOUT THE SERIES EDITOR

Edward Yourdon is an internationally recognized consultant, lecturer, and author/coauthor of more than 25 books, including *Managing High-Intensity Internet Projects, Death March, Time Bomb, The Rise and Resurrection of the American Programmer, Modern Structured Analysis*, and others. Widely known as the lead developer of the structured analysis/design methods in the 1970's and the popular Coad/Yourdon object-oriented methodology in the early 1990's, Edward Yourdon brings both his writing and technical skills as Series Editor while developing key authors and publications for the Just Enough Series/Yourdon Press.

# Contents

Preface  *xvii*

Acknowledgments  *xxi*

## CHAPTER 1
## What is CRM and Why is it Important?  *1*

Express Version  *1*
What is CRM?  *2*
Elements of CRM  *3*
The Benefits of CRM  *6*
    Cost Savings  *6*
    Customer Satisfaction and Loyalty  *6*
    Increased Profits  *7*
    Increased Internal Accountability  *7*
    Employee Satisfaction  *7*
    Better Business Intelligence  *8*
    What Should you Expect for your Implementation?  *8*
Can CRM Technology Conquer All CRM Challenges?  *9*
CRM Nirvana—What Is It and Is It a Worthwhile Goal?  *10*
Why Does CRM Fail So Often?  *12*
    Politics  *13*
    People  *13*
    Process  *14*
Is CRM Just for the Big Guys?  *14*
Can CRM Work If It's Not Integrated?  *15*

Does CRM Deliver Applications or a Tool Kit?   *16*
What's the Place of IT in CRM Initiatives?   *19*

# CHAPTER 2
# Auditing your CRM System   *21*

Express Version   *21*
The Big Question: Do You Need A New CRM System?   *22*
The 5-Minute CRM Test   *23*
   Scoring   *26*
Detailed CRM Inventory   *26*
   CRM Process   *27*
   Ease of Use—For Customers   *31*
   Ease of Use—For Internal End-Users   *33*
   Ease of Maintenance   *38*
   Metrics   *39*
   Cost   *40*
Bad Reasons to Get a New Tool   *41*
   Bad Reason #1: I Saw a Cool Demo   *42*
   Bad Reason #2: We Need to Keep Up With the Joneses   *42*
   Bad Reason #3: I Don't Have The Latest Technology (But the Current Tool Works)   *43*
   Bad Reason #4: I Got A Call From A Sales Rep   *43*
Good Reasons to Get a New Tool   *43*
   We Have No CRM Tool   *44*
   We Use A Homegrown Tool   *44*
   We Have No Customer Portal   *44*
   Our Tool Is Really Slow   *45*
   Our Vendor Disappeared   *45*
   We Have Time And Resources To Do A Good Job   *46*

# CHAPTER 3
# Overview of CRM Selection and Implementation   *47*

Express Version   *47*
A High-Level View of the Entire Process   *48*
Success Factors   *49*
   Think Small, Dream Big   *49*

  Stay In the Box *52*
  Get Users Involved *56*
  Measure Success *58*
 The Three Phases of CRM Projects *60*
 How Long Will it Take? *61*
  Project Complexity *61*
  Timeline for Simple Projects *63*
  Timeline For Moderately Complex Projects *66*
  Timeline For Complex Projects *67*
  Why Timelines Cannot Be Compressed Easily *69*
  Why Vendors Substantially Underestimate Timelines *70*
  Layered Implementations *72*
 How Much Will It Cost? *73*

## CHAPTER 4
# The CRM Project Team *77*

 Express Version *77*
 What's a Good CRM Project Team? *78*
 The Executive Sponsor *80*
  Role *80*
  Requirements *81*
 The Project Manager *84*
  Role *84*
  Requirements *86*
 The Business Owners *88*
  Role *88*
  Requirements *89*
 The Super-Users *91*
  Role *91*
  Requirements *92*
 The IT Owner *96*
  Role *96*
  Requirements *97*
 The Technical Staffers *99*
  Role *99*

Requirements   *101*
How Many Resources Does It Really Take?   *102*
   New Support-Tracking System, Small Company   *103*
   New SFA System, Medium-size Company   *105*
   New Integrated CRM System, Medium-size Company   *107*
   New Support-tracking System, Large Company   *110*

# CHAPTER 5
# Requirements Definition   *113*

Express Version   *113*
Why Define Requirements?   *114*
   How Detailed Should Requirements Be?   *115*
Creating a Requirements List   *116*
   Gathering Requirements   *116*
   Ranking the Requirements   *117*
   When Do I Start Shopping?   *120*
Structure of the Requirements List   *121*
The Vendor   *122*
   Success is not All About Features   *122*
   Vendor Requirements   *123*
Technical Architecture   *124*
   Not Just a Matter for IT   *124*
   Technical Requirements   *126*
Functionality   *129*
   Who Determines the Functionality Requirements?   *129*
   Techniques for Specifying Functionality Requirements   *130*
   Functionality Requirements   *131*
   Cross-Functional Requirements   *132*
   Marketing-Automation Requirements   *144*
   Sales-Tracking Requirements   *144*
   Support-Tracking Requirements   *146*
Implementation and Maintenance   *147*
Budget   *149*
Template Requirements Checklist   *150*

## CHAPTER 6
## Shopping for CRM Systems  165

Express Version  *165*
Shopping with a Purpose  *166*
Creating the Long List  *167*
    Categories of CRM Tools  *170*
    Name, Names, Names!  *178*
Evaluating Candidates  *180*
    Keeping Track  *180*
    To RFP or not to RFP?  *180*
    Setting Up Productive Vendor Meetings  *182*
    Tough Questions for CRM Vendors  *188*
Creating the Short List  *190*
    It's a Gradual Process  *191*
    Scoring the Requirements  *191*
    Define Weights  *191*
    On or Off the Short List?  *192*
Sample RFP  *193*
    Cover Letter  *194*
    RFP Instructions  *194*
    Company Information  *195*
    Vendor Qualifications  *196*
    Product Overview  *197*
    Technical Requirements  *197*
    Functional Requirements  *198*
    Implementation and Support Requirements  *198*
    Pricing  *199*

## CHAPTER 7
## Buying CRM Systems  201

Express Version  *201*
The Home Stretch  *202*
Checking References  *203*
    Why Do a Reference Check?  *203*
    When to Check References  *204*

Picking a Good Reference  204
Whom to Ask  207
Are References Impartial?  207
Who Should Do the Reference Check?  208
What to Ask  209
Seeing a Demo  214

Negotiating the Contract  215
When Should You Negotiate the Contract?  215
Who Should Negotiate the Contract?  216
Contract Points to Consider  216

Getting the Best Price  222
Discounts are Meaningless  222
Use Good Old Competition  222
Understand the Sales Rep's Compensation  223
Play the Clock  223
Negotiate Now, Buy Later  223
Site Licenses  224
Focus on Maintenance and Support  224
Pay Late  226
Odds and Ends  226
Are Used-Car Buying Techniques Worthwhile?  227

Preparing an ROI Justification  228
Costs  228
Benefits  230
Are ROI Analyses Realistic?  235

# CHAPTER 8
# Selecting an Integrator  237

Express Version  237
What's An Integrator And Do I Need One?  238
When Do I Start Looking for an Integrator?  240
Tool Vendor or Third Party?  241
Mix and Match?  243
Are Certified Partners Better?  244
Implementation Scenarios  245

Finding Integrators  *248*
  Is Small Beautiful?  *249*
Evaluating Integrators  *249*
  Integrator Requirements List  *250*
  Evaluating the Integrator  *254*
  Checking Integrators' References  *254*
Negotiating With Integrators  *259*
  Fixed Price or Time and Materials?  *260*
  Contract Checklist  *261*

## CHAPTER 9
# Implementing CRM Systems  *263*

Express Version  *263*
Implementation Overview  *264*
The Kickoff Workshop  *265*
  What Should It Cover?  *266*
  Who Should Be There?  *270*
  How Long Should It Be?  *270*
  Where Should It Be Held?  *272*
  Who Should Drive It?  *272*
  Managing A Successful Workshop  *273*
A Few Technical Notes on the Implementation  *275*
  Development/Test/Production Environments  *275*
  Data Migration  *276*
Testing  *277*
  Use Cases  *277*
  Functionality Testing  *279*
  Load Testing  *280*
Training  *280*
  What Should the Training Cover?  *280*
  Who Should Create the Training  *281*
  When Should It Be Delivered?  *282*
The Rollout  *283*
Successfully Managing an Implementation  *285*
  Milestones  *285*

Status Reports  *286*
  Keeping the Tool Vendor in the Loop  *287*
Care and Feeding of the Integrator  *287*
  Make the Staffers Productive Onsite  *288*
  Make the Staffers Productive Offsite  *288*
Involving the Users  *289*
Internal Promotion  *290*
Customer Promotion  *292*
  Focus on Benefits  *292*
  Use Many Channels  *292*
  To Limit Access or Not?  *293*
  Leverage Customer Usage  *294*
Handling Implementation Problems  *294*
  You Can't Expect a Trouble-Free Implementation  *294*
  Resolving Issues  *295*
  Should You Ever Give Up?  *296*
Post-mortem Review  *296*

# CHAPTER 10
# Measuring Success  *299*

Express Version  *299*
Why Metrics Matter  *300*
  Didn't We Talk About ROI Already?  *301*
Types of Metrics  *301*
  What Makes a Good Metric?  *302*
  Tangibles vs. Intangibles  *303*
  Strategic vs. Operational  *304*
  Short-Term or Long-Term?  *305*
Garbage In…  *306*
  Get the Logging Religion  *307*
  Make it Easy to Log  *307*
  Capture Customer Satisfaction  *308*
Don't Be Average  *310*
Slicing and Dicing, Babushka-Style  *311*
More is Not Better  *312*

Marketing and Lead Generation  *312*
　　　Sales  *313*
　　　Support and Service  *313*
　The Dashboard Concept  *314*
　　　It's Short  *314*
　　　It Shows Key Metrics Against Targets  *315*
　　　It Shows Trends  *315*
　　　It's Visual  *315*
　Streamline Delivery  *316*
　　　Make Metrics Widely Available  *316*
　　　Use Subscriptions  *316*
　　　Make Them Timely  *316*
　　　Make Them Automatic  *317*
　　　Make Tweaking Easy  *317*
　　　Make Spreadsheet Analysis Easy  *317*
　Suggested Metrics  *317*
　　　Lead Generation Analysis  *318*
　　　Telesales Productivity  *319*
　　　Sales Pipeline  *320*
　　　Sales Productivity  *321*
　　　Support Productivity  *321*
　　　Support Issue Distribution  *322*
　　　Support Case Aging  *323*
　　　Knowledge Base Productivity  *324*
　　　Customer Satisfaction  *325*
　　　Support Financials Summary  *326*
　　　Top 10 Customers  *327*
　　　Knowledge Base Usage  *327*
　Where do I Go From Here?  *328*

## CHAPTER 11
# Rescuing a Failing CRM Project  *331*

　Express Version  *331*
　Project Failures  *332*
　Step 1: Assess  *332*
　　　Why Projects Fail  *332*

The Assessment Session  *333*
Can the Project be Saved?  *337*
Step 2: Restructure  *338*
Step 3: Restart  *340*
Budget and Schedule  *340*
The Process  *340*

# CHAPTER 12
# CRM Resources  *343*

Web Sites  *343*
Sites for CRM Information  *344*
Sites for Sales and Marketing  *344*
Sites for Support And Service  *345*
Sites for IT  *345*
Magazines and Trade Publications  *346*
Magazines for Sales and Marketing  *346*
Magazines for Support And Service  *346*
Magazines for CRM  *346*
Magazines for IT  *346*
Books  *346*
Analysts  *347*
Conferences  *348*

# Glossary  *349*
# Index  *361*

# Preface

## What's the Book About?

This book is a practical guide for business users on how to select and implement CRM tools successfully. Despite frequently repeated claims that CRM projects are more likely to fail than to succeed, I believe that well-thought out, well-run CRM projects do succeed, and I'm ready to share the techniques and approaches used by successful CRM project managers.

The book focuses on CRM tools but it's difficult to discuss the tools without considering the larger context of the business processes and the organizations that use the tools. In fact, limiting one's vision to the tools while neglecting the surrounding processes and the people who use the tools is a recipe for disaster, so there will be plenty of discussion of how to integrate the tools into the processes and into the organization.

Here are the tasks you can expect to master by reading the book:

- Appreciate the relative roles of process, technology, and implementation in the success of CRM.
- Audit the performance of your current CRM tool.
- Create an appropriate plan for CRM selection and implementation with logical phases and sequencing.
- Select an effective team for a CRM selection or implementation project.
- Select a CRM system that fits your unique requirements by leveraging customizable checklists and following a systematic selection strategy.
- Identify a solid good implementation partner by asking the right questions of the candidates and of the references.
- Manage a CRM implementation project to a successful conclusion.
- Measure success during and after implementation.

The book focuses on mid-sized implementations for companies that have between $10 million and $500 million in revenues, although the same ideas can be applied to both smaller and larger organizations. Larger companies will typically require more in-depth process analysis than is described here, while smaller companies can make do with simple packages that require minimal customizations—unless of course they are planning a rapid expansion in which case they should proceed as mid-sized companies would.

The book focuses on what can be a very technical process, selecting and implementing CRM tools, but it's not a technical book. Instead, it takes the point of view of a technically savvy business user. Technology is never discussed for technology's sake, but always in the context of how it can influence business results, whether in the positive or the negative. So, for example, it doesn't discuss how to create Java code, but it mentions when it's a good idea to ask the vendor about Java code. This is not about cool, leading-edge technology; it's about meeting your business goals.

This book is also useful for IT personnel who want to be a partner with the business users to deliver successful CRM implementation projects. It gives practical recommendations for creating a CRM team that unites the efforts of the business team and the IT team and for leveraging contributions from both sides throughout the project.

# How Do I Use the Book?

You may choose to read the book in a linear manner or focus on specific topics. Here is how the chapters are organized:

Chapter 1, "What is CRM and Why Is It Important," sets the stage by inventorying the many components of CRM systems, listing the benefits of CRM, and answering many dilemmas about CRM implementations. Start there to get oriented to the field of CRM, especially if you are skeptical about whether CRM can benefit your organization.

Chapter 2, "Auditing Your CRM System," is a great place to start if you already have a CRM system installed but you are not sure that it's as good as it can be. You'll find some practical tools to evaluate whether your system is up to par and whether issues may be stemming from other causes such as faulty processes.

Chapter 3, "Overview of CRM Selection and Implementation," gives you an orientation to the entire process. Start there if you are just beginning to think about CRM and you need a general orientation to what it takes to implement a successful project. Also start there if you are involved in a CRM project that's in its infant stages.

Chapter 4, "The CRM Team," describes the elements of a successful implementation team, including who should be on it, when it makes sense to hire help, and what technical and personal characteristics to look for in the various team members. In many ways the team makes or breaks the project, so don't skip this chapter.

Chapter 5, "Requirements Definition," discusses the first phase of CRM projects. It contains a template of a detailed requirements checklist as well as a process for creating your own custom checklist.

Chapter 6, "Shopping for CRM Systems," gives an alternative to the standard request-for-proposal (RFP) model. It contains advice on how to get enlightening demos from vendors and helps you avoid time-wasting standard sales presentations while getting more accurate answers to your evaluation questions.

Chapter 7, "Buying CRM Systems," focuses on the negotiation phase of the project to get the best deal in the short and long-term. It includes tough questions to ask the vendors and the references, as well as a step-by-step guide to negotiating the terms and conditions of the contract and the price.

Chapter 8, "Selecting an Integrator," describes how to find a solid integrator to implement the system. The best course of action is almost always to engage an outside party to assist with the tool implementation. This chapter discusses how to conduct the integrator selection concurrently with the tool selection and what to look for.

Chapter 9, "Implementing CRM Systems," walks through a CRM implementation, demonstrating how to integrate rapid-development techniques and early customer acceptance. If you have already selected a tool, read this chapter before the start of the implementation phase. This is a chapter you will come back to again and again during the implementation phase.

Chapter 10, "Measuring Success," is all about metrics. It discusses how to define metrics to measure both the success of the CRM project itself and the health of the business, leveraging the metrics capabilities of the tool to maximize the benefits you derive from it. This chapter is useful both during and after the implementation.

Chapter 11, "Rescuing a Failing CRM Project," talks about handling a failing project. It gives a three-step process for deciding whether a project is worth saving and how to restart it so it can be successful. Start here if your project is not working well, or if you inherited a sick one. Most projects can be salvaged, but not without making appropriate changes.

Chapter 12, "Resources," contains additional information sources, be they books, web sites, conferences, and magazines. The CRM field is very dynamic so it's important to know where to find the current information, beyond this necessarily static book. Chapter 12 gives you a rich set of references to continue your education in the CRM field.

The book also includes a glossary of all the key words used in the book for your reference.

## About Express Versions

Your time is valuable. For all of you skimmers each chapter starts with an executive summary that gives you a one-page summary of the concepts covered in the chapter. If you'd like more details, just read the relevant parts of the chapter.

Welcome to the occasionally puzzling but wonderful world of CRM. Happy trails!

# Acknowledgments

Many colleagues and friends helped me create this book and I thank them for dedicating many hours to review draft after draft, clarifying ideas, smoothing the flow, and throwing in encouraging comments to boot.

Andrew Marks shared the reality of implementation projects based on his long experience directing CRM projects to successful conclusions. I also thank him for his input on RFPs.

Naval Gupta kept my feet and my words on firm ground for the technical side, patiently untangling concepts until I got them, and generously sharing his implementation experience as well. I looked forward to his feedback that always contained positive comments regardless of the amount of red ink.

Ralph Wilson must read every tidbit of information about CRM, for he brought to my attention many ideas and facts I was not aware of. He also has a knack for divining clear thinking and clear sentences out of my muddled drafts. (Any remaining muddle is all mine.)

Richard Farrell took the time to discuss each and every chapter in a leisurely conversation, encouraging me to discuss big ideas and not to get stuck in the nitty-gritty. He spotted many opportunities to improve the overall flow of the book.

Thank you also to A.C. Ross, John Houtsma, Lyle Ekdahl, Mitch Bishop, Paul McGhee, Richard Kline, and Susan Munne for their suggestions and help.

# What is CRM and Why is it Important?

## Express Version

- This book focuses on Customer Relationship Management (CRM) as a tool set that exists within a larger context of processes and functions.
- The benefits of CRM include decreased costs and increased customer loyalty combining to create higher profits, as well as increased internal accountability, employee satisfaction and better business intelligence. Some of the benefits are hard to quantify, and hence are rarely measured (but they can and should be, as we will see in Chapter 10).
- Despite the tool vendors' claims, CRM technology is not enough for success. It has to be embedded into solid processes.
- CRM nirvana is a completely integrated set of tools that support all customer-focused activities in the company. However, partial solutions can be very successful, whether or not they eventually merge into a fully integrated solution. Piecemeal approaches are also much more likely to succeed than long, complex projects.

- Despite well-publicized failures, most CRM projects are successful. Following the techniques described in this book will greatly improve your chances for success.
- Mid-sized enterprises can derive great benefits from CRM, although they should not necessarily follow the complex and expensive approaches that larger companies use.
- Successful CRM implementations bring IT and business functions together into the CRM team. This book focuses on a non-technical approach to CRM that can be used by both business and IT managers.
- The CRM field is dynamic so updating your knowledge through current articles and conferences is important.

# What is CRM?

CRM stands for *Customer Relationship Management* and is used quite loosely to refer to three things:

- The entire field of Customer Relationship Management, that is, all customer-focused functions such as marketing, sales, and customer support.
- The tools used by such functions such as sales force automation (SFA).
- Something in between the two, usually the processes involved in managing the relationship with the customer.

This sloppy use of the term CRM to mean many things can get pretty confusing, and unfortunately few articles and books clearly define the specific meaning they are using, while others use more than one meaning within the same piece. It's a mess!

The CRM name and abbreviation were invented specifically to refer to the then-emerging class of tools that automate the customer-contact functions. This book focuses on CRM tools, bringing in discussions of the surrounding processes only as they relate to the success of the tool project itself. However, we will see that there are plenty of opportunities to discuss the larger context since technology by itself cannot make a CRM project successful, regardless of the claims some tool vendors make about it.

# Elements of CRM

CRM has grown into a dense and tangled field, and many vendors that provide only a small piece of the puzzle call themselves CRM vendors, making it difficult to sift through the claims. In addition, many back-office systems are sprouting customer portals and other features close to CRM functionality, so the boundaries are not as clear-cut as they were. Here's a survey of classic functionality categories for CRM systems (Figure 1.1).

- **Sales force automation (SFA)**. Some call it the star of the lot, and it was one of the two early drivers of the CRM field, the other one being support tracking. SFA tools track prospects, contacts, and activities, allowing managers to follow leads through the pipeline, forecast revenue, and catch bottlenecks. Many systems include aids to the sales process such as proposal and quote generators. Because of the revenue-forecasting requirements, SFA has always emphasized metrics even more than other areas of CRM..

A unique characteristic of SFA is the requirement for supporting mobile, disconnected users. Field sales reps need to download relevant account information to their PCs, update it while away from the office, and then upload it back into the shared system. This calls for robust synchronization capabilities so the downloads and uploads can hap-

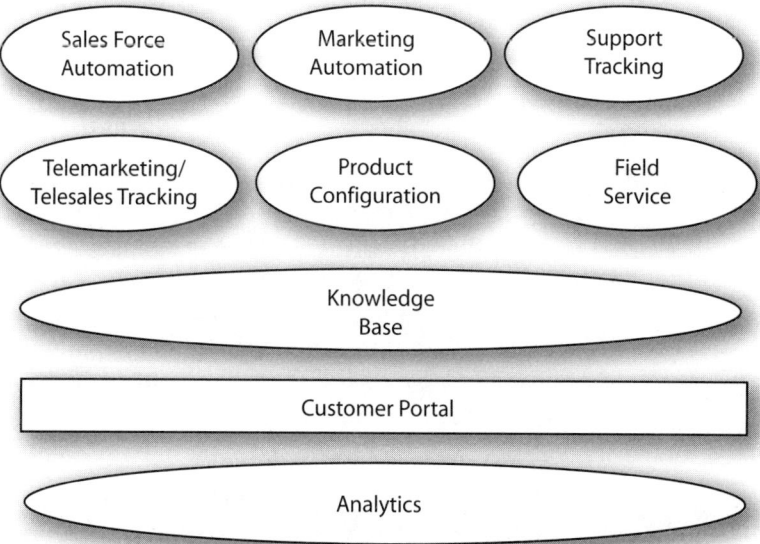

**FIGURE 1.1**
Elements of CRM

pen quickly and maintain data consistency even if multiple updates occur.

- **Telemarketing and telesales tracking**. Although they can be considered a part of SFA, tools for telemarketing and telesales operations tend to be quite a bit different because telemarketers often work from scripts, or at least in a much more structured environment. They do not need mobile, disconnected functionality. In many ways, their requirements are closer to those of support tracking and indeed many vendors offer contact center modules that can serve both inbound and outbound contact centers. ("Contact center" is the modern and accurate term for what used to be known as a call center).

  Part of the functionality of a contact center application is computer telephony integration (CTI), which allows information to be shared between the phone system and the CRM application. Typical applications of CTI include routing calls, either based on the incoming phone number or on information entered by the customer into the phone system as directed by menu choices, and the ability to display screens containing the caller's information a split second ahead of delivering the call (so-called screen pops). CTI can also manipulate the phone system based on information in the CRM database, for instance it can dial phone numbers as displayed on a user's screen.

- **Product configuration**. Product configurators are tools that allow users to customize complex products to their exact requirements. Product configuration used to be an activity that took place off-line and outside the interactions with the customers, but now configurators are part of many CRM suites. This is partly due to the influence of e-commerce, which requires that instant configurations be available to customers.

- **Marketing automation**. Often called campaign management, marketing automation allows the design, execution, and management of campaigns. Depending on the sophistication of the tool, the campaigns may use a variety of media and include segmentation and list management capabilities. Marketing event planning is another potential component of marketing automation.

- **Support tracking**. With SFA, support tracking is the other historically important part of CRM. Basic support-tracking features include the ability to track the history of support requests from inception to resolution, including routing, ownership, escalations, and transfers. Integration with phone (CTI, described above) and electronic communication systems (e-mail and the customer portal, described below) is often provided, although by no means a given. Another important area is the provision of a customer database to track service contracts. The contracts area is where integration with the sales system or with the accounting system may come into play.

- **Field service**. Field service has different requirements than service that is provided from a support center, much as a telemarketing group needs different features than a field sales force. Like field sales, field service employs a mobile workforce and it has special requirements such as the management of parts and spares. Many field service tools allow users to communicate through wireless communications.

- **Knowledge base**. Knowledge base functionality is useful in all areas of customer-focused functions. There are really two different types of functionality here. One is the ability to expose the knowledge base to the users through a variety of search capabilities. The other, more important in many ways although less discussed (I think because it doesn't demo well), is the ability to support the creation and maintenance of documents. Knowledge creation and maintenance becomes very complex with large amounts of information.

  Knowledge base functionality serves both internal and external users through a permission scheme that allows only selected documents to be exposed to external users. Tools that separate internal and external knowledge base systems create a lot of extra work and miss the point of a knowledge base, in my opinion.

- **Customer portal**. Web-based customer access to the CRM system is now an absolute requirement. Basic customer portals allow access to the knowledge base and to the request-tracking system, but more and more sophisticated functions are expected including branch locators, electronic downloads, online chat sessions, and so forth. Proactive e-mail alerts are often conceived as being part of customer portals. Customer portals and the functionality around them are sometimes called eCRM and the subsystems are called e-sales, e-marketing, or e-support.

  A lot of attention is now placed, and rightly so, on personalized portals, where customers can control what they want to see. Customer portals are also going wireless to serve customers that do not have access to traditional browsers.

  The customer portal should not be confused with the ability of internal users to access the CRM system through the web. Modem tools offer what's called thin-client functionality, whereby they can be manipulated through a web browser even by internal users. Older tools offer a thick-client interface in a traditional client-server setup, requiring installation of the client on each user's machine. (And, for complete confusion, older tools with modern ways offer both thin-client and thick-client interfaces, often with different functionality, not to mention different looks.) We will discuss the pros and cons of both types of interfaces in Chapter 5, "Defining Requirements for a CRM System."

- **Analytics**. One of the benefits of CRM is an improved ability to view and analyze customer-related activities. Once a poor relative of other CRM functionality, analytics have become big business and are often sold separately as a value-added option. Although clever reporting is important, the main success factor for analytics is to have good data, so make sure that the data you need is indeed captured by the system, and that users are indeed entering it as required.

Some tools live on the fringes of the CRM world. For instance, workforce management tools provide functionality to schedule staff in customer contact centers, integrating sophisticated requirements about shift length, skills, and logistical constraints. Another example is monitoring tools that allow contact centers to record interactions for security or quality monitoring purposes.

# The Benefits of CRM

It's true that the benefits of CRM are often overstated, especially by vendors, but it doesn't mean that CRM tools are useless. Properly implemented, they can and should bring a whole set of tangible benefits.

## Cost Savings

This is often the first goal that is reached for (if not always attained) during CRM initiatives. The idea is that the technology will make it easier to reach customers, to sell to them, and to service them. Self-service tools are often sold solely with a cost-saving rationale, but most other CRM tools, from quote generators to internal knowledge bases, are also likely to produce cost savings by boosting employees' productivity. We will revisit this topic when we discuss return on investment (ROI) for CRM implementations in Chapter 7.

## Customer Satisfaction and Loyalty

Good CRM tools make it easier for customers to do business with you, whether it is through the flexibility of self-service, by being able to get what they need faster because employees can be more efficient thanks to the tool, or by receiving targeted information that is immediately useful.

Several studies[1] have shown that highly satisfied customers are not merely happy: they buy more, cost less to service relative to what they buy, are less price-sensitive, and are happy to spread the word about the vendors they favor. So there is a distinct business advantage to cultivating loyal customers.

## Increased Profits

Profits are the ultimate test and a consequence of both the cost savings and the increased customer loyalty described above. It's not always easy to tease out the part CRM plays in increased profits, however, since by the time profits show up many underlying variables have changed beside the new CRM system. So it's particularly important to devise strategies to measure the increase in profits attributable to the CRM tool.

## Increased Internal Accountability

By assigning and tracking tasks, the CRM tool makes it possible for everyone to follow the flow of requests from owner to owner, to analyze adherence to SLAs (service-level agreements) and to note any delays or errors. This is helpful both for managers who want to evaluate their teams' performance and also for function owners who need to coordinate with other functions. No more wondering about who owns a particular issue, whether something fell through the cracks, or whether there is a systemic problem when issues are handed off from one group to the other.

## Employee Satisfaction

Few CRM implementations bother to quantify their impact on employee satisfaction, perhaps because employee satisfaction is rarely measured, and in any case apportioning the effect of CRM implementations on employee satisfaction is very difficult. The reality is that the availability of good tools makes a big difference to employees, especially the employees who are eager to deliver better value to customers (in other words, the more valuable employees). Employee satisfaction matters because satisfied employees vote with their feet: they stay and reduce costly turnover. Satisfied employees also are likely to be more productive.

---

1. *The Loyalty Effect: The Hidden Force Behind Growth, Profits, and Lasting Value* and *Loyalty Rules! How Leaders Build Lasting Relationships in the Digital Age*, both by Frederick H Reichheld Harvard Business School Press 2001.

## Better Business Intelligence

Another benefit that is difficult to quantify, better business intelligence means that you can get to know your customers better so you can adapt your products, marketing strategies, and support levels accordingly. The more modern CRM tools tend to have much better built-in analytics so you can really take advantage of the customer data that is stored in them. The main obstacle to getting better business intelligence is actually not the tool itself, but rather the fact that the existing data is not exploited as well as it could be. For instance, there are many support organizations that don't have a process to identify and address the top issues that customers call about, even though it would quickly translate into large cost savings.

## What Should you Expect for your Implementation?

What benefits can you reasonably expect from a CRM implementation? All of the above, although the extent and timing will depend on the scope of the implementation. For small-scope projects such as self-service support, you may see significant savings within a few weeks of rollout as the caseload drops significantly, especially if most support requests are straightforward. Generally speaking, all CRM projects should result in cost savings, although rarely so quickly.

Improved customer satisfaction can be more elusive than cost savings, not so much because of weaknesses in the tool itself but because the customer is not always put at the center of process definition. In other words, many projects view the customer as an entity to be managed rather than as a volunteer who will gladly participate if the CRM offering is attractive and delivers tangible benefits. Not surprisingly, customer satisfaction may drop if the net effect of the CRM implementation is to put a barrier between customers and their human helpers within the company.

Profits should follow cost savings and increased customer satisfaction, but you need to be patient. Even after months of implementation work, it takes time for the users to fully master the new technology and even longer to see tangible benefits, again depending on the scope of the project. It will take many months to a year before you see increased profits on larger projects, but the good news is that the profits can be significantly larger than for a small-scale project.

In any case, if you want to establish and quantify tangible benefits from your CRM project you must set quantitative goals and a baseline before you start so you can keep a scorecard of the impact of the project. We'll come back to this later.

It's now time to address common questions and negative perceptions about CRM, all issues that may be on your mind as you decide whether to take the plunge. We'll discuss the following:

- whether CRM technology can conquer all CRM issues;
- whether CRM nirvana is a good goal to have;
- the true failure rate of CRM projects;
- why CRM is important for all companies, not just the very largest;
- why you should get going with CRM even if all you do is a small piece;
- when CRM technology should be viewed as a tool kit rather than as an application;
- the proper roles of IT versus the business owners in a CRM project.

# Can CRM Technology Conquer All CRM Challenges?

We've already visited the multiple meanings of CRM, so we know that CRM can mean many things. The real question is whether CRM technology can bring order to chaos in customer-focused functions. Despite what the CRM vendors say, the answer is a clear *no*: CRM tools by themselves do not solve customer management problems.

Indeed, many companies with excellent systems for managing customer interactions use very simple tools, and moreover their tools may be a little behind the times. They don't try to automate all customer interactions. They don't put either the tool or even the process at the center of things. Instead, they define processes around customer needs and they position the CRM tools as aids to the telemarketer, sales rep, or support rep, offloading routine tasks such as generating and approving quotes, checking order status, or tracking support inquiries. You can be successful at managing customer relationships with minimal tools.

Successful CRM projects recognize that the tool is only one piece of the puzzle when it comes to managing customers. The tool needs to model and support a reasonable process, whether the process pre-dates the tool or, more likely, the process is reshaped to match both the existing environment and the technology. But the tool does not dictate the way the process works, either for the customer or for the internal user.

As a consequence, there is no one perfect tool out there that will fit every need. A tool that functions well in one environment may not fit another with different requirements. Think for instance of how a good business-to-consumer sales tool would fail in a business-to-business selling environment. And even a perfectly well suited tool can be implemented poorly and therefore fail to meet the goals. A simple example of that would be a clumsy custom user interface on an otherwise well-designed application.

CRM technology is only one piece of the larger CRM challenge. There is no magic tool that will handle all customer management issues in and of itself.

## CRM Nirvana—What Is It and Is It a Worthwhile Goal?

Like all great ideas, CRM has been oversold. The vision in the early days (the early 1990s) was for a completely integrated customer relationship universe, from which each employee would have a perfectly transparent view of each customer interaction. While very few implementations have reached this peak, those that have often prove that complete integration has its problems, as the level of detail available through integrated implementations can be overwhelming. For example, it's easy enough for a sales rep about to visit a customer to check the system and see that the customer has two support cases open. But for complex issues it may be difficult to correctly gauge their severity, requiring a call to the support team to clarify the situation, or worse, walking into a minefield at the customer site because of a failed interpretation of the notes in the system. More data is not always helpful.

Beyond integrating the various customer-focused functions (for example, giving sales reps the ability to monitor support cases) lies another thorny problem: integrating the customer-focused functions with the back-office systems (allowing sales reps to have access to the accounts receivable records of the customer, for instance). In a funny way, as employees start to enjoy the benefits of tracking customer interactions, they may suffer more acutely from being unable to easily access information that is required to work with customers, such as accounting information or production information, but is stored in other systems.

Finally, the vision from the early days now needs to include the web and the requirement that the systems be open to customers. Today's CRM nirvana includes appropriate portals so customers can buy online, access their buying history, interact with support online, and conduct all their business electronically if they need to.

If we combine all of the factors above, CRM nirvana would be a completely integrated tool:

- bringing together all customer-focused functions (so customer-focused employees can access all customer-related interactions through a single interface, at least within the limits of their authorization levels);
- linking seamlessly to back-office data (so customer-focused employees can access any corporate data required to respond to a customer inquiry through a single interface, again as limited by authorization schemes);
- providing online customer access (so customers can seek their own answers through the same systems, within the constraints of their authorization).

No one said nirvana was easy!

CRM nirvana is not a bad goal in itself, although I'll come close to making that statement later in the chapter. But most companies can be very successful with a more modest approach. For example, many companies with a long, complex sales cycle can often isolate the sales process and issues quite successfully from the service side. Once the customer makes a purchase, they simply record that customer in the (separate) service-tracking system, ideally at the time of purchase but sometimes only at the time of the first service request, and take it from there. Service never sees the details of the sales cycle, and that's just fine. In such a setting, installing a sales-tracking tool that is not accessible from other systems or functions can be very successful.

Even in environments where a completely integrated approach is required, starting with isolated pieces that are eventually brought together is often the right thing to do. This is because ambitious projects bring more risks because of their sheer complexity and the lack of a coherent executive sponsorship, which will be discussed at more length in later chapters.

So CRM nirvana may be a good theoretical goal, but it's not essential in every case, and it should not be used to block a project just because the project is not comprehensive. Start your CRM project where it hurts and concentrate on getting that particular area taken care of. Ensuring that each individual piece fits in the larger picture is a secondary goal, although important in the long run, especially from the point of view of a CIO.

## Why Does CRM Fail So Often?

It's become almost fashionable to talk about the high failure rate of CRM projects. For instance, an often-cited Gartner study from late 2001[2] claims that over half of CRM projects fail to deliver on expected savings and business advantages. Is CRM the kiss of death? I think not. If we look behind the numbers we find much more encouraging facts.

First, many projects that are classified as failures, including in the famous Gartner study, are not failures at all in the normal sense of the word. They simply "failed" to set objective, quantifiable objectives from the start and therefore cannot claim to have achieved any specific objectives. It's certainly sloppy to start projects without defined goals, but I will let others who have never sinned throw that first stone!

Second, even projects that fail to reach their stated objectives may not be complete failures. Let's say that an SFA implementation project targeted a 10% decrease in sales costs, but finds that the decrease is only 8%. Is that a failure? Yes, in the sense that it did not achieve the goal, but the organization did save money, and a sizable amount of money at that. Considering the level of guessing, padding, and maneuvering that takes place during goal-setting sessions, especially for long-term projects, I would be tempted to consider such a project a success.

So it's not true that most CRM projects fail. But some do fail, and I've certainly seen my share of failures. Some projects don't make it to completion and are halted before deployment because of technical or other issues. Some projects are deployed but cancelled shortly afterwards because of grave shortcomings. Yet other projects are deployed and stay deployed but fail to serve their users, whether employees or customers, and are usually widely reviled as such. All those are failures in the real sense of the word. You will notice that I don't include projects that simply cost too much, and that is because I have yet to find a system that is embraced by its user community but is unaffordable. In other words, expensive failures tend to be all-around failures. Real failures are obvious.

Why do CRM projects fail? In my experience, failures occur because of the three P's: people, process, and politics, either as a single factor or, frequently, combined for a more lethal effect.

---

2. As reported on 9/10/01 at the CRM Fall Summit in Orlando, Florida.

## Politics

Politics can be a great hazard for CRM implementations. Simply put, there needs to be a clear political will to make a CRM project a success. This means that there should be a so-called executive sponsor, someone with the appropriate organizational and political clout to make the project happen. Ideally, this person should also be the business owner for the function(s) covered by the implementation. Right here, we can see that for a cross-functional implementation this is going to be difficult! Since companies tend to be organized by functions, a cross-functional implementation will require that a general manager be the business sponsor, and these people are often busy with other things.

Even if an appropriate executive sponsor can be found, some stability is required, as CRM projects tend to be long. We'll come back to this point in Chapter 3 but you will need at least a few months for a one-function project with relatively limited goals. Furthermore, there will be obstacles along the way, which will create wonderful opportunities for opponents to reopen the discussion of whether proper choices have been made. Will the executive sponsor have the tenacity and the patience to push the project through to the end? Will the executive sponsor still be around by the time the project is done? Will the executive sponsor refrain from delegating the project down so low in the hierarchy that it may lose its momentum?

## People

People, even when not involved in political ploys, can easily derail CRM projects. First, there's the great fear of change. CRM implementations always require some amount of change, sometimes a lot if process changes are extensive. Some employees will resent that. Then, there is the Big Brother effect: employees can get nervous when asked to document their actions and they are not above boycotting the new system, often citing irreconcilable difficulties with the user interface. And finally there is the problem of mastery: there is almost always a dip in productivity as the new system is implemented since the users have to get used to the new system. That creates a vulnerable time when even supporters can go through a period of doubt.

In addition, CRM projects often involve a whole team of outside contributors to help select (sometimes) and implement (almost always) the system. There can be people failures with them too, although I prefer to treat them as process failures.

## Process

Process failures are another source of CRM project failures. Even with good executive sponsorship and an enthusiastic team, projects may fail because they are not properly driven. It is my hope that this book will help you avoid process failures, so let's start by analyzing the various ways the process can fail.

The most important process failure is failure to designate an appropriate project owner. Not the executive sponsor we discussed above, the project owner is hands-on, creates the plan, assembles the team, manages the work, and reports progress and exceptions to the executive sponsor. Put an unskilled project manager in that role and you've pretty much guaranteed failure for the entire project.

Process failure can also stem from a bungled approach to the task, for instance believing that the choice of the tool is everything and neglecting the implementation, or failing to involve both the technical team and the users from the start. Leaving out IT may result in a perfectly tailored interface on top of a hopelessly underpowered server and network infrastructure. And leaving out the users may get you a well-tuned system, but with so few actual users it would be hard to tell whether it would actually work well in high-load conditions. Both approaches are a big waste of time and money.

Most CRM projects succeed despite the obstacles. What makes the difference for successful projects? They have an executive sponsor who passionately believes that it needs to be done and it can be done. There is a strong and well-communicated business need behind which employees can rally. And there is a cohesive and effective project team, including a strong project manager, to shepherd the project through successful implementation. The focus of the book is to describe how to bring together the executive sponsor, the business need, and the project team to deliver a successful project through practical and effective strategies.

## Is CRM Just for the Big Guys?

CRM is for everyone! Although we tend to hear about multi-year, multi-million-dollar implementations from large corporations, mid-sized enterprises need CRM just as much. Even tiny enterprises benefit from CRM systems. My neighborhood pizza place has a great system that remembers our name, our preferred toppings, even the fact that we usually phone our order ahead so we don't have to wait at the restaurant. The system resides, as it often does in small businesses, in the memory of the owner. I'd rate it as perfect.

Businesses that are larger than one person can't use the "all in the head" approach, and even the one-owner business may need help tracking customer information. The problem for non-huge enterprises is that the massive projects that are standard and required by the large corporate players are simply overwhelming for smaller players and do not match either their resources or their requirements. This book outlines a practical blueprint for mid-sized companies, adapting the same good principles used at the top to a more reasonable scope.

Don't shy away from CRM because you think you are too small. Many of the good tool ideas that were initially developed for the largest players have been adapted down to smaller, cheaper, and more manageable packages that are just right for more modest means and do not sacrifice essential functionality in the process. In this instance, larger enterprises are a great testing bed for innovation.

An advantage of CRM systems for smaller environments is that they allow them to function in many ways as larger players, which has its sweet rewards. For instance giving customers meaningful around-the-clock self-service web access to the enterprise is absolutely within the reach of mid-sized and even small companies and allows them to deliver service that would simply not be possible without automation.

# Can CRM Work If It's Not Integrated?

As discussed earlier under "CRM Nirvana", the ideal CRM system is integrated both between the various customer functions and with the back-office systems so that customer-focused staffers can access all the information about customer interactions and all the information required to meet customer requests within a single interface. However, many companies find that piecemeal projects work very well. Why is that?

- For one thing, almost all integrated approaches require custom work to link disparate systems. That makes them very expensive not just for the initial implementation but also for maintenance since the various pieces don't always evolve harmoniously together. It's very difficult to get a return on investment if you start with a large outlay.
- Integrated approaches take a lot of time, partly because of the integration work (to get the various systems to talk to each other), but also

because of the amount of coordination required to implement a larger-scope tool with many more stakeholders even when no integration is required. So integrated approaches require patience and are inherently riskier because they take more time.
- Perhaps the thorniest problem of integrated CRM is, who will lead the monster? Can we find an appropriate executive sponsor? Turf battles can and do extinguish integrated CRM projects more readily than more modest approaches.
- Finally, if you select a CRM suite to avoid having to do custom integration between the customer-focused functions (you would still have to do back-office integration, if required), you automatically restrict yourself to a much smaller set of vendors. What may sound like a great way to get to a short list usually translates into less than best-in-class functionality for any given function, an older architecture, and higher pricing. So you may end up without the leading-edge features that you want while paying a hefty price.

Therefore, it can be better to start with smaller, function-focused pieces. You can select best-in-class features for each of them separately, the selection process can be driven by a single business function, and the implementation process is a lot quicker.

If the various customer functions are quite separate, staying with distinct, non-integrated pieces for CRM may be just fine in the long run. And if you need some integration you will likely find that only a small percentage of data and processes need to be truly integrated, and perhaps not through the most delicate and expensive simultaneous update scenarios.

Many companies function happily with disconnected CRM modules and even find advantages to that route. Good CRM does not mean complete integration, although to be fair it probably requires some integration for the key areas.

## Does CRM Deliver Applications or a Tool Kit?

While tool vendors promise complete solutions, they sometimes deliver no more than a tool kit to create a complete solution. And customers want both the convenience of a ready-to-use application and the comfort of full customizations, which require powerful customization tools. What can and should you expect from a CRM tool?

Most newcomers to CRM think of it as a set of ready-made applications that handle sales, or marketing, or service. It's a pretty accurate characterization of the lower-end offerings, which require almost no work to make them usable, only what I call personalization, that is, customization that stops short of requiring any programming. Personalization includes:

- Populating drop-down lists and other sets of value to match specific requirements. For instance, a support issue could have default statuses of open and closed, but the customer may want to have values of new, in process, and closed.
- Renaming fields to match local usage. For instance, a "customer" may be known as a "client" or an "organization".
- Hiding certain fields that will not be used. For instance, the tool may be able to record the industry segment of the customers but you may decide it's not a piece of data you want to maintain.
- Hooking up the tool to other basic systems, for instance, allowing it to receive and send e-mail.
- Making minor adjustments to the look and feel of the display such as adding the company logo (usually in a pre-determined area) or dropping a style sheet on the web pages.
- Entering data such as knowledge base documents.
- Creating user accounts and authorizations.

All tools allow some level of personalization. Lower-end tools allow the least scope for personalization but on the other hand they often offer wonderful implementation tools, GUI-based tools that a non-technical user, say a business manager, can master easily and quickly. Lower-end tools also have the distinction that they can almost always be used right out of the box, before any personalization occurs, if you are willing to go with the default values.

One level up from personalization is customization, which I will distinguish from personalization as requiring a technically knowledgeable individual to perform and usually involving some programming. Customization has a much larger scope than personalization, including such elements as:

- Drastically changing the layout and look of the screens.
- Adding, modifying, and deleting fields to change the data model. This goes further than merely hiding fields, which can typically be handled without programming, at least in the more modern tools. Note that many tools allow adding certain fields that capture details very easily

and without programming, so the line is somewhat hard to draw between personalization and customization on this point.
- Altering the workflow of the tool such as manipulating the way issues are passed from one owner to the next, authorizations gathered, etc. This is beyond the scope of the simpler tools (in which one may be able to manipulate statuses, but not the underlying workflow). Some tools offer powerful workflow editors to accomplish this. Others will require a more brute-force approach.

The lower-end tools often restrict severely the amount of customization that is possible. If you want to get rid of a piece of functionality, or you want to extend the tool in any way, you simply won't be able to do it. Lower-end tools are usually fairly rigid applications, but they can also be used right after installation, without any additional work.

On the other hand, high-end tools can be little more than tool kits that allow you to build custom applications, but don't really offer much to the end-user right out of the box. It is a disconcerting feature of some tools that they simply cannot be used *at all* without a lengthy customization period. To be fair, this situation is much rarer than it was several years ago, but it's something to watch out for during product evaluation. All vendors demo applications, but it's up to you to determine whether the applications come ready made or are the product of their tool kits.

The better tools combine the best of both worlds: a complete, usable, well thought-out application that can be used as-is or after only minor personalization work, and a tool kit to extend and adapt it to specific needs. That way, you can select applications that do most of what you need and only have to change them in specific, limited areas.

Yet another aspect of customization is integration: making the CRM tool work with other tools such as the e-mail server, other business applications, the phone system, etc. Integration is always custom work and can range from the simplistic (adding a button to call up another application) to the very complex (seamlessly merging the sales system with the payment system). We'll come back to the fact that it's critical to assess your specific needs before taking the plunge since complex integrations are terribly expensive.

Although simple integrations can be done with almost any tool, more complex projects are greatly facilitated by the existence of an application programming interface (API), that is, a predefined set of routines to hook into the CRM tool. This is yet another area worth looking for when shopping for a CRM tool even though it will not deliver any immediate benefits.

# What's the Place of IT in CRM Initiatives?

Should IT be kept away from CRM projects because CRM projects are really all about the business function? No, that would be a big mistake for three reasons.

1. Business users typically lack the technical knowledge and expertise required to evaluate and implement CRM systems. (By the way, vendors know this, and some may take advantage of the situation if you try to do it alone.)
2. IT almost always has a role in implementing the system, be it by providing system administration for the machines used by the CRM system, database administration for the underlying database, or network tuning required by the implementation. If IT is not involved early on or at all, it will be difficult to get cooperation and the long-term future of the tool will be threatened.
3. IT is the logical place where the overall company CRM plan can be created and nurtured, so if you have any hope to one day integrate the various pieces, at any level, you'd better invite IT to play early in the game.

Should IT be at the center of CRM projects? No, again that would be a big mistake because CRM projects cannot succeed without strong and direct business user sponsorship, guidance, and feedback. IT should not attempt to drive CRM projects because buy-in from the users is critical. However, IT should suggest CRM solutions to functional managers who may not have the time or the expertise to delve into automation issues.

Ideally, IT and the business function owners should work on CRM projects as equal partners, each concentrating on their area of expertise. The role of IT increases for enterprise-wide deployments since IT often provides some of the coordination required between the various functions, but I would strongly caution against IT playing a lead role in enterprise-wide projects for fear that the functional owners will disengage. Political will from the functional owners is the first requirement for the success of CRM projects.

CRM implementation can bring both tangible and intangible rewards to your organization, whatever its size. Your chances of success are excellent as long as you follow a sensible strategy, as will be outlined in the rest of the book. CRM nirvana may be a completely integrated system, but you can be very successful with a piecemeal approach, provided that the right players are involved. Let's begin.

# Auditing your CRM System 2

## Express Version

- Perceived problems with CRM systems are often due to poor underlying processes or poorly thought-out customizations of a basically good tool. Since implementing a new tool takes lots of time and resources, thoroughly investigate whether the tool is the root cause of the problems before making the decision to select a new tool. Use our easy test to facilitate the audit process.
- Don't decide to switch tools based solely on a sleek demo. Any tool can look wonderful in a demo.
- One size does not fit all. Don't base a decision to get a new tool on a recommendation from a colleague who may be facing different challenges.
- Do get a new tool if you are still using a homegrown tool. You will be amazed at the functionality you've been missing and you'll save money too, at least in the long run.

- Do keep up to date on new tools and new technologies. If your current tool vendor is lagging behind and even future releases fail to include new technology ideas, it makes sense to explore alternatives.
- Tool implementations work best when you have adequate time and resources. Be wary of embarking on a tool change if you are pressed for either.

# The Big Question: Do You Need A New CRM System?

If you have absolutely no tool in place to track customers' interactions, you need a new CRM system. Save yourself some time and proceed directly to the next chapter.

If you do have a tool in place but are not satisfied with it, take a good look at it before deciding to start over. Why? First, because problems that appear to be tool problems may stem from other causes. Second, because implementing a new tool requires significant amounts of time and money, and requires retraining customers and staff to use it. You don't want to embark on such a project without having a clear requirement to do so.

What other areas could cause what appear to be tool issues?

Very often, the root cause is poor processes rather than the tool itself. Processes that are inefficient, not customer-friendly, or plain confusing need to be fixed before any tool can be successful. It's true that a tool implementation process will (should!) expose process issues, giving you an opportunity to fix them, but it's really an expensive and roundabout way to address process issues. Fix the processes first, and then worry about the tool.

The second root cause, which is often difficult to isolate, lies with the specific implementation of the tool. In other words, you can have a tool that's basically sound, but the particular implementation (customization) you are running with is poor. It's not that hard to twist a good tool into a poor customized version thereof (although it's not possible to contrive a good implementation of an ill-suited tool). Poor implementations cause poor day-to-day performance, and typically more headaches and problems when it's time to upgrade to the next version, so they are a very big issue.

What follows are two different instruments to evaluate your current CRM tool and to untangle the root cause of issues you may encounter.

The first one (the five-minute test) is very quick and focuses on a handful of critical questions to determine how well your tool is performing and whether any shortcomings come from process or implementation weaknesses rather than the tool itself. It's a good starting point, especially if you have already done some research in this area.

The second one (the detailed inventory) is much more thorough and explicit and is meant for 1) those hurried souls who went through the five-minute test and want to explore specific areas in more detail and 2) those of you who prefer an in-depth approach. The detailed inventory includes more questions and, for each question, explains why it's important, how to go about evaluating that particular area, and how to identify root causes.

The chapter ends with a list of good and bad reasons to get a new CRM tool. This is the place to go if you are tempted to make a move although your current tool is working well just because you saw a cool demo or you want the latest technology. By the end of the chapter, you should have a good idea of whether you need a new CRM tool.

## The 5-Minute CRM Test

For those of you who like to make quick assessments, here is a short test that will help you pinpoint whether your CRM system is successful, and whether it makes sense to think about a replacement, or whether the issues have root causes in other areas. Experience shows that quick assessments are often just as accurate as lengthy ones, but if you'd like a more thorough and detailed version of the test, please skip ahead to the next section.

To get the most accurate results on this test, respond as candidly as possible to each question rather than trying to figure out what the "right" answers may be. If you are not directly involved in customer-focused activities, you will need to involve the managers responsible for those groups to complete the test. They should also be encouraged to be candid. To make sure that they are not overly optimistic in their responses, spot-check a few with individual contributors in the various groups.

Some questions may simply not apply to you (for instance, if your CRM system does not have a support component, questions about support don't apply.) Just skip them.

**TABLE 2.1** The 5-Minute CRM Test

| | | Disagree Strongly | Disagree | Agree | Agree Strongly |
|---|---|---|---|---|---|
| 1 | Customers know how to contact the sales team (by phone or electronically). | | | | |
| 2 | Customers know how to contact the support group (by phone or electronically). | | | | |
| 3 | Sales reps know how customers should contact the support group. | | | | |
| 4 | Support reps know how customers should contact the sales group. | | | | |
| 5 | There are existing, documented (written) processes for handling customer queries. | | | | |
| 6 | Sales and support reps can locate the documented processes for their area within 2 minutes if they are unclear about them. | | | | |
| 7 | There are well-defined metrics for customer-focused activities. | | | | |
| 8 | Customer-focused employees have formal objectives that relate to the metrics. | | | | |
| 9 | There is a defined, documented (written) process for creating new knowledge base documents. | | | | |
| 10 | The knowledge base is growing daily. | | | | |
| 11 | When you hire someone, it takes less than one business day to create a new account for that individual. | | | | |
| 12 | The tool improvement request with the highest priority is less than 3 months old. | | | | |
| 13 | You are using a commercial CRM tool. | | | | |
| 14 | You are running your tool on a release that is currently supported by the vendor. | | | | |
| 15 | Important customer information is accessible within the tool (rather than in a file cabinet or unrelated system). | | | | |

**TABLE 2.1**  The 5-Minute CRM Test *(continued)*

| | | | | | | |
|---|---|---|---|---|---|---|
| 16 | There is a customer portal available to conduct sales and support business. | | | | | |
| 17 | Customers require no training to use the portal. | | | | | |
| 18 | Your CRM tool supports a knowledge base. | | | | | |
| 19 | Line managers are getting regular metrics that are immediately meaningful for them (with no Excel massaging required). | | | | | |
| 20 | E-mail from customers is automatically loaded into the system (no manual cut and paste). | | | | | |
| 21 | Knowing the name of a customer, a sales employee needs less than 1 minute to locate the assigned sales rep, pending deals and existing support cases. | | | | | |
| 22 | Knowing the name of a customer, a support rep needs less than 1 minute to locate the assigned sales rep and existing support cases. | | | | | |
| 23 | It takes less than 4 hours to train a new hire to use the system. | | | | | |
| 24 | Creating a new account in the system can be done in less than 5 minutes by someone without a programming, technical background. | | | | | |
| 25 | Sales reps can enter a new prospect into the system in less than 2 minutes. | | | | | |
| 26 | Support reps can enter a new case for an existing customer in less than 2 minutes. | | | | | |
| 27 | A support manager can get a list of the current open support cases in less than 2 minutes. | | | | | |
| 28 | A sales manager can get a current forecast in less than 2 minutes. | | | | | |
| 29 | A marketing manager can get a hit rate of the last 3 campaigns within 2 minutes. | | | | | |
| 30 | The current system costs less than $1,000 per employee per year to maintain. | | | | | |

## Scoring

Add up the checkmarks in the Disagree and Disagree Strongly columns. If you have more than ten you have a CRM problem. Read on to determine what might be the root cause.

Questions 1 through 12 address customer processes rather than the tool. If many of them are rated on the Disagree side (either Disagree or Disagree Strongly), concentrate on fixing the processes rather than the tool. Once the process issues are addressed, take the test again to determine whether a tool change is also required.

Questions 14 through 30 are both about the tool itself and how it has been customized for you. Questions #14 (running on a current release), #19 (useful metrics), and #30 (cost) are usually good indicators of how well the customization is working rather than the tool.

Questions 21 through 29 (speed of doing various common tasks) are not silly time trials. Because tools won't be used if they are not efficient, it's important to see how quickly common operations can be performed. Problems in those areas can be caused by specific implementations as well as by the tool itself.

Question 30 is highly sensitive, since most companies do not track maintenance cost per seat to begin with, and since many normal variations occur as a result of the intricacies of the customizations on the one hand and the size of the user base on the other (a small user base means a higher cost per seat, all other things being equal.) Include in the cost figure: any depreciation costs on the license that you are still carrying; support and maintenance fee to the vendor; the same costs for the server, database, and other tools required by the CRM system; and the compensation costs for your internal support team. I deliberately chose a low number to make you think about how much you're spending so don't despair if your cost is only slightly higher than $1,000 per year.

# Detailed CRM Inventory

Perhaps the five-minute test whetted your appetite for more, or you simply like a more detailed approach. In either case, the inventory below expands on the quick test and gives you more details on what is important and why.

The format for the inventory is an annotated list. For each item—some present in the five-minute test above, some new—comments are available on why it is relevant in the first place, how to go about rating it, and what the outcome may mean in terms of the tool, the underlying processes, or customization.

Rate each item in the inventory using the same scale as was used for the five-minute test (Disagree Strongly, Disagree, Agree, Agree Strongly). Here again, be as candid as you can on your responses: the candid answer is always the right answer. Although this is the "long" test, try not to spend more than a couple of hours at the most on it. Taking more time may increase your desire to rate higher and your imagination to do so, distorting the whole exercise.

Note each area that you rate on the Disagree side (including Disagree Strongly and Disagree). What is the root cause? Is it a weakness of the tool itself or with the way it's customized? Is it a process issue or a tool issue?

## CRM Process

Items in this section are related to process rather than the tool. If there are issues in this area, they should be addressed prior to making any tool change decision, since the tool can only assist with the process, not guide it (although it's true that a well-run tool implementation would uncover process issues, it's considerably cheaper and easier to fix them first!)

- Customers know how to contact the sales team and the support group (by phone or electronically).

    Is there an organized process to communicate such basic information to customers? If your current tool lacks a portal where that information can be made available, is the information given to customers in other forms? Such a basic "how-to" process is required regardless of the technology you are currently using.

- Sales reps know how customers can contact the support group, and conversely support reps know how customers can contact the sales team.

    One of the biggest complaints customers have with their vendors is that the left hand doesn't seem to know what the right hand is doing. Although the distribution of cross-departmental information can be facilitated by a CRM tool, employees in one customer-focused group should understand the value of being able to direct customers to the right place and should know how to help customers access other services within the company even if there is no integrated tool.

- There are existing, documented (written) processes for handling customer transactions.

    The process documents don't need to be long or formal. Actually, overly complex documents often signal a gap between the formally documented process and the way things are normally handled. The process should be written in simple English (or whatever language you use in your company) and should be clearly understandable to an outsider (as opposed to a senior employee). The process should take the transactions from beginning to end and clearly indicate routing and handoffs.

For a more meaningful test, take a few customer transactions through the entire cycle. Do they follow the process? If they deviate from it, is there a bona fide exception to be made?

The ultimate test is whether the process makes sense to both the customers and the employees. Many otherwise well-documented and properly applied processes are cumbersome and wasteful of time and resources. A common weakness is to require multiple layers of processing—whereas state-of-the-art processes shoot for a "one-owner" approach—as well as formal authorizations along the way, rather than letting the staffers make independent, fast decisions, which can be audited later if a review is required.

- Sales and support reps can locate the documented processes for their area within 2 minutes if they are unclear about them.

The ease of access to the documented processes is an important test of the value attached to it. If reps routinely choose to "wing it" rather than to check the proper way of doing things, you can be sure that adherence to the process is neither important nor rewarded.

- There is an owner for each customer-focused process.

Is the owner identified within the process itself? Spot-check a few documents to verify that the owner is still with the company and is still the owner of the specific process.

Processes change over time, which is a good thing since they need to adapt to new circumstances and they should be improved through experience. Assigning processes to specific owners makes it more likely that required maintenance will actually happen. Also, since many times it is the hands-on staffers who spot potential changes and improvements, it makes sense to make it very clear to them whom to report suggestions to. Bonus points here if there is a clear process for process maintenance, especially if it includes feedback to individuals who provide suggestions.

- The processes were updated in the last six months.

Following up on the point above, finding evidence that processes are indeed updated means that that they are important. You may think that processes that do not change mean good processes (they don't change because they don't need to change because they are perfect in the first place). The reality is that processes that don't change don't change because no one cares about them. Changes need not be very significant.

- There are well-defined metrics for customer-focused activities.

  Do you think that metrics are a function of the tool rather than the process? I beg to disagree. Although a good tool makes the computation of metrics much easier, metrics should exist independently of the tool.

  Ideally, metrics should capture actual results (qualified leads, actual sales, happy customers) rather than simple measures of activity (number of campaigns, sales calls, or support cases). We'll discuss this topic in much more depth in Chapter 10.

- Customer-focused employees have formally-defined objectives that relate to the metrics.

  Measurements are one thing. Making sure the measurements matter to the staffers who work with the customers ensures that the metrics are attended to. What gets measured gets done, which is yet another reason to pick good, meaningful metrics. Do you really want your team to compete on how many sales calls they make? I think not!

- There is a defined, documented (written) process for creating, reviewing and posting new knowledge base documents.

  Here again, a good tool will make knowledge creation much easier, but you still need to have a clear process to create documents. A state-of-the-art process will have some way of gleaning documents from the front-line staffers, either by encouraging them to write documents themselves, or by having a system through which they can request and suggest new documents.

  Also, there should be some kind of timeline system to ensure that documents are posted promptly (ideally, within a couple of days of their creation), Audit a few recent documents to see how long the full cycle took from creation to posting. It's useless to create documents that take weeks to post.

- There is a defined, documented (written) process for maintaining knowledge base documents.

  Knowledge maintenance, often neglected compared to its more glamorous knowledge creation sibling, increases in importance with the size of the knowledge base. Poorly done, it is the main reason why knowledge bases are not used: why bother using a knowledge base where many documents are obsolete or plain wrong?

  At a minimum, the maintenance process should collect user input on problematic documents and act upon the input swiftly, within a couple of days at the most. It's best if the input is unobtrusive, that is, the user should not have to fire a specific e-mail to the document owner or the knowledge base owner to get a document changed: instead, it should be possible to post the feedback right from the knowledge base environment.

Beyond reactive maintenance processes, it's even better to have a systematic review process through which documents are reviewed periodically regardless of specific user feedback, both singly and in comparison to others in the same category. Documents that are not used much, overlap with others, or obsolete can be discarded or fixed up.

- The knowledge base is growing daily.

This is a great test of the overall quality of the knowledge-creation process, and would more accurately be stated as "the knowledge base changes daily" since changes and deletions are just as important to the quality of the knowledge base as additions. Of course, if your organization is tiny, *daily* growth is a tough requirement, but the idea is to see constant growth, not sudden increases on the days the one knowledge base reviewer suddenly decides to pay attention to the knowledge base.

- When you hire someone, it takes less than one business day to create a new account for that individual.

Even a very cumbersome tool will allow creating a new user in minutes. The point here is whether there is a process to bring the account creation request to the right person and have it executed within a business day, as a matter of routine and not just because you happen to be benchmarking. CRM tools are useless if one cannot access them.

- The tool improvement request with the highest priority is less than 3 months old.

Another good benchmark test, the aging of improvement requests is a sign of 1) whether anyone is bothering to generate improvement requests (if no one's using the system, you can be sure no one's bothering to request improvements) and 2) whether anyone is paying attention to the requests. Unattended improvement requests will surely lead to no more improvement requests, and a tool that doesn't change is a tool that is dying.

By the way, if you should find that there is no formal list of improvement requests, or that improvement requests are filed away in the e-mail folder of some lucky individual, the support mechanism for the CRM tool is not functioning properly. This is not necessarily a weakness of the tool itself, although I would question why such an informal record-keeping mechanism is used when, presumably, the tool should be able to track its own enhancement requests and bugs, at least if it includes a support-tracking component.

## Ease of Use—For Customers

Items in this section focus on the customers' use of the system through some kind of portal. Problems in this area can be related to either the tool or its implementation. Older tools tend to be weaker in this area, although they are making progress as customers demand more e-commerce functionality. In some cases, existing customer-facing functionality is not implemented because of fears that customers can't enter support cases properly or would use online order information to their advantage. Such issues have little to do with the tool itself, but instead should trigger revisiting the business choices that were made around customer access.

- There is a customer portal available to conduct sales and support business.

    A customer portal is a basic requirement today and if your tool doesn't offer it, it's time to shop around. I must say that I have encountered many situations where existing portal functionality is not implemented. Three types of reasons are cited for this (to me) amazing situation: lack of resources to implement and maintain the portal; a concern that existing functionality is insufficient compared to what customers want; and finally a fear that the portal would be "misused" by customers.

    If your tool offers a customer portal that is not deployed because of resource constraints, you should know that customer portals reach ROI in the shortest amount of time compared to other CRM functionality, so you need to find a way to work around the resource limitations. If the underlying issue for the resource gap is that the tool provides only a tool kit, and therefore requires *lots* of resources to implement the portal, then you have an argument to find a better tool.

    Regarding the concern about limited functionality: sure, we would all like an all-powerful, all-encompassing portal, but even basic functionality is better than nothing, and customers certainly understand this. Implement what you have.

    The third concern, about customers' potential misuse of the portal, is not well grounded and stems from a misconception that creating a more transparent relationship with customers will create abuse. Barring the real issues of security, which need to be addressed, opening up systems to customers is actually a breath of fresh air. Just as an example, support groups often shudder at the thought of letting customers log support cases electronically. Will the descriptions be complete? And how can we allow customers to determine the priority of their issues? Well, it turns out that customers actually do a great job of describing issues in writing, and are remarkably restrained in choosing priority levels, so the concerns are misplaced.

Assuming now that you do have a functional customer portal, there are certainly degrees of excellence. A basic portal with online information is just that, basic. You really want to aim for an interactive experience where customers can search for information and conduct at least simple transactions online such as placing repeat and add-on orders, checking on existing orders, and logging and checking on support issues. In order to safely conduct personalized transactions, the portal should include an identification scheme (with a password).

Check whether the portal is customer-focused rather than department-focused. I have seen many portals where training and support are described in completely different areas, probably because two totally different departments handle them, whereas customers think of them under the common umbrella of "services."

If there is no portal, or if functionality is lacking in the portal, first confirm whether you are using all the functionality provided by the vendor in this area. If not, explore whether your organization is too timid in letting customers conduct business online (an issue with process or politics) or if the tool is too awkward to make deployment possible (a tool issue). If you are using all available functionality and your portal is weak, then the issue lies with your tool. Weak portal functionality is an indication to select a better tool.

- Customers require no training to use the portal.

  Using the portal should be intuitively obvious. A portal is just a web site, and like any other web site it should be user-friendly. Anyone should be able to navigate and operate the various functions with no training whatsoever. While an online help function is a definite plus, it should be possible for a novice to figure things out without having to resort to it. Clearly, the requirements for simple use are even more stringent if your customers tend to be more technologically naïve.

  If your portal functionality is particularly rich, it's fine to offer a tour of the portal, either self-guided or through a webinar (an online seminar), to make sure that customers do not overlook specific, perhaps unusual functions. But navigating and operating the portal should be easy to do without specific training.

If your portal requires training for successful use, you may have an issue with the tool itself, but often it's really with the customization of the tool. Most companies choose to customize the customer portal. Sometimes, to be honest, it's because the portal functionality provided by the tool vendor is nothing more than a tool kit! However it's not rare that misguided customizations create difficulties in using the portal. If you have a chance to see other portal implementations for the same tool vendor, which is often possible since portals have more public exposure than internal systems, check whether any of them are better than yours. If so, you have a customization issue, and you should work on that. If not, the underlying tool is to blame and this is a potential reason for finding a new one.

## Ease of Use—For Internal End-Users

Items in this section focus on the employees' use of the system. Problems in this area can be related to the tool, its implementation, or more rarely process issues. Older tools have clunkier user interfaces, but don't be put off by less visually appealing interfaces. If they allow quick manipulation of the data, they can be quite effective and many items here focus indeed on speed of common operations rather than pure sleekness of the tool.

- Desk-bound staffers keep the application up on their screens at all times.

  A major issue with CRM system is user adoption. If desk-bound staffers (in support and telesales functions, for instance) live and breathe the tool, it's a positive indication that it is being used. If they do not, this could signal everything from a tool issue, to a customization issue, even a process issue if customer transactions are not faithfully recorded. Look for clues in the other entries of this section.

- Important customer information is accessible within the tool rather than in a file cabinet or unrelated system.

  I'm not talking here about having *all* the information in the company available in the tool (although it would be handy, if potentially overwhelming). I only mean that basic information needed to do the work on a daily basis is available. For instance, if I'm providing support, can I tell whether a particular customer has failed to pay the maintenance bill and should therefore be denied support? (But I don't really need to see the detailed state of the customer's receivables.) If I'm a sales rep, can I see what products the customer bought last year? (But I don't necessarily need to see the actual contract that was signed at the time.)

If customer-focused staffers must hunt down basic information, their efficiency decreases, but more insidiously their desire and likelihood to use the tool also decrease. In particular, if you find "feral" tracking systems for important information, especially if it would be fairly easy to track within the tool, you have a good clue that something is not quite right with the CRM tool. For instance, a support group that tracks requests to a tier 3 group in a separate tool would be a red flag.

Issues in this area can be created by the tool. For instance, if the tool doesn't include a function to record purchases, even at a high level, then accessing a purchase history will not be possible. However, problems can also be a matter of process or implementation. For instance, if there is no process to record purchases or if there is no process to transfer purchase information from the back-office system to the CRM system, even a tool that *would* be able to show a purchase history will not be able to do so. We'll come back to this point when we talk about integrations. A good strategy is to focus on frequently used data and to find integration and automation solutions for them rather than trying to get all systems to share all data seamlessly.

- Knowing the name of a customer, a sales employee needs less than 1 minute to locate the assigned sales rep, pending deals and existing support cases.

There are many time-based questions in this inventory, and the reason is simply that frequently performed tasks must be very efficient. Note that access to selected pieces of information from other departments needs to be quick, too (for sales employees, it might be getting a list of support cases).

Issues in this area can arise for a variety of reasons. If the navigation required to perform the tasks is awkward, it can either be a tool issue or a customization problem. If it is a tool issue, you may be able to work around it through clever customization, but I would question the wisdom of pouring resources into a tool that doesn't do the basics right.

If it takes time for the system to process the request, it can be a limitation of the tool itself, or it could be a configuration issue. If you have severe performance problems invite the vendor to conduct a performance audit. They should be able to suggest a different configuration to ease the problem, or they may spot inefficiencies in the ways customizations were programmed. You can then evaluate the cost of the prescribed remedies, weigh them against the likelihood that the tool can indeed perform against your requirements once they are implemented, and decide whether the tool needs replacing.

- Knowing the name of a customer, a support rep needs less than 1 minute to locate the assigned sales rep and existing support cases.

  This is the same issue as the one above but viewed from the perspective of a support staffer.

- Sales reps can enter a new prospect into the system in less than 2 minutes.

  This is another common task that must be performed very quickly and efficiently. Watch for the number of keystrokes required. Also watch for automatic data quality check. Does the system let you enter a new prospect called "ABC Systems" if there is a customer by that name? If there is a customer called "ABC"? Such simple mechanisms go a long way in ensuring data integrity, and data integrity can be a big issue in CRM implementations.

  Entering a name is one thing, but can the sales reps enter all the relevant information about the prospect? For instance, can the tool track the data collected through the sales methodology they use?

  Problems here are mostly attributable to the tool, although ugly customizations can also be a problem.

- Support reps can enter a new case for an existing customer in less than 2 minutes.

  This is the same issue as above, but in the support world. The key here is how easy it is to find the customer record. Look for built-in aids to find customers with similar spellings and word case, and look for multiple ways to locate a customer by name, name of contact, customer number, e-mail address, etc. This is particularly important if you have a very large base of customers.

- The most commonly used screens have no elements that reps say are "useless" or "never used."

  This will require a bit of research on your part, but it will give you a good feel for how easy it is to use the tool. Sure, staffers can and do ignore unused fields, but it's a strain to have to constantly differentiate between useful and useless fields.

  If you have problems in this area, you may conclude it's all about the implementation. Why not just get rid of those fields? Point well taken, but the real issue may be why those fields are there in the first place. And, if they were not removed as part of the implementation, is it because removal is difficult and hard to undo, which would also be a tool issue?

- E-mail from and to customers is automatically loaded into the system (no manual cut and paste).

   This is a good indicator of whether the tool handles the low-level, repetitive actions that it should handle, freeing staffers to do the creative part of the job. Ideally, the system should automatically load incoming e-mails into the system, associate them with existing issues as appropriate, and route them correctly. And staffers should be able to send outgoing e-mails directly from within the tool, with the e-mails being captured into the system. Note that you do need a facility of this sort even if you attempt to conduct most of your business through a portal.

   Although most tools do have such an e-mail connector, it's not always implemented, sometimes because it's not easy to do so, which would be a tool-based issue.

- It takes less than 4 hours to train a new hire to use the system.

   Ideally, someone with decent computer skills should be able to use the system without any training, much as is the case with the customer portal. The reality is that each system exists within a process and it makes sense to have some formal training available to use the system in the most efficient way possible.

   If the training requirements are much greater than 4 hours (if your CRM covers multiple business functions, it would be 4 hours per function, not for the whole thing), then the system is too complicated. Is that the tool's fault? Perhaps. Check the vendor's end-user materials, if any exist. If they require more than a half-day to cover, then the tool is too complex. Strange customizations certainly add to the training requirements. Long training requirements are an immediate drag on productivity, but most importantly they signal that the tool is not as user-friendly as it could be.

- There is an end-user self-paced training document that is less than 10 pages long.

   This is another take on the training issue, because high training requirements say a lot about what it's like to use the system on a daily basis. So even though you may choose to provide instructor-led training for new hires, it should be possible to learn how to use the system from a self-paced, reasonably short written tutorial. The 10-page limit is by business function.

If such a tutorial doesn't exist, question why. It could be that the tool is so difficult to use that it requires a human instructor. It could also be that no one thought of creating one, which would be a simple process issue.

As reinforcement for the initial training, and to support a self-training option, it's good to have an online help facility available. In many cases, the online help system that comes with the tool (if there is one) is very difficult to update to accommodate customizations made to the tool. This is a common reason why online help is rarely truly helpful.

- Your CRM tool supports a knowledge base.

  CRM systems are not just transaction tools; they should offer a knowledge base function that allows your staff to store important information so it can be retrieved when needed, whether by internal users or customers.

  If your tool doesn't support a knowledge base, you may want to rethink your choice, although you can certainly purchase an add-on tool and perhaps integrate it with the CRM tool.

- The knowledge base provides multiple search mechanisms for end-users, including keyword searching, category searching, and special-attribute searching such as looking for a document created within the last week.

  This item tries to qualify the degree to which a user is likely to find a relevant document in the knowledge base. Successful searches are not that common, especially for the so-called naïve users, who may not be using the exact keywords contained in the documents. Be sure to benchmark this item both for internal and external users.

  Weaknesses here are mostly due to the tool itself.

- The knowledge base allows users to refine searches and/or ranks retrieved items in order of likely relevance to narrow the search results.

  While the previous test item focused on retrieving all the documents that meet the search criteria, this one focuses on not having to wade through pages of potential hits. This is a very difficult criterion to meet, and the larger the database the more difficult it is to isolate the most relevant documents.

  Weaknesses here are again due to the tool itself.

- It takes a reviewer no more than 2 minutes to retrieve documents waiting for review and post them into the knowledge base.

  Cumbersome document posting mechanisms are the bane of otherwise efficient (that is, search-efficient) knowledge bases. Most of the time, issues with the review mechanism lie squarely with the tool, since little or no customization is done on that area of the tool. The tools that are most successful for document creation are those that treat it like issue handling, providing queues, statuses, owners, and alerts. Unfortunately, there are few such tools.

## Ease of Maintenance

Items in this section focus on the support and maintenance requirements of the tool. This is an important section since a tool with extraordinarily high maintenance requirements will cost more. It is also likely to be less well maintained, which results in decreasing functionality and usage over time.

- You are using a commercial CRM tool.

    At this point in time, there's simply no reason to use a homegrown tool. Yes, a homegrown tool is perfectly tailored to your exact needs. Yes, the initial cost of a commercial tool is high. But there's no way that a homegrown tool can compete with commercial functionality over time.

    So if you are using a homegrown tool, and even if it is performing well against other items in this inventory, you should consider replacing it with a commercial tool.

- You are running your tool on a release that is supported by the vendor.

    Why does this matter? Because if you are behind the times you are 1) running the real risk of encountering an issue that would stall your work for significant periods of time and therefore 2) demonstrating that the CRM system is not very important for the health of your company.

    Most companies that run outdated releases do so because they don't see any exciting new features in the newer releases or because the burden of upgrading is too large. If you can't see anything worth upgrading to in newer releases, question the wisdom of staying with a vendor who is so out of touch with new tools and technology. And if you are overwhelmed by the resources required to upgrade, I totally understand. It's a well-known issue that upgrading a CRM system is difficult, costly, and long, and even more so when extensive customizations are at stake. This point is often skirted by vendors during the evaluation phase with misleading guarantees that upgrades are painless. True, upgrades can be painless when no customizations are involved, but porting customizations is often a real chore.

    If you find yourself in a situation where upgrading is more than you can bear, consider starting over instead. If upgrading is very difficult, a new start may require only slightly more resources while leaving you with a system that will be easier to upgrade in the future.

One last piece of advice: if upgrading is a bear because you did extensive customizations, remember the lesson and refrain from customizing the new tool any more than absolutely necessary. Ask the vendor to provide a written customization strategy that minimizes the pain of future upgrades.

- Creating a new account in the system can be done in less than 5 minutes by someone without a programming, technical background.

New hires cannot be productive until they can use the tool (if they can, the tool is not at the center of the process, and that's a large problem in itself). Therefore the process of defining new users should be simple, and it should not require a skilled programmer—ideally a non-technical line manager should be able to do it, ditto for account terminations or changes of privilege levels. Note that we had an item in the Process section that stated that new hires should be authorized in less than a day. This is more of a focus on the technical process of authorization.

Problems here indicate a tool issue.

## Metrics

- Executives are getting regular metrics that are immediately meaningful for them (with no Excel massaging required).

Metrics have been the neglected stepchild of CRM implementations. One vendor actually went for several releases with absolutely *no* canned reports, under the justification that all customers wanted custom reports anyway.

If executives do not get regular and meaningful metrics, you are missing out on a big benefit of CRM systems. Typically metrics that will be meaningful to executives require some customization, regardless of how good basic metric reports may be—and they are often not good.

A terrible reason for the absence of good metrics is if the underlying data are not available in the tool. If that's the case, determine whether the tool cannot track the data at all or if the data is not being entered properly and reliably. If the former, question the vendor on why that's the case, as it could be a symptom of a deeper mismatch between your business needs and the tool. If the issue is with the way the data is entered, which is most likely the case, it's either a process issue or an issue with the usability of the tool, which you would have detected by using the items in the sections above.

- Line managers are getting regular metrics that are immediately meaningful for them (with no Excel massaging required).

This is a more stringent test than the one above because executives are typically catered to much more than line managers. Make sure to survey the first-level managers as well.

Additional points can be gained here if managers can define the types of metrics they receive, how often they receive them, and through what medium by using an online system. If the online metrics delivery system is built into the tool, all the better! Mega points if the needs of your first-level managers are actually fulfilled by using out-of-the-box reports. Most organizations find that custom reports are required, and this is almost always the case for large organizations where some slicing and dicing is required.

One word about Excel massaging: there's nothing wrong with it really, and it's most desirable to be able to load CRM data directly into a spreadsheet for analysis. However, if managers have to do any processing before they can use basic metrics, almost assuredly they will put it off, thereby missing out on the benefits of good data.

## Cost

- The current system costs less than $1,000 per employee per year to maintain.

If you do not know the aggregate maintenance cost of your CRM system, you are not alone! If you can compute it in a few hours, good for you. Include all the costs, internal and external. Start with the depreciation costs for the license, if you are still carrying them. Add the maintenance costs paid to the vendor, which is a recurring expense. You need to do the same for all the pieces of the CRM tool, including hardware and software such as the underlying database. (Don't bother about allocating shared expenses such as network expenses; this should remain a back-of-the-envelope exercise.) Finally, add the cost of your internal support team for the CRM tool, and any outside consultants you use for that purpose.

The reason for this benchmark is that you can find a reasonably powerful ASP (Application Service Provider) solution for about that amount of money. (An ASP is a vendor that offers business solutions through a rental arrangement rather than through a classic packaged license.) Although ASP solutions are typically limited in terms of how much customization they can support, it's always interesting to compare your cost to an ASP cost.

What if you come up with a much higher figure? If you are blissfully happy with all other aspects of the system, that may be just fine for you. Also, if your system includes extensive integrations, you are likely to exceed this figure regardless of how easy it is to maintain the tool itself, and you would never be able to get that level of customization from an ASP. It may make sense to review whether all the integrations are required, however.

Another area to scrutinize is very involved customizations. They cost more to maintain day-to-day than the vanilla tool, and they also create much greater challenges for upgrades, as described above. If you absolutely need the customizations, fine, but you may find that very similar benefits can be derived from much more constrained customizations, following the familiar 80/20 rule that states that 80% of the benefits can be gained through 20% of the effort, if that effort is directed judiciously.

Finally, excessive costs can be caused by the tool itself. It may be that the tool is simply hard to maintain, requiring expensive programmers to make any changes, for instance. This would be a good issue to discuss at user group meetings to get a feel for what others are spending on maintenance. And don't forget to study your maintenance bill carefully. You may be paying for more users than you need, or for a level of support you no longer require.

Is high cost by itself a reason to change tools? Probably not. In my experience, most companies start questioning the cost of a system only after they uncover usability problems. So if you're basically happy with your tool, but horrified at the cost, start working on trimming the costs through fewer customizations and integrations, and a more aggressive stance on containing maintenance costs.

# Bad Reasons to Get a New Tool

There is something truly exciting about getting a new tool, similar to getting a new car. It's new, it's "leading edge," and there's the promise that it will smooth away the bumps in the road. While a new tool can indeed solve current issues and propel you to new levels of speed and efficiency, there are plenty of bad reasons for replacing an existing tool. Let's look at four of them.

## Bad Reason #1: I Saw a Cool Demo

Perhaps you went to a business conference and saw a really well done demo. The business scenario was such a good match to your own, the screens were uncluttered and colorful, and the tool looked intuitive and powerful. Or you took advantage of one of the popular webinars to get a glimpse of the tool and came away thrilled after a few glimpses. The sales rep said that implementations typically take only a few weeks with an ROI to match. Should you jump?

Probably not if you are basically satisfied with your tool and you saw the demo only by chance. Let's face it: demos, for the most part, look great. If there's a good product manager, the business scenario will be realistic and sometimes eerily close to your own situation, and sleek screens and good workflows can be put together easily to match the scenario *even if they are not part of the basic tool*. This is a key point: demos can show anything, and it's often very difficult even for practiced eyes to distinguish between what's part of the out-of-the-box tool and what's customized. Chances are that the out-of-the-box tool does not have those very screens and workflows that you admired so much in the demo. (In Chapter 6, "Shopping for CRM Systems," we'll discuss how to get realistic demos.)

On the other hand, if you saw the demo because you determined, perhaps through one of the tests above, that your tool is indeed weak and in need of a replacement, then a positive outcome means that you should consider the tool in more detail. Because demos can lie so easily and powerfully, as discussed above, you need to temper your enthusiasm with serious research before you make a decision. But a good demo makes for a tool that's worth investigating and we will show you how in the chapters to come.

## Bad Reason #2: We Need to Keep Up With the Joneses

So your good friend, colleague, and rival tells you that her company just invested a good seven-figure sum into a new CRM tool that is now up and running, gives your friend great metrics, and, you surmise, is generating plenty of positive attention for her from the rest of the management team. You are running on a basic, older tool. Should you upgrade?

If your only motivation is to keep up with your friend, the answer is no. Go buy yourself a new car or whatever else will make you feel better. Revel in the knowledge that you can invest the big bucks your friend spent into something else such as a new advertising campaign, a bevy of sales reps, or a brand-new reproduction lab for support.

On the other hand, if you have determined that you need to upgrade, your friend's experience is a great opportunity to get an unbiased demo with plenty of information on the real requirements for a successful implementation. You should investigate other tools since your requirements may be different, and you will definitively end up with a different implementation even if you do choose the same tool, but direct hands-on experience is always precious during the selection phase.

## Bad Reason #3: I Don't Have The Latest Technology (But the Current Tool Works)

This is similar to bad reason #2 above, but with a twist. You're not so much jealous of a particular colleague, but you suffer from a simple case of technology envy. (In other words, it's not the new BMW in your neighbor's driveway you are lusting after; it's the knowledge that such a beautiful driving machine exists).

It may be that you do indeed need the new technology. For instance, if your tool doesn't support chat and your customers are asking for it, *loudly*, you may well need to implement a chat solution. But if your impetus comes solely from your love of technology, then you should just sit tight. After all, new technology typically requires a few years to settle down and it's always wise to leave to others the experience of the bleeding edge.

## Bad Reason #4: I Got A Call From A Sales Rep

You got a cold call, and you actually took it, and the sales rep was very persuasive and told you that this new tool would simply revolutionize the way you do business. Time to jump?

Call me cynical, but your buying the tool would primarily revolutionize the sales rep's commission. Remember that, by itself, a tool cannot solve all problems. If you do not have a CRM tool problem today, then your time is better spent on other issues.

# Good Reasons to Get a New Tool

But enough negativity! There are plenty of good reasons to get a new tool. Here are six situations that should prompt you to seriously consider a change.

## We Have No CRM Tool

Let's face it: you're behind the times. There are so many ways in which a CRM tool can improve the way you work with your customers while helping the bottom line. Are you afraid that it's going to take lots of time and money? This book is here to guide you through the process.

## We Use A Homegrown Tool

Once upon a time, there were no commercial CRM tools and companies built their own. Now that CRM vendors have had years to refine their technology and offerings, it's very rare to find a homegrown tool that combines good functionality with affordable upkeep. In my experience, most homegrown products are hopelessly old-fashioned because it costs too much to keep maintaining them properly.

So if you are using a homegrown tool, and unless you are ecstatically satisfied with it, you should consider going mainstream. True, you will lose the ultimate customized look and feel of homegrown, but you will gain affordable maintenance and timely adoption of new technology since the cost is spread among thousands of clients.

While going through the selection process, keep an open mind to changing the way you do business to match the capabilities of the new tool. The most common mistake people make when switching from a homegrown tool is to overcustomize. It's costly, of course, but more importantly, when the next release comes, upgrading requires almost as much work again, and you're back in the mode of overspending on maintenance. So if you are switching from a homegrown tool, remember to keep customizations to a strict minimum.

## We Have No Customer Portal

A telltale sign of an old, obsolete tool is a complete inward focus. If your tool offers no customer portal, or one that's so limited and painful to set up that it's not functional, it is a not-so-subtle sign that you need to move on. Good portal functionality is not merely "cool," it's that wonderful kind of technology that's truly useful. So if you cannot get a clear commitment from your vendor on when it will become available, start looking elsewhere. And even if you get an acceptable commitment, you should question your vendor's ability to keep up with new ideas. Portals are not this year's new, new thing!

If your tool does include acceptable portal functionality, but you have not deployed it, go find a way to get it done right away. You can't use your inability to act as a ticket to get a new tool.

## Our Tool Is Really Slow

While lack of functionality is the #1 reason why internal users shy away from using a CRM tool, slow performance is a close second. I've seen implementations where it took a full minute (that's 60 seconds) to refresh a screen. No wonder the real work took place on paper!

If your tool is really slow, do not immediately conclude that it needs to be discarded. Request a performance audit from the vendor (this is better than having an independent third-party perform the audit because there are fewer directions in which to point fingers). The vendor should be able to identify hardware and configuration changes to improve performance. If no relief is possible (or none without massive additional investment) it's probably because you have exceeded the capabilities of the tool, or the underlying architecture does not scale well. Either way, it's time to go shopping.

## Our Vendor Disappeared

The CRM world has seen enormous numbers of acquisitions, outright failures, and strategy changes over the past few years, to the point where my customers sometimes have trouble recalling the name of the vendor of the CRM tool they use daily. While many such changes occur without causing long-term damage to the underlying products, you may well be a victim of an orphan tool. What to do?

If you find that your tool is being "end-of-lifed" or is being described by some other polite, death-suggesting understatement, don't immediately conclude that an immediate uprooting to a different tool is necessary. Take the opportunity to reassess your tool strategy rather than blindly following the path the vendor is suggesting. There's no need to rush into a decision; typically orphaned tools are supported for several months to several years, giving you enough time to make a rational choice.

If the tool is orphaned because of an acquisition, you will probably be given the option to "upgrade" to the acquiring party's tool. Carefully weigh the benefits and costs of the upgrade, which is really a migration. As in any tool migration, you are facing what will almost certainly amount to a full re-implementation. It's likely that the vendor will provide special implementation assistance for the migration to retain the customer base. The vendor may provide special incentives and attention to the accounts that upgrade early, and they will need to be balanced against the additional level of experience that will be gained during the early upgrades and leveraged for later ones.

The ownership of the license typically carries over but do ask about potentially higher maintenance fees based on a different license price structure. Maintenance costs should also weigh in your decision.

If you are not happy with your current tool, and the features of the new one are not appealing either, you should be able to get a good deal from another vendor eager to capture some of the accounts in transition away from their suddenly larger competitor.

## We Have Time And Resources To Do A Good Job

It's best to make tool changes when you are not under the gun. If your tool is working fairly well, but you anticipate issues with functionality, performance, or vendor stability to impact you within a year or two, it's a good idea to start looking now. Although quick implementations are certainly possible, giving yourself several months for the initial tool selection phase makes for a more enlightened, less stressful, and more economical choice.

By now, you should have a good idea of whether you need a new tool. Let's see how to go about selecting, acquiring, and implementing one.

# Overview of CRM Selection and Implementation

## Express Version

- A critical success factor for CRM projects is to "think small, dream big." While a comprehensive plan helps avoid coordination nightmares down the road, it's best to use a layered approach with 60- to 90-day goals rather than massive projects that carry a lot of risk.

- In the same vein, don't try to do more than the tool can do, or to expand drastically the scope of a project once it starts. It's usually better to relegate newly discovered requirements to a future phase.

- Early and continuous involvement of users, including individual contributors, and preferably top performers and informal leaders, is a tremendous help in getting user acceptance, as well as getting high-quality input for the technical requirements, customizations, and testing.

- Create and communicate tangible measurements of the success of the project.

- To determine high-level time and resource requirements, it's useful to classify projects as low, medium, or high complexity depending on the scope of functions and applications being automated, the number of users involved, and the number of integrations.
- Typical timelines from the initial tool selection to implementation vary from 3 to 9 months for low-complexity projects, from 6 to 12 months for medium-complexity projects, and from 10 to 24 months for high-complexity projects.
- Ways to speed up the timeline include keeping the various functional groups focused and working together (most important for the tool selection phase) and narrowing the number and scope of customizations and integrations (for the implementation phase).
- Typical budgets depend both on the complexity of the project, but also on the number of users (since the large cost of integrations and customizations can be spread over the total number of users). Count on at least $10K per user and up to $50K with extensive customizations. Except for very simple projects, the cost of the CRM license is only a fraction of the total cost.

## A High-Level View of the Entire Process

You have decided to implement a new CRM tool, whether you are starting from scratch or replacing an existing tool that doesn't make the grade, as confirmed through the audit process described in the previous chapter. This chapter describes an overall blueprint for the entire selection and implementation process, including key success factors and typical time and resource requirements for projects of various complexity levels, as well as recommendations for decreasing complexity when appropriate.

This is a good place to start to get an overall idea of what it takes to be successful with a CRM implementation. The upcoming chapters will expand on each step of the process so you can delve into the details. This is a more theoretical and high-level chapter than the rest of the book but it still contains plenty of practical advice.

We'll start with the key success factors for CRM projects.

# Success Factors

While there are many techniques that deliver a successful CRM project, they derive from just a few general principles or success factors: "Think small, dream big" (have a general plan, but take small steps), "stay in the box" (don't overreach), "get users involved" (user buy-in is key), and "measure success" (set a solid goal and prove you are succeeding).

## Think Small, Dream Big

While some see CRM projects as multi-year projects that affect the entire organization and require massive change both to infrastructure and process, I believe such mega-projects are very risky and that many of the public failures we hear about are caused by overlong, over-complex projects. Huge projects have many weaknesses.

- **Changing requirements**. The competitive environment in which your organization exists changes quickly, so that requirements defined today are likely to be inadequate two years from now, even if they were carefully crafted. Requirements defined for 90-day deliverables are much more likely to remain valid by the time the project rolls out.

- **Scope creep**. Scope creep is the phenomenon through which additional features and requirements are added to a project after the initial requirements have been defined and agreed upon. It's pretty easy to banish scope creep from a short project, both because there's little time to generate additional requirements and also because there's simply no time to fit them in. With massive projects, on the other hand, change requests are often required since conditions do change over longer periods of time. And with an extended schedule it's tempting to accommodate the changes, with the hope that the time can be made up. So the already massive scope of long projects tends to get more massive over time.

- **Sponsorship stability**. CRM projects need a strong sponsor at the executive level. The longer the project, the more likely that the sponsor will lose interest, change roles, or leave the company, obliterating the chances of the CRM project.

- **Technical complexity**. While short-term projects can be complex, they usually don't get as complex as longer ones. More importantly, they provide a discipline that encourages tackling the technical challenges one at a time, along with short-term milestones to assess success and to refocus the strategy as needed.

- **Technical obsolescence**. Over the course of a long project, the technical components do not sit still. For instance, over a two-year project the CRM software itself is likely to go through *eight* or so maintenance releases and one or two major upgrades. And this is only the beginning: there will be upgrades and changes in the underlying network, servers, desktop equipment, browser software, wireless devices, and all the other technical pieces of the CRM project.

  Don't think you can simply ignore the upgrades. Vendors will stop supporting the older products after several years, so you will be forced to upgrade multiple times throughout the project. Ugly!

- **Project management complexity**. The amount of coordination required by massive projects is staggering and the complexity increases by an order of magnitude with the length of the timeline and the size of the staff involved. The more complex the project, the more likely breakdowns can develop and remain undetected for long periods of time. Smaller-scope projects are incomparably easier to manage.

- **Cheerleader fatigue**. Enthusiasm and optimism are important components of successful projects. It's much harder to sustain them for two years as compared to three months. If the scope of a project requires a multi-year schedule, proceeding with a series of three-month mini-projects ensures tangible positive outcomes each quarter that should help recharge everyone's batteries and sustain the team throughout the extended schedule.

Huge projects are risky. This is not to say that long-term plans are not useful. Without a long-term plan the organization can make shortsighted mistakes. For instance, a single-minded focus on solving the issue of handling incoming customers' e-mail may bring a great e-mail processing system that fails to connect with any of the other systems in place, creating an unhelpful island of information. With a long-term plan, the organization can select a tool that has an integration component, even if the integration doesn't happen for a while.

Take the time to create a high-level plan (the "dream") to coordinate the various CRM efforts. At the same time, avoid analysis paralysis: it does not make sense to create a detailed five-year plan since one can't even begin to imagine where CRM vendors will be then. Don't wait for the perfect tool to plug into your perfect dream.

Once you have a long-term strategy in place, think small when it comes time to defining an actual project. It's much easier to shepherd small projects to a successful conclusion, and over time they are more effective than large projects.

They are much easier to manage. There are fewer people involved, so there is less potential for communication breakdowns, and there's also less time to mess up. It's also a lot easier to adapt to changing circumstances when each step is small.

Small projects make it easier to meet the users' expectations. It's easier to define realistic expectations on small projects to begin with, and because of the short duration, expectations don't have much time to inflate or change significantly.

As a consequence, small-scope projects are less likely to fail than larger projects. When something goes wrong the feedback comes quickly, before much damage is done. It's much easier to fix a short-term deliverable than one that was months in the making.

Small-scope projects do have drawbacks, although I think they are more than offset by the advantages described above.

Isn't it more expensive to work with multiple small deliverables compared to one big deliverable? It's true that there is a fixed minimum overhead associated with any deliverable, so that a project with many small steps carries more overhead than one with fewer steps. However, large-scope projects have a much higher communication and coordination burden, so the difference is not that great in the end.

Note that this optimistic assessment assumes the all-important point that you have created an overall strategy and you are deploying against that strategy. If you are taking small steps in an uncoordinated, haphazard approach, you run the risk of having to redo some of the steps when you realize that they don't fit well together, and that would be a very great expense indeed.

Does it take more time to work through small steps? In a way, yes. If you could do everything perfectly with one large-scope project, you would probably do it faster than if you use multiple small steps. The reality is that the likelihood that a single large-scope project would be done perfectly is very low to nil, even with strong project management, because what makes a CRM system really work is the tuning that can only happen once the users are actually using it. It's more realistic to implement small steps quickly and to go through several tuning exercises rather than to implement one big step that needs no tuning.

And now for the big question: can small steps really be used for large organizations with complex needs, or is it a technique that can only be used for small-scale deployments?

Certainly, if your needs are complex you will find that even small steps are bigger than small steps suitable for a small organization with simple needs. However, I would argue that it's especially important for large deployments to be structured through smaller steps, each providing a complete solution to a particular issue, and each allowing a realistic validation by the end-users before proceeding. Only the initial step in the project should be significantly longer for large deployments to allow for the development of the overall data model (what data is tracked in the system and how it is organized) and of the system architecture.

So go ahead and have big (coherent) dreams, but implement them in small steps.

## Stay In the Box

There's the old story of the people who want to repaint their kitchen and fall prey to the "while we are at it" syndrome:

- While we are at it (repainting), we should redo the floor.
- While we are at it (redoing the floor), we should change the stove.
- While we are at it (changing the stove), we should get all new appliances.
- While we are at it (getting new appliances), we should redo the cabinets.
- While we are at it (redoing the cabinets), we should get a bigger window.

After many months and many, many times the cost of a fresh coat of paint, they get a new kitchen, the walls of which we can only hope are painted the right color. And they may keep going and decide to push a wall out (add two months), creating their own monster project.

The same thing can happen to CRM projects. Here are some typical examples of the "while we are at it" syndrome.

- While we are at it, we should customize the screens so they all conform to our internal web format standards.
- While we are at it, we should extend the rollout to the channel sales group, not just direct sales. ("Rollout" or "deployment" is the last phase of the implementation during which the system is made available to end-users as their primary work environment as opposed to a test situation.)

- While we are at it, we should integrate the CRM tool with the ACD (automatic call distributor) so we can do intelligent routing and automatic dialing.
- While we are at it, we should review all the documents in the knowledge base and not roll out the system until the review is absolutely complete.
- While we are at it, we need to train all staffers on a new sales methodology, or advanced support skills.

It's important to address new issues and ideas encountered during the project, but it's usually best to keep pretty much within the scope defined at the beginning of the project and to defer new items to a second phase. Let's analyze the examples we just saw.

- On the issue of customizing screens to conform to a corporate standard, the answer is a clear "yes" for the customer interface. Customers should not be aware of jarring differences between CRM portal pages and other pages on your web site. This requirement should be identified right at the beginning of the project, and it should be relatively easy to achieve, at least with modern CRM tools that allow applying templates to the portal screens.

    It's a different story for internal users. While consistency is visually pleasing (your corporate standards are visually pleasing, right?), and while consistency makes for greater efficiency, changing dozens of screens to conform to an ever-evolving corporate standard is a waste of resources in my mind. By all means make the easy changes such as including your logo on the page or matching your color scheme, but focus your precious resources on making sure that the screens are efficient and uncluttered rather than matching the corporate standard. Find other ways to make friends with your Corporate Identity department.

- Extending a rollout to another sales organization (from direct sales to channel sales) will probably require revising the workflow and making changes to some data fields and screens. Does it make sense to include the channel sales organization in the planning so there can be one combined rollout for both sales organizations? If the entire company is moving from direct sales to channel sales, then yes, you must change your plan. If that's the case, we are not talking about a "while we are at it" issue, but about a "just found out I must" issue, which has a completely different urgency.

    Barring such a drastic change, I recommend completing the rollout to the direct sales force as planned and considering the needs of the channels sales force in a second phase. Making the system usable for channel sales may (or may not) require changes to the data model as well as changes to the application itself, but such changes and any impact they have for the direct sales team can be handled in a later phase.

Even if it's known from the start that both sales organizations need the CRM tool, it may still be a good strategy to tackle one organization, then the other. In that case I would definitely start by defining a data model that meets the needs of both organizations.

- Extending a rollout to include an integration with another tool, in the example the ACD, is usually a kiss of death. Integrations are costly in both time and resources, they add significant risk to the project, and if you integrate the CRM tool with other tools before the end-users have had a chance to try it hands-on, you may well integrate the wrong functions entirely. Better to roll out the CRM tool without the integration first, work out the kinks, and then do the integration when it's very clear what functionality is needed.

There are good reasons to include an integration in a CRM project *if the decision is made upfront*. One such situation is if the integration is the one tangible benefit of the project. If you are changing the CRM system specifically to allow integration with the phone system and there is no other major benefit to the project, then the integration *is* the project.

Another reason to include an integration in a project is funding. It may be a lot easier to go to the well once, albeit with a much larger request. Even in this case you should seriously consider deploying in two phases, the first one without the integration and the second one being the integration, once you have some production experience. The CFO should be amenable to a two-step approach to minimize risk.

- Delaying the rollout of a tool because of concerns about the quality of the documents in the knowledge base is almost always a mistake. The tool by itself cannot overcome weaknesses in your document creation and publication process, although it can be a big help in making the process function more efficiently.

If the documents you are concerned about have been accessible all along in their imperfect and unreviewed state, why not roll out with them? In parallel, accelerate the review process, perhaps by giving the reviewers a clear incentive (read: a bonus) to complete the review quickly.

If, on the other hand, the concern is that unreviewed documents will be exposed to customers who did not have access to them before, then you have a problem, but one that should be solved by withholding (through the tool's permission scheme) the potentially offending documents until they are reviewed. As before, expedite the review process through judicious incentives to avoid having to roll out with an empty knowledge base.

Finally, seriously consider putting all the unreviewed documents in the big round file in the sky and starting over. I once spent close to a year paying overtime compensation to support staffers to review old documents we could not bear to throw away. In the end we salvaged only a handful of documents, definitely not our money's worth. Your experience is likely to be similar in fast-changing environments where any document older than two years is likely to be truly obsolete.

- Is it wise to delay a rollout to train the users on new methodology? It's often the case that a CRM project uncovers gaps in the underlying business skills of the staffers who will use the tool. If the issue is that the users are not as competent as first thought on the existing sales methodology or the existing troubleshooting protocol, I would roll out the tool anyway and conduct the training when time and resources become available. The tool is *not* the solution to the entire issue of customer management so it should not be held hostage to the methodology training.

On the other hand, if learning the new methodology is required to use the tool, then the training should be a part of the rollout, and that should have been identified early in the planning process. You should hold the methodology training before the rollout (and remember the problem for the post-mortem analysis).

If you hold training on the methodology separate from the tool training, use the sessions to reinforce each other. If the methodology training comes first then the tool training should showcase how the tool helps the users follow the steps in the methodology. If the tool training comes first then the methodology training should show how the tool can help put it in practice.

These examples illustrate situations where new requirements occur during the actual project, but the same rule of "stay in the box" applies to defining the initial requirements. For instance, if your CRM project is focused on adding an online sales tool but you also find that it would be good to improve the sales methodology, the marketing materials, and the color of the Palm Pilots, I very much recommend limiting the CRM project to implementing the online sales tools, at least if the sales methodology is clearly identified and agreed to before selecting the tool. Once the tool is launched (or in parallel, if you have enough resources), attack the other issues.

Don't torture the tool. If you're trying to do something that's simply alien to the way the tool was designed, the results will be 1) expensive and 2) never quite right. By conducting a reasonable selection process, as will be described in the upcoming chapters, you should end up with a tool that does most of what you need. Bring your current process with you when you evaluate systems and evaluate the demos through the lens of the process. Aim for a good overall fit between your process and the tool (without being obsessed by a complete, 100% fit: perfection is not of this world).

In the same vein, if your process does not fit well with the tool, consider changing your process rather than the tool. This is particularly true if your process doesn't seem to fit with *any* tool that you see. Yes, it's possible that you have discovered a secret way to do things that's better than everyone else's. On the other hand you could be driving the wrong way on the freeway, which is why everyone else is going the other way. If all the tools do things a certain way, chances are it is a best practice and you should simply adopt it.

Keep customizations to less than 10%. This is an arbitrary number, for sure, but it illustrates that you should shop for a good overall fit for the tool and keep customizations to a minimum. Customizations are expensive and do not port well to new releases, so they are very expensive in the long run. As long as you have a good overall fit between your process and the tool, first consider adapting your processes to the tool rather than automatically customizing the tool.

## Get Users Involved

One of the key tests of the success of a CRM initiative is whether the users actually use the system. The problem is that, even when the new tool has clear advantages over the old one, it's difficult to switch to a new tool where familiar things are no longer familiar and even routine operations may require checking the handy cheat-sheet that was provided during the training sessions. By getting users involved early, you have a chance to build up enthusiasm and support for the benefits of the system that will help overcome the barriers to adoption.

Take care to avoid overselling the system. No, the new tool will probably not double the users' productivity (let's face it, it will probably lower productivity in the short-term as users get used to it). No, the new tool will not allow 50% of customer requests to be fulfilled automatically (at least if the requests you get are reasonably complex). And no, the tool will not contain all the data the users ever need to do their job. Instead of overreaching claims, present a nuanced picture of realistic benefits: they will be able to see your pipeline at the touch of a button; they will be able to automatically attach interesting documents to customer e-mails, etc.

Besides the advantages of psychological preparation, the other benefit of involving users early is that they are the ones who know how to do the job and what's needed to do it. End-users—not their managers, not some mythical "super-user," and certainly not ersatz process managers—need to be a part of the entire project cycle, from selection to implementation, to keep everyone honest. Certainly it's neither feasible nor desirable to involve *everyone* in each step. Have you ever tried to hold a demo for 500? And what about stopping all sales activities for two days while we debate the tool workflow? You can't get everyone involved every step of the way, but you need to involve actual end-users, and ideally some of the best-performing ones, at each crucial juncture.

You may find that end-users are not very interested in the project because, especially if they are top performers, they are busy selling customers or helping them resolve service issues. Find the right levels of stick and carrot to get them to participate. In particular, understand that their time is valuable and make sure they are asked to participate only in high-value activities. For instance, if a vendor is doing a daylong dog-and-pony show, end-user input may be best spent on the demo portion. Even then, their participation may be required only if the tool is a real contender (did the CIO nix it because of vendor viability concerns?) and only if the demo can be interactive (we'll come back to techniques to get the vendor to deliver the information that you want in Chapter 6, "Shopping for a CRM System").

Another characteristic of top performers is that they are usually good readers. Don't spend 30 minutes giving them "background information" when they could read it in ten minutes when it's convenient for them. They also like to be kept informed (again, not in a long and tedious meeting). Why was the tool they liked so much not selected? Why are we behind schedule and what is being done to catch up? They'll want to know.

In addition to top performers, it's well worthwhile to involve the group's informal leaders, who may not be top performers themselves but who have a lot of influence on the group and command respect and admiration. It's a challenge because they tend to be busy, but they will spread the word on the project very well, better than top performers who may be more of the loner type.

There is tremendous value in getting individual contributors involved, not just managers. The nature of their job is different, and it's quite common that managers don't have a very good sense of what individual contributors in their groups do all day. If there are subgroups that are likely to use the tool differently (say, focused on different markets, or different products), make sure you get representatives from all groups, at least until you prove to yourself that the requirements are similar. We'll come back to this topic in more detail when we discuss the project team in Chapter 4.

It's a mistake to assume that IT staffers or even process managers can substitute for actual end-users. Even when these individuals are well aware of the requirements of the end-users, they simply cannot have the same level of awareness about what really matters on a daily basis that the actual end-users have. Don't assume that IT or the process group can be a complete substitute.

## Measure Success

Human beings like to have tangible feedback for their efforts. This is particularly true of long-term, large-scope projects where it's hard to tell whether one is really making a difference. Setting up a system to capture and communicate progress on the project will help sustain the enthusiasm of the participants. At the same time, since there is always a contingent of skeptics attached to any CRM project, the same information can be used to contain their criticisms, if not to generate their enthusiasm.

Metrics are typically the responsibility of the project manager, although on larger projects this can be delegated.

How does one measure the success of a CRM project? We'll see detailed metrics suggestions in Chapter 10, "Measuring Success," but here are some high-level points.

**Start Early**   Establishing metrics that are meaningful and acceptable to all parties before the start of the project makes them more credible in the long run, avoiding any suspicion of manipulation. It's fine to set only high-level targets when you start. You can then assign specific quantitative targets only when the implementation starts, once you have a better idea of what the tool will really be able to do.

**Be Simple**   Using 12 different calculations, or anything that requires knowledge of advanced statistics to understand, is counterproductive. Stick with three to five high-level measurements, each of them a simple arithmetic computation (you can use averages, but standard deviations are probably not required to make your point).

**Measure Results, not just Activities**  Having reviewed 10 vendors (an activity) is nowhere as important as having narrowed down the list of candidates to two (a result). During the implementation phase, having completed 80 test items (an activity) is an interesting achievement, but even better is having passed 78 of the test items (a result). In the same vein, measuring projects by elapsed time is nowhere near as useful as using milestones, which, if well defined, refer to actual results. Measuring for results implies the use of targets—i.e., how much did we accomplish versus what we were planning. Make sure that the results you measure are meaningful both for customers and for internal users.

Now for some examples for long-term (not project-oriented) business goals:

For a marketing organization:

- Reaching 2000 customers within 2 months is an activity goal.
- Creating 20 qualified leads within 2 months is a better goal.
- Creating leads that generate sales of $X within 2 month is a good result goal.

For a sale organization:

- Entering all pending deals within 24 hours is an activity goal.
- Creating complete forecasts daily is a better goal.
- Increasing forecast accuracy to within 10% in the last week of the quarter is a good result goal.

For a support organization:

- Entering 2000 documents into the knowledge base is an activity goal.
- Increasing knowledge base usage by 50% is a better goal.
- Decreasing the case/customer ratio by 20% is a good result goal.

**Report Good and Bad**  One eerie characteristic of failing CRM projects is the incredible disconnect between the status reports and reality. While the status reports include vaguely-worded and minor delays and difficulties, the implementation team is overwhelmed with problems, its members either screaming at each other or no longer communicating at all, and so frustrated they are barely able to drag themselves to the office in the morning. The disconnect can be sustained for amazingly long periods in larger organizations with many layers and many people involved—thankfully, that's not usually the case in smaller organizations.

To gain credibility, share both good and bad news. This includes areas of potential over-investment. For instance, if you planned for a testing period of four weeks and you're done in two, could it be that the planners were sandbagging? Is it possible that the testing that was accomplished was insufficient? Meeting the goal by a mile should raise questions, not only congratulations.

**Be Transparent**   Status reports are meant to be shared widely. A wide distribution is a great incentive to create accurate reports as well as a vehicle to get them corrected quickly when needed. In particular, special reports to the executives can bring confusion and misinformation. If they are required because the regular status reports are too long, then they should also be shared downwards to benefit from the effects of a wide distribution.

While we will see many more practical pieces of advice as we work our way through the book, the top four success factors: "think small, dream big," "stay in the box," "get users involved early" and "measure success" are our guides to CRM success.

# The Three Phases of CRM Projects

At the highest level, there are three phases to implementing a CRM system:

- **Selecting the tool**, which includes defining requirements (covered in Chapter 5), shopping for the tool (Chapter 6), and negotiating the purchase (Chapter 7).
- **Selecting the integrator.** Most of the time, as we will see, it makes sense to contract out at least part of the tool implementation, since integrators can leverage their experience to make the implementation both faster and less error-prone. It doesn't mean you should completely give up control, however, as we will discuss in Chapter 8, "Selecting an Integration Partner." Some newer, mid-range tools may be able to be implemented without outside help. We will discuss when to make that decision in Chapter 8.
- **Implementing the tool.** This is typically the longest phase by far, and its success depends much on how well the two other phases went. Chapter 9 expands on activities and recommendations for this phase, whether you are working with the vendor, a third-party integrator, or alone.

Although the three phases are described sequentially, it doesn't mean that they occur strictly sequentially. In reality, there is quite a bit of overlap between the tool selection and the integrator selection phases: It's impossible to make a final decision on an integrator without having chosen a tool, and it's also very unwise to select a tool without having appropriate integrator candidates identified for the implementation. Moreover, there are many situations where implementation constraints influence the selection of the tool. For instance, you may choose to withdraw from consideration tools for which they are few qualified integrators available based on your evaluation of integrators.

Even the implementation phase is not completely separate from the tool and integrator selection phases. While actual implementation cannot start until after the tool and the integrator have been chosen, there's much that can be put in place for the implementation before the other two phases are completed. One of the most important is selecting team members for the implementation, as you will want to include additional individuals who were not already involved with the selection phases.

Although it's convenient to think of the three phases—tool selection, integrator selection, implementation—as separate events, remember that they all overlap and interact in important ways.

# How Long Will it Take?

This is the most popular question I get about CRM projects, and it's even more popular than another popular question: what does it cost? Like all important questions, how much time is required is not an easy question to answer. The most accurate answer is "It depends." I've personally witnessed a *successful* one-month project from beginning to go-live date, as well as projects that took close to two years to complete. Unfortunately not every long project was successful, so time spent is not a guarantee for success.

One way to approach the time forecast is to start with the overall complexity of the project. Although a complex project can sometimes be accomplished faster than a straightforward one, given a good team and relentless focus, project complexity is a fairly reliable indicator of how long it will take. Let's start by defining what makes a project complex.

## Project Complexity

Project complexity depends on the following eight factors:

- **The number of business functions** involved. If you are looking for a CRM system for just one function, such as sales, it will be easier to select a tool and faster to implement it than if you are looking for an all-encompassing solution for sales, marketing, and support. Coordination between the departments, finding a proper project sponsor, and finding appropriate technical solutions all are more difficult and time-consuming when multiple functions are involved.

- **The scope of the automation**. In the same vein as above, the scope that's being automated has a direct effect on complexity. If you simply want to track sales contacts, your task will be a lot easier than if you also want to implement a scheduling package, a product configurator, and a proposal generator.

- **The size of the organization**, the size of the employee population affected, and, to a lesser extent, the size of the customer base. For starters, it is a simple fact that any project that involves lots of people takes more time to complete (even if it's not a straight line increase). There is also a technical component, as massive numbers of users mean higher performance requirements along with more complex applications, typically requiring extensive configurations and at least some customizations. Finally, very large customer databases create performance and functionality challenges.

- **Geographical dispersion** of the users and, most important, of their leadership. Having to coordinate with geographically dispersed users means that decisions will take longer. It also creates more pressure on performance tuning and deployment issues.

- **Multi-lingual requirements**. You can add many more complexity points if the users are speaking different languages. It's not only a matter of translating the screens and messages, but also handling different holidays, time zones, currencies, tax calculations, and potentially processes too. If you must provide multi-lingual screens to internal users, the complexity increases even further.

- **The requirements for integrations with other systems**. Because integrations are always custom, they necessarily require lots of time to implement. In the future, each time any of the integrated systems changes the integration will have to be revisited and perhaps adapted. This does not mean that integrations should be avoided, simply that they add to the complexity of a project and therefore its ultimate cost. They should always be weighed against the benefits they bring.

- **The customization requirements**. This criterion may appear unreasonable, since it's pretty difficult to estimate customization requirements when you haven't even started looking for a tool! However, you can make a reasonable guess of the customization requirements by observing—or mandating—how open you will be to adapting your process to the one modeled in the tool as opposed to capturing your exact requirements into the tool. If you are using a unique process and you are unwilling to adapt it to match a potential tool, you automatically add to the complexity of the project.

- **The target timeline**. This again sounds like a chicken-and-egg criterion since we are establishing the complexity index precisely to establish a timeline. What I mean is that, as we know, projects expand to fit the timeline, so if you allocate an overly generous timeline you can be sure that the project will expand to it. To be fair, an overly tight timeline has the potential for explosive failures. Rushed projects often fail to meet their objectives, if not the target deadline itself, and after they fail they need to be redone at great additional cost and with a considerably less enthusiastic staff.

  Be realistic when establishing a target timeline, but don't be afraid to be a little ambitious compared to the targets discussed below. Be on the shorter side rather than the longer side. In the same vein, you should also set deadlines for the important milestones of tool selection and integrator selection to avoid being behind even before you start the implementation.

A low-complexity project targets the main applications for one business function only, for a moderate number of users (no more than a couple hundred). Users are distributed within a single geographical entity (one center, one country, or at the most one continent) with no multi-lingual requirements. Only a couple of integrations are required, and there is flexibility to process change to match the tool to avoid customizations.

A medium-complexity project may target more than one business function and it provides a pretty full complement of applications for each function. There are hundreds of users who are geographically dispersed. Some customer language adaptation is likely to be required. Several integrations are involved. Because of the size of the project, it's clear that customizations will be required.

A high-complexity project targets multiple business functions, with very complete coverage of the applications for each function. It has thousands of users, they are dispersed, and there are multi-lingual requirements. Many integrations are required.

Let's see what typical timelines look like for various levels of complexity.

## Timeline for Simple Projects

Here are timeline estimates for a simple project (that is, one that targets the main applications for one business function, has no more than a couple hundred users, no more than a couple of integrations, and minimal customizations.)

The tool selection could take from one month to three months, depending on the availability of key personnel and their prior knowledge of the CRM field. It can also be helpful to purchase the tool at the end of the vendor's financial quarter (more on this in Chapter 7, "Buying a Tool") so in this instance slower can be better! Simple projects are ideal candidates for accelerated tool searches, as described in Chapter 6, "Shopping for a Tool."

The process of selecting an integrator should be shorter than with the more complex projects because the requirements are simpler, but sometimes it's difficult to find good, reliable integrators for smaller-scope projects. With a simple project, you may consider doing the implementation yourself. It's always a good idea to at least get some guidance from someone who implements that particular tool day in and day out, not just once in a while. Count on one to two months to find an integrator, much of which can be accomplished simultaneously with the tool selection process. For a simple project, the vendor should be able to either provide implementation assistance or point you to an experienced implementation partner.

Implementing the tool is much faster for simple projects and this is where the timeline gets dramatically shorter. Count on anywhere from two to five months, with the higher figure required if integrations are involved. If you follow our recommendation for layered implementations, you should be able to do the first rollout within 90 days, leaving the integrations to a second phase.

| 0 | 1 | 2 | 3 | 4 | 5 | 6 | 7 | 8 | 9 |

Tool Selection (1-3 months)

Integrator Selection (1-2 months)

Implementation (2-5 months)

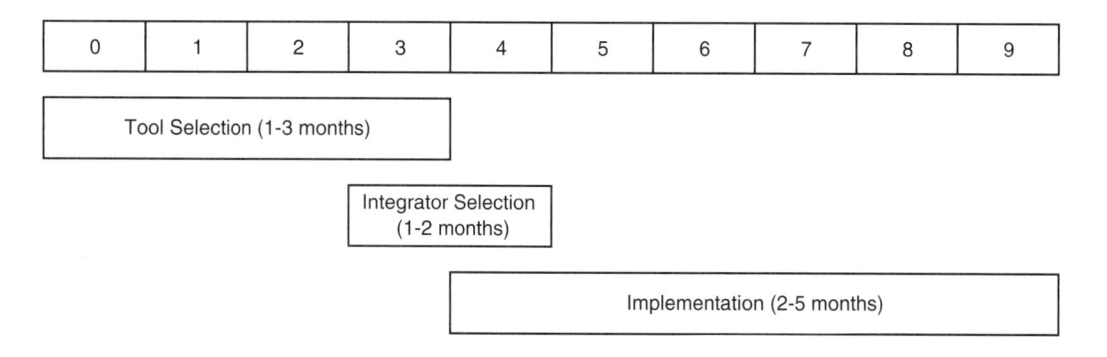

**FIGURE 3.1**
Timeline for Simple Projects

Overall, to complete a simple project from selection through implementation, you are looking at a minimum of three months and up through nine months, with the higher figure reflecting both a thorough tool search as well as more complex integration requirements (see Figure 3.1). Again, while faster is not necessarily better, longer timelines tend to breed delays and issues, so if you are considering a simple project it would be best to aim at something like a six-month deliverable, with the tool selection itself happening around the two-month mark.

What about very short timeframes? I mentioned earlier I had been a part of a successful one-month project, so it's possible to be successful with ultra-short deadlines. If you are tempted by a near-instantaneous solution, here are some points to consider.

- Don't be obsessed with speed. If there is no real business requirement, you must realize that a super-fast project will deliver a limited solution with no customizations. In particular, if your current tool is performing reasonably well, there is no reason to go for a super-fast project.
- Accept that you will not do an exhaustive search. There is no way to do that and an implementation within a couple of months. You can see demos of lots of different tools, but you cannot perform the kind of in-depth study that would allow you to make a fully informed decision
- Use your network. Because you cannot do an exhaustive search, it's particularly important to get others to help you with the initial winnowing. Why take a chance on a tool no one has heard of? Focus on colleagues with businesses similar to yours and eliminate any solution that requires a long implementation.
- Get a coach. There are consultants, including yours truly, who specialize in helping companies select CRM solutions. These people stay well informed of the market and can provide you with a first-cut selection appropriate to your requirements. Make sure you understand any financial gain the consultant may derive from a particular selection so you are aware of potential conflicts of interest. Select someone who has experience in your specific market because you have no time to spare. For instance, if you are looking for an e-commerce retail solution, someone who has been working exclusively with financial services companies would not be a good fit.
- Dedicate a small cross-functional team (users and IT staffers) to the project for the duration. We will talk in more detail about how to select the team in the next chapter, but the operative word here is dedication: with a short project, the team cannot be expected to do anything else.

## Timeline For Moderately Complex Projects

Here are timeline estimates for a medium-complexity project, that is, one that targets one or two business functions with a full complement of applications, has hundreds of users who are geographically dispersed, and requires some integrations and customizations.

The tool selection could take from two to four months, depending mostly on how well the different functions involved coordinate with each other. Moderately complex projects can be candidates for accelerated tool searches, as described in Chapter 6, "Shopping for a Tool." Reference checking is very important when projects cease to be simple, and onsite, hands-on reference checks, which take time, become very desirable. Try not to spend too much time on the selection process, however, since the real work is still ahead and you should be able to identify the top candidates reasonably quickly.

Selecting an integrator is required for moderate-complexity projects. Although it's always a good idea to have your own staff participate in a hands-on manner, it's very unlikely that you will have the trained resources required to actually pull off the project. Count on one to three months to find an integrator and much of the selection process can be accomplished while you complete the tool selection process. Note that the timeline does not differ much from that of a simple project.

Implementing the tool can take from four to nine months, and even longer if many integrations are required before rollout. With a longer schedule, I strongly recommend using a layered implementation, with regular deliverables every 60-90 days rather than one "big-bang" delivery. One popular approach is to roll out by function. However, this approach can be frustrating for the early users who typically have to wait until the entire rollout is completed before their immediate usability issues can be addressed (and there will be some, no matter what).

Adding it all up, a moderate-complexity project will take from six to twelve months (see Figure 3.2). While it is perfectly possible, if aggressive, to achieve a timeline on the lower end of the range, being successful in less than six months is unlikely with a moderate complexity project. Here are some pointers to achieve a speedy rollout with a moderately complex project.

- Do all you can to ensure that the various functions or groups involved work together harmoniously. Tool selection can be a very tense experience when multiple functions are involved. Single vendors are unlikely to satisfy all parties equally on the one hand, yet going with different vendors means you will need to do some integration work. If you have a terribly tight deadline and you are working with more than

```
0 | 1 | 2 | 3 | 4 | 5 | 6 | 7 | 8 | 9 | 10 | 11 | 12
```

Tool Selection (2-4 months)

Integrator Selection (1-3 months)

Implementation (4-9 months)

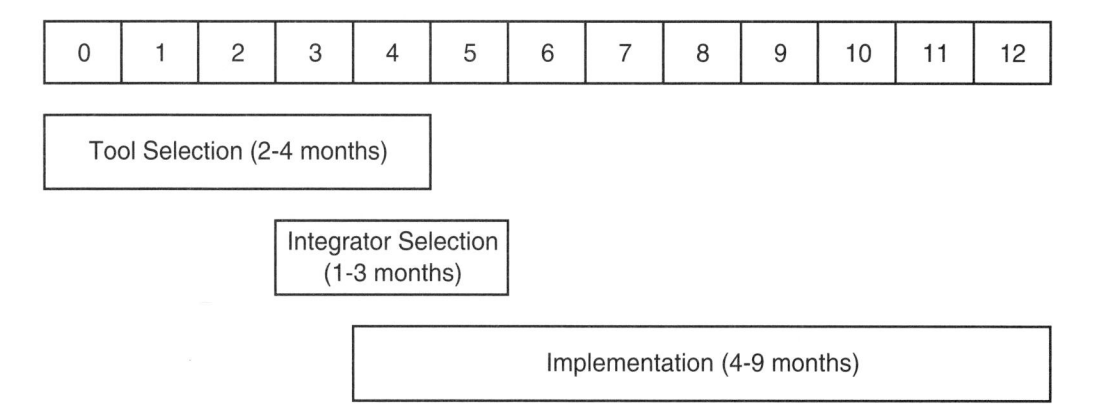

**FIGURE 3.2**
Timeline for Moderately-Complex Projects

one functional group, you most likely will have to mandate using a single vendor, and one or both parties will not get all the functionality they are dreaming of.

- Minimize the complexity of the customizations and integrations involved. This makes for a shorter rollout timeline as well as streamlined maintenance requirements in the future. Remember (and remind the groups involved) that customizations and integrations that are not achieved today can always be added on later, and that a better selection of customizations and integrations may be achieved after the users have had a chance to work with the system.

- Get skilled project management. Even the shorter project timelines are long enough to afford plenty of opportunities to miss something or forget a dependency. If the project manager comes from the system integrator, as is often the case, you will need to carefully evaluate the individual who will work with you.

## Timeline For Complex Projects

Here are timeline estimates for a high-complexity project, one that targets multiple applications for multiple functions, with thousands of dispersed users, multi-lingual requirements, and many integrations.

The tool selection could take from three to six months and will require good coordination among the functional groups and IT. Make sure that everyone buys into the decision, as you're sure to hit some problems later on. It's not unusual for a group to break ranks or attempt to sabotage the project because they were not part of the initial decision. At the same time, don't oversell the project because you don't want participants to have an overly rosy expectation. Without an appropriate-level executive sponsor, success in this phase alone is unlikely. All this is true of any project but it becomes particularly important for complex projects since the likelihood of problems is much higher.

Selecting an integrator is an absolute requirement for complex projects. The good news is that a project of this size should be highly attractive to potential integrators. The bad news is that few integrators have the required resources and experience to bring complex projects to a positive conclusion, so spend plenty of time checking references, both for recently-completed projects and projects that are still in progress. Because you will be working with large integrators, you can never be sure exactly who will work on your project, which is too bad since it makes such a big difference. Ask the references who worked on their project and who was especially valuable.

Count on two to three months to find an integrator. Some of the process can be accomplished simultaneously with the tool selection process. For a large project the integrator may need some time to assemble the team that you need so there may be some waiting time involved.

Implementing a complex project can take years! Focusing on the initial rollout, we will use a range of six to eighteen months, although six months would be particularly quick (and desirable!) while eighteen months would be dangerously long for the first step in the rollout.

It's essential to use a layered implementation strategy so that you get regular deliverables that allow you to test the system as you go. Nevertheless, the first deliverable may not happen for six months or so since you will probably need to customize the data model and the basic screens. Data migration (moving data from existing systems to the new system) is always an issue with larger projects and it also adds to the timeline.

Adding it all up, a complex project will take 10 to 24 months or more (see Figure 3.3). This is huge and perhaps you would like to aim for something a little shorter. If so, try these strategies.

- Dare to do an accelerated tool search as described in Chapter 6, "Shopping for a CRM Tool." Usually large projects are conducted with traditional RFP methods that are thorough but time-consuming, but if you are in a hurry you may want to be bold.
- Seriously consider a suite tool. Having some level of pre-integration should save you significant time during the implementation.

| 0 | 1 | 2 | 3 | 4 | 5 | 6 | 7 | 8 | 9 | 10 | 11 | 12 | 13 | 14 | 15 | 16 | 17 | 18 | 19 | 20 | 21 | 22 | 23 | 24 |

Tool Selection (3-6 months)

Integrator Selection (2-3 months)

Implementation (6-18 months)

**FIGURE 3.3**
Timeline for Complex Projects

- If you do select different tools for different functions, work out the integration strategy early on, ideally before making the final decision on the tool selection.

- Once the tool selection is completed, work on a joint data model, then proceed with parallel implementations by business function. This method will allow you to 1) meet urgent needs first; 2) work around the scheduling constraints of various groups, for instance avoid deploying a new SFA tool in the last fiscal quarter of the year; and 3) spread out the integrator staffing requirements better, which may allow you to increase the quality of the staff

## Why Timelines Cannot Be Compressed Easily

We discussed various ways to keep the timelines to a minimum and those techniques will help. But does it have to take so long? Yes, because there is a fair amount of waiting time. For instance, when we talk about tool selection, it will take some time to arrange for a vendor demo. It will take some time to assemble your evaluation team, not to mention scheduling around the team members' requirements (this is one of the reasons why smaller companies and smaller teams move so much faster). It will take time for the reference checks, which is certainly not the place to cut corners. Negotiating the purchasing contract is another area where some patience will be amply rewarded. Even if you know what you want, it's unlikely you can complete the selection step in less than a few weeks without paying close to list price, which is definitely not a good outcome for CRM purchases. Much the same is true of integrator selection. Here, the additional issue is scheduling. The best people tend to be busy, and there can be a real advantage to waiting for the particular individual you want to become available for the project.

Interestingly, the implementation phase is one that can often be compressed, although not all activities within the implementation phase are good candidates for compressing. We'll discuss this at length in Chapter 9, "Implementing Your CRM Tool." For now, suffice it to say that any activity related to customization or integration can potentially be shortened, cut out altogether, or scheduled for future phases. Other areas are *not* amenable to compression, including planning and testing. Planning is essential to make the right decisions on what should or should not be done. We will see how to conduct an effective planning session in Chapter 9. As for testing, many otherwise lovely CRM applications cease to function properly under high load conditions, so don't skimp on testing if you want to be successful.

## Why Vendors Substantially Underestimate Timelines

Ask almost any CRM vendor how long it takes to implement their solution and you're likely to hear "under 60 days" or, if they are really hedging, "We have several customers who have gone live in less than 60 days." The reality is that most customers take months to implement CRM solutions. What's going on here?

- Some customers do go live in very short order. They typically have a burning business need and are willing to sacrifice customizations and a perfect fit to get to their goal. Most of the time, the super-fast rollouts are followed by more or less extensive re-implementation efforts, sometimes starting immediately after the initial rollouts, to handle all the customization issues that could not be addressed the first time around.

- Customers with low-complexity projects can roll out much more quickly, as described earlier in this section. Even without a pressing business need, simple projects go faster. If your requirements are complex you simply won't be able to achieve the same results.

- Even customers who complete their rollouts within reasonably long timeframes may bring the tool up quickly, perhaps to a small pilot group, before they work on the customizations and integrations they need. They do implement, in a fashion, in 60 days, but it's not a full and complete rollout as most people would define a rollout.

- On the other hand, a sizable number of customers suffer protracted implementation schedules because of political issues, project management weaknesses, or lack of technical resources completely unrelated to the underlying tool. Understandably, vendors don't wish to include such experiences in their records.

- Vendors know very well that customers are afraid of long implementations, therefore it is in their best interest to minimize the time required to go live.

What should you do to get a better picture of typical implementation times for tools you are considering?

- **Ask a friend**. Your network is the best resource for unbiased information about implementation requirements.
- **Keep informed**. Trade magazines and web sites are full of "war stories" about CRM implementation (Chapter 12 lists many such resources). Although you need to use your usual caution about overly fawning or, on the other hand, gloom and doom articles, you should be able to get more reasonable estimates from these sources. Be sure to consider projects that are similar to yours in complexity. What took Giant Company 36 months to achieve may have little bearing on what you are doing.
- **Ask the references** supplied by the vendor. Clearly, the vendor will not give you negative references (and, if they do, run!) but you should be able to get realistic assessments through simple questions. We'll come back to this in Chapter 7, "Buying a CRM Tool."
- **Ask for details**. When the vendor says 60 days, ask for a written commitment. Ask for the names of a few customers who rolled out in that period of time, then ask if you can talk to them. Ask what modules they deployed, and how many users they had. Ask who the integrator was. Good investigators know that plenty of congruent details indicate that the underlying stories are true.

  If the vendor will provide the implementation services, don't sign the license agreement without a detailed statement of work for the implementation piece, including a schedule and a resource estimate.
- **Multiply vendor estimates** by two or three. This crude method yields surprisingly accurate results, and it's certainly faster than any of the techniques above.

What if the vendor makes some outrageous claim, such as implementing in a week? Using our handy-dandy multiplication rule above, you know that it really means a month, but still, a month is a really short time. What's going on? It could well be that you have stumbled upon one of the new-wave vendors who offer simple but powerful applications. Assuming you can verify the claim, you can be sure that the tool will be very easy to implement, maybe not in a week, but within weeks, not months, and also that you will be limited in the amount of customization you will be able to do. If that meshes with your requirements, you will be rewarded with a quick rollout, and an inexpensive one too! Just don't hope to make extensive integrations and customizations, either now or later, with such a tool.

## Layered Implementations

Layered implementations, whereby features and customizations are delivered through repeated, relatively short-term deliverables, are an excellent strategy to counter-balance long implementation timelines required for complex projects. They are the practical application of the small steps prescribed under the "think small, dream big" principle described in the section about success factors.

It's somewhat difficult to define layered implementations in terms of what they are. So let's see what they are *not*.

- They are not **feasibility studies**. Although there may be changes to the tool and its customization as a result of a deliverable, each deliverable is a step towards the goal, not a test of whether to proceed with the project.
- They are not **pilots**. They are part of a formally approved program on a formally adopted tool.
- They are not **testing vehicles**. Each deliverable is a fully-tested whole, although it will often be used as a test environment to determine what enhancements are most important.
- They are not **cop-outs** from more grandiose plans. You know the story: it's two weeks before rollout and three major features just are not working. In addition, there's no way that screens can be customized to fit the new color scheme. So the features are cut, the screens left as-is, and code is rolled out on the target date, although it's code that bears little resemblance to the plan. This scenario is not a small step; it is a partial and incomplete deliverable. Not necessarily a bad thing under the circumstances, but it lacks the planned aspect of a layered strategy.

Most implementations benefit from a strategy of layered implementation. Layered implementations allow you to build on success while minimizing failures (and making it easier to recover from failures).

# How Much Will It Cost?

Now that we have a general idea of how long it takes to complete a CRM project, it's time to tackle the second most popular question: how much will it cost? The key idea around cost is that, although the cost of the tool itself can be frighteningly high, the technology cost is a small portion of the overall cost. Cost estimates range widely depending on the complexity of the project, but it's safe to say that you will spend *at least* one or two times the cost of the software in implementation costs alone, and this doesn't include such items as the cost of the hardware, IT staff salaries, training, etc.

Let's start with an inventory of costs associated with a CRM project:

- **License costs**. Assuming that you are buying licenses outright (you could choose an ASP strategy instead), this is probably the most obvious cost. We will see in Chapter 7, "Buying a CRM System," how to negotiate for the best price, but you should count on at least $2000 per seat just for the software with a mid-range package, going way up with high-end packages. You will pay relatively more per seat if your group of users is small.

- **Maintenance and support costs**. They are tacked on to the license costs and, unlike them, are recurring (you get a new bill each year). Count on paying about 20% of license costs towards maintenance, starting at the time of the purchase (long before the solution is actually implemented, although this is one of the many items you can negotiate). Also, many vendors compute maintenance from the list price of the software, which can be much higher than your actual price depending on your negotiating skills and what the vendor's pipeline looked like the day you bought.

- **Hardware and other tools** required for the CRM system such as a database. You will probably need to purchase a number of dedicated machines to run the system, including a separate one for the customer portal. If you don't already have the database system licenses the system will need, you will need to purchase them, too. You may also have additional costs such as a web server, middleware, a report writer, and other add-on tools. The costs can be higher than the CRM license itself depending on the requirements.

- **Implementation costs**. This is a big one! For most systems, you will need to hire an integration partner, who will provide both technical staff and project management. If you are not hiring the CRM vendor to do the work, you may also want to invest in technical reviews by the vendor for both the implementation plans and the actual application prior to rollout. Implementation costs are very dependent on your particular requirements, but it's safe to assume that you will spend at least the amount you spent on the tool for a simple project and several multiples of that number for a complex project.

- **IT staff**. Typically the integration partner can only do so much (and you don't want to leave your IT infrastructure unattended in any case). You may not think of IT staff's salaries as additional out-of-pocket expenses, but they add up and you may need to hire additional personnel to maintain the system.
- **Other staff**. Although the integration partner will typically provide a project manager, you need to have some direct overseeing authority and responsibility throughout the project. This will be a dedicated individual (or team) for larger projects, potentially a part-time assignment for simple projects.
- **Training**. The creation and delivery of training needs to be accounted for. Tool vendors usually provide training for the implementers and the administrators (for a fee) but not for the end-users since end-user training is (and should be) very process-oriented and specific to your implementation. The integration partner may be able to do the work, or your internal training group can do it, or you can contract it out. In any case, there will be some expense associated with the creation and delivery of end-user training, not counting travel expenses for the attendees, or their salaries during the training.

So what's the large number on the bottom of this addition? In a mid-2002 report by Deloitte (reported in CRMdaily.com on 7/11/02 under the title "Setting a Realistic Budget for CRM"[1]), the following prices are quoted:

- For a simple project, count on (take a deep breath) $15k per seat for 100 users to $10K per seat for 5000 users. It makes sense that the per-seat price decreases for larger number of users, since product pricing is better for more users. More importantly, although implementation work is more complex for a larger user base, the additional cost is not directly proportional to the size of the user base.
- For a moderate complexity project, prices go up to $30K per seat for 500 users, graciously sliding down to $10K per seat for 5000 users.
- Finally, complex projects require $50k per seat for 1000 users down to $15K per seat for 5000 users.

---

1. http://www.crmdaily.com/perl/story/18559.html

Should you believe these high numbers? Undoubtedly, there are companies out there that spend that kind of money on CRM implementations. It's also true that many companies fail to track expenditures properly so that they don't really know how much they spend, and therefore tend to seriously underestimate their costs. And finally there are companies that spend significant amounts of money on projects that never make it to deployment, which are the most expensive projects of all.

That being said, it's absolutely possible to spend drastically less than the numbers above while deriving real benefits from the project. I have been a part of many implementations that did not even come close to the $15k per user that the study reports for simple projects. To minimize your cost, try the following approaches.

- Consider a **mid-range tool**. Gone are the days when mid-range tools ran out of gas with more than a few dozen users. If you have no more than a couple hundred internal users, a mid-range tool should be able to handle it in terms of pure performance. You may or may not be happy with the more limited functionality, however.

  The beauty of mid-range tools is not only that the license fee is much less, but that the implementation is a lot cheaper because there are fewer features and fewer customization opportunities.

- **Minimize complexity**. Scrutinize each customization and each integration by asking what the benefit will be versus the cost. Only allow those that have a good cost/benefit ratio.

- Use a **layered implementation** approach. While the layered approach won't necessarily save you money, as discussed above, it will bring a more rational approach to the implementation through which you can decide at each step how much more to invest into the tool, and where that investment will do the most good.

- **Negotiate** hard with the vendors. We'll give you specific tools to do that in Chapter 7, "Buying a CRM System." There's typically a lot of leeway in pricing for CRM systems. You can also negotiate with integrators (see Chapter 8) although there's less flexibility with them.

- **Stay on top of the implementation**. If your project is at all complex, the implementation is where the big bucks can be squandered. You must get regular, complete information about the project at least on a weekly basis. Using a layered approach will help here in the sense that you won't be more than one step behind, but you need to do better than that. Chapter 9 gives a blueprint of how to conduct an effective implementation.

- **Consider using an ASP.** You won't have to pay for the software upfront, so your implementation cost will be less. The ASP has lots of experience with the tool and you will have fewer customization options; therefore you should be able to roll out paying much less for implementation than your first-year subscription fee. Your other internal costs will be nil or greatly reduced. Over the long run—more than four or five years—ASPs are more expensive, however.

Now that we understand key success factors, typical timelines, and typical budgets for CRM projects, the upcoming chapters will focus on each aspect of the project, starting with the all-important project team.

# The CRM Project Team 4

## Express Version

- In many ways, the quality of the CRM team determines the outcome of the project. Therefore it's important to assemble the right people for the job.
- The most important member of the CRM team is the executive sponsor. The executive sponsor sells the project to all the stakeholders within the company before, during, and after the project, and removes political and other obstacles in the path of the project. The ideal executive sponsor is the business line manager for the function(s) being affected by the project.
- Next in order of importance is the project manager. The project manager orchestrates the planning and running of the project and its communication, which require both a strong project management background and PR skills. The project manager can be a consultant, although if that's the case it's important to have a robust overseeing process in place under the eye of the executive sponsor.

- The business owners are the line managers in charge of the business functions affected by the project. They are responsible for driving the project from a business function perspective.
- Actual end-users must be included in the projects. Because of the time requirements, it can be difficult to persuade end-users, and especially top producers, to participate, but it's essential for the success of the project. Their time must be carefully guarded and their participation leveraged for maximum impact.
- The IT owner is the counterpart of the business owners, representing the IT side. The IT owner coordinates the internal technical resources and should be involved whether or not the implementation of the tool is outsourced.
- The programming and technical staff may be hired out, although it's important to plan for continuity so you can maintain the system once it's in place. Beware of completely outsourcing the implementation to the point that no one internal to the organization quite understands what was done.

# What's a Good CRM Project Team?

If you want your CRM project to succeed, you must create a great team to work on it. The quality of the team is the most important component for success and is even more important than the financial resources you have. After all, a great team should be able to justify getting the appropriate resources; conversely, it's quite possible for a well-funded project to fail for lack of a good team, for instance if there is not a committed executive sponsor. This chapter describes the various roles required on the team, who can play these roles, what roles can be contracted out and what roles should not, and how many people resources you need to complete a successful project.

Let's start with an overview of the various roles on CRM teams. Depending on the type of project, its complexity, and its length, the various roles described here may be assigned to part-time contributors, to people working full-time on the project, or to multiple individuals for the larger projects. Some of the roles, such as the executive sponsor role, are by definition part-time roles and may not increase significantly in scope even as projects get very large. In smaller projects, some roles will be so abbreviated that you can dispense with them or combine them with others. And some roles will almost always be outsourced regardless of the type or size of the CRM project. We'll see details in upcoming sections. For now, let's inventory the roles regardless of whether they are played by employees or by contractors, whether they are part-time or full-time, or even whether they exist at all.

- **The executive sponsor.** This is the executive who shepherds the project from beginning to end and who has both the vision to make it happen and the proper understanding, power, and influence to sell it and nurture it to a successful conclusion. This role is absolutely key to the success of the project.

- **The project manager.** This is the individual who makes the project work by creating the project plan, driving day-to-day activities, and addressing issues as needed. This is obviously an important role but as we will see it's less key than the executive sponsor, and you can hire a consultant to do it if needed.

- **The business owners.** They are the line managers in charge of the business functions affected by the project. Unlike the executive sponsor, the business owners may not have the vision or political savvy to push the project into existence, but they are the ones who need to embrace it so their teams embrace it, and they also will need to provide the input required to define good quality requirements for the project.

- **The super-users**. They are end-users who are part of the project team and help define requirements and conduct user testing. The role is different from that of the business owners in that the super-users are hands-on practitioners of the particular functions being automated. You can't get away with involving only the business owners if you want real-life feedback on usability. Super-users also play a critical role in creating acceptance for the new system, which can be half the battle of CRM projects.

- **The IT owner.** The IT owner is the counterpart of the business owners, representing the IT side. While it may be true that no CRM project can succeed when driven only by IT management, I have personal experience with several that failed because IT management was not involved early enough and deeply enough. IT management must be involved whether or not the project is outsourced.

- **The technical staffers**. They include programmers, system administrators, database administrators, security specialists, and other individuals as required by the specific project. Many technical resources can and really should be outsourced, as it's unlikely that you will either have the required specialists on staff, or that you will need them for the long run.

Let's now examine each role one by one, analyzing its specific requirements and how they can be met in various project configurations.

# The Executive Sponsor

The executive sponsor is the crucial member of the team since, without an executive sponsor, no project has even a remote chance of being successful. This is especially true of complex projects that are more likely to run into technical and political issues both because of their scope and because they will take longer. CRM projects need a champion at the executive level to succeed.

This is not to say that one cannot inspire a successful CRM project from a position other than the executive level. It simply means that one cannot carry out a successful CRM project without the active assistance of an appropriately placed executive. If you are not in an executive position but you think that the issues within your organizations could be solved by implementing a new CRM system, do your homework (including finishing this book), create a recommendation, and pitch it to your favorite executive.

## Role

The executive sponsor defines the vision for the project, either by creating it from scratch or by getting inspired by the vision of others in the organization, or through some combination of both. The important thing is not so much how the vision comes into being, but rather that the executive sponsor has completely embraced the vision and is committed to realize it no matter what.

The vision should not be only a technical vision, but rather a comprehensive view of how business will be run once the tool is in place. The vision for the CRM project should be completely integrated with the other business goals of the organization. The executive sponsor must have both a clear vision for the project and a grasp of the tangible (high-level) deliverables.

Besides creating and sustaining the vision, the second big responsibility of the executive sponsor is to communicate the vision and to sell the project throughout the company. This includes convincing the organization as a whole to invest in the project, and that can be a large investment indeed, as discussed in the previous chapter. The executive sponsor must motivate the owners of the business function(s) targeted by the project to participate in it and to support it even as it requires hard work and sacrifices such as diverting precious staff members to work on it, as well as reducing the financial resources available to achieve other goals. The executive sponsor may have to convince other executives, whose departments will probably be impacted in some way by the project without reaping direct benefits from it, of the long-term value of the project to the company as a whole.

Selling the project is not a one-time event. There's selling the idea that the organization should embark on a CRM project in the first place. Then, there's selling the decision to use a particular tool and selling the accompanying investment in the tool itself and in the implementation, both in terms of budget and people. Repeated selling is required throughout the implementation period so everyone "keeps the faith", especially at rollout time when there's almost always some struggling with the new system. Selling continues to be required beyond the immediate rollout, when it becomes clear that the new system will not solve all the problems of the organization, and perhaps not even all the problems it was intended to handle.

Finally, the executive sponsor is the champion of the project throughout its existence. Although the project manager looks after the day-to-day issues, the executive sponsor must make time to check on the project on a regular basis, probably daily even if it's only for a few minutes. The executive sponsor doesn't merely read or listen to the project status reports, but also asks the difficult questions that can expose hidden issues. In other words, looking for trouble is a good strategy for the sponsor. The sponsor also helps the project manager anticipate political issues that can arise during the project, which the project manager can be blind to since he or she doesn't function at the executive level on a daily basis. Finally, the sponsor helps the project manager resolve practical and political issues, either by coaching the project manager on what to do or by directly handling the issues that require executive attention or influence.

The executive sponsor must be available to the project manager for quick questions and for brainstorming ideas. The effectiveness of the teamwork between the two individuals is much lessened if the executive sponsor cannot be available on very short notice, as many issues can worsen quickly if not caught and handled promptly.

## Requirements

So what kind of person are we looking for here? The main requirement is that the executive sponsor must the highest-level executive for the business function(s) being automated. For example, if the project targets an SFA solution it must be the VP of Sales. For deployments that affect multiple functions, it has to be a general manager type. Why aim so high?

- Because the top executive can terminate the project at any time. To avoid the potential of a veto from the top, you need unequivocal support from that individual from day one of the project. The executive sponsor can delegate much of the actual work, as we will see, so we are only talking about sponsorship there, not hours and hours of hands-on work.
- Because lots of business decisions will need to be made that only the top executive can make. If the executive sponsor cannot make the decisions directly, it takes too much time. You need a direct line to the top executive.
- Because selling the project within the targeted organization is much, much easier if the executive sponsor happens to also be the top executive for the functions involved in the project.
- Because the top executive for a particular function has the ideal scope and credibility to sell the project outside that particular group.

The executive sponsor needs to be politically savvy to sell the project throughout the entire organization as well as to anticipate and deflect political attacks against it. The executive sponsor also needs to be credible within the entire organization. If the top functional executive happens to be perceived as weak, even if only because of too short a tenure, try tapping the executive at the next higher level instead. If that fails, it's probably not a good idea to pursue a CRM project, at least until the political support solidifies.

An important success factor for the executive sponsor is the ability to create and communicate a solid, rich vision of how the project will bring tangible business benefits. A charismatic style is a great help for the communication part of the role, but an executive with a well-established record should do just fine without it.

Top executives are busy, so one of the hardest requirements is making enough time available for the project. Many duties can be delegated but the essence of executive sponsorship cannot be, or you lose the concept of the executive sponsor. By making time to meet with the project manager on a regular basis and by being available on short notice when needed, the executive sponsor nurtures a positive relationship with the project manager. Under such circumstances significant issues with the project are likely to be brought up promptly, before they get ugly, while no time is wasted on items of low importance.

What can be delegated? Except for very small projects in small organizations where the executive sponsor may also serve as a project manager, the day-to-day supervision of the project can and should be delegated, either to the project manager or to a staff manager who can filter appropriately. Be careful about too much filtering, as it can obscure potentially relevant issues. Another potential area for delegation is communication. Although the executive sponsor must deliver key communications about the project throughout the organization, the creation of the presentations, memos, and other communication vehicles can be done by others (with the condition that they are reviewed and vetted by the executive sponsor, as with any other key piece of communication). Finally, and especially in larger organizations, other individuals can analyze project-related issues and come up with solutions before they are presented to the executive sponsor for a decision.

By definition, executive sponsorship is a part-time role, since the very idea of making it a full-time job would run counter to the idea of executive sponsorship. The good news is that, unless the executive sponsor also plays other roles in the project, as is often the case in smaller companies, executive sponsorship should not blossom into a significant proportion of the executive's time, even for large projects. A few hours a week should be enough, except for specific events such as creating the initial requirements, approving the top vendor candidates, creating the implementation requirements, and approving major milestones. The savvy project manager schedules such key activities to fit the schedule of the executive sponsor.

Because the executive sponsor is so important to the success of the project, there is a great risk to the project if the sponsor moves on, even if the project is doing well. The risk is heightened if the move is caused by perceived weaknesses in the sponsor, even if the weaknesses have nothing to do with the project. It's easy to blame problems on the departed, and the project's opponents may try to push their advantage if the sponsor leaves, regardless of the state and health of the project.

To protect a CRM project through a transition, organize a very meticulous handoff from the old sponsor to the new one, covering both vision and ongoing management. The chances of survival are much better if the new sponsor can indeed take the vision as his or her own. It's not unusual to find a certain amount of refocusing and repurposing in the project as the result of the change in sponsorship.

# The Project Manager

The project manager is the individual who carries the project through by creating the project plan, managing day-to-day activities, and addressing issues as needed. Although a weak executive sponsor has the very real potential of sinking a good project with a skilled project manager, it's hard to think of a successful project that doesn't have a skilled project manager at the helm. Actually, a skilled project manager would probably spot a weak executive sponsor quickly and work to find a better one!

## Role

The project manager creates and refines the project plan. Creating the project plan involves coordinating with many different parties, both technical and business-oriented. As we will see in Chapter 9, "Implementing a CRM System," the project plan is best initiated in a team workshop, bringing together all the stakeholders so issues can be identified and decisions can be made on the spot. It's important to acknowledge that experienced CRM project managers are not able to make all the decisions required for a project by themselves, and must consult with the other members of the team to reach solid, well-informed decisions. It is precisely this team approach that makes the difference between a so-so project manager and a truly successful one.

Once the plan is created, the project manager drives it through project completion. Project management requires a firm hand to avoid scope creep and delays while allowing genuine issues to be handled appropriately. Here again, the project manager may need to consult others on the team to make decisions, but should know enough about the technical and business environment of the project to decide when to make an independent decision and when to request assistance, and from whom.

The project manager assembles the project team. This is perhaps the most delicate activity, since it requires attention to both skills and personalities, particularly when it comes to choosing which end-users will become the super-users. Especially on larger projects managers can show a great deal of reluctance to assign resources that will be consumed for weeks on end by the CRM project. The project manager must be prepared to identify the best candidates together with backups and to be persuasive when recruiting them. He or she must convince the managers of the benefits of their staff's involvement, knowing when to pull in the heavy artillery (the executive sponsor) if essential resources are not forthcoming.

Once the project plan is defined and the team is recruited, the project manager manages to the plan. This requires daily contact with all team members to make sure things are on track. If there are technical issues beyond the complete understanding of the project manager (and there will almost always be some such issues, regardless of the skills and experience of the project manager), appropriate detective work must be performed to confirm both good and bad news.

As problems arise, the project manager handles them by assigning team members to resolve them, by escalating them to the executive sponsor, or by working with individuals outside the project team. This triage of issues is an essential skill of the project manager, one where both technical skills and an understanding of the business environment are required to recognize what issues are important, and to determine how best to handle them. Most of the big problems I have seen in CRM projects stemmed from the inability of the project manager to recognize that certain issues existed at all, or to realize that they would seriously affect the outcome of the project. The difficulties often arise because the project plan and milestones were poorly laid out in the first place and failed to expose key issues. At the same time, the project manager should not panic at every little problem for fear of wearing out the team and the executive sponsor's welcome, so there's a difficult balancing act inherent in problem management.

The project manager chooses to conduct meetings as appropriate to bring everyone up to speed and facilitate cross-pollination. Special attention must be given to scheduling the meetings so as not to interfere with the actual work being done. (I find that a set weekly meeting for the entire team is often the best way to proceed.) The project manager must also orchestrate meetings so that key resources find them to be a productive use of their time, or else they may not show up the next time around.

As the project manager is managing the project, there's a component of people management as well, keeping the team members engaged, reasonably happy and motivated, and free of having to work on pestering issues outside their scope. This is not a mere cheerleading job, and actually many team members, being very technically-oriented, will resent being cheerled, if there is such a word. Rather, it's a matter of attending to individuals and removing obstacles in their way, knowing when to provide the compliments, the reassurance, the motivation, or simply peace and quiet to do the job at hand. I've found that most people treasure having someone else who will think through the logistics for them. They can come in and do their work without having to worry that they have the proper version of the browser, a key to the bathroom (don't laugh, it's often a big issue for contractors!), or the password required to do the testing. This level of detailed management is a good example of the essential difference between the responsibilities of the project manager and those of the executive sponsor.

The project manager also communicates the plan and progress against the plan to the team and to the larger organization. A bit of PR is always welcome here, avoiding dry status reports without becoming so slickly cheerful that suspicions start developing. For all but simple projects, a comprehensive approach to communications is best, blending regular status reports, presentations, updates through various established communication vehicles, and probably a dedicated web site for the project that curious individuals can access for the latest news. In larger projects, the project manager can choose to delegate the implementation of the communication strategy to a specialized individual.

Finally, the project manager collects feedback and lessons about the project from the various participants and the end-users. The goal of such a "key learning" or post-mortem exercise is to make subsequent projects smoother, and for CRM projects there almost always is a subsequent project, often with many of the same participants, to address issues that were left aside in the initial deployment.

## Requirements

So, apart from walking on water, what kinds of skills are we looking for when recruiting a project manager for a CRM project?

It's obvious that a successful project manager needs to have excellent project management skills. Even excellent organizational skills will be put to the test by complex projects that include dozens of subtasks and insidious dependencies all over the place. There is also a very large component of people coordination. Even individuals who are assigned to the project on a part-time basis (and so, presumably, have a full-time manager somewhere else) may spend weeks on the project, and their efforts need to be planned and coordinated with others' contributions. There is the issue of making the team feel and function as a team even though it is temporary and many of its members are only participating in it on a very part-time basis. In short, for all but the simplest projects, formal project management training and successful experience with similar projects is a requirement.

The second requirement is to find someone who understands the technical side of the project at least at a managerial level. Although there's no need for the project manager to be able to tune the web server, it is very important that the project manager 1) understands the need for tuning the web server and 2) have a rough idea of how long it should take. So if the web server administrator asks for ten weeks to do the tuning the project manager must be able to determine that it is, or not, a reasonable estimate. Here again, experience with similar projects is invaluable.

The third requirement is an understanding of the business issues around the project so that problems can be recognized early and circumvented with just the right amount of effort. This particular requirement seems to scream against using a consultant in the role, since deep knowledge of the organization appears to require having worked in that organization for a while, but it's not that simple. We'll come back to that in just a moment.

The fourth requirement is solid communication skills. This goes way beyond communicating with the team members, which was mentioned above and is quite an undertaking in itself. This is about formal communication outside the project team, reaching out to end-users and to the larger organization. The mix between the communications requirements and the technical project management requirements is often uneasy and many project managers are much stronger on one side or the other. If I were to compromise on either one I would favor strong technical project management skills for the project manager and get help with the communications side.

Should you hire a consultant to be the project manager or must the project manager be an insider? The requirement of understanding the business issues seems to mandate an insider, and a long-time, well-informed one at that. However, the very first requirement we listed, successful experience driving similar projects, is very rarely found within the organization since companies rarely conduct back-to-back CRM projects in-house. What should you do?

If you do not have an individual with the appropriate project management experience on staff, go with a consultant, whether one working for a system integrator or an independent one. Experienced consultants understand business issues quite well since there are many similarities across companies, and they know what questions to ask to get the inside scoop on the specific issues within the company. If you choose to use an outside consultant as the project manager, be sure to provide access to the executive sponsor and business owners to gather information. You should also include an extra level of supervision to ensure that business considerations are properly understood, and that the project manager is putting the best interest of the company ahead of his or her employer's.

So far the discussion has proceeded as if there is only one project manager and the role is full-time. It doesn't need to be. For a simple project in a small organization, the executive sponsor, business owner, and project manager may be one and the same person. Projects with a small scope can do well with a part-time project manager, either an employee or an outside consultant, reporting to the business owner. Projects of medium or higher complexity require a full-time project manager. Very complex projects require a small team of project managers to ensure that all components are appropriately managed.

# The Business Owners

The business owners are the managers of the business functions targeted by the project. They give direction and feedback to the project and they also contribute to selling the project within the team.

## Role

The business owners are part of the team both because the project would not survive without their support, just as it won't survive without an executive sponsor, and because they need to give specific input to the requirements definition phase.

To address the first point, it's pretty clear that implementing a tool that all staffers of a particular functional group will use simply cannot be done without the participation of the management team for that group. Actually, it's often the case that the business owners provide the impetus for the project in the first place, selling it upward to the executive sponsor. If that's the case, the main issue may be to restrain their enthusiasm as contract or technical issues delay the rollout of what they already believe will make their lives easier.

On the other hand, if the tool project is initiated outside of the business group, a certain amount of skepticism may reign amongst the business owners. Will the tool really work? Will the proclaimed business benefits really take hold? When will the tool be ready? Will it be properly tested? Will it be easy to use? Will it make their jobs easier? (Yes, I've been on their side too!) Part of the role of the executive sponsor and of the project manager is to provide timely, realistic information to the business owners about what benefits are reasonable to expect from the project, what the requirements are for their organization, what risks exist, and what risk mitigation efforts are planned.

The second aspect of the participation of the business owners on the team is to provide input and feedback, most of which is required during the requirements definition phase, but occasionally throughout the project as business decisions need to be made. Unlike the executive sponsor, who may be somewhat removed from the day-to-day routine, the business owners are directly involved with the CRM tool. It's essential that they have a say in its features and customization. Even when their teams (the super-users) make the most of the detailed recommendations, they are the ones who need to approve the decisions as they are made. The project won't get very far without the business owners getting behind it.

An interesting characteristic of the business owners is that there are almost always several of them, so the decision process can be challenging within that group. One of the functions of the executive sponsor is to resolve conflicts that cannot be handled by the business owners and the project manager.

The business owners also designate and make available the super-users. This is a critical function since the super-users provide the detailed functional specifications for the project. The business owners often resent having to give up key individuals to the team, even if they are generally in favor of the project. It's much easier to get the appropriate super-users assigned to the team if the business owners are well informed about the project and feel it's well run and will succeed. The project manager and the executive sponsor both may be required to invest their time and persuasive skills to convince the business owners of the wisdom of assigning solid super-users.

Finally, the business owners have a responsibility to share information and enthusiasm for the project within their team. While the savvy project manager helps the business owners by providing appropriately packaged information that they can pass on, there is no substitute for the functional managers talking about and promoting the project with their team.

## Requirements

It's important that all relevant business owners be a part of the project team, simply so that decisions can be made quickly and are less likely to be overturned later. The good news is that business owners do not need to devote large chunks of time to a CRM project. Their time is required mostly:

- To define initial requirements, which requires a few hours over several days, more if it's a large project or the number of business owners is large.
- To evaluate the candidate tools, which requires a few hours for each candidate, plus travel time if required.
- To define the implementation requirements, which is the big chunk: a day to a week depending on the complexity of the project.
- To review and approve milestones, a few hours for each.

There is no substitute for having the business owners represented on the team. It's certainly possible to function with only a subgroup of active business owners on the team, but it's critical to get everyone's approval for each main milestone. Experience shows that business owners who don't take part in the decision process tend to raise issues at approval time, all of which must be reviewed (which takes time). Some of the issues are so pertinent as to require revisiting the decisions based upon them (which takes even more time). You might as well push to include everyone on the team in the first place.

In particular, resist the tendency to include only the local business owners on the project team because it's so much easier to communicate with them than to brave distance, time zones, and language barriers to include the business owners in remote locales. If you want to reach solid decisions and to gather acceptance throughout the organization, include *all* the business owners. Revel in the beauty of technology such as conference calls and web conferencing, and don't hesitate to vary the meeting times so that remote participants don't always have to stay late or start early to participate. There's nothing quite like a 7a.m. Pacific Time meeting to remind Left Coasters that Europe is an important part of the world. As an added bonus, early meetings won't conflict with their other commitments!

In larger organizations, it may be tempting for the business owners to delegate their role to someone on their team, and a certain amount of delegation is sometimes required and can work just fine. If decisions tend to be revisited when the delegators get involved, however, it's time to go back to the original plan and to demand that all the business owners participate on the project team themselves. Often, the reluctance of the business owners can be overcome if the project manager can ensure that their precious time is used appropriately, not taken up by long, content-light meetings.

If you are working with a large group, try a level-laddering approach where the different geographies and subgroups are represented by managers from different levels in the organization. Have some director-level owners, some second-level managers, and some first-level managers, making sure all the geographies and subgroups are represented. The benefit of level laddering is that it lessens the burden on the top managers while allowing the project team to have a cross-section view of the organization, and giving developmental opportunities to lower-level managers.

# The Super-Users

The so-called super-users are end-users of the tool who have been chosen from among their peers, who are too numerous to involve en masse, to participate in the CRM project. Their role is to give detailed input and feedback on how the job is done and how the tool can support the job. They have a role in defining requirements, evaluating the tools, and conducting usability testing. They are expected to be representatives of the larger user community, so they will likely poll their colleagues on various issues and give informal status reports in return.

## Role

The main function of the super-users is to give detailed input to the project team on how the tool will really be used day-to-day. Although the functional managers are involved on the team (they are the business owners discussed above), there is often a big difference between the way end-users interact with a tool and the way their managers use it. Therefore, it's essential to go to the actual end-users to get accurate information, especially in larger organizations.

The super-users should be able to describe:

- the data they use to do the job, including data that may be hard to come by today, but should be supplied more easily through the new tool;
- the way the information should be presented to make the most sense to them;
- how the process flows;
- what information is needed at each step;
- the most common tasks, which are the ones that should be streamlined in the finished product.

The super-users should also be able to prioritize project options to match their priorities on the job.

Occasionally the super-users' priorities will conflict with those of the business owners, which is always an interesting event during a CRM project. Such conflicts can be a great opportunity to identify process bottlenecks, if handled appropriately by the project manager. (I should have mentioned that project managers must be great diplomats on top of everything else!)

The super-users have the important task of defining the business testing criteria, often called the "use cases." This awkward phrase hides a very useful concept: defining a comprehensive set of criteria that the tool must meet even before any customization is created (or, in some cases, even before the tool is selected, although that is a bit extreme). The super-users have the required hands-on experience to define the criteria, which are task-based, and, down the line, to perform the hands-on testing. It's always a good idea to ask other end-users to participate in the testing, as the super-users have become too familiar with the tool to be truly objective by the time the testing is performed.

The super-users are also the natural team to test the training program and documentation for the tool. As for the testing of the tool, the super-users know entirely too much about the tool to be good judges of either by the time the training is developed. It helps to bring in some additional, fresh volunteers at that point to make sure that the level is right for people who have never used the system. Whatever their limitations may be when testing the training materials, the super-users make good trainers or trainer assistants since they understand the process being automated and have intimate knowledge of the new tool within the business context. They can also be of great help in the early stages of the rollout to provide ad-hoc support to their peers.

Although super-users will provide a lot of the input straight from their experience, sometimes they will have to consult others in their groups. The project manager should be sensitive to this specific need and should select individuals who are willing to work with the rest of the team. The project manager should also provide the super-users with the practical tools they need to gather feedback from their team. For instance, the project manager should make it easy for end-users to access the development or testing system when required to give feedback to the super-users. This issue of access is one of the big headaches of CRM implementations.

Super-users also serve as the project's informal ambassadors within their teams. The savvy project manager understands that keeping them informed and reasonably happy can go a long way towards creating a positive attitude in the larger team.

## Requirements

Whom should you pick as super-users? First and foremost, super-users should be real and current users. Taking an individual from the field or the support center and placing him or her on the project team on a full-time basis is going to be a disaster. Within a few weeks of the transition, the individual gradually forgets the specific rhythm and frustrations of the job, while processes and conditions change in the field or the support center without the individual being aware of the changes. Whatever you do, do not remove the super-users from their day jobs.

This can cause interesting dilemmas, since, after all, real end-users have real responsibilities, some of which are sure to conflict with the very real work of being a super-user. Some scheduling finesse is required here. The project manager should be sensitive to the ebb and flow in the super-users' workloads, while the business owners must schedule some slack in the super-users' duties for the duration. For example, it's not a bad strategy to assign to super-user status an individual who, for whatever reason, needs a breather, perhaps because of travel burnout or a specific personal situation that requires a limited schedule. Just make sure that the individual is indeed performing a real end-user job when not playing super-user.

An added difficulty is that the super-users should be chosen from among the high performers. Business owners can be tempted to volunteer marginal contributors since they will be missed less than their high-contributing peers. The problem with that approach is that there are reasons why the marginal contributors are marginal. One reason may well be their lack of knowledge of how the job should be done when done well. The last thing you want is to replicate that lack of knowledge in the tool. Additionally, marginal contributors rarely generate any respect from their peers, so putting them on the team deprives you of the important ambassadorship aspect of their role.

Which brings us to another aspect of selecting super-users: tapping into the informal leadership of the group to select those individuals who have the respect of others without necessarily having a special title or place in the hierarchy. If the project manager is not familiar with the group, as would be the case for a consultant, the business owners should help identify the informal leaders and choose within that group the ones that would make good super-users.

Using informal leaders has two advantages. First, and obviously, because they are well connected to others, informal leaders will bring better information into the project, and they will be very effective in spreading the word about it. Second, informal leaders reach that status in part because they do their jobs in ways that are recognized by others to be superior, so that when they share their techniques with the project team to be automated in the tool, they contribute techniques that are likely to work for everyone. On the other hand, top performers who are not informal leaders often use techniques that are highly idiosyncratic and may not be suitable for others, so that modeling them into the tool may be counter-productive. If you happen to find informal leaders that are also top performers, you've hit the jackpot!

How many super-users should be on the team? One factor is the user population. If there are four different groups using the system, the right number of super-users is higher than four. Another factor is the maximum desirable size of the super-user team. Twenty super-users are too many, at least if they are all focused on the same specific tool. The right number of super-users is one or two per business owner, and business owners can't be many more than a half-dozen. As long as you identify high-performing informal leaders, adding more will not increase the quality of the project, only the confusion and coordination overhead, so know when to say enough.

One short note here about dissenters. You may find that some informal leaders can be thorns in the side, always having an opinion about everything and always raising issues. They don't belong to the school of only speaking out when it's important: they find something to speak out against in each and every initiative! If you find that you have such dissenters among the informal leaders, I recommend placing them on the super-users' team under the theory of tackling problems early.

Here I'm talking about dissenting informal leaders, not lone dissenters, who can be identified and handled by the business owners as they see fit. Dissenting informal leaders happen to have an audience, which is a sure sign that at least on occasion they are right on, and they are right on in a way that is recognized by others. Placing them on the super-user team makes for much more interesting team meetings, to be sure, but with enough attention from the project manager and the business owners the dissenters can bring you two wonderful benefits.

- Because they are contrarians they will identify problems that no one else has thought about. Sometimes, the problems will turn out to be moot, but often enough they will turn out to be absolutely critical. Dissenters have a talent for identifying neglected issues and small but insidious problems, and they do great testing. The quality of the end product will be much improved through their contributions.
- The second benefit is that, if you can bring them to the point that they are actually happy with the system (not totally happy, it's not their style!), then you will have effectively disarmed a lot of the negative reactions from the user community.

Bring dissenting informal leaders into the team. They will increase both the quality and the acceptance of the project, the two reasons why you need super-users in the first place.

How much time should the super-users schedule for their work on the project team? Quite a bit, and quite a bit more than the business owners although their participation should never reach the point of full-time involvement since the whole idea is to involve actual, current users of the tool. Let's take an inventory.

- Super-users must be a part of defining the initial requirements, which will take several hours to several days. They will spend more time than business owners because of the level of detail required.
- Super-users should evaluate the candidate solutions. A decent strategy might be to have a couple of super-users participate in the initial review for each candidate, only involving the entire group when a particular candidate is deemed promising. Thoroughly investigating one vendor may take a couple of days. This is, again, significantly longer than business owners must spend since there is more hands-on work required.
- Super-users must participate in the implementation requirements workshop: a day to a week depending on the complexity of the project, just like the business owners.
- Unlike the business owners, super-users need to be involved throughout the implementation to test the system and to give feedback on technical decisions. The time requirements can be high, as each testing session requires several hours, and this doesn't include the work required to get feedback from their teams.

If testing requires travel to the development center, time adds up quickly. I believe that the project manager should set up the necessary environment to cut down on travel. Yes, there are lots of benefits to getting the super-users together physically in one room, but I don't believe you can recruit the best super-users if you require big chunks of their time doing low-outcome tasks such as sitting in a plane.

Although the testing time required is high, super-users have very little to do during focused development periods, so the scheduling for the more intensive requirements such as testing can be done so as to minimize conflicts with their real jobs.

Overall, a serious super-user may spend 20-30% of his or her time on the CRM project, although this will vary from none at all (during coding period) to full-time (during testing, for instance). It is a significant burden.

# The IT Owner

In many ways, the IT owner is the counterpart of the functional business owners. During the project, the IT owner gives direction from the technical side, just as the business owners do for the business side. In the long run, just as the business owners are responsible for the usage of the tool, the IT owner makes sure that the tool is appropriately maintained and enhanced.

## Role

The first part of the IT owner's responsibility is to give technical input to the project. Typically the functional managers on the project (the business owners) are quite unaware of the technical aspects of tool selection and implementation. Therefore it's important that they collaborate with the IT owner to make the best overall choices that meet both technical and business requirements. The IT owner provides input about:

- Architectural requirements. The tool should run on the corporate hardware, use the corporate database, and offer integration possibilities with other tools likely to require integration (or at least incompatibilities should be known upfront and budgeted and planned for).

- Standards adherence. Being aware of the corporate standards, the IT owner can require them in the selection process and compromise as appropriate. There's no reason to pursue a tool that has good functionality but doesn't fit in the overall corporate standards.

- Implementation requirements. Although business fit dictates a great part of the implementation complexity, technical considerations can make or break a project. The IT owner can coordinate the requirements including the availability of skilled implementation contractors.

- Maintenance requirements. Although often neglected during the initial phases, maintenance requirements make an enormous difference in the total cost of ownership (TCO) in the long run. Knowing the IT resources both present and planned, the IT owner can define the maintenance requirements for the tool.

Once the technical requirements are in place, the IT owner ensures that the technical side of the project runs smoothly. This includes vetting the tools being considered to make sure that they match the technical requirements, and if they do not, assessing the extra costs associated with handling the gaps. The IT owner is often involved not only in demos and technical discussions with the vendors but also in reference checking. There's no better way to get the inside story on the technical side than to get the IT owner to talk to the reference's IT owner.

The IT owner is also front and center in the selection of the integrator, as business owners are typically not well-versed to what makes a good integrator or a good working relationship with an integrator. The IT owner is likely to have a good rolodex section for integrators, and, barring that, a rolodex full of colleagues who may have worked with the integrators suggested by the vendor.

It's critical that the IT owner fully embrace the project, hand in hand with the business owners. Even if the IT owner has doubts about the vendor selection, once the organization has made a choice that meets the functionality requirements and the IT standards, the IT owner must not be a barrier to success.

The IT owner is busy during the implementation phase making sure that appropriate IT resources are applied to the project and that the integrator is delivering appropriate deliverables from the technical angle. There is also a great deal of staging work required from the IT staff itself, so a lot of coordination work is required from the IT owner, as, at least for larger operations, a number of separate IT functions need to be involved.

During the implementation, the IT owner also plans for the time after the rollout. How will the tool be supported? Does the IT organization possess the proper skills to support the tool? To perform system administration functions? What about enhancement requests? Depending on the situation, the solution may require anything from a simple readjustment to the existing IT processes all the way up to creating a complete support structure from scratch, including hiring dedicated support and maintenance staff members.

Just like the business owners, the IT owner remains involved beyond the rollout date to ensure that the new system is appropriately administered, supported, and maintained. It's smart to plan for a period of very high availability from the support and maintenance staff right after rollout, when issues and good ideas are likely to surface, even with a good planning process. Of course support and maintenance will need to be provided throughout the life of the tool.

## Requirements

To be successful, the IT owner needs to have a good general view of current IT capabilities and processes, IT architecture, and future plans. Although the technical details can be handled by the IT staff on the project, the IT owner should know enough to assign the right individuals to the right issues and to estimate the requirements of each assignment. Since the project involves many different IT functions, the IT owner must be able to coordinate with the various groups involved on a project that may entail myriad details over many weeks and months.

Because the IT owner role spans functions, and because it requires a strategic vision, there is an argument to be made that the head of IT (let's say the CIO, for the sake of this discussion) should be the IT owner. Indeed, if the project is significant, as CRM projects often are, the CIO should be involved in the requirements definition and the tool selection. However, it rarely makes sense to have a CIO involved in the day-to-day technical management of a CRM project, except in a smaller company where there is no other strategic-level IT owner.

Typically the IT owner for a CRM project will have a title such as "Business Applications Manager" or something similar. The IT owner does not have the top IT job but must have:

- The support of the CIO.
- Enough seniority and experience to bring a strategic technical viewpoint to the project.
- Enough clout to accomplish the multi-disciplinary coordination required.
- As much as possible, a direct stake in the long-term support and maintenance of the tool.

The time requirements for the IT owner depends mostly on how much of the implementation work is handled by an outside party. Here's a breakdown of time requirements for the IT owner:

- Defining the technical requirements for the tool (a few hours to a few days).
- Evaluating the candidate solutions, which requires several hours for each candidate, plus travel time if required.
- Evaluating the integrators, which is very much the domain of the IT owners, and which requires several hours per candidate, and several days for the finalists.
- Defining the implementation requirements, which can take a day to a week for the kickoff workshop itself and another few days to iron out the technical details.
- Coordinating the IT resources during the implementation, which could be a few hours a week for a simple project handled by an integrator or a full-time job for a complex project done in-house. In any case, much

time is required at the beginning of the implementation to make sure that all the IT requirements are covered and to oversee the scheduling of resources, and again near the end of the implementation timeframe to ensure that the application is appropriately rolled out.

In-house deployments and large deployments make for a full-time IT owner's role. But even if the requirements are lighter, it's critical to have an appropriate IT owner on the team, even if there is a strong project manager and a strong integrator. At the end of the day, the tool must become a part of the overall infrastructure of the company. IT participation is required from the start to ensure that the project is actually feasible within the IT architecture (whether it's the current architecture or if the architecture needs to change to accommodate the project). The IT owner also makes sure the appropriate IT resources are made available so that the project is indeed incorporated into the IT offering.

# The Technical Staffers

The technical staffers on the project are responsible for installing and customizing the system, handling the setup and administration of the various systems involved, testing, rollout support, and performing ongoing support and enhancements. There are many ways to set up the technical team. How you do it depends on how much the integrator can do, what can be handled by the internal IT staff, and how much you want to farm out.

## Role

A critical and sometimes overlooked role of the technical staff is to contribute to the requirements definition and to the selection of the tool and of the integrator from a technical perspective. Much of the technical work during the selection process can be handled by the IT owner, but it's likely that he or she will want to confirm specific points with specialists on the IT team, or sometimes with outside consultants. It's also a good strategy to allow the technical staffers to work directly with the vendor's technical team; experience shows that technical workers are often remarkably candid when talking to their technical peers.

During the implementation phase, the technical staffers may be called upon to play a variety of roles depending on how much the integrator is doing. This includes:

- Providing system configuration and administration services. There can be minimal requirements for the IT group during the coding phase if the work is done at the integrator site, but that still leaves open the issues of the testing environment and the production environment. (We'll come back to why having three environments for development, testing and production is ideal; see Chapter 9, "Implementing a CRM System.")

  The need for system configuration and administration typically heats up towards the end of the implementation cycle as the full system nears deployment. System administration needs extend from the server to the network, the database, and desktop or laptop systems. Significant tuning requirements may exist as well.

- Installing the tool. This can be a rather involved operation, and almost always is for high-end systems. It is best attempted with the vendor's or the integrator's assistance.

- Customizing the system. This is often the prerogative of the integrator, but even when an integrator is involved there's a lot of value in having IT staff members participate in the design and coding of the system. If nothing else, they will have to provide support for the customizations in the long run. Customizing the system almost always involves coding, although some simple customizations may be done through a simple interface with no coding required.

- Integrating the system with other systems. If integration is required with a legacy or other system, the expertise for those systems often comes from the IT group. Unlike the IT staffers who work on other parts of the customization, the system specialists bring their knowledge to the integrator's team rather than learning from them.

- Testing the system. Just as the super-users have a hand in creating use cases that capture the business requirements for the tool, the technical staffers create the criteria for load testing as well as the use cases for administering the tool. The technical staffers run the tests, or at least check they have run successfully, throughout the project.

- Support for the rollout and beyond. The technical staffers are completely or partially responsible for supporting the tool. Support requirements at rollout are usually very high as users may stumble a bit despite the training, and problems may develop despite the testing that was done. Technical staffers are also on the frontline when it comes to providing ongoing support, including reviewing and incorporating enhancement requests.

## Requirements

The requirements for the technical staffers are as varied as their responsibilities. Except for very simple projects, many different functions participate in the project:

- System administrators for all the systems involved.
- Database administrators.
- The network managers.
- The application programmers for the CRM tool itself and for all the tools that may be linked to, in any way, by the project, whether a complete integration is required or something lighter-weight.
- UI specialists, especially for the customer portion of the rollout.
- Web designers.

It's obvious that complex projects need many, many more technical staffers than modest ones. At one extreme, for a minimalist project and a very user-friendly tool, the IT staff may only need to provide a machine to install the tool while the business function handles all the customization and maintenance work. Very few projects are that simple. One of the key decisions that should be made before the project starts, and therefore well before a tool is selected, is the level of technical resources that can be applied to the project. This requirement will shape the selection of the tool: don't overreach.

Beyond the total size of the technical team, the big issue for the IT staffers is to define the respective responsibilities of the integrator versus the in-house IT staff. Generally speaking, it's a good idea to farm out the customization work. The expertise is rarely available in-house and the volume of resources required is huge: why hire a whole bunch of people for a time-limited project? However, even if an integrator is involved, it's critical that in-house technical staffers be an active part of the project if it is to succeed in the long run. In particular:

- The IT staff must play an active role in selecting the tool. No integrator can ever understand your IT landscape as well as you do, so no integrator should be allowed to make the decision for you. Remember that all tools are "easy" for integrators since they work with them everyday.
- The IT staff must participate in the requirements definition for the implementation phase. They have or can find answers to many of the questions that will come up about how the tool can be integrated into the IT environment. Working with the IT owner, the IT staffers can provide many technical details about the inner workings of the IT infra-

structure, anticipating the issues that must be resolved in order for the project to be a success.

- Even if the integrator is handling all customizations, and even when the in-house application programmers must start from scratch and go to vendor-sponsored classes, they must be involved in the coding part of the implementation. It may seem strange to apparently delay the project for the sake of bringing non-key programmers up to speed. The reason for doing this is that a few weeks' apprenticeship with the programming staff of the integrator is invaluable both in terms of learning how customizations are really done and to provide a smooth handoff to the support phase.

- The IT staff must be involved in setting up the environment required for testing and production. They can be assisted by the integrator, to be sure, but they need to fully understand the setup so they can support it. Moreover, many companies restrict access to their internal systems for security reasons.

- Unless the integrator will provide full support after the rollout, which is very rare, the IT staffers will have to provide ongoing maintenance after the rollout. This should be planned during the project so that appropriate staff can be hired, trained, and brought up to speed on the customized application.

The individual time requirements can be quite small for each technical staffer. For instance, the requirements of the network administrator are likely to be limited to only a few days during the entire process, but skipping that step may lead to real problems later.

## How Many Resources Does It Really Take?

Even after going through detailed guidelines for each member of the team, it may be difficult to visualize what the CRM project team should look like when you combine all the ingredients. To help you define the scope and shape of what you may need for your own specific project, here are some typical CRM project scenarios and their matching teams, together with comments on why and how the choices were made and what could be done differently depending on the particular circumstances. The scenarios are composite case studies, drawn from real-life situations that illustrate different aspects of CRM projects but without the restrictions or confidentiality issues of actual case studies.

You may read through all the scenarios to gather inspiration and then design your own team. If you're pressed for time, start with the scenario that's closest to your particular situation and adjust from there.

## New Support-Tracking System, Small Company

**The Context**   In this small company (300 people) the support team only has 15 people. The simple support-tracking tool that was put in a few years ago when there were only two people on the support team is bursting at the seams, and, most problematic, doesn't support an integrated knowledge base. It seems that a good strategy is to upgrade to a more powerful, more modern system that supports an integrated knowledge base and a customer portal.

The support group reports to a support director who in turn reports to the VP of Services. He is relatively new to the company and is the one who spotted the requirement to upgrade the tracking system shortly after his arrival. There's only one support center for now, although a satellite center will be opened in Europe within the year to support local customers.

**The Team**   This is a relatively straightforward project, with only one business function involved, a small number of users, and a focused strategy. The project team is, therefore, small and simple.

- The executive sponsor should be the VP of Services. The only potential issue is that he is a new player, but with a project of this size it shouldn't be a problem.

  The other potential candidate is the support director, but since the director did not identify the problem prior to the arrival of the VP of Services, she may not have the level of strategic vision required, nor may she have the required skills and connections to get the budget approved. However, considering that the project is squarely limited to the support team, it may be a good opportunity for the support director to get a first taste of executive sponsorship. This setup can work provided she has appropriate visibility and business savvy, and if the VP of Services is willing to step back and to provide coaching and assistance. It would be a great developmental project for a manager at that level.

  Because the scope of the project is limited, it does not make sense to have the CEO be the executive sponsor, although it sure would not hurt to have the CEO be squarely in favor of this project!

- In such a small organization, everyone is very pressed for time, and no one has managed the deployment of a support tool before. The VP of Services has hired an independent consultant he has worked with in the past who will be responsible for the selection phase of the project. Once the tool is selected, and depending on the specific requirements for the deployment, the consultant may be asked to stay on and manage the implementation.

  It would be possible for the support director to be the project manager (but it looks like she's already over-scheduled), or for an IT owner to play that role (but it's very unlikely that there would exist a business applications manager in a company this size.)

- The business owners are the support director and the support managers. They are all conveniently located in one location and are working so closely together that it will probably be easy to get them to agree on requirements. The only question marks are 1) whether they will be able to ignore the constraints that have been imposed by the current tool and "dream big" and 2) whether they will adapt to the customer-openness model that the VP of Services is driving for and that modern tools support. This last point is a clue that the VP of Services should probably be the executive sponsor, unless the support director has internalized that vision.

- The super-users will be three support reps taken from the three support teams. One is quite new but she has worked with one of the tools being considered in her last job. The other two are senior members of the team and highly respected by all members of the support center.

  Note here the addition of a junior person on the team of super-users. She will probably be more sensitive to the requirements of less experienced reps, which is a good thing since the group is expanding. Watch out if the tool selected is not the one she used to work with. There could be some level of disappointment or even resentment.

  If the European support center were already in existence, a support staffer from Europe would need to be on the team, even if it meant enrolling the one and only European staffer. It's essential that all geographies be represented.

- The IT owner will be the director of IT and the only manager in that department. The main issue will be to ensure that the tool that's chosen fits into the corporate standards and won't require much maintenance. This goal matches the goal of the support team, which has had a hard time getting any help for the old tool from an overburdened IT group and wants to find a solution they can administer themselves.

An important note here is that the IT owner must be persuaded to devote enough time to the project and to fully commit to the selection. Even with the goal of no IT involvement there will necessarily be some level of resources required from IT and it's essential that IT not throw up any roadblocks. A good relationship between the IT owner and the executive sponsor is important in securing appropriate mind share.

- Although the goal is to require very little help from the IT group, the IT staff will need to be involved at some level to set up machines, help with the testing, and provide ongoing support. Any actual coding or customization work required will be farmed out to the vendor.

## New SFA System, Medium-size Company

**The Context**   In this medium-sized company, the direct sales organization includes about 120 people scattered throughout the U.S. and Europe. There is no sales-tracking system in place today, although various forecasting spreadsheets exist, developed in conjunction with the financial analysts. The goal of the project is to facilitate lead tracking and improve forecasting.

All the account managers report to the VP of Sales, who herself reports to the CEO. There are four regional sales directors, one in Europe and the other three in the U.S., organized geographically. There is a small Sales Operations organization that processes orders, located at the headquarters in the U.S.

**The Team**   There are many ways to organize the team for this project, depending on the available talent within the organization. Here's a typical team, with comments on other potential configurations that could be used.

- The VP of Sales is the executive sponsor. This is pretty much a requirement, although it would be possible to have the CEO be the executive sponsor. If the VP of Sales is strong enough, it's better to make her the sponsor since the project is focused on the sales team.

   Because the VP of Sales is very busy and travels widely, especially at quarter-end, she has asked the Sales Operations manager, who is located at headquarters and doesn't travel as much, to serve as her right arm on this project. This is quite common and will work properly as long as the Sales Operations manager has the respect of the sales directors (better check on that early on) and is able to quickly pass on issues that need her attention to the VP of Sales.

- The project manager for the implementation phase will be supplied by the integrator and so will have done such implementations before.

There is no one in the company that has gone through a project of this magnitude before, so it makes sense to get outside help. For the first phases of the project, the tool selection and integrator selection phases, the IT director will serve as the project manager since this is a high-profile project within the company. He will use one of the business analysts on staff in his group to put together the initial requirements.

It's not unusual to change horses mid-stream, as it were, and to use different project managers for the selection and implementation phases, at least when there is no in-house resource capable of managing the implementation. It's really not that much of a problem, assuming that a good transition can be done, and specifically that requirements gathered at the beginning can be safeguarded and then enhanced for the implementation. Here, continuity will be ensured since the IT director will continue to be part of the project under another role, the IT owner (see below).

- The business owners are the four regional sales directors as well as the Sales Operations manager. Some area sales managers (who report to the directors) will be participating as well, including one who went through a similar exercise with a prior employer just last year.

  The business owners are eager to get involved and reasonably enthusiastic about the benefits of the project, but they are concerned about their and their teams being asked to put significant time into the project, especially during quarter-end periods. This is a critical concern that must be addressed by the project manager. In this case, the project manager set things up so that the requirements definition workshop will take place during the first month of the quarter. A lot of sales training is occurring at that time too, but the time is better than quarter-end. Any testing and deployment efforts will also be scheduled outside the last month of any quarter.

- The super-users have been identified as seven individuals, two from Europe and five from the U.S., including one sales operations rep, with a range of experience levels and tenure. All super-users were identified by their managers as good performers with an optimistic view of the project, except for one sales rep from the Central region, who is quite a skeptic. He is on the team because he's felt to be one of the informal leaders among the sales reps; if he can be won over he will influence many more to follow him. He's a good example of a dissenting informal leader. The situation has been discussed with the project manager, who had specifically requested that informal leaders be placed on the project team.

- The IT Director, who reports to the CFO, is the IT owner for the project. There is a Manager of Business Applications reporting to him, but the IT Director is concerned about the visibility of this project. He decided it would make sense for him to be actively involved in the project, especially since the Manager of Business Applications was promoted from an individual contributor's position just a few months ago and needs some seasoning on the political side. Over the course of the project the participation of the IT director is likely to drop once he is satisfied that the manager can handle it. The IT Director feels that most of the value he can bring to the project himself is in the tool selection phase since he has a lot of experience negotiating contracts.

- Most of the technical resources will come from the integrator, although the database administrator, network administrator, and system administrators from the IT group will be required to devote some time to the project. One of the individuals in the Business Applications group will be apprenticed to the integrator's team during the implementation so she will be capable of maintaining the system single-handedly after the rollout, as well as performing minor upgrades as required. She won't have enough time available to handle major changes in the future, but she would be capable of directing contractors.

## New Integrated CRM System, Medium-size Company

**The Context**  In this largish company, the sales organization has been run with ACT and Excel systems, and fairly successfully as far as these tools can go. With over 250 people now, things can get out of hand in crunch times, however. A big unresolved issue is that most sales are to existing customers and sales reps frequently find themselves unknowingly calling on accounts that have service issues because their access to the support system is very limited. They are forced to use an old, custom-made interface that makes it very difficult to extract the strategic issues even if all the details are captured.

On the other hand, the service team (close to 50 people) has used a traditional client-server tool for years. The customer portal is severely limited, as is often the case with older tools, but after layers and years of customizations it's working. The support team is pretty much happy with the tool, except for a few mavericks who think that a migration to a new-wave integrated system is long overdue. The Client Services VP is not one of the mavericks. He used the same system at his old company for years and feels it does the job just fine. He doesn't want to upset things by doing a switch.

A VP of Quality was hired a few months ago after the executive team unsuccessfully struggled with serious customer satisfaction issues and slow growth for close to a year. She has identified the lack of a common customer-tracking system and especially the barriers between the service and sales groups as a major reason for the corporate problems, and she has convinced the CEO to make a major investment to resolve the issue. The goal is to implement a unified, transparent system through which everyone would have access to all account information, whether sales- or support-related.

The Sales VP, who had previously showed great unwillingness to adopt a costly tool that would require many process changes, has now rallied to the initiative and has committed to pushing new technology through his group, along with a massive sales training initiative that pushes solution sales. The sales team as a whole is not nearly as enthusiastic. The Client Services VP is very skeptical of the new project and doesn't think there is enough corporate will to accomplish the grandiose plans. In any case, his team is working very efficiently with the current tool and customers are happy with service, even if they are dissatisfied with the lack of responsiveness from the rest of the company.

**The Team**   This team is interesting to assemble because of the large political component of the project.

- The executive sponsor must be the CEO, who is the only individual with enough clout, or at least enough power, to make the project happen. It would be a mistake to make the VP of Quality the executive sponsor since it's more than likely that there will be serious pushback from the Client Services VP, which she would not be in a position to handle fully. Even the Sales VP who seems so eager today may turn reluctant when resources requirements are defined or when the demands of the tool project conflict with the huge training program being undertaken.

    Without the political complications it would be possible to imagine the VP of Quality serving as the executive sponsor, but I for one would avoid that setup because she simply does not have the required political power. She could, however, serve as second-in command on the project for all practical purposes, as she will undoubtedly do even in this instance.

- The project manager is an outside consultant with the appropriate background and experience, and plenty of business savvy, chosen by the VP of Quality. The VP of Quality has taken great pains to make sure that the project manager can work well with the CEO and has appropriate access to him when needed.

    The VP of Quality could serve as the project manager if, and this is an important if, she had the appropriate experience with such projects. Otherwise, a better role for her would be as a business owner (owner of the customers, in particular) and substitute and helper for the CEO who is the executive sponsor.

    Another possibility for the project manager would be a very strong Business Applications Manager from the IT group, if there were such an individual. It's not clear that there is given the state of the current CRM tools, although the weakness may be due solely to the strategic choices of the business owners. If there is a Business Applications Manager in place and if that individual has enough political visibility to both main business owners and has the appropriate project management experience, then the project manager job belongs there.

- The business owners are the Client Services VP and the Sales VP, and their management teams. The divergent views between the services and sales groups could create interesting conflicts, which is why the choice of the project manager is so important (not to mention the choice of executive sponsor!). With appropriate focus on solutions and outcomes, the project manager could be pleasantly surprised that the two executives and especially their teams may welcome the new tools if they can see clear business benefits.

- The IT owner can be the Business Applications Manager if there is indeed someone with this title, and if there is not, it's probably time to create that position. The IT owner must be sensitive to the political situation with the business units, especially to create trust with the Client Services VP, so the Business Applications Manager may need assistance from a higher-up IT executive. A good setup would be for the CIO to serve as the IT owner through the tool selection decision, and for the Business Applications Manager to take over afterwards. However, the CIO cannot completely abdicate involvement in a key political project, especially if the Business Applications Manager is new.

- The technical staffers will include a blend of in-house IT staff and copious numbers of consultants. All the pure customization work should be farmed out for efficiency, making sure the individuals who will provide support and maintenance are involved for a smooth handoff.

## New Support-tracking System, Large Company

**The Context**   This large company is about to get much larger because of a recent acquisition. The two support teams are to be merged. They both have traditional support-tracking systems in place, but one tool is on the verge of becoming orphaned after multiple acquisitions of its original vendor. The other has not kept up with modern technology and lacks basic amenities such as an integrated knowledge base and a functional customer portal.

The two Services VPs agreed early on in the merger process that this would be a good opportunity to start fresh with an integrated system that is more robust and has a better future than either of the ones in place today. They discussed the issue with the CIO who agrees that they should replace what's in place today. Further, he thinks that they should proceed independently of the sales and marketing groups who are busy migrating the acquiring company to the existing system in the acquired company (which is much superior to the one that was used in the acquiring company). Eventually the support-tracking system and the sales-tracking system may be merged, but the CIO considers that it's best to go for a best-of-breed solution for support.

The support teams are large (over 400 people altogether) and because of the merger there are multiple support centers in the U.S., Europe, Asia, and an outsourcer located in India. Part of the business strategy is to close some support centers and to merge others, but in all likelihood there will be multiple centers for a long time to come, maybe forever. Furthermore, the support team includes technical account managers, many of whom work out of sales offices or even from their homes.

Both organizations are pretty open to a new system, since the old ones are not that good, but at the same time there is a lot of uncertainty about the mergers. There are also a lot of other issues to attend to, including reassuring customers that they won't be left behind.

On the IT front, the acquired company has a fantastic Business Applications Manager, who is the one who coordinated the selection and implementation of the sales-tracking system the company is now making standard. Her next target was a support-tracking project, so she's well versed in the topic already. She is not well known in the acquiring company, which is a problem, and furthermore she is located far from the new headquarters.

**The Team**   It's not unusual for CRM projects to arise out of mergers. Indeed, the acquiring company in this case is migrating its sales-tracking system. Is it too much to take on both the sales-tracking system and the support system? It is a lot, but it looks like the support systems just won't last, so once the sales-tracking project is on track there's no choice but to pursue a unified support-tracking tool.

- The executive sponsor should be the new Support VP (that is, the Support VP for the merged support teams). There's no need to involve the CEO directly in this project since the project focuses on only one business function, and since there seems to be a surprisingly small amount of political heat around it. The new Support VP will undoubtedly be busy with other issues, but it would not be appropriate to delegate the executive sponsorship downward in this case since the CRM project is critical to the success of the merged teams.

   If the choice of the individual who will run the support team is contentious, the CEO may need to become the executive sponsor, but it doesn't sound like a reasonable alternative; better for the CEO to concentrate on choosing a strong Support VP in the first place.

- The project manager can be the Business Applications Manager, with two conditions. One, the sales-tracking project must be in good enough shape to allow her to devote enough time to the support project. Second, there is the issue of the remote location. It shouldn't matter so much with modern communication techniques, but it's essential for the Business Applications Manager to build the proper alliances and to be visible, both of which will be much easier to accomplish with frequent visits to headquarters, and perhaps a temporary move there for the duration of the project.

   If the Business Applications Manager cannot be available enough for the support project or cannot bridge the distance gap, it's possible to instead hire an outsider to manage the project. An outsider may be better accepted by both sides, and may also be more visible at headquarters. I would prefer to go with the Business Applications Manager if her workload allows, both to make a positive statement that the acquired company matters, and because she has such a good track record.

- The business owners are the support managers. Their involvement is particularly critical for three reasons. They already have solutions in place so the new tool must at least do better than the status quo. They come from two different groups, so getting to common ground is more delicate. It will be their first project as a merged team so it needs to be successful.

   Because the project manager comes from the acquired side, it's critical that the support managers on the acquiring side be very involved with the project, since the project manager presumably is more aware of and

more sensitive to the other side. Also, any time the project manager is from IT, the business owners must make sure that decisions include the business side, not just the technical side.
- The IT owner will be the Business Applications Manager, with potential assistance from other individuals on the team depending on her workload. If she needs assistance, it would be good to pick someone who is located at headquarters. She should be able to play the role of the IT owner even if she is not the project manager since the IT owner's role is less time-consuming than the project management role.
- Most of the technical work will be done by a system integrator. The existing support and maintenance staff for the current support-tracking applications will be given first priority to interview for a spot on the support and maintenance team for the new support-tracking tool and will be trained on the new tool. They are not expected to produce much of the customization work, only to receive enough on-the-job training to be able to handle the maintenance. System administration work will be handled by other existing IT personnel.

One last thought about selecting the team. Although this chapter may create the impression that the team is neatly identified and assembled prior to the start of the project, reality is rarely as well ordered. For starters, while it would be crazy to initiate a project without an executive sponsor, it's not uncommon for a business owner to create the initial inspiration so for a brief moment the project team may have a business owner but no executive sponsor. Once the executive sponsor is in place, the other key team members can be recruited: the project manager (for the selection process at least), the key business owners, and the IT owner. The first task of that small team would then be to identify the remaining team members, namely the other business owners, the super-users, and the technical staff, all selected to serve at least for the selection phase. Once the decision is made on the tool and the integrator, changes are often made to the team, and especially the project manager and the technical staffers as requirements become clearer. It's a very rare event indeed when the project team is assembled from the get-go and never changes throughout the life of the project.

Once the team is assembled, it's time to get going with the project. The next chapter focuses on the very first step, requirements definition.

# Requirements Definition 5

## Express Version

- Taking time to define requirements before embarking on the project avoids wasting time on inappropriate tools and limits completely inappropriate decisions.
- Although the process is shown as linear, with requirements definition preceding product selection, the two are interleaved. Especially if you are starting from scratch, it's best to do some research about what features are available before nailing down the requirements.
- Although technical requirements make up much of the requirements checklist, also include requirements for the company you will be doing business with. The competitive landscape changes quickly in the CRM field so if you'd like to keep your vendor for the long run you should do some due diligence into its financial and strategic stability.
- The second piece of the requirements checklist is about architecture and adherence to technical standards, since you don't want to waste time evaluating candidates that won't match your IT requirements.

This is one of the reasons why the IT group must be a part of each CRM project from the start.

- The third piece of the requirements checklist is the business functionality proper. It often makes sense to see a few tools before creating the functionality portion of the requirements, especially if it's been some time since you looked at CRM systems. Some of the features that are now standard in mid-range systems were rarely seen a few years ago, even in high-end systems.

- Include implementation and maintenance requirements so you don't get caught with a new system that you can't use without extraordinary effort. It's easy to get dazzled by features and to forget that more features almost always bring more complexity.

- Do set a budget from the start, although it will probably change later. There is a limit to what you can spend, and knowing what it is will help you target the right candidates.

- Getting the team to rank requirements so the top ones are clearly highlighted makes it easier to evaluate candidates quickly and thoroughly. It's a critical responsibility of the project manager.

# Why Define Requirements?

If you want to buy a house, you don't go to all the open houses in the area until you find the one you want, do you? And you certainly can't go to all the open houses all over the country. Instead, you sit down and you think about how many bedrooms you need, how much of a commute you can take, and whether special features such as a gated community or a pool would be desirable or something to avoid. You also think about how your needs may change in the future, how much you can afford, and whether you would be willing to buy a fixer-upper.

Although it is said that the top criteria for houses are location, location, and location, you know that in the end the layout of the rooms, the state of the plumbing system, and the size of the closets will have a big impact on how satisfied you will be with the house, and you'd better think about such detailed requirements before you start shopping and while you are shopping. When my family moved to a new area a few years ago, a very wonderful real-estate agent started by taking us on a full-day tour of ten very different kinds of houses, all having the requisite number of rooms and all within our price range, just to see what kinds of houses would be more likely to "work" for us. With her help, we were able to go way beyond the room number and price requirements and create a detailed checklist of must-have, nice-to-have, and "absolutely hate" criteria. (We live in such a house today, which she found for us in less than a month– thank you, Enis.)

A CRM project is no different. This chapter takes you on that full-day requirements definition tour, all from the comfort of your reading chair. With it, you will be able to create a custom requirements list and to rank the requirements on your list so you can distinguish the must-haves from the nice-to-haves. The requirements list will be your tool during the selection process to screen candidates in or out and to rank the serious contenders. It can even be transformed into an RFP (request for proposal) if you wish to use a formal process. We will discuss both RFPs and a less formal alternative in Chapter 6, "Shopping for a CRM System."

## How Detailed Should Requirements Be?

A common question I get from my clients when creating a requirements list is how detailed to get. This is not a trivial question. On the one hand, the requirements list drives the project, so if it's vague or incomplete you will likely make the wrong choice. Because the requirements list will be used during the evaluation phase to score how well each vendor meets each requirement on the list, you want each requirement to be precise enough to allow you to score the candidate tools against it. On the other hand, defining requirements is a time-consuming task that gets ever more time-consuming as requirements get more detailed.

If you were creating a requirements list for a house, you might specify lots of storage space, or lots of light, or a safe yard for kids. That's much better than a standard "3 bedrooms, 2 baths" description, and certainly more useful when trying to decide whether a particular house is suitable. On the other hand, requiring a 5x6 closet off the master bedroom, a living room painted yellow, or a fenced sandbox in the backyard is probably too much detail unless you absolutely needed those specific features. (And at least the yellow paint is easily attainable in just about every house!)

For a CRM requirements list, don't use vague language that you might find on a marketing brochure, such as "the system should scale well." Instead, state how many users the system should support and what kind of response time they should expect. Whether you elect to perform a stress test as part of the evaluation process or to simply rely on references is your choice, but you should have a good idea of what you are testing against.

Don't go for too much detail. A requirements list is not the detailed specifications document that will be created at the start of the implementation phase to direct the customization work. For instance, a requirements list should not include screen specifications. If it did, you would probably not find a tool with those exact screens anyway so the list would be of little value during the evaluation phase.

The level of detail of the requirements list and the amount of effort you choose to put into creating it should match the overall scope of the project. Simpler projects do quite well with straightforward lists, lists that are fairly high-level, pretty short (say, no more than a few pages), and that can be put together within a few meetings of the project team, each lasting a couple of hours. More ambitious projects must have longer, more detailed lists that may require several weeks of work by the project team to gather, evaluate, and rank. This segues nicely to the topic of the process required to build the requirements list.

# Creating a Requirements List

## Gathering Requirements

The requirements definition process depends on both the scope of the project and the knowledge of the project team about CRM tools. For a small project with a well-informed team, a relatively informal meeting of the project team may suffice to transform the template checklist at the end of this chapter into a custom checklist suitable for proceeding to the tool evaluation phase.

As projects become more elaborate, requirements definitions also get more complicated. The most efficient way to proceed is to alternate between working with the whole project team and letting individuals and subteams work on specific portions of the checklist. The overall process flows as follows:

- Start with a kickoff meeting for the entire team to go over the process of defining the requirements and to organize the work. At this point, the project team may be a skeleton team consisting of only the business and IT owners (and the project manager and the executive sponsor, of course!) and without the super-users or technical staffers.

  The requirements definition process is a great opportunity to identify who should be on the team. If you can't complete a significant piece of the requirements, then you know you'll have to engage a specific resource to do it (smaller pieces can be farmed out as needed without requiring the specialist's presence on the team for the duration of the project). The requirements definition process is also a great opportunity to observe the individuals on the team and to make appropriate substitutions either immediately or for the implementation phase if expertise or enthusiasm is lacking.

- Parcel out the various sections of the requirements list to the appropriate groups or individuals and let them research them independently. The project manager must keep a tight rein on the schedule so you don't spend inordinate amounts of time on the selection phase. Going back to the schedules discussed in Chapter 3, "Overview of CRM Selection and Implementation," you should be targeting anywhere from one to six months *total* for selecting the tool, depending on the complexity of the project, so don't let the requirements definition take up more than a week to a month depending on the complexity of the project.

- Once each subgroup has completed the work on individual sections, bring the whole team together again to validate and approve the entire set of documents. It may seem strange to ask individuals who know little about a particular topic to validate the choice of the specialists, but it's a powerful technique for both team building and quality assurance. On the team-building side, cross-reviews allow all the members of the team to understand, at least at some basic level, all the aspects of the tool project. Cross-reviews also make for better quality, as individuals who are not directly involved with a particular area often raise relevant questions and suggestions during the review, deepening the specialists' thinking about their findings, catching incompatibility issues between sections, and sometimes steering the research in a new and improved direction.

  The validation meeting is a good time to handle the ranking of the items on the team. We'll discuss this activity next.

## Ranking the Requirements

Most requirements-gathering efforts result in an overabundance of requirements, as the team gets hooked by the intriguing bells and whistles offered by vendors. The team that started out wanting a simple sales-tracking tool may wind up "needing" a full quoting and proposal-generating system with wireless integration after getting some inspiration from the creative CRM marketplace. Is there any harm in trading up?

Sounds like a potential disaster to me, not to mention an *expensive* disaster. The sad reality is that a team that was perfectly sized and equipped for a straightforward project can rarely be scaled up, either in quantity or in sophistication, to deliver a significantly more complex project. And even if it were possible to bring the more ambitious project to fruition, it's not clear that the functionality that was added in the frenzy of requirements gathering would actually be used or useful.

Fortunately, gross inflation in the scope of a project during the requirements definition phase is usually cured quickly when the team finds out that the larger project cannot be achieved with the budget at hand. Hence the importance of including a budget in the requirements definition.

How can you avoid creating a requirements monster in the first place? By asking the team to prioritize the requirements. The prioritization exercise should be conducted in a group meeting of the entire team, both to get buy-in from everyone and to get good cross-pollination as described above. For larger projects ask the subteams to prioritize their areas before the group meeting to make it more efficient.

The main problem during the prioritization exercise is to keep the team members from deciding that everything is top-priority. This is true whether you have a few priority levels or many, so I recommend using just three levels.

- **Top priority**: must-have, can't live without it. These are the features that really make the system. Usually they can be directly related to the initial impetus for the project, to the vision. They should all have a direct link to the tangible goals for the project. For instance, if your goal is to have all customer information in one place, a top-priority item would be that the tool include a customer database suitable for the kind of customer (such as consumer versus corporate).

  Anything that is labeled as top-priority but that cannot be related to the original concept for the project should be questioned, taking into account that the level of details of the requirements list is much greater than the vision. For instance, if your goal is to ensure that all sales reps have instantaneous access to their customers' data at any time, from anywhere, and your reps tend to be on the road most of the time, one of the functionality requirements may be that you need the system to support wireless data synchronization. The business goal said nothing about wireless synchronization, but it's the way (one of the ways, we'll come back to this point) to accomplish the goal.

  If the project is replacing an existing system, it's likely that the functionality of the existing system will show up in the must-haves, and that's usually a good thing since you don't want to deliver less than what the users already enjoy today. However, don't be afraid to discard existing functionality as appropriate. For instance, the current tool may boast a heavy-duty customization tool, but you may not need one if you can find a tool that supports most of the required functionality out-of-the-box.

- **Medium priority**: should-have, would have a tangible business benefit, but could do without. This can be a difficult category to populate, as articulate team members can make a good case that requirements that have business benefits are really essential to the accomplishment of the vision. The should-have requirements are often the foundation of future implementations.

  Let's revisit the wireless data synchronization example above. Perhaps your sales force is somewhat less mobile, and perhaps a once-daily data synchronization—that can be performed from a fixed location—is sufficient to bring them fresh information and to allow them to send updated information to the central system. In that case, good old non-wireless data synchronization would suffice and would be the top-priority requirement, while wireless data synchronization would be downgraded to a medium-priority requirement that may be implemented in a second phase of the project if needed.

- **Low priority**: nice-to-have, can definitively do without it. Low-priority items are those items that are useful, sometimes really attractive to the members of the team, but cannot be linked to tangible business benefits. The link between low-priority requirements and the vision is tenuous. They are often generated by cool vendor demos and datasheets rather than by the team members. Their absence should never be used to reject candidate tools, although they can be icing on the cake for the winning tool.

  Going back to the example of wireless data synchronization, if sales reps start their day in the office and therefore can sync up their data with the central system from the office, wireless data synchronization may be only a low-priority requirement. Certainly it's nice to have for those occasions when a sales rep skips the office start, but it would not impact the goals of the project if it were omitted.

Some project managers like to trim down the requirements list by completely dropping the low-priority items from the list. My heart is with them, but I've found it doesn't work well with project teams who usually have a strong emotional attachment to *all* the requirements on the list. I usually keep all the requirements even those tagged low-priority. You can always sort them out of view in the spreadsheet when required and you will have them handy for future use.

The requirements prioritization exercise can be painful, so it's a good test of the project manager's ability to work with the team. Useful techniques include reviewing the overall vision for the project, encouraging dialog between the technical and business users, and gently questioning the top-level requirements that are particularly difficult to meet. It's fine to keep tough requirements in the top-priority category if they are indeed essential, but only if everyone agrees that they are.

The outcome of the requirements prioritization is a "final" list of requirements, one that should be shorter than the initial draft and that clearly identifies the top priority items.

## When Do I Start Shopping?

Although it's realistic for the requirements list to undergo some changes and refinements during the early stages of the tool selection process, don't initiate serious talks with vendors until you have at least a draft of the requirements list. As long as you don't know what you want you may waste time with unsuitable candidates (visit houses you would never buy) and you may ignore potential candidates (that townhouse would put you so close to the office). You could also fall for the first tool you see without fully thinking through what you really need (buy the big house in the new development when that little bungalow close to town would be a better fit for your lifestyle).

That being said, if the project team is very new to the CRM world, it may be very difficult to create the requirements list without doing any shopping at all, since no one has a good feel for what's out there. If you are in that situation, try some light browsing of existing systems without spending much time on the browsing and without making an emotional commitment to any one vendor. If the timing works out, a great way to browse is to attend a suitable conference that features an exhibit hall, for two reasons:

- You can see all the tools, or at least a nice variety, in one go;
- In a public setting the tools you will see won't be customized to your exact needs, so it's easier to avoid falling in love with a particularly well-tailored demo only to realize later that most of it was handcrafted specially for you.

Barring a conveniently scheduled conference, a good alternative is to sign up for web-based seminars with a handful of tool vendors. So-called webinars often contain lots of PowerPoint slides and only a short demo, so you may have to suffer through some low-yield moments, but at an hour a pop they are still pretty painless. They will give you an exposure to a variety of approaches to handling customer-related functions as well as a feel for how slick tool demos can be. Such browsing is not truly shopping and can safely be done before the requirements checklist is created.

## Structure of the Requirements List

A requirements list for a house includes a mix of factors, from the number of bedrooms (functionality) to the type of floor plan (architecture), to the long-term prospects for the neighborhood (strategic value and fit), to whether you can move right in (ease of implementation), and of course the price. Some of the requirements are for the short term (the distance from your office) and some are for the long term (the age of the roof).

It's the same for a CRM requirements list. Some items are tactical and some are strategic; some are technically driven and some are business-focused. Tool vendors typically focus only on functionality and technical architecture, but you need to think more broadly. Organize the requirements in five buckets, each weighing about equally in the final decision.

- **The vendor.** What kind of company do you want to do business with? Is it a stable vendor? Are they innovating?
- **Technical architecture.** Is the tool's architecture appropriate for your needs? Will the tool be compatible with other parts of your IT architecture?
- **Functionality.** This is where the actual features of the tool come into play. Does the tool include all the functionality that you need? Are there some features that could put candidate tools over the top?
- **Implementation and maintenance.** What will it take to actually make the tool work in your environment? Can the tool be customized to the extent you want and need? What are the long-term requirements? How hard is it to upgrade your customizations?
- **Budget.** You don't want to waste time considering alternatives you can't afford, so you should set a high-level budget upfront including the tool, its implementation, and long-term maintenance costs.

The rest of the chapter discusses each of the categories in depth, and includes a summary checklist at the end to help you create your own customized list.

# The Vendor

## Success is not All About Features

The relationship with your CRM vendor doesn't end when the contract is signed. Some would even argue that the relationship *starts* at the time the contract is signed. And the relationship doesn't end when the implementation is complete, either. In fact, you are looking at many years of working with a CRM vendor as the tool goes through several upgrades, additional customizations, and integrations. Once in place, CRM tools often outlast key stakeholders, organizational structures, even business models. So the choice of the tool should be viewed as the choice of a long-term partner, not as a mere decision on features and functionality.

The interesting dilemma in the CRM field is that a lot of the creative, leading-edge functionality originates from small vendors, who are inherently less stable than more established players. The CRM field has seen a large number of mergers and some outright failures. When a vendor disappears entirely, its customers are placed in a difficult situation: they suddenly find themselves with unsupported systems, perhaps at critical times for their needs, while they must consider another large investment to purchase a replacement that will be supported in the long run. If they had chosen an ASP solution, they may even become unable to access their data (let alone use the system) from one day to the next.

Outright failures have been relatively rare, but mergers are common. Tools from vendors that undergo mergers are typically supported "as is" (with no enhancements) for many months, sometimes years, and occasionally forever, if there is such a concept in the technology arena. In the case of an acquisition by a competitor, the typical scenario is that the acquiring company provides support for a year or so, then offers to migrate customers to the other tool. Migrating systems is not a trivial affair. As discussed in Chapter 2, "Auditing your CRM System," facing a migration should trigger a reassessment of your CRM strategy rather than an automatic agreement to proceed with it. In the case of a migration inspired by a merger, at least you would not be in a situation where you would be left completely stranded with no notice.

What should you do if you need a specific functionality that is only provided by a smaller, less stable vendor? One possibility is to wait a little while. There is a great deal of leap-frogging happening on functionality, so if there's a good idea out there, it will eventually be picked up by a larger, more stable company. Sometimes such a vendor acquires the smaller, innovative vendor, but not always. In a leapfrog environment, what counts most is the ability of the vendor to pursue a long-term strategy of continuous product improvements. An important part of assessing your vendor's stability is to look beyond the current features or the current size of the company and to evaluate the vendor's commitment to product marketing and innovative development (which depends in part, but in part only, on financial stability).

Always include vendor requirements in your list, even if you need to bend them later on.

## Vendor Requirements

What should the vendor requirements cover?

- **Financial viability**. Is the company successful and likely to remain successful? If the vendor is a public company, it's easy to get a hold of its financial results and, assuming they are properly audited, to analyze its prospects. Private companies are more challenging. While some may be willing to share some financial information under a non-disclosure agreement during the sales cycle, it's a lot more difficult to evaluate this information. In the end, you will have to make a leap of faith based on your analysis of their success in the market. Remember that all successful, large, public CRM companies started as small, private outfits (as did hundreds of others that did not make it).

- **Customer references**. This is, for me, an essential criterion, unless you are willing to take a chance on a wonderful and unique technology—and you have a good backup plan in case things don't work out as you had hoped. With smaller vendors, check references early in the evaluation phase so you don't waste your time on candidates that do not have appropriate references.

  An appropriate reference is a customer in a field similar to yours, using the tool in approximately the same way as you will, and with about the same number of users. For example, if you provide financial services, a reference from a software company is not that useful. If you are looking for a marketing automation system, a support-tracking reference is not what you want. If you want to implement with 300 users, a reference with 20 users is insufficient. (The opposite is not that great either: the 300-user reference is likely to have vastly more resources available to implement the solution, and they may need complicated features that would just get in the way of your small organization.) We'll come back to the art of getting meaningful references in Chapter 6, but it suffices to say that you should define the kind of references you would seek as part of the requirements checklist.

- **Geographical presence**. Although I can't imagine picking a vendor solely because it is in your backyard, there's much to be said about accessibility, both in the short term and long term. Taking this point to extremes, would you buy a system from a vendor that's headquartered on the other side of the world, with no local sales force where you are? If you had a choice of two vendors, one local and one remote, would you be more likely to go with the local vendor? Be sure to consider not only the availability of the sales force, which is often quite good, but also the availability of support and other post-sales services for the long-term.
- **Business model**. Is ASP acceptable? Desirable? Required? Is a dual model (ASP and packaged) important?
- **Technical vision**. Can the vendor articulate a technical vision? Does the vision make sense? Does it match your needs? Do you believe the organization is likely to sustain the technical vision? For instance, is there a strong CTO? Do you see a depth of technical leadership within the company beyond a key individual? (This last point is important for a small vendor: if the CTO were to leave, would the company survive?)
- **Business vision**. Is the marketing and business development strategy attractive? Does it put you and your needs in the center of the vendor's focus, or on its margins? If you like the business vision, do you think the vendor is likely to be successful with it?
- **Attention to customers**. Better vendors use a better sales process, provide more customized responses to RFPs and other requests, and in general lavish more attention on their customers. Don't mistake pre-sales attention for post-sales support quality (we will address post-sales support quality in section 8) but do take into account the quality of the pre-sales process when evaluating the vendor.

For convenience, all the requirements discussed in this and future sections are summarized in checklist format at the end of this chapter (section 9).

# Technical Architecture

## Not Just a Matter for IT

It's important to define the technical requirements for the tool so you don't find yourself with a tool that simply cannot function properly within the technical infrastructure of your organization. Clearly, defining the technical requirements is going to require much input from the IT group. However, it's easy to focus too much on the technical side and to forget the business implications of the technical choices. This is where a strong IT owner can orchestrate the contributions of the various technical staffers while adding the proper amount of business acumen and strategic thinking. The IT owner's contribution is essential in at least three ways:

- The technical staffers may focus only on "cool" technology and prefer the leading edge, which they see as more fun and better for their resume. In fact, established technology may be a better choice for the organization if it combines a lower risk with "good enough" technical power. Note that the IT owner may have the same weakness!
- The technical staffers may be unaware of the longer-term goals for IT. While the CRM project must be grounded in the present reality, it also needs to fit within the future framework. The IT owner should be able to bring that knowledge to the team. Also, it may be appropriate to accelerate some IT initiatives to accommodate the project. This kind of decision-making responsibility needs to be done at the IT executive level, by or through the IT owner.
- Finally, there are occasions when the CRM project will trigger objections and changes to the IT infrastructure model. This is where an experienced IT owner will really shine. First, the IT owner should be able to recognize whether the technical requirements are inappropriately preventing a reasonable business choice for the CRM system, as opposed to reasonable technical requirements placing reasonable limits on the business choices. For example, if none of the good CRM systems out there run on the particular operating system that you support, perhaps your supported list needs changing. On the other hand, if only some CRM systems fail to support your preferred operating system, it's probably fine to just eliminate them from consideration.

If the CRM project triggers revisiting the corporate IT strategy, the IT owner should have the wherewithal to drive the decisions required to make changes through the organization, and to do so quickly enough to avoid delays to the project.

The technical architecture area is one where asking all the team members to review all the requirements yields plenty of benefits for teamwork. If the business owners can understand why the technical requirements are restrictive, and if they can be convinced that the restrictions make sense, they will be more open to discarding some otherwise tempting candidates that do not include appropriate technical requirements.

## Technical Requirements

Technical requirements include the technical platform, scalability, integration capabilities, and the all-important development environment. If you are a business owner and you're tempted to skip this section, try to read on: you should be able to follow the description easily and it will help you understand what your IT counterparts are concerned with.

- **Technical platform**. It's usually best if the CRM system can conform to established standards within the organization, including hardware, operating systems, database, web servers, etc.

  Standards are useful in two ways. First, they capture some level of tested and approved quality. The organization believes that the standards that were chosen allow it to function properly; inferior solutions are not included in the standard platforms. Second, there's a great advantage to minimizing the number of competing technologies being supported at any one time because it is so much easier to maintain staff and training to handle a few different technologies as opposed to many different ones. So this is about simplifying the IT universe rather than keeping out inferior solutions.

  Would you consider adding platforms and protocols to the list of standards as part of the CRM project? If so, are there any restrictions to what you would accept? Most organizations strongly prefer or mandate open standards, for instance.

  One important aspect of the technical platform is whether the tool offers a thick client or a thin client. Older tools were built with a client/server model, in which client software must be loaded onto each user's machine and performs significant tasks for the user. That software is the client in client/server and is now often called a *thick* client. In contrast, newer tools can usually be run with a *thin* client, which handles only the user interface and the navigation, not the business logic. It is very lightweight and usually (though not always) embodied in a web browser. Web-based clients are much easier to deploy, since there's less need to fiddle with each user's machine. You may need to use a particular web browser, or to set up specific options in the web browser. Thick clients, on the other hand, can pack lots of processing power into the clients, thereby allowing faster processing, and they offer a richer set of widgets (drop-down menus, buttons, automated charts, clickable graphics, etc.). Of course, some type of thick client is required if users must interact with the system without a connection to the network, for instance, field sales reps using the system offline.

Carefully qualify your requirements for thin clients if you decide to go that route. Most vendors require specific browsers, specific versions of the browsers, and large amounts of memory, which may require checking, configuring, or even upgrading each machine to ensure that it meets the requirements. That can mean a lot of work, especially if your users are not sophisticated and cannot do it themselves. Also, some vendors require significant downloads, either during the first session with the tool on a given machine, or every time the user logs on. That process would have an impact on usability and should be noted in the requirements. Finally, vendors that offer both thin and thick clients may offer only a subset of functionality through the thin client, so make sure your requirements specify what functions should be available through the thin client.

- **Scalability**. This has to do with whether the tool can support the number of users you need to serve, and how well it can adapt to serving larger numbers of users. Scalability is of course a very important issue, but make sure to use reasonable scenarios in your evaluations. One of my clients spent months and lots of IT cycles to conduct large-scale trials to determine whether a particular tool could support *ten times* its current number of users, only to find out that the grandiose user projections never came close to being met. In this area as with other areas in the requirements, it's best to stay within a reasonable timeframe of a few years' time. Who knows what you will need and what software you will require in five or ten years?

    Starting with the number of users you need to support today, use a two-year projection. Consider where the users are located. If everyone is a LAN connection away from the server, life will probably be pretty good. If your users are dispersed, then you need to specify that in the requirements. High-end tools typically provide a three-tier architecture to support a large number of dispersed users, through which the thin clients on the desktops interact with an application server, or one of many application servers used for distributed processing or for redundancy. The application servers then interact with a database server. While your requirements should describe the business requirements (support X number of users located in Y areas) rather than dictate a particular architecture, it's likely that the IT owner will like to see a three-tier architecture.

- **Availability.** Availability refers to the ability of a system to continue to perform despite underlying failures. Is it critical that the tool be available at all times, even in the event of something like a database failure?

If that's the case then the tool should support continuous synchronization with backup servers to minimize downtime. What kind of clustering does the tool support? Is it compatible with the existing IT infrastructure?

As you make your decisions about the availability requirements, keep in mind that high-availability is complex and expensive, and may not be worthwhile in all situations. Because of the complexity, high availability may be a good candidate for a second phase. High availability is expensive, not only because you need to purchase and set up much more hardware and software, but also because it slows down processing time, which may be more expensive than anything else. Don't blindly check off the high-availability requirement without fully considering your options. It would be a shame to disqualify candidates that would otherwise provide a good fit just because they don't have high-availability features you may never exploit.

If some amount of down time is acceptable if the system crashes and therefore you decide to forgo a high-availability strategy, you still need a viable backup and recovery component to get the system back up after a crash. Make sure that the tool provides an acceptable recovery strategy.

- **Integration**. Unless you are looking for a small, isolated system, you will need to integrate the CRM tool with other tools within the organization. The tools may be already in existence (such as your accounting system). They may be acquired concurrently with the CRM tool as part of the CRM project (for instance, a computer-telephony interface for the phone switch), or they may appear later as part of a separate project (for example, an analytics system).

  Specifying the integration requirements for the tools that are currently in existence is easiest, although the level of integration required is rarely obvious at the time of the requirements definition and may demand a detailed analysis later in the cycle to make a good decision. The requirements for future tools are even more challenging.

  If you anticipate tight integration requirements, you will want to require a fully defined API (application programming interface). It's best if the API is based on industry standards and allows access to all the objects within the tool, but you will find that some APIs are proprietary or only allow partial access. Especially if future integration needs are unknown, you would have the most leeway with a standard API and an exposed data model.

For the integrations you are planning, it's a good idea to require production references. It's true that each integration is custom, but the fact that other customers managed to make it work bodes well for your success. You should get more details on what was done from the individuals who created the integration to get a full picture of what is required.

Many CRM vendors have established partnerships with the vendors of tools that are often integrated with theirs. Partnerships are great, but be sure to fully evaluate the depth of the partnership during the evaluation phase. You presumably need partners that have accomplished more than merely paying a fee to be listed as partners.

- **Development environment**. Unless you are considering a very simple tool, you can expect to have to make some customizations, and therefore you will need a development environment. Development environments can be the neglected stepchildren of CRM systems, so make sure you define and later evaluate your requirements in that area.

  You may need to modify the data model, the workflows, and the screens, so consider development facilities for all three areas. Wherever possible, prefer widely-used standards to proprietary toolkits. Older tools often require the use of little-known scripting utilities that require specially trained staff and are not useful outside that particular context, while newer tools may offer easier-to-use, but sometimes less powerful screen-driven tools.

  Consider that in most instances you will have separate systems for development, testing, and production. Cleanly migrating changes from one environment to another is critical, and yet few tools offer any robust assistance in this area.

# Functionality

While functionality (the features) is not the one and only piece of the requirements list, it's clear that no CRM system will ever be successful without the appropriate functionality. Sure, you could love the vendor, the technical architecture, the services offered, and the price, but in the end the functionality is the impetus for the project.

## Who Determines the Functionality Requirements?

The business owners and the super-users are the team members who have the best expertise to design the functionality requirements. I'm not saying that the business owners can do it single-handedly. While the business owners can see the strategic goals for the organization and how the CRM tool can meet these goals, they are removed from the day-to-day tasks of the average individual contributor, especially in a large organization, and they may miss critical functionality.

I remember a Support VP who focused obsessively on how well the support-tracking tool could help him manage escalations, which was the customer-related task that filled the most hours in his days, but somehow neglected to bring the same level of attention to how support cases were created in the tool, a task which clearly was the most-frequently performed task in the support group as a whole. The tool ended up with a complex and slow case creation process (which was the out-of-the-box process, to be honest) when it should have been clear that this common task needed to be optimized in priority. No super-user would have neglected the case entry screen!

## Techniques for Specifying Functionality Requirements

It's often difficult for super-users and business owners alike to get to the functionality requirements because they find it difficult to translate business processes into tool requirements. Here are some suggestions for how to proceed, from basic ideas useful when processes are already well-defined and working well to more exotic strategies that may be required if the processes are in need of formalizing or changing. Chapter 9 revisits these ideas from the perspective of the detailed implementation requirements definition.

A simple and very effective way for the super-users and the business owners to organize their requirements definition is to diagram the business processes. Pictures are worth many words and a simple diagram of the sales process, with the various stages and owners, should make quite clear what routing is required, what level of collaboration is required amongst the sales team, and how the tool should handle generating proposals, to name but a few examples.

There are many formal methods for diagramming processes and you should feel free to use the ones you like. My experience is that business users respond better to a simple and informal approach to diagramming as opposed to funny-looking boxes and spaghetti-like multi-page diagrams, so let them doodle and encourage them to stay with a relatively high-level diagram (say, one page).

Such a casual approach may not suffice with larger, more complex organizations, or organizations that have never used formal processes but now need them. If that's the case, you may want to proceed to a formal task analysis, where roles and tasks within the organization are explicitly defined. Task analysis can be combined with diagramming techniques, of course.

You may encounter a deeper issue. Sometimes both business owners and super-users share a certain lack of imagination about what the tool *could* do as opposed to what the current tool *does do*. Worse, they get hung up on *how* the current tool does things. Often the best way to do something (track a sale, manage the knowledge base, hand off a case) is not to reproduce the current process, especially if the process is manual, but rather to approach the task in a new, more efficient way. You don't want to write your functionality requirements to read, "do what the current tool does", especially if the current tool is not working well! What you need is a touch of re-engineering, a fancy and somewhat fad-sounding concept for creating new processes. While a full discussion of re-engineering techniques is beyond our scope here, you can use the following easy techniques to get the business users going on a more inventive road.

- Include on the team some individuals that have used other tools in other jobs, preferably the types of tools that are likely to be considered during the selection process as opposed to older or homegrown tools. Such individuals should be able to contribute fresh ideas, that are implemented in an existing CRM tool so they have a good dose of reality in them.
- Ask the IT owner or other knowledgeable technical resource to work with the business team. It's useful to choose someone who has experience with other CRM tools, but a good facilitator who can ask "how else?" and "why?" questions can do very well with minimal knowledge.

The business owners may have trouble thinking in the abstract terms of functionality and features and they may want to draw screens at this point. Now is not the time for screens (we'll get there in the implementation phase), so the project manager or the IT owner may need to lend a hand to elevate the debate as required. It's fine to specify uncluttered screens or one-click functionality for specific tasks as long as you stay away from screen layouts.

## Functionality Requirements

The discussion of functional requirements below is formidably long because CRM systems are formidably rich. Remember that this is an inventory and you do *not* need each and every requirement listed. For starters, entire sections may not apply: don't bother with marketing automation if you don't need that, and don't bother with wireless communications if you don't need them.

Even for sections that do apply to you, take only what you need: most functional requirement lists are way too long! Focusing on the essentials not only accelerates the selection process, it also increases significantly the quality of the fit of the tool that's chosen. It's best to spend more time exploring fewer requirements in more depth than lightly touching hundreds of requirements and running the risk of missing some important points in the process, when some of the requirements are just wishful thinking or perhaps won't ever be implemented.

Another key point to keep in mind when defining functionality requirements and when evaluating potential candidates against the requirements is that simplicity wins. Fancy, convoluted solutions are usually not the best because they can be too complicated for users. Whenever possible, strive for solutions that require as little effort as possible.

The first section is about those areas that pertain to all functional groups (marketing, sales, support) and is followed by sections for each functional group.

## Cross-Functional Requirements

This section includes requirements that may apply to any business function. We start with communication channels since a basic requirement for CRM systems is to handle the channels you currently use when communicating with customers such as email and phone, and perhaps some additional ones that you want to add as part of the CRM project (and some CRM projects focus solely on adding channels, such as chat).

**Phone Integration**   If you have call centers, whether for marketing, sales, or support, you may want to integrate the CRM tool with the phone switch through computer-telephony integration (CTI) software. This would allow you to validate and route customers based on information gathered by the phone system; to do screen pops, that is, to have screens painted with appropriate customer information a split second before the call is presented on their phone; and to automatically dial phone numbers, either for a specific customer or as part of a list.

- Specify exactly what kinds of interactions you are looking for, as you will want to check at that level of detail during the evaluation phase. Do you wish to do entitlement checking? Screen pops? Outbound dialing?

- If you already have a switch or CTI software, check whether the tool supports them unless you are open to changing them.

### E-mail Support

- **E-mail integration**. Do you want users to send e-mails from within the CRM tool? Should the messages be logged into the system? Are you open to using the CRM's native e-mail system or do you need to link to the existing e-mail system? Should outgoing e-mails be tagged in particular ways (typically so they can be recognized from a response)? Do you wish to send bulk e-mails from within the tool?

   Should incoming e-mails be automatically loaded into the system? What processing, if any, needs to be done on those messages (such as creating a new prospect or a new support case, or adding e-mails to an existing record)? Since you are probably behind a firewall, what kind of firewall compatibility do you require?

- **E-mail processing**. Do you need automatic acknowledgements on e-mails? Do you want the tool to route e-mail requests? Based on what? This item is directly related to whether you want to encourage customers to place requests via e-mail or via a portal. Portal communication is much more structured than e-mail so I would de-emphasize e-mail routing in favor of a more powerful portal. You may feel differently, especially if your customers are used to communicating via e-mail and would balk at switching to a portal.

   Are you looking for a tool that supports canned response templates from which the users can select the appropriate one manually? Or do you want the tool to suggest the proper answer? Or do you want the system to dispense entirely with humans when it "knows" the answer and to send automatic responses?

- **E-mail utilities**. Is spell checking available for outgoing e-mails? What formats are supported? (This is moot if you require integration to your e-mail system, of course). Do you need e-mail templates? Should attachments be allowed?

**Customer Portal**   Customer portal functionality is a very special channel because it's so rich.

- **Authentication and security**. Although the knowledge base is often accessible without barriers, you may want to protect even that part of the portal with an authentication scheme if you feel it would provide too much information about your products to your competitors.

Would you like to use an existing authentication scheme from another part of your web site? What kind of signup functionality would you like? (Self-registration? Manual registration?) What type of authentication scheme is required to maintain security? More stringent schemes are required if you must protect sensitive personal information.

Once customers have access to the portal, do you need a flexible permission scheme, for instance granting more privileges to your partners (to see more documents, or to see their customers' records for instance)?

- **Personalization.** Do you want to deliver a different portal experience based on customer characteristics? What would the characteristics be? How deep should the personalization go?

- **Knowledge base**. Can the customer access the knowledge base from the portal? What types of search functionalities are required (FAQs, text search, natural language processing, tree search, advanced search)? We'll talk about the knowledge base more in an upcoming section.

- **E-commerce**. Should the CRM tool allow customers to shop and place orders? What integrations, if any, are required there? Note that few CRM tools offer fully featured online shopping environments, although some may be adequate for simple stores.

- **Order tracking**. Should customers be able to track their orders online? What integrations are required to make that happen if the order records are not in the CRM database? Should customers be able to modify their orders online?

- **Service/support case entry**. Do you want to allow customers to place requests for customer service or technical support from the portal? Probably yes: this creates significant cost savings in service and support operations. If you decide to go this route, you may want to de-emphasize e-mail issue logging.

- **Online case management**. Should customers be able to view the progress of their cases online? If so, you will want to require some facility to hide sensitive (or boring!) bits of the case records from customers. Pay close attention to how flexibly this can be done. Can customers add comments to cases, or is it a read-only facility? Can they close cases online? Reopen them?

- **Customer forums**. Would you like customers to collaborate to discuss or resolve issues? What kind of control do you wish to have on the forums? Do you wish to name special users as moderators?

**Wireless Support**   Wireless communication may be required for either customers or internal users. Full support of wireless devices is not a common feature for all tools, so carefully weigh what you must have versus what would be nice to have so you don't find yourself having to discard otherwise suitable candidates.

- **Supported devices and protocols**. If you already have wireless devices in place, inventory what they are. If you will be purchasing wireless devices as a part of the CRM project, define your preferences.
- **Wireless messaging**. Many CRM tools allow simple outbound communications such as signaling a wireless device as the result of an alert within the system. Do you also need treatment of inbound messages?
- **Wireless real-time access**. Can users interact with (usually a significantly reduced subset of) the system through a wireless device? Is this a fully formed application or can it be accomplished solely through a customization effort using a tool kit?
- **Data synchronization**. Unlike the point above, this one focuses on disconnected users. That is, do your users need to download information from the system to their wireless devices? If they do that, should they be able to make updates on the wireless devices? And can the updates be uploaded at some later time back into the main database?

**Chat Support**   Chat (instant messaging) is a potentially costly, but very powerful way to communicate with online customers, often used for collaborative selling and sometimes for customer service and support. While chat is a wonderful tool, you may not need it. If you have no plans to use it soon, it would be a mistake to exclude from consideration tools that do not provide a chat environment. If you plan to introduce chat after the initial rollout, include it in the requirements so that you don't have to go out and get yet another tool to be integrated with the CRM system later on.

- **Integrated chat support**. Do you have an existing chat environment that you need to link to the CRM tool or are you looking for the tool to provide a chat environment?
- **Chat environment**. What kinds of user experience are you looking for? Do you want to be able to define response templates? Adjust windows? Route and queue chat requests in any particular ways? Do you want to provide chat support from designated locations on your web site or throughout? Does the tool have restrictions on what kinds of pages chat can be activated from? Does the tool work properly across firewalls and what kinds of arrangements do you need to make to

install it (this is a potential security issue)? Do you need records of all chat communications?

- **Advanced features**. Do you want your internal users (employees) to be able to push pages to customers? To take control of their browser entirely (this is useful for technical support situations, for instance)? Many CRM tools provide only basic messaging features, which may or may not be sufficient for you.

**Voice over IP (VoIP)**  Voice over IP is a technique that allows transporting voice over the computer network, eliminating the need for a telephone. It's a tempting option if your customers are consumers who may only have one phone line when they are using the web. For all others, it's an interesting idea but still a technical challenge so it is not widely used. Here again, do not unnecessarily disqualify candidates that don't offer VoIP just because you think it's cool.

The main issue for VoIP is to check that the tool can use existing protocols that you use in-house. This is a good example of an issue that requires input from a technical specialist—here the telephony specialist—who may not be needed more than a few hours during the selection phase.

**Multichannel Support**  Above and beyond supporting a variety of channels, you probably want the tool to deliver a consistent experience to the users regardless of what communication channels they use. This section explores those issues.

- **Consistent experience**. A fancy phrase to mean that users, both internal and external, can initiate conversations in any medium and pursue them in other media, as needed, while being able to access all the information gathered in previous conversations. In other words, the customer can e-mail asking for some information, receive a response by phone (perhaps because a more precise description is needed), and then later open a chat to ask for further details. At each step in the process the internal user (and, ideally, the customer) would have full access to the entire request history without having to jump from one system to the next to get it.
- **Universal queuing and logic**. This means that, once in the system, issues coming from any communication channel can all be handled in the same way. For instance, if you define routing logic based on keywords for e-mail, the same logic should be usable for routing chat. This makes for a much more productive organization of labor.

**Customer Database**  Keeping track of your customers is a key function of the CRM tool, and it can be more challenging than you think.

- **Comprehensive records**. What information would you like to record about customers and prospects? Is there anything unusual you need to track? In particular, are your customers corporate entities or consumers? For corporate customers, do you need to track multiple contacts with different roles for a single customer? Do the roles change over the life cycle of a customer? Do you need to keep track of special relationships among your customers such as households or reseller/end-user entities?
- **Custom fields**. Even if you are lucky enough to find a CRM tool that has a customer database that actually includes all the fields you want to track, you will probably want to add some in the future, modify existing ones, and delete or hide others. It's very useful if the tool can allow that. Specifically investigate how such changes can be done. Do they require programming? What restrictions exist on the type of fields that can be added (such restrictions *always* exist, although they can be mild) or deleted (you can be sure you won't be able to remove the customer number)?
- **Link between databases**. Where should your customer data reside? There are many good answers to this question, including making the CRM system the master customer database, using the accounting system as the master database and linking the two in some way, and using a so-called federated model where customer data is held in several systems with appropriate links and synchronization. While the only really bad answer to where the customer data reside is "we don't know," it's very important to define a strategy for the data repository early in the project and, if required, processes to keep everything and everyone in sync. No need for details at this point, but you can't make much progress without a strategy.

   If you are using the CRM tool for marketing campaigns, you may want to load prospect lists into it and maybe do some processing and cleansing of the lists. Specify what's needed.
- **Customer history**. It's very useful to have immediate access to the products a customer has purchased, whether you are trying to build a marketing campaign, do follow-up sales, or support the customer. Determine whether that type of information should be kept in the CRM system, whether that should be the master record within the company, and if multiple repositories exist what kinds of synchronization mechanisms are required. Don't go overboard with the synchronization: if your sales volume is low a simple manual entry into the CRM

system after the purchase is recorded in the accounting system may be just fine.

**Employee Database**  Similar issues apply to the repository of employee information. In particular, the employee information is likely to be stored elsewhere, perhaps in an HR system or in the corporate e-mail system, so there's the question of integrating and synchronizing information from another master database.

In addition, CRM-specific items such as the permission scheme need to match your needs. Are permissions based on roles? Does the tool need to have a concept of the reporting hierarchy for routing and escalating issues and for reporting purposes?

**Knowledge Management**  The knowledge base is the set of documents that help your employees answer customers' requests and help your customers help themselves. The knowledge base used by sales reps is often called the marketing encyclopedia and is mentioned in the sales section, but the same concepts are applicable to it.

- **Document creation**. Do you need a way to create new documents? Who will do this? How easy does it need to be? If some documents will be created using existing objects (such as support cases), do you want to be able to migrate the objects into the knowledge creation process? Is a spellchecker important? Do you need templates? Can documents have customized attributes, such as the author's name or product category, that may be essential for searches or document maintenance? What document formats are supported (some tools only support simple text, which is insufficient for most applications)? It's best to find a tool that allows newly created documents to be visible immediately without requiring special processing (beyond going through the review process).

- **Heterogeneous knowledge bases**. If you are using documents created outside the CRM tool, must they be brought into the system or can they be searched anyway? If the documents must be brought into the tool, does it require manual processing or are automated loading facilities available? What document formats do you need to support? Are they restricted in the tool? What do you need in terms of support for attachments?

- **Knowledge creation workflow**. Beyond creating new documents, you will need a process to review the documents and eventually post them for the users. What kind of workflow do you need? Some CRM tools provide limited support for creation workflows. If you need multiple review steps, or you want to have full support for queues, status changes, and alerts during the document creation process, you will need to state that. Make sure that you can control who can do reviews and post documents through the permission scheme.

Keep in mind that your knowledge creation workflow may change over time. Will the tool be able to accommodate adding steps to the review, for instance?

- **Document maintenance**. This is often a weak area in CRM tools, so be sure to specify what you need. If you are planning for a pretty small knowledge base (say a few hundred documents) robust document maintenance tools are probably not that important since one person can easily wade through all the documents and decide whether they are still valid. As your knowledge base increases in size, so do the maintenance requirements.

  Do you need a planned obsolescence model, through which a review date is included at document creation date? Do you intend to create buckets of documents within the knowledge base, so that each bucket can remain of reasonable size and be maintained by one individual? If so, make sure that the requirements say so.

- **History trail**. Do you want to capture everything that went on with a particular document? It's very useful for the knowledge base manager to have a full history trail available for documents so that it's possible to figure out who reviewed a particular document, or who the original author was.

  Many tools offer very limited history trails, sometimes limited to the author, the creation date, and the last update date. Other tools provide a history of events on each document that shows who took what action on what date. Very few tools provide more than that, and in particular very few tools provide a full version control environment. If you need such a level of control, you probably will have to purchase a tool focused on document management and integrate it to a CRM tool. Carefully define the level of sophistication that you need.

- **Self-learning features**. Some tools leverage the use of the knowledge base to improve the quality of the documents. For instance, the tool may display documents in order of their popularity, either how often they were accessed or how often users rated them as useful. The tool may allow you to run reports on failed searches, information that's useful to a knowledge base manager when deciding where to add content. Self-learning features are very important since they allow you to use "free" resources to improve the knowledge base and also because they allow you to capture information you would not be able to obtain easily otherwise.

When deciding on self-learning requirements, be sure to consider the needs of both internal and external users. For example, internal users (employees) may need and actually use functionality that allows them to flag questionable documents to the knowledge base owner, while that would make no sense to external users (customers) who, after all, should be able to benefit from a fully vetted set of documents and may find it confusing to be offered the ability to set error flags.

- **Search capabilities**. The proof is in the pudding, and for knowledge bases the truth is in successful searches. There are many ways to go about searching, so you should think about both your users' level of sophistication and the volume of your knowledge base. Small knowledge bases, those that contain up to a few hundred documents, can be explored quite successfully with relatively basic tools. As the volume of documents grows, simplistic techniques become insufficient. User queries may fail to retrieve existing documents (perhaps because users are not aware of the magic keywords they should be using). Perversely, queries may also return too many documents, creating an overwhelming set of potential solutions that users are unable or unwilling to explore.

Start with a brutally honest evaluation of the likely size of the knowledge base on the one hand, and the sophistication of your users on the other. With a very small knowledge base, a simple FAQ strategy would work. Even with a few hundred documents, offering a tree-based search (by topic and sub-topic) and a search engine should cover most user requirements. The more sophisticated users would benefit from an advanced search mechanism, for instance one that allows searching on document attributes (the author of the document, or its topic category) in addition to a text search.

If you anticipate a large knowledge base or unsophisticated users, you may want to go further. For instance, having the knowledge base automatically present documents in order of popularity, as discussed under self-learning features, would be critical. With unsophisticated users, the ability of the search system to interpret natural language and synonyms would remove frustrations. With huge knowledge bases, the ability to refine searches when the result set is large would be a great asset.

My warning here is not to fall in love with any particular feature that vendors show you without analyzing it in the context of your business needs. The ability to manually enter synonyms into the search system so that naïve users are accommodated sounds wonderful, but if you don't have the resources to maintain the list of synonyms, you just bought yourself a very expensive paperweight. If your users are all internal employees with plenty of relevant training, they will know the specific terminology to use in searches and may not need guided searches.

- **Leveraged searches**. Many times the knowledge base will be used as part of working on a customer issue. The knowledge base can be leveraged for productivity to handle such tasks as automatic suggestions (suggesting potential solutions to the user based on the description of the issue), auto-response (sending an automated response to a known query), and linking documents with other objects such as deals or support cases. You may also want to use specialized tools such as case-based reasoning or CBR, through which resolution is achieved by reusing or adapting solutions that were used to resolve similar issues in the past.

- **Permissions and authorizations**. Whether on the knowledge creation or knowledge search side, you need to manage access to the documents in the knowledge base. This is definitely required if you make the documents available to customers through a portal. Here are some points to think about around permissions and authorizations.

  Can permissions be defined as group profiles that regulate creation, modification, review, posting, and access, with the profiles then being applicable to individuals? Group profiles are handy since you can just say that John Doe has a "sales rep" profile, and therefore can read all the documents in the knowledge base but cannot review or post, rather than having to define John's profile individually.

  Since some individuals will undoubtedly have special roles, it's helpful to be able to apply multiple profiles to a single individual (for the multi-taskers), and also to create truly custom profiles as needed. Otherwise, you would be stuck creating profiles that apply to just one person, a big waste of time.

  Moving to permissions, you probably want to be able to assign permissions to individual documents rather than to buckets of information. Otherwise you would need to move documents from bucket to bucket as they get reviewed, which is a pain. You should be able to define permissions separately for internal and external users. If you have partners or other "special" customers, having an intermediate level between internal user and customer would be extremely handy.

- **Subscriptions and alerts**. The knowledge base may be used in push mode to send alerts to users, either to all users or to some subset understood by the system (say, all users of a particular product, or all sales reps in the West). This can be leveraged to automatically send updates or newsletters to customers. Alerts are usually sent via e-mail, although a potential use for this technology is to post news on the customer portal.

  Users may also want to subscribe to particular documents or categories, so they automatically get updated when the document is changed or documents are added to the categories they are interested in. This feature is useful for both internal and external users. The nice thing about subscriptions is that they are completely automatic and can deliver timely information without requiring any overhead from the document creation function.

**Metrics**   Measuring and displaying results is a huge undertaking, to the point that there are now vendors that focus exclusively on CRM metrics tools (analytics). This is a delicate area of the requirements since metrics tend to be very customized, so you will rarely find exactly what you want in the out-of-the-box products. If you already know what you want in terms of metrics, great! Otherwise, don't bother creating exact requirements yet (you should do it at the start of the implementation phase, as will be discussed in Chapter 9), but instead focus on the following four areas.

- **Data availability**. If you want to measure how quickly leads are acted upon, you'd better look for a system that stores timestamps on lead creation and activity. The same is true for tracking closure times for support reps. Make a list of items you want to report against and beware of add-on (custom) fields, as reporting against them can be a lot more difficult.

- **Customizable templates**. CRM vendors will proudly state they support 72 different canned reports (or 372!). The reality is that 72 reports won't help you if they don't include the ones you use every day. As much as possible, take time to define the key reports you will be using ahead of time. Are they available as templates? (Don't worry about the pretty stuff; do the templates extract the data you need in a way that's useful to you?) Customizable templates are ideal so you can easily change a few details rather than having to start over. They should also allow you to do the slicing and dicing required for larger organizations.

  Look for templates for graphs and time-based reports.

- **Report creation tools**. Unless your needs are very simple and you are very lucky with your tool choice, you will have to customize reports. Look for GUI tools that can be manipulated by business users. On the other end, if you will have complex reporting needs, being able to integrate a full-featured reporting tool is required.

- **Report distribution system**. Can the system push reports to users? It's ideal to have a self-service environment where users can subscribe to the reports they need within the limits of their authorization level. What formats do you require for output?

  Do you need a way to populate spreadsheets? (I think you do!) To feed into a data warehousing system? If so, do you need periodic updates to that system? Will updates be made though an existing interface or through a separate customized piece?

  How will the production of reports impact the normal use of the system?

**Internationalization** You may have internationalization needs in your near future even if they are not a concern today. If your needs are in the distant future, be flexible here since a true localized system is very complex and few systems support the facilities you would need to build one, let alone offer an out-of-the-box solution.

- **Language support**. Do internal or external users need to use non-English languages, and which ones? Double-byte languages such as Japanese are supported more rarely than single-byte languages such as German. If you need support for double-byte languages check it out early during the evaluation phase. Data entry is one thing; data manipulation is another. In other words, it's pretty common for tools to accept entries in, say Spanish, but not so common for tools to properly sort Spanish words, handling non-English sort order and accents.

- **Foreign currency support**. Do you need to keep forecast, quotes, and other financial information in multiple currencies? If you also need to report on mixed currencies, specify that.

- **Interface localization**. Do you need to localize some screens of the application? Usually it's pretty easy to do that for the customer portal but not so easy or even impossible for the internal user interface. (Most tools offer English-only interfaces out of the box.)

- **Time zones**. Even something as seemingly simple as correctly displaying and manipulating time zones can be difficult. Many tools work with and display only "server time," which may be confusing to workers around the country and around the world.

## Marketing-Automation Requirements

These requirements are specific to the marketing function.

- **Campaign design**. Is it easy for a non-technical user to create a campaign? Can the tool support promotion codes? Does the tool support dynamic campaigns?
- **Customer targeting**. Can campaigns be targeted to customers based on all aspects of the customer relationship? Does the tool support permission-based marketing and handle automatic opt-in/opt-out mechanisms?
- **Campaign delivery**. Does the tool support recurring, multi-step, or event-triggered campaigns? Can the campaign be adapted to several environments, in particular e-mail and phone-based campaigns?
- **Campaign analysis**. Does the tool allow you to determine who got the messages and distinguish between different types of responses?
- **Lead distribution**. How are leads distributed to the sales force?

## Sales-Tracking Requirements

These requirements are specific to the sale function and cover both field sales force and telesales functions.

- **Opportunity management**. The tool should track each potential deal from beginning to end including products, key contacts, milestones, competitors, and other information relevant to your environment. The tool should support routing deals as needed for your environment (by geography, product, industry, for example). Complex routing rules dictate a more robust rules engine. It's likely that you will change the rules over time so the tool used to define rules should be as easy to use as possible.
- **Contact management**. You want to look for a tool that can track all interactions with the customer, regardless of the media (phone calls and face-to-face meetings will be logged manually by the sales rep). Additional features may include the ability to schedule appointments and to manage to-do items. This may require integration with existing tools.

  You may be looking for full workflow management, perhaps to match your particular sales methodology. You may need to add alerts for specific events within the sales cycle, whether or not you implement full workflow support.

Another useful ingredient of contact management is the ability to manage collaboration with multiple actors. This functionality is not that common, however.

In addition to contact tracking, the tool may also provide a number of job aids. This may include assistance in creating tailored presentations or proposals from existing templates in the knowledge base. Expense report management is another possibility.

- **Marketing encyclopedia**. This is very similar to the knowledge base functionality mentioned earlier. The marketing encyclopedia provides a comprehensive set of marketing tools that sales reps can use for presentations, RFPs, and other sales actives.

- **Quoting**. Sales reps probably need assistance to create quotes, get approval on them, and deliver them to the customers. If your product set is complex, you may need a significantly robust pricing and configuration tool as well. Such tools may need to be accessible to customers from the portal, either in self-service mode or while working with a sales rep.

- **Account management**. This set of functionality addresses post-sales activities, from product delivery to follow-up sales to existing accounts. Account management can be a rather neglected aspect of CRM functionality so take time to define how you would use this feature.

- **Forecasting tools**. Many SFA efforts are directly connected to a need for faster, more accurate forecasts. What kind of forecasting do you like to do? What kind of reports do you require? While most tools let you build any report you want, it's even better if you can find canned reports to address your specific needs.

- **Disconnected usage**. Field sales reps may require the ability to download relevant information from the CRM tool into a portable device (typically a laptop, but sometimes a wireless device). They need to be able to work on that disconnected device (ideally with an interface that's reasonably similar to the connected mode) and to upload changed data back to the database (the dreaded "synchronization").

If you need good synchronization functionality, make sure you check references in great detail, as it's an area that's very difficult to do properly. One of the common issues is that synchronization takes too long, hence doesn't get done, so you lose valuable information. Clever ways to download only the information that's required and to handle data transfers make the difference between an unusable solution and a good solution.

Similar functionality may be needed for field service reps.

## Support-Tracking Requirements

This section describes requirements for support and service organizations.

- **Flexible case attributes**. All tools will track the basics including case categories, priorities, and statuses. If you need specific values for these fields, typically to match the ones in use today, make sure the tool can support them. Many support organizations have specific case attributes they need to run the business such as internal and external priorities, case closure codes, and the like. It's a good time to determine which ones are critical for the business.

- **Case creation and entitlement**. Case creation is a very common task, so it's worth checking that it's really easy. If the support center checks entitlement (for instance, registered customers), specify what kind of entitlement data and scheme are required. Do you sell case packs? Do you work with annual contracts? Do you have different levels of support with different entitlement policies? Many tools are weak in this area so be sure to check the entitlement item early on.

- **Routing, rules, and alerts**. Unless the support center is very small, there is some kind of routing algorithm in place. What is it? Make sure the tool can handle it. Routings based on any one item, be it geography or product line, are usually easy to implement with any tool. Multi-criteria routing is more problematic. Tools may or may not support automatic (or forced) assignments of cases to individuals.

  Do you need some kind of automatic processing on particular events? Most support centers use alerts and escalations based on case aging and most tools support time-based rules. If your criteria are more complex, carefully evaluate both the requirements and how the tool can meet the challenge since many tools are not completely flexible on this point. Also define whether the business owners need to be able to change the rules and therefore need a simple configuration tool.

- **Workflow support**. All tools support open and closed statuses, and the idea of case ownership. Most support groups need something a little more sophisticated, from more descriptive case statuses to full workflow support, through which each step in the process opens up a predetermined number of possible next steps. Be warned that workflow engines can be inflexible and hard to use so evaluate the modeling tool even if you are not planning to make workflow changes right away. You will probably have to make some changes in the future and you don't want to be blocked by a difficult modeling tool.

- **Defect and enhancement tracking**. Such systems may be considered within or outside the scope of the CRM system. If within, make sure you have the proper level of workflow support (light support is often enough). If outside, what integrations are required?
- **History trail**. To do case analysis, run metrics, and other tasks, it's useful to have a full history trail for cases, ideally transaction-based. CRM tools often provide fairly good support for history trails on cases, in contrast to knowledge base documents.
- **Collaboration and escalation**. Many times cases require more than one person to work on them. All CRM tools support case ownership changes and almost all support escalations to the next level. Check out how they model your own escalation scheme.

  The next degree of sophistication is true collaboration, whereby the case owner can engage others, either individuals or groups, in the resolution of the case without surrendering ownership. The collaboration threads can be made visible to the customer when appropriate. This is an important feature in high-complexity support centers, but it's rarely supported by traditional CRM tools.
- **Field service**. If you have a field service workforce, you need to consider either disconnected usage or wireless usage. All the considerations under disconnected usage by sales and under wireless support apply. Please refer to those sections.
- **Customer satisfaction surveys**. Do you survey customers after cases are closed? It could be as simple as an outgoing e-mail on case closure (which most tools can handle with minimal programming) and as complex as a web-based input and reporting mechanism with tunable sampling mechanism. Choose what works for you.

# Implementation and Maintenance

Just when you thought you were done, you still have to think about what it will take to actually implement and maintain this monster, I mean the CRM system. It's often a matter of trade-offs between the functional and technical requirements on the one hand and the implementation and maintenance requirements on the other. The more functional and technical requirements you have, and the more sophisticated they are, the more difficult and costly the implementation and maintenance will be. You may need to compromise.

I strongly recommend setting firm limits on implementation and maintenance requirements right from the start, and refusing to consider tools that require more than you can afford. Remember that vendors usually downplay implementation and maintenance resources required, so any tool that is advertised as requiring more than you can invest in it should be firmly discarded. Consider the following elements when defining implementation and maintenance requirements.

- **Time**. How much time are you prepared to spend on the implementation? If you have an urgent business need, you can't afford to take a chance on a tool that does not have a proven track record of being implemented within your timeframe.
- **Implementation assistance**. Does the vendor provide implementation assistance, either directly or through third parties? During evaluation, check whether implementers are readily available or if there is typically a waiting period. (And if so, are they swamped or are the skills required so arcane that no one wants to learn them?) Check if training is available, where, and with what level of advance notice, both for tool administrators and end-users.
- **Maintenance policies**. What level of maintenance support do you need? Think about how long old releases should be supported (most vendors only support a couple of releases and discontinue support for older ones). During evaluation, check what the vendor policy might be for certifying their software on new versions of the operating system, database, and other ancillary systems. If your database vendor pushes you to upgrade but your CRM vendor is not certified on the newer release, life will be unpleasant for a while.

  Is there a warranty period?
- **Support program**. What level of technical support level do you expect? What support hours do you need? Are there specific support-level agreements (SLAs) you need? Does the vendor provide patches for urgent problems? Check that the vendor provides a knowledge base for technical problems and that the knowledge base is complete and user-friendly.
- **Long-term tool maintenance**. Who will be responsible for ongoing administration of the system? Do you expect that business users (that is, non-programmers) will handle simple tasks such as authorizing new users, changing business rules, running metrics, etc.? If so, look for tools

that offer user-friendly user interfaces for such tasks (and even the technical staff will appreciate easy interfaces for the simple tasks).

Are upgrades complex? What tools are available to facilitate migrating to newer releases?

Even if you use an integrator for the initial implementation, your internal resources are likely to be responsible for ongoing maintenance, so always evaluate the power and ease of use of the customization and integration tools. They will determine the level of resources that will be required to maintain the system and also, more importantly, how likely you will be to get important customizations and integrations done. In other words, poor customization and integration tools often mean a poor implementation because it's just too much of a hassle to make changes to the tool.

# Budget

I've never seen a CRM decision made solely on price, that is, that product X is chosen over product Y solely because product X is cheaper. On more than one occasion I have seen a particular tool selected even though it's *slightly* more expensive than the initial target budget because it has particular strong functionality that is thought to justify the additional expense. But it's rare that a tool is selected despite being *considerably* more expensive than the budget allows. You need to define a budget for the tool purchase and implementation as part of the requirements definition so you don't waste your time evaluating candidate tools that you can't afford.

When creating the budget, be sure to consider all the costs, including:

- **The tool purchase cost**. In the next chapter we'll see how to negotiate well to minimize what you have to pay. Consider costs for add-on products or underlying hardware, database management systems, etc.
- **The implementation costs**. It's difficult to create a specific budget until you have chosen a tool and defined the extent of customizations and integrations required, but you'll need to take your best guess. Include compensation for the internal resources and training costs.
- **The maintenance costs**. Include the vendor's support fee and any other support fees for associated hardware or software. What's the planned increase over time? Can you get guarantees on fee increases? Include your internal costs, which may include permanent staff and contractors.

One last note about the budget. Some CRM projects end up costing considerably more than either the initial target budget or the approved budget. Although an increase between the initial target and the approved budget can be justified by higher business achievements afforded through better functionality, large overspending during the implementation is always a bad thing. The goal of this book is to give you practical tools to create reasonable budgets in the first place, and to keep to them throughout the implementation cycle.

## Template Requirements Checklist

The following pages contain a template requirements checklist for you to customize to your exact needs. All the items in the template are described above in the text, so please refer to the appropriate section if any item is unclear.

The template checklist is very long because it covers all aspects of CRM tools. Only consider those sections that apply to you and disregard the rest.

Do not use the checklist "as is." Just because a particular item is on the list does not mean that it is required in your case, even if it's in a section that you are interested in. Think of the template as one of those preprinted shopping lists you find in supermarkets: you don't buy each item on each shopping trip, do you?

The checklist is built to accommodate weights for each item that represent the priority levels for each requirement and can be adjusted as needed to weigh the various requirements categories against each other. All weights are set at "1" in the template but you need to adjust them to your specific needs.

It's very handy to use the list in a spreadsheet format. You can find a spreadsheet version of the checklist on my web site at www.ftworks.com/JustEnoughCRM.htm. It will be updated from time to time to reflect new technology and contributions from you, the readers.

# Template Requirements Checklist

| # | Item | Weight | Vendor 1 | | | Vendor 2 | | | Vendor 3 | | |
|---|---|---|---|---|---|---|---|---|---|---|---|
| | | | Score | Rating | Comments | Score | Rating | Comments | Score | Rating | Comments |
| | | 256 | | | | | | | | | |
| 1 | Vendor Requirements | 7 | 0 | | | 0 | | | 0 | | |
| 1.1 | Financial stability | 1 | 0 | | | 0 | | | 0 | | |
| 1.2 | Customer references | 1 | 0 | | | 0 | | | 0 | | |
| 1.3 | Geographical presence: sales and post-sales support | 1 | 0 | | | 0 | | | 0 | | |
| 1.4 | Business model. ASP/licensed? | 1 | 0 | | | 0 | | | 0 | | |
| 1.5 | Technical vision | 1 | 1 | | | | | | | | |
| 1.6 | Business vision | 1 | | 1 | | | | | | | |
| 1.7 | Customer focus | 1 | | | | | | | | | |
| | | | | | | | | | | | |
| 2 | Technical Requirements | 15 | 0 | | | 0 | | | 0 | | |
| 2.1 | Technical platform | 5 | | | | | | | | | |
| 2.1.1 | Compatible hardware | 1 | 0 | | | 0 | | | 0 | | |
| 2.1.2. | Compatible OS | 1 | 0 | | | 0 | | | 0 | | |
| 2.1.3 | Compatible database | 1 | 0 | | | 0 | | | 0 | | |
| 2.1.4 | Compatible web server | 1 | 0 | | | 0 | | | 0 | | |
| 2.1.5 | Thin or thick client | 1 | 0 | | | 0 | | | 0 | | |
| 2.2. | Scalability | 2 | | | | | | | | | |
| 2.2.1 | User load and distribution | 1 | 0 | | | 0 | | | 0 | | |
| 2.2.2 | 3-tier architecture | 1 | 0 | | | 0 | | | 0 | | |
| 2.3 | Availability | 2 | 0 | | | 0 | | | 0 | | |
| 2.3.1 | High-availability features | 1 | | | | | | | | | |

## CHAPTER 5 ▸ REQUIREMENTS DEFINITION

| | | | | | | | | | |
|---|---|---|---|---|---|---|---|---|---|
| 2.3.2 | Backup and recovery requirements | 1 | | | | | | | |
| 2.4 | Integration | 3 | | | | | | | |
| 2.4.1 | Required integrations | 1 | | | | | | | |
| 2.4.2 | Standard API | 1 | | | | | | | |
| 2.4.3 | Fully exposed data model | 1 | | | | | | | |
| 2.5 | Development environment | 3 | | | | | | | |
| 2.5.1 | Customization depth required/power of customization tool | 1 | | | | | | | |
| 2.5.2 | Standard script/programming language | 1 | | | | | | | |
| 2.5.3 | Support for migrating customizations to production | 1 | | | | | | | |
| | | | | | | | | | |
| 3 | Functional Requirements | 203 | 0 | | | 0 | | 0 | |
| 3.1 | Cross-functional requirements | 139 | 0 | | | 0 | | 0 | |
| 3.1.1 | Phone integration | 4 | 0 | | | 0 | | 0 | |
| 3.1.1.1 | Screen pops | 1 | | | | | | | |
| 3.1.1.2 | Entitlement checking | 1 | | | | | | | |
| 3.1.1.3 | Outbound dialing | 1 | | | | | | | |
| 3.1.1.4 | Support of specific phone switch | 1 | | | | | | | |
| 3.1.2 | E-mail support | 16 | | | | | | | |
| 3.1.2.1 | E-mail integration | 7 | | | | | | | |
| | Logging of outbound e-mails | 1 | | | | | | | |
| | Link to corporate e-mail system | 1 | | | | | | | |
| | Tag outbound e-mails | 1 | | | | | | | |
| | Bulk outbound e-mails | 1 | | | | | | | |

| | | | | | | | | | | | |
|---|---|---|---|---|---|---|---|---|---|---|---|
| | Automatic load of incoming e-mail | 1 | | | | | | | | | |
| | Automatic processing of incoming e-mails | 1 | | | | | | | | | |
| | Firewall compatibility requirements | 1 | | | | | | | | | |
| 3.1.2.2 | E-mail processing | 5 | | | | | | | | | |
| | Automatic acknowledgements on e-mails | 1 | | | | | | | | | |
| | Routing of incoming e-mails | 1 | | | | | | | | | |
| | Canned response templates | 1 | | | | | | | | | |
| | Automatic response suggestions | 1 | | | | | | | | | |
| | Automatic responses | 1 | | | | | | | | | |
| 3.1.2.3 | E-mail utilities | 4 | | | | | | | | | |
| | Spell checking | 1 | | | | | | | | | |
| | Supported formats | 1 | | | | | | | | | |
| | E-mail templates | 1 | | | | | | | | | |
| | Attachments (inbound/outbound) | 1 | | | | | | | | | |
| 3.1.3 | Customer portal | 24 | | | | | | | | | |
| 3.1.3.1 | Knowledge base | 2 | | | | | | | | | |
| | KB access from portal | 1 | | | | | | | | | |
| | Search capabilities from portal | 1 | | | | | | | | | |
| 3.1.3.2 | Authentication and security | 5 | | | | | | | | | |
| | Authentication required? | 1 | | | | | | | | | |
| | Link to existing scheme? | 1 | | | | | | | | | |
| | Signup control (self/manual) | 1 | | | | | | | | | |

|  |  |  |
|---|---|---|
|  | Authentication scheme | 1 |
|  | Flexible permission scheme, e.g., for partners | 1 |
| 3.1.3.3 | Personalization | 2 |
|  | Required? | 1 |
|  | Types of personalization | 1 |
| 3.1.3.4 | E-commerce | 3 |
|  | Online shopping | 1 |
|  | Online order taking | 1 |
|  | Integrations required | 1 |
| 3.1.3.5 | Order tracking | 3 |
|  | Online order tracking | 1 |
|  | Integrations required | 1 |
|  | Online order modification | 1 |
| 3.1.3.6 | Service/support case entry | 1 |
| 3.1.3.7 | Online case management | 5 |
|  | Online viewing of existing cases | 1 |
|  | Management of confidential information | 1 |
|  | Adding comments | 1 |
|  | Closing cases | 1 |
|  | Reopening cases | 1 |
| 3.1.3.8 | Customer forums | 3 |
|  | Required? | 1 |
|  | Monitoring requirements | 1 |
|  | User moderators? | 1 |
| 3.1.4 | Wireless support | 8 |
| 3.1.4.1 | Supported devices and protocols | 1 |

## Template Requirements Checklist

| | | | | | | | | | | | |
|---|---|---|---|---|---|---|---|---|---|---|---|
| 3.1.4.2 | Wireless messaging | 2 | | | | | | | | | |
| | Outbound alerts | 1 | | | | | | | | | |
| | Inbound messages | 1 | | | | | | | | | |
| 3.1.4.3 | Wireless real-time access | 3 | | | | | | | | | |
| | Required? | 1 | | | | | | | | | |
| | Essential subset for function | 1 | | | | | | | | | |
| | Customization required | 1 | | | | | | | | | |
| 3.1.4.4 | Data synchronization | 2 | | | | | | | | | |
| | Downloads to device | 1 | | | | | | | | | |
| | Upload changes? | 1 | | | | | | | | | |
| 3.1.5 | Chat support | 9 | | | | | | | | | |
| 3.1.5.1 | Integrated chat support or link? | 1 | | | | | | | | | |
| 3.1.5.2 | Chat environment | 6 | | | | | | | | | |
| | Response templates | 1 | | | | | | | | | |
| | Control of window size | 1 | | | | | | | | | |
| | Restrict chat access to certain pages | 1 | | | | | | | | | |
| | Chat works on all types of pages | 1 | | | | | | | | | |
| | Firewall compatibility and requirements | 1 | | | | | | | | | |
| | Records of chat communications | 1 | | | | | | | | | |
| 3.1.5.3 | Advanced features | 2 | | | | | | | | | |
| | Push pages to customers | 1 | | | | | | | | | |
| | Browser control | 1 | | | | | | | | | |
| 3.1.6 | VoIP | 2 | | | | | | | | | |
| 3.1.6.1 | Inbound/outbound? | 1 | | | | | | | | | |
| 3.1.6.2 | Compatibility with standards | 1 | | | | | | | | | |

| | | | | | | | | | | | |
|---|---|---|---|---|---|---|---|---|---|---|---|
| 3.1.7 | Multichannel support | 2 | | | | | | | | | |
| 3.1.7.1 | Consistent experience | 1 | | | | | | | | | |
| 3.1.7.2 | Universal queuing and logic | 1 | | | | | | | | | |
| 3.1.8 | Customer database | 11 | | | | | | | | | |
| 3.1.8.1 | Comprehensive records | 3 | | | | | | | | | |
| | Consumers/corporate customers? | 1 | | | | | | | | | |
| | Multiple corporate contacts | 1 | | | | | | | | | |
| | Special customer relationships, e.g., reseller/end-user | 1 | | | | | | | | | |
| 3.1.8.2 | Custom fields | 3 | | | | | | | | | |
| | Fields required | 1 | | | | | | | | | |
| | Restrictions on creation, deletion | 1 | | | | | | | | | |
| | Ease of creation/changes | 1 | | | | | | | | | |
| 3.1.8.3 | Link between databases | 3 | | | | | | | | | |
| | Customer master | 1 | | | | | | | | | |
| | Synchronization requirements | 1 | | | | | | | | | |
| | Data cleansing | 1 | | | | | | | | | |
| 3.1.8.4 | Customer history | 2 | | | | | | | | | |
| | Records needed | 1 | | | | | | | | | |
| | Synchronization requirements | 1 | | | | | | | | | |
| 3.1.9 | Employee database | 4 | | | | | | | | | |
| 3.1.9.1 | Records needed | 1 | | | | | | | | | |
| 3.1.9.2 | Concept of organizational hierarchy | 1 | | | | | | | | | |
| 3.1.9.3 | Synchronization requirements | 1 | | | | | | | | | |

# Template Requirements Checklist

| | | | | | | | | | | |
|---|---|---|---|---|---|---|---|---|---|---|
| 3.1.9.4 | Permissions | 1 | | | | | | | | |
| 3.1.10 | Knowledge management | 42 | | | | | | | | |
| 3.1.10.1 | Document creation | 8 | | | | | | | | |
| | Required in tool? | 1 | | | | | | | | |
| | Easy process | 1 | | | | | | | | |
| | Migrate CRM objects to documents? | 1 | | | | | | | | |
| | Spell checking | 1 | | | | | | | | |
| | Document templates | 1 | | | | | | | | |
| | Custom document attributes | 1 | | | | | | | | |
| | Document formats | 1 | | | | | | | | |
| | New documents available on the spot | 1 | | | | | | | | |
| 3.1.10.2 | Heterogeneous knowledge bases | 4 | | | | | | | | |
| | Migrating documents to the knowledge base | 1 | | | | | | | | |
| | Searching on external documents | 1 | | | | | | | | |
| | Supported formats | 1 | | | | | | | | |
| | Attachments support | 1 | | | | | | | | |
| 3.1.10.3 | Knowledge creation workflow | 5 | | | | | | | | |
| | Custom document statuses | 1 | | | | | | | | |
| | Permission-based reviews | 1 | | | | | | | | |
| | Support for review queues | 1 | | | | | | | | |
| | Review alerts | 1 | | | | | | | | |
| | Adding review steps | 1 | | | | | | | | |
| 3.1.10.4 | Document maintenance | 2 | | | | | | | | |
| | Expiration date | 1 | | | | | | | | |

# CHAPTER 5 ▸ REQUIREMENTS DEFINITION

|  |  |  |  |  |  |  |  |  |  |  |
|---|---|---|---|---|---|---|---|---|---|---|
|  | Document categories—how many levels? | 1 |  |  |  |  |  |  |  |  |
| 3.1.10.5 | History trail | 1 |  |  |  |  |  |  |  |  |
| 3.1.10.6 | Self-learning features | 4 |  |  |  |  |  |  |  |  |
|  | Popularity rankings | 1 |  |  |  |  |  |  |  |  |
|  | User ratings | 1 |  |  |  |  |  |  |  |  |
|  | Report failed searches | 1 |  |  |  |  |  |  |  |  |
|  | Flagging errors | 1 |  |  |  |  |  |  |  |  |
| 3.1.10.7 | Search capabilities | 7 |  |  |  |  |  |  |  |  |
|  | FAQ | 1 |  |  |  |  |  |  |  |  |
|  | Tree-based search | 1 |  |  |  |  |  |  |  |  |
|  | Full text search | 1 |  |  |  |  |  |  |  |  |
|  | Searching on document attributes | 1 |  |  |  |  |  |  |  |  |
|  | Natural language queries | 1 |  |  |  |  |  |  |  |  |
|  | Case-based reasoning | 1 |  |  |  |  |  |  |  |  |
|  | Refining existing searches | 1 |  |  |  |  |  |  |  |  |
| 3.1.10.8 | Leveraged searches | 2 |  |  |  |  |  |  |  |  |
|  | Automatic suggestions | 1 |  |  |  |  |  |  |  |  |
|  | Linking documents with other objects | 1 |  |  |  |  |  |  |  |  |
| 3.1.10.9 | Permissions and authorizations | 5 |  |  |  |  |  |  |  |  |
|  | Group profiles | 1 |  |  |  |  |  |  |  |  |
|  | Combine group profiles | 1 |  |  |  |  |  |  |  |  |
|  | Individual profiles | 1 |  |  |  |  |  |  |  |  |
|  | Permissions on documents or categories? | 1 |  |  |  |  |  |  |  |  |
|  | Permissions for internal/external users | 1 |  |  |  |  |  |  |  |  |
| 3.1.10.10 | Subscriptions and alerts | 4 |  |  |  |  |  |  |  |  |
|  | Send alerts to uses | 1 |  |  |  |  |  |  |  |  |

# Template Requirements Checklist

|  |  |  |  |  |  |  |  |  |  |  |
|---|---|---|---|---|---|---|---|---|---|---|
|  | Alerts to subgroups of users | 1 |  |  |  |  |  |  |  |  |
|  | Users subscriptions to documents | 1 |  |  |  |  |  |  |  |  |
|  | Users subscriptions to categories | 1 |  |  |  |  |  |  |  |  |
| 3.1.11 | Metrics | 12 |  |  |  |  |  |  |  |  |
| 3.1.11.1 | Data availability | 2 |  |  |  |  |  |  |  |  |
|  | Required fields | 1 |  |  |  |  |  |  |  |  |
|  | Reporting against custom fields | 1 |  |  |  |  |  |  |  |  |
| 3.1.11.2 | Customizable templates | 3 |  |  |  |  |  |  |  |  |
|  | Key reports | 1 |  |  |  |  |  |  |  |  |
|  | Graph templates | 1 |  |  |  |  |  |  |  |  |
|  | Time-based report templates | 1 |  |  |  |  |  |  |  |  |
| 3.1.11.3 | Report creation tools | 2 |  |  |  |  |  |  |  |  |
|  | Easy to use tools | 1 |  |  |  |  |  |  |  |  |
|  | Integration to external report writers | 1 |  |  |  |  |  |  |  |  |
| 3.1.11.4 | Report distribution system | 5 |  |  |  |  |  |  |  |  |
|  | Self-service subscriptions | 1 |  |  |  |  |  |  |  |  |
|  | Output formats | 1 |  |  |  |  |  |  |  |  |
|  | Dump to spreadsheets | 1 |  |  |  |  |  |  |  |  |
|  | Link to data warehousing system | 1 |  |  |  |  |  |  |  |  |
|  | Impact of reporting on system | 1 |  |  |  |  |  |  |  |  |
| 3.1.12 | Internationalization | 5 |  |  |  |  |  |  |  |  |
| 3.1.12.1 | Language support | 2 |  |  |  |  |  |  |  |  |
|  | For data entry | 1 |  |  |  |  |  |  |  |  |
|  | Sort order | 1 |  |  |  |  |  |  |  |  |
| 3.1.12.2 | Foreign currency support | 1 |  |  |  |  |  |  |  |  |

| | | | | | | | | | | |
|---|---|---|---|---|---|---|---|---|---|---|
| 3.1.12.3 | Interface localization | 1 | | | | | | | | |
| 3.1.12.4 | Time zones | 1 | | | | | | | | |
| 3.2 | Marketing automation | 12 | | | | | | | | |
| 3.2.1 | Campaign design | 3 | | | | | | | | |
| 3.2.1.1 | Easy to use for a business user? | 1 | | | | | | | | |
| 3.2.1.1 | Support promotion codes | 1 | | | | | | | | |
| 3.2.1.3 | Dynamic campaigns | 1 | | | | | | | | |
| 3.2.2 | Customer targeting | 3 | | | | | | | | |
| 3.2.2.1 | Query universe | 1 | | | | | | | | |
| 3.2.2.2 | Permission-based marketing | 1 | | | | | | | | |
| 3.2.2.3 | Automatic opt-in/opt-out | 1 | | | | | | | | |
| 3.2.3 | Campaign delivery | 4 | | | | | | | | |
| 3.2.3.1 | Recurring campaigns | 1 | | | | | | | | |
| 3.2.3.2 | Multi-step campaigns | 1 | | | | | | | | |
| 3.2.3.3 | Event-triggered campaigns | 1 | | | | | | | | |
| 3.2.3.4 | E-mail and phone-based campaigns | 1 | | | | | | | | |
| 3.2.4 | Campaign analysis | 1 | | | | | | | | |
| 3.2.5 | Lead distribution | 1 | | | | | | | | |
| 3.3 | Sales Tracking | 24 | | | | | | | | |
| 3.3.1 | Opportunity management | 5 | | | | | | | | |
| 3.3.1.1 | End-to-end tracking | 1 | | | | | | | | |
| 3.3.1.2 | Track products | 1 | | | | | | | | |
| 3.3.1.3 | Track milestones | 1 | | | | | | | | |
| 3.3.1.4 | Track competitors | 1 | | | | | | | | |
| 3.3.1.5 | Deal routing | 1 | | | | | | | | |
| 3.3.2 | Contact management | 9 | | | | | | | | |
| 3.3.2.1 | Track all interactions | 1 | | | | | | | | |

| | | | | | | | | | | |
|---|---|---|---|---|---|---|---|---|---|---|
| 3.3.2.2 | Schedule appointments | 1 | | | | | | | | |
| 3.3.2.3 | Manage to-do items | 1 | | | | | | | | |
| 3.3.2.4 | Supports sales methodology | 1 | | | | | | | | |
| 3.3.2.5 | Collaboration | 1 | | | | | | | | |
| 3.3.2.6 | Presentation creation | 1 | | | | | | | | |
| 3.3.2.7 | Proposal generation | 1 | | | | | | | | |
| 3.3.2.8 | Proposal template | 1 | | | | | | | | |
| 3.3.2.9 | Expense reports | 1 | | | | | | | | |
| 3.3.3 | Marketing encyclopedia | 1 | | | | | | | | |
| 3.3.4 | Quoting | 4 | | | | | | | | |
| 3.3.4.1 | Quote creation | 1 | | | | | | | | |
| 3.3.4.2 | Approval workflow | 1 | | | | | | | | |
| 3.3.4.3 | Pricing tool | 1 | | | | | | | | |
| 3.3.4.4 | Configurator | 1 | | | | | | | | |
| 3.3.5 | Account management | 1 | | | | | | | | |
| 3.3.6. | Forecasting tools | 1 | | | | | | | | |
| 3.3.7 | Disconnected usage | 3 | | | | | | | | |
| 3.3.7.1 | Synchronization | 1 | | | | | | | | |
| 3.3.7.2 | Ability to download/ upload selected data | 1 | | | | | | | | |
| 3.3.7.3 | Functionality in disconnected mode | 1 | | | | | | | | |
| 3.4 | Support Tracking | 28 | | | | | | | | |
| 3.4.1 | Flexible case attributes | 2 | | | | | | | | |
| 3.4.1.1 | Custom values | 1 | | | | | | | | |
| 3.4.1.2 | Custom fields | 1 | | | | | | | | |
| 3.4.2 | Case creation and entitlement | 4 | | | | | | | | |
| 3.4.2.1 | Easy/quick case creation | 1 | | | | | | | | |
| 3.4.2.2 | Case packs | 1 | | | | | | | | |

| | | |
|---|---|---|
| 3.4.2.3 | Annual contracts | 1 |
| 3.4.2.4 | Support multiple entitlement strategies | 1 |
| 3.4.3 | Routing, rules, and alerts | 6 |
| 3.4.3.1 | Single-criteria routing | 1 |
| 3.4.3.2 | Multi-criteria routing | 1 |
| 3.4.3.3 | Automatic (forced) assignments | 1 |
| 3.4.3.4 | Alert on screen/e-mail/pager | 1 |
| 3.4.3.5 | Escalations | 1 |
| 3.4.3.6 | Easy-to-use rule engine | 1 |
| 3.4.4 | Workflow support | 4 |
| 3.4.4.1 | Special case statuses | 1 |
| 3.4.4.2 | Full workflow support | 1 |
| 3.4.4.3 | Powerful and flexible workflow engine | 1 |
| 3.4.4.4 | Business users can modify workflow | 1 |
| 3.4.5 | Defect and enhancement tracking | 2 |
| 3.4.5.1 | Functionality in the tool | 1 |
| 3.4.5.2 | Integration with other systems | 1 |
| 3.4.6 | History trail | 1 |
| 3.4.7 | Collaboration and escalation | 4 |
| 3.4.7.1 | Automatic and user-controlled escalations | 1 |
| 3.4.7.2 | Asking for collaborators | 1 |
| 3.4.7.3 | Record collaboration | 1 |
| 3.4.7.4 | Make collaboration visible to customers | 1 |

# Template Requirements Checklist

| | | | | | | | | | | |
|---|---|---|---|---|---|---|---|---|---|---|
| 3.4.8 | Field service | 2 | | | | | | | | |
| 3.4.8.1 | Disconnected usage | 1 | | | | | | | | |
| 3.4.8.2 | Wireless usage | 1 | | | | | | | | |
| 3.4.9 | Customer satisfaction surveys | 3 | | | | | | | | |
| 3.4.9.1 | Transaction-based | 1 | | | | | | | | |
| 3.4.9.2 | Sampling mechanism | 1 | | | | | | | | |
| 3.4.9.3 | Opt-out | 1 | | | | | | | | |
| | | | | | | | | | | |
| 4 | Implementation and Maintenance Requirements | 22 | | | | | | | | |
| 4.1 | Time | 2 | | | | | | | | |
| 4.1.1 | Maximum allowable | 1 | | | | | | | | |
| 4.1.2 | Phased implementation | 1 | | | | | | | | |
| 4.2 | Implementation assistance | 7 | | | | | | | | |
| 4.2.1 | Vendor | 1 | | | | | | | | |
| 4.2.2 | Third-parties | 1 | | | | | | | | |
| 4.2.3 | Certified partners | 1 | | | | | | | | |
| 4.2.4 | Waiting period | 1 | | | | | | | | |
| 4.2.5 | Training for administrators | 1 | | | | | | | | |
| 4.2.6 | Training for programmers | 1 | | | | | | | | |
| 4.2.7 | Training for end-users | 1 | | | | | | | | |
| 4.3 | Maintenance policies | 4 | | | | | | | | |
| 4.3.1 | Length of support for old releases | 1 | | | | | | | | |
| 4.3.2 | Certifications on new O/S | 1 | | | | | | | | |
| 4.3.3 | Certifications on new DB versions | 1 | | | | | | | | |
| 4.3.4 | Warranty period | 1 | | | | | | | | |
| 4.4 | Support programs | 5 | | | | | | | | |

| | | | | | | | | | | |
|---|---|---|---|---|---|---|---|---|---|---|
| 4.4.1 | Support hours | 1 | | | | | | | | |
| 4.4.2 | SLA | 1 | | | | | | | | |
| 4.4.3 | Availability of patches | 1 | | | | | | | | |
| 4.4.4 | Technical knowledge base | 1 | | | | | | | | |
| 4.4.5 | Ceilings on fee increases | 1 | | | | | | | | |
| 4.5 | Long-term tool maintenance | 4 | | | | | | | | |
| 4.5.1 | Tasks that can be handled by business users | 1 | | | | | | | | |
| 4.5.2 | Friendly user interfaces | 1 | | | | | | | | |
| 4.5.3 | Customization tools | 1 | | | | | | | | |
| 4.5.4 | Easy upgrades | 1 | | | | | | | | |
| | | | | | | | | | | |
| 5 | Budget | 9 | | | | | | | | |
| 5.1 | Initial costs | 3 | | | | | | | | |
| 5.1.1 | License | 1 | | | | | | | | |
| 5.1.2 | Hardware | 1 | | | | | | | | |
| 5.1.3 | Add-on products | 1 | | | | | | | | |
| 5.2 | Implementation costs | 3 | | | | | | | | |
| 5.2.1. | Integrator | 1 | | | | | | | | |
| 5.2.2 | Internal resources | 1 | | | | | | | | |
| 5.2.3 | Training | 1 | | | | | | | | |
| 5.3 | Maintenance costs | 3 | | | | | | | | |
| 5.3.1 | Support fees for associated hardware or software | 1 | | | | | | | | |
| 5.3.2 | Internal costs | 1 | | | | | | | | |
| 5.3.3 | Costs for add-on purchases | 1 | | | | | | | | |

# Shopping for CRM Systems

## 6

## Express Version

- Shopping for CRM systems includes creating a long list of candidates, evaluating them against the criteria in the requirements list, and selecting the best two or three for the final evaluation and negotiation process.
- There are so many CRM vendors that it's useful to organize them in categories and to restrict your search to the categories that best match your requirements.

  CRM systems can be mid-range or high-end. Mid-range systems have a good set of functionality and scale fairly well, but they have limited customization capabilities. They are easier and faster to implement than high-end systems. High-end systems have extensive customization capabilities and scale best, but they also require much more time and many more resources to implement. Unless you clearly need the additional functionality and customization tools of high-end solutions, it's best to stay with a mid-range tool.

CRM systems can be suites, covering several business functions, or point solutions that focus on a particular piece of functionality. Although suites deliver pre-integrated solutions, you may need to patch together several point solutions to get the ultimate best-of-breed solution.

Some vendors offer so-called vertical solutions that are customized for specific industries, while most tools are general-purpose. If you need a high-end system you will find that high-end vendors often offer vertical solutions, which should save you some customization work.

CRM systems can be purchased as packaged products or in an ASP arrangement. Some can be purchased either way. If you have reasonably limited customization requirements, need a solution quickly, and do not mind the idea of an ASP arrangement, it may be the best solution for you.

- The traditional RFP process is slow and costly. You may want to substitute a lighter version in which you use the requirements checklist as a scorecard for the vendors.
- Take an assertive approach to driving vendor presentations and demos to minimize fluff and focus on what matters to you—your requirements.
- The key issue in CRM selection is to be perfectly clear about what is part of the product and what is customization. It's often difficult to tell during demos.

## Shopping with a Purpose

Once your requirements list is complete, it's time to go shopping. As mentioned earlier, don't start shopping seriously until you have a fairly good idea of your requirements so you don't waste time evaluating unsuitable vendors on the one hand and you don't ignore potential good fits on the other.

It's useful to organize the shopping process into four stages:

- **Creating a long list**. There are hundreds of vendors that claim to be CRM vendors so it makes no sense to attempt to evaluate them all. The first step in the process is therefore to create a so-called long list of likely candidates by performing an abbreviated evaluation of vendors' capabilities against the requirements list.
- **Evaluating the candidates** against the requirements. Through a structured process, you perform a more thorough evaluation of the candidates on the long list against the checklist, rating them as you go.

- **Creating a short list**. Using the results from the evaluations, you narrow down the list of vendors to the two or three best candidates. Creating the short list is usually fairly simple, as leaders emerge rather naturally.
- **Negotiating the best deal**. After the evaluation is complete, you need to check references and negotiate the best possible agreement.

This chapter covers creating the long list, evaluating candidates, and creating the short list. Checking references and negotiating the best deal will be covered in the next chapter.

# Creating the Long List

The long list guides the selection process. It should have the following two characteristics:

- Focus on candidates that have a realistic chance of meeting your requirements. For instance, the candidates on the long list should fit within your price range and should offer the high-level functionality you require, whether it's marketing automation or VoIP integration.
- Be diverse enough to include a variety of approaches and philosophies. The long list should not be too short: limiting yourself to a couple of candidates at this stage may cause you to overlook interesting ones. In particular, if you did some vendor browsing as part of creating the requirements list and even if you really liked some of them, you should try as much as possible to consider a wide sample of candidate vendors when you create the long list.

Use a combination of approaches when creating the long list: it's a kind of brainstorm and you want to generate a wide list, so be creative. Below are six different approaches with proven results. Use as many as you can to expand your horizons.

- Visiting the exhibit hall of an appropriate **business conference**, as suggested in the last chapter, is a good way to see many vendors in one go. The level of detail of what you can see in an exhibit hall is ideal for creating the long list—even though it's absolutely insufficient for completing the evaluation step. Seeing systems side by side also allows you to contrast the vendors' positioning easily. The amount of customization is limited because vendors have to address many potential clients, so you are less likely to be confused about what's in the product and what's custom. The experience of seeing that all vendors have slick demos should help immunize you against being taken in by pretty looks during the evaluation phase. Not to mention that you will enjoy collecting the inventive give-aways that are standard fare in that kind of event. (Need another free T-shirt?)

- Study the articles and ads in your favorite **trade magazine or web site**. This is a decent substitute for the trade conference exhibit hall, although the amount of information available in an article is, by necessity, limited while CRM tools are pretty complex. Ads are even shorter than articles but they are interesting because they force vendors to target just one benefit so you will quickly see if the vendor's technical and business vision matches your requirements. See Chapter 11 for suggestions for suitable publications and web sites.

- Sign up for **vendor webinars**. In an hour and without leaving your favorite workstation you can get a high-level picture of a tool. Webinars are often painfully short on exposure to the actual product, devoting half of the typical one-hour length to an "expert" disserting on some lofty topic, another fifteen minutes to a fluffy presentation about the company and its strategic direction, and a scant five minutes to a quick demo. Q&A is fairly short and questions are answered at the discretion of the emcee, so your questions may not be addressed at all. Despite the limitations, webinars are just right for checking on the overall fit. You will find them helpful to build the long list but don't expect to complete a full evaluation through a public webinar.

- Get **suggestions from colleagues**. This is in many ways the best approach since it will yield advice beyond just names. On the other hand, it's limited to your network. It may not uncover the newest tools, depending on your colleagues' appetite for the bleeding edge. If colleagues suggest in-depth evaluations at this stage, politely decline and return when and if their recommendations make it to your long list.

- Get **suggestions from staff members**. Unless your entire staff has been with you forever, it's likely that some staffers have used other tools in other organizations relatively recently. Both positive and negative suggestions are helpful, provided that you take the time to understand the reasons for the enthusiasm or lack thereof (since your needs may be different from the organization they came from) and also the role of the author of the suggestion (since end-user experiences can be totally different from those of administrators or executives).

- Work with **analysts**. CRM analysts are extraordinarily well informed (or should be!) about the CRM world and the relative strengths and weaknesses of the players. In particular, they have a pretty good grasp of who the stronger vendors are and what vendors may survive for the long haul.

The problem with analysts is that they know nothing about your requirements. The point of CRM tool selection is not to select "the best" or "the leader" in the field, but rather the one that fits your needs most closely. Don't be mesmerized by quadrants, rankings, or waves; dig deeper into the unique strengths and weaknesses of each offering, matching them to your requirements list.

As you gather suggestions, what is it exactly that you should be considering when deciding whether a particular vendor should be added to the long list? Since you're not in a position to check each candidate in detail at this stage, stick with a handful of high-level criteria. If the list is getting too long (ten candidates would be a lot), add more criteria from the requirements list. If you can't find any suitable candidate, drop some of the criteria. The following criteria work well for building the long list:

- **High-level business functionality**. This one is obvious: if you are looking for a marketing automation tool, don't bother with CRM solutions that don't offer that. If you need to handle Spanish text, then reject solutions that cannot work with international languages. Make sure you only consider functionality that cannot be customized or somehow added on. For instance, let's say you want to support chat. While it would be ideal to find a solution that includes chat, you should be able to add chat as a point solution to another tool that provides the other functionality you require. On the other hand, you can't "add on" international language support or multichannel support.
- **Scalability**. If you are planning for a few dozen users, almost any CRM tool will do. As the number of users increases, the range of tools that can support that many users decreases. Eliminate tools that do not have an established record of supporting twice as many users as you are planning for.
- **Price**. At the long list stage, you are very far from negotiating a final price, but there's no reason to consider candidates that are way above what you can afford. So if your budget is $100k (for the tool, not the implementation) don't waste your time on $500k tools, but don't discard the $200k vendors either, since you can always exercise your negotiating muscles later to get close to or even under your target. We will see in the next chapter that CRM prices can be very flexible.
- **Implementation time**. If you have a short-term implementation goal, some of the more powerful and complex tools are out. Although all vendors claim their tools can be implemented in a few weeks or

months, the more complex tools simply are not amenable to aggressive implementation timeframes. If you need to be up and running in 60 days and the vendor says that they've had implementations as short as 60 days, you probably want to pass on that particular tool unless you are very sure that you can live with a minimal implementation.

## Categories of CRM Tools

The CRM field is so wide as to be overwhelming as you enter the long list stage, so it's useful to organize it into a number of categories that meet specific needs. We will look at four useful dichotomies: traditional versus new wave, suite versus point solutions, vertical versus general-purpose, and packaged software versus ASP.

**Traditional versus New-Wave**   Some CRM tools have been around for a while and some are rather recent. The traditional tools have had years to accumulate features so they offer very rich functionality, although the features tend to be piled up in a historical rather than a slick or organized manner. With traditional tools, the architecture and customization tools require longish implementation cycles, but they allow extensive amounts of tailoring if you are willing to undertake the work required.

On the other hand, new-wave tools are streamlined, having adopted a smaller subset of features. The better new-wave tools focus on exactly the essential features, so the loss of functionality may be almost invisible. New-wave tools allow for limited tailoring but on the other hand customization and deployment are easier. Choosing between traditional and new wave tools often boils down to how much customization and integration you need.

Here are characteristics of traditional CRM tools:

- They include **lots of features**. This means that almost anything you may want will be there. For instance, whereas a new-wave CRM tool may lack a CTI integration, a traditional tool will usually offer several options, all of which used by several customers in production settings.

  But lots of features could be a problem. You will probably have to spend significant amounts of time and resources turning off or hiding features that you don't need. And if you choose not to, your users will complain that the application is confusing and hard to use.

- Partly as a result of the abundance of features, and partly because the original thick clients allowed and encouraged it, traditional tools offer **busy screens and can be hard to use** and hard to learn because of the complexity of the underlying application. End-users will typically need a couple days of training to use the tool properly. This is not a big problem in an environment where staffers use the application a lot and turnover is low, but for staffers who are new or who are intermittent users, the training investment is large.

- Traditional systems **encourage using best practice functionality**, honed over long periods of time. This can be a great incentive to abandon or modify quirky business processes. Actually, if your business model is hard to fit into an existing, traditional tool, your first impulse should be to question your model rather than the tool.

  However, there are instances where the built-in tool workflow simply has to be modified for your needs. Traditional tools make it very difficult to change the workflow, and some changes are simply impossible. For example, collaboration, where multiple individuals contribute to a particular issue, is often desirable from a business perspective. But it's very challenging to build it in an environment that relies on a paradigm of one owner per issue, which is the way most traditional tools function.

- Despite the limitation described above, traditional tools **can be customized to do almost anything**—as long as the workflow model is not tinkered with. This makes them very flexible indeed, to the point where you may not recognize the underlying tool as you check references. Each implementation may not only look but even function in a totally different way.

  The customization possibilities come at a cost. It takes time and resources to customize, for one thing. Another interesting consequence is that the traditional vendors, knowing that almost all customers will perform customizations, adopt a lackadaisical approach to perfecting the out-of the box application and screens, leaving them cluttered and confusing. Worse, they may deliver an "application" that is completely unusable prior to customization; that is, they deliver a tool kit rather than a complete application. If you are in a hurry to get going, a traditional tool may simply not be what you want.

- Traditional tools can also **be integrated to many other systems**. As a bonus you're likely to find reference accounts for many integrations, which is always a nice omen, although not a guarantee that it will work for you too.

  Integrations are costly because there is always some custom work required, so having the potential for integrations may not be such an attractive proposition for you. It's almost always a mistake to select a particular tool over another, simpler one, only because it has integration capabilities that you might exploit in the future but for which you have no specific plans.

- Traditional tools are **expensive and slow to implement**. If you need the richness of their features and their customization capabilities, the cost is probably worthwhile. If you only need something simple they may be a waste of money and resources, and they may saddle your organization with a tool it cannot sustain in the long run.

New-wave vendors take a different approach.

- They usually contain **basic, major functionality**, and are well suited to modest requirements. The better new-wave tools offer an uncannily well chosen subset of functionality: just what you need, and no more. This is much better than having to remove or hide features in a traditional tool.

  As well chosen as the functionality may be, you may find that your needs are much greater than what you can find in a new-wave vendor. If you have to add a lot of functionality that would be bundled in a traditional competitor, it may be easier, cheaper, and even faster to select a traditional tool. As careful as you are with customizations, it's hard to beat the long-term maintainability of built-in features.

- New-wave tools have **less built-in structure**, which can be an advantage if you are trying to implement something different. On the other hand, if you want to enforce a standard best practice, a traditional tool delivers everything you need in a neat package.

- New wave tools sometimes **offer unique features**, both because they come from newer, nimbler companies, and because some new-wave tools are built from the ground up to deliver entirely new functionality. For instance, when chat first became popular for sales and service, a number of vendors appeared that offered pure chat functionality—that is, without a customer repository, the whole focus being on the communication channel. To this day the "chat only" vendors such as divine/eshare have been much more innovative in their domain than the traditional vendors, even the vendors who have incorporated some chat functionality into their products.

  Over time, the most useful and popular new features get integrated into the traditional tools, as chat did, and the inventive new vendors may add more robust CRM features to the new functionality (but chat vendors have not). So if you are looking for unique new features you may have to go with a new-wave solution.

- New-wave tools are **easy to use**, or at least much easier than the traditional tool. This is a consequence of the much smaller feature set to be sure, but the user-interface and the user paradigm are also significantly different. Rather than designing for an expert user who uses the tool daily for years, new-wave vendors design for the user who is computer-savvy but may be new to the application. For instance, they use popular user interface (UI) standards rather than creating an idiosyncratic, complex user experience.

- New-wave tools are, on the whole, **easier to implement than traditional tools**. This is not just because they offer limited functionality, but more a matter of philosophy. Traditional tools are built on the idea that IT help is required and available for tool implementation projects. New-wave tools have a realistic view that IT resources are always limited and they put many tasks within the reach of an educated, but non-technical, business user. Almost all new-wave tools require highly skilled IT resources for the initial implementation, however.

- New-wave tools may have **limited customization facilities**. This is not an issue if you are planning to keep customizations to a minimum and if the base functionality meets your needs by itself. But if you absolutely must have specific functionality that needs to be built expressly for you, new-wave tools may be too restrictive.

- **Integration kits can be missing** or you may find that no customer has implemented the specific integration you are interested in. Here again, your requirements may be such that the limitations do not matter, but if you need specific integrations you will need to carefully evaluate what's available and what's proven.

So should you choose a traditional vendor or a new-wave vendor? Carefully consider your needs for customization and integration. If they are high, chances are that you will be more successful with a traditional tool, but only if you are ready to invest the necessary time and resources to make it work. If your customization needs are modest, or you have limited resources, a new-wave tool that offers a good set of functionality is probably the best bet, even if you have to give up on some less essential features, since the implementation requirements are much lighter.

**Suite or Point Solution**   Another way to look at CRM choices is whether to select a suite offering or a set of specialized tools. A suite offering gives you an integrated solution with different modules that address each business function. A point solution covers one particular area or one particular set of functionality very well, but requires additional tools to deliver a complete solution.

Suite offerings are very tempting.

- They deliver a **pre-integrated solution**, so sales, marketing and service can easily share information. Sharing information is certainly possible with cobbled solutions, but it requires integration work.

  There are a few drawbacks, however. One is that suites do not, in general, solve the issue of integrating with back-end systems such as accounting. The other is more insidious. Whereas point solutions are created with the assumption that they will be integrated with other tools, and hence offer nicely open architectures that conform to industry standards, suites can be weaker in their integration capabilities.

- They usually have a **consistent user interface across functions.** Consistent interfaces make it easier to train users. This may seem immaterial since sales reps rarely morph into service reps or vice-versa, but it does make it easier for reps to research information in other departments.

  Interfaces are not always consistent since some of the suite vendors grew through acquisitions and have not chosen to make the interfaces consistent across functions.

- They usually offer **weaker functionality** in some areas, particularly for the more leading-edge features. If your feature requirements are high, suites may be disappointing.

  In particular, if you are considering adding modules to an existing CRM suite, you may find that a point solution delivers better functionality and is a better choice despite the integration requirements.

- Most suites are offered by **traditional vendors**, so they have the advantages and disadvantages described above.

- Even as traditional tools, suites are **faster and easier to implement** compared to creating custom integrations between best-of-breed tools. If you need a completely integrated solution but are short on time, a suite is your best bet, although you may have to sacrifice some functionality in the process. For the same reason, it may make sense for you to use the same vendor for front-office and back-office functionality.

- Suites are **easier to maintain**, since the maintenance team only needs to learn one tool and only needs to interact with one vendor's support organization. This is tempered by the fact that suites, being traditional tools for the most part, tend to have more complex maintenance tools.

- Point solutions focus on just one area or one particular feature set.
- They deliver the cool functionality and the **specialized or leading edge features**. Some features will eventually be delivered by the suite vendors, but it could take years. Point solutions do what they do extremely well and are often referred to as "best of breed" for that reason.
- With restricted scope, point solutions are usually **easier to implement and to maintain**. But if you need to put together several point solutions, each with a different customization and maintenance environment, what you gain in simplicity may be lost with the synergy of a suite environment.
- Moreover, many, although by no means all, point solutions are also **new-wave tools**, which means their implementation is easier. They also have the drawbacks of new-wave tools.
- If your requirements are narrow, the **limited scope** of the point solutions is not an obstacle. If your requirements are wide and you also need tight integration, then you will need to integrate multiple best-of-breed solutions, a long and resource-intensive process.

Suite or point solution? If you are targeting a single business function, you might as well go for best of breed, at least if you have no plans to expand to other functions in the medium-term. If you need a solution to cover multiple functions, consider both suites and point solutions. If your needs are fairly simple and you are looking for a quick implementation, a suite is your best bet, although you will have to live with the feature limitations.

On the other hand, if your needs are complex and you either are willing to invest in costly integrations or you need only loose integrations, then cobbling together a bunch of point solutions will give you the best of both worlds, high-end features and integration.

**Vertical or General-Purpose**   In an effort to minimize the customization work required to implement their tools, some CRM vendors offer vertical packages that are targeted to a specific industry segment such as health care, financial services, government, etc. Vertical tools are often built with a set of templates applied to a base product, but there are stand-alone vertical tools as well.

If you find a vertical tool with a good fit for your needs you will find that the customization requirements are much reduced. Therefore the implementation time is much faster and the maintainability of the end product is much better. On the negative side, vertical tools are often traditional tools, and therefore harder to implement and to maintain. Mid-range vendors tend to stick with general-purpose tools, so you will probably have to select a high-end vendor if you want a vertical tool. That may be outside your price and timeframe range.

By all means investigate vertical solutions appropriate for your industry, but unless your needs are fairly complex you should be able to do well with a general-purpose tool.

**Package or ASP** CRM tools have traditionally been sold as licensed software, however some are now packaged as ASP (application software provider) offerings through which the software is rented rather than bought outright. Some vendors offer only ASP solutions, some vendors offer both, and yet others allow third parties to offer the tool in an ASP arrangement while they stick to the licensed software model. Virtually every CRM tool is available through an ASP arrangement. What are the pros and cons of choosing an ASP arrangement?

- **Initial costs are much lower** with an ASP. This is less of a benefit than it seems since you can arrange for a loan arrangement to purchase software. However, if you need a solution only for the short-term, perhaps until you have time to deploy a long-term, comprehensive solution, an ASP will be more advantageous.

  Before you make a decision, run the numbers. Even with an ASP, you will incur significant costs for the initial startup and you may be required to sign up for a lengthy commitment.

- ASP vendors offer pre-packaged customizations, and they have a lot of practice with customizations; therefore **the startup time is remarkably short**. The other side of the coin is that ASP vendors restrict the scope of potential customizations, so you are in a situation that's quite similar to the one of new-wave tools versus traditional tools: startup is easier and faster, but the scope is more limited.

  Be sure to consider the kinds of reports that you need. An ASP can probably create anything that you need, but at a price.

- An ASP solution can **support fluctuations in the user base** more flexibly than an in-house solution. This is true of the infrastructure (no need to purchase or install servers for instance) and of the pricing structure. For instance, if you buy licenses for 100 users and find that you really need 120, you will have to go and buy 20 more, often at a high price because it's not a large purchase. If you only need 80 you can't really return the extra 20. An ASP is able to adapt to ups and downs better.

- In some circumstances it may make sense to **start with an ASP solution and migrate it in-house later** (using the same tool). This is easiest if the ASP happens to also be the vendor. If you are considering such an arrangement, be sure to negotiate the terms for the migration from the ASP model to the licensed model so it has the financial benefits of a rent-to-own situation.
- ASP vendors often offer **prepackaged integrations**, sometimes offering suite-like functionality through integrated best-of-breed tools. This is an ideal situation if you want the best of both worlds, although finding an ASP vendor that offers precisely the set of tools you want can be a small miracle.

  If you want to integrate the system with your existing back-end systems, an ASP solution may prove unworkable.
- ASP vendors offer **streamlined upgrades**, both because they can leverage their experience to many customers and because they tend to support fewer customizations, so upgrades are easier.

  If you want to integrate the system with your existing back-end systems, an ASP solution may prove unworkable.
- ASP solutions are **usually cheaper in the short-term** than licensed solutions, but more expensive in the long run. Make sure you understand all the charges both at startup and in the future, and any back-end charges.
- That being said, ASP solutions **do not exist for low-end packages**. If your budget is very limited, buy a low-end package that will deliver limited functionality, very limited customization capabilities, but a very easy implementation at a low price.
- If you are considering an ASP solution, you will need to consider the important **issues of data ownership, data security, and data migration**. It's a weird feeling to hand overy our precious data, especially customer data, to a third party. You will want to work out ways to ensure that data is regularly backed up and somehow made available to you so that you can continue your operations should there be any issue with the ASP.
- Test and re-test the **performance** of the application if you are considering an ASP. The tool has got to perform well over the network.
- Even more than with a licensed software vendor, double- and triple-check the **stability of the ASP vendor**, since you don't want to find yourself brutally deprived of service.
- You may want to go as far as **designing an exit strategy** if you choose

an ASP. It's comforting to know that you have options should the ASP not work out.

To ASP or not to ASP? The case against ASPs could be as simple as having a corporate policy against them (usually because of data ownership and security concerns). For small and medium companies, however, ASP solutions can be very liberating, allowing the company to focus on its core competency, which is rarely IT. The limits of ASP solutions can actually be quite helpful, since they discourage fanciful customizations that often have limited paybacks.

Packaged solutions are cheaper in the long run, so if you know you will use the solution for a long time, it's best to go that route.

## Name, Names, Names!

Naming names in the CRM field is a risky business. The incredible vitality of the field makes for an ever-changing landscape of vendors and tools, and mentioning each and every vendor that exists today would require pages and pages. Therefore the vendor lists below are by necessity partial and there are many perfectly good CRM vendors that are not included. The lists are accurate as of late 2002. For updated lists, please consult www.ftworks.com/JustEnoughCRM.htm.

The best-known names in the CRM world are traditional vendors with high-end offerings such as Siebel, PeopleSoft, and Amdocs. Just to illustrate how common acquisitions are in the CRM field, Siebel offerings include some of the old Scopus line (my ex-employer). PeopleSoft bought Vantive. Amdocs bought Clarify, which was for several years part of Nortel before being spun off. All three vendors offer suites with roots in the front office.

There are relative newcomers to the world of the traditional, high-end vendors such as Oracle, which is trying to leverage its strengths for back-end applications (and the database, of course). Oracle CRM has less of a track record than other vendors, however. Another example is SAP, which could be a good solution if you are already using it for back-office functions.

New-wave high-end offerings include Epiphany—which started in the analytics and marketing automation business and then bought Octane, a service-tracking tool—and JD Edwards, after its acquisition of YOUcentric. Parts of Kana's offerings such as the old Silknet are squarely in the high-end realm, while others are mid-range. All Kana offerings are in the service-tracking arena.

In the mid-range, GoldMine, originally a sales-tracking tool, bought HEAT, a longtime support-tracking tool to deliver a mostly-integrated suite under the FrontRange brand. Onyx, Pivotal, and SalesLogix (now owned by Best Software) also have roots on the sales side but also offer support-tracking functionality. Saratoga Systems is another, smaller player.

The mid-range new-wave field is very exciting, with vendors packing much power into their offerings while allowing for quick and easy implementation—well, at least significantly easier than other CRM tools. Salesforce.com is one example. Salesforce.com is an ASP that started on the sales side, as is obvious from its name, but now also provides basic support-tracking functionality and a decent, if basic, knowledge base. Upshot is a direct rival. And RightNow Web offers a sturdy support-tracking tool with integrated knowledge base and self-service functionality both under an ASP model and a licensed software model.

The big unknown and potentially giant gorilla in the mid-range, new-wave field is Microsoft, which has announced a solution to be available in 2003. The expectation is that the solution will be easy to integrate with other Microsoft tools, including e-mail and perhaps even its accounting offering (Great Plains). It remains to be seen what functionality will be available and how easy the tool will be to implement.

There are also many contenders in specialty areas of the CRM world including collaboration (ePeople, Tightlink), chat (Cisco, divine), knowledge base management (AskJeeves, Banter, Kanisa, Primus), and automated self-service (NativeMinds, ServiceWare) workforce management (Blue Pumpkin), and monitoring tools (Nice, Witness).

The approaches described so far should allow you to create a solid, manageable long list of vendors from which to start the evaluation. It's always possible to remove candidates from the list after you find out that they are lacking some essential feature, or to add a candidate that was discovered late but seems very solid. Experience shows that CRM teams rarely make additions to the long list because their hands are full evaluating the candidates on it, so if you have to err on either side it's best to include more candidates on the long list and be prepared to drop the weaker ones quickly rather than creating an overly short list and missing out on potential good matches.

## Evaluating Candidates

The crux of the selection process is the evaluation of the candidates. Evaluating candidates can be extremely time-consuming so it's important to make good strategic and tactical choices on how to conduct the evaluation so you can achieve a good decision in the length of time you allotted to it. The goal of this section is to discuss how to gather all the information that you need in the shortest amount of time.

### Keeping Track

Evaluations can be confusing, especially if you are evaluating lots of different vendors. Keeping good records avoids mistakes and saves time, and it doesn't need to take lots of resources. Record keeping is the project manager's responsibility. Since the end goal is to evaluate each aspect of the requirements matrix for each vendor, a good strategy is to summarize all the information in that matrix, keeping supporting arguments arranged by vendor and requirement number. Keep the records centralized so all team members can access them.

### To RFP or not to RFP?

The traditional process for evaluating candidates is to use an RFP. The CRM project team prepares a detailed document (the RFP) that defines the tool or service being requested, what kind of information the vendor should provide, and how it should be packaged, and sends the RFP to all the vendors under consideration. The vendors prepare detailed responses to the RFP that are then evaluated by the organization. Based on the results of the evaluation the organization can create a short list of best-fit vendors.

The RFP process is very useful in at least two ways. First, it forces the team to create a complete and detailed requirements list. If you are following the recommendations in this book that won't be a problem but I cannot overemphasize the benefits of knowing what you want before you go shopping. Second, the RFP process naturally creates a formal record of promises made by the vendors. The results of the RFP are usually attached to the sales contract and can be referred to later on if there is a problem with the deliverable. RFPs are almost always used for government contracts and very large contracts for that reason.

If you want to use an RFP process, you can refer to the RFP template at the end of this chapter for inspiration. The template may also be useful if you are not planning to use an RFP: you can use some of the questions as a guide when meeting with the vendors.

Despite its strengths, I find that the RFP process often fails to deliver the benefits one expects, for a number of reasons.

- It takes an **enormous amount of time**. Creating the requirements list is something you should do anyway, so that's not so bad. But the level of detail and completeness you need to achieve to use the list in the RFP is much greater than what you would need for internal use, so it takes much more time than the requirements list itself.

    You also need to give the vendors several weeks to respond to the RFP—and if you give them too little time, the responses will not be as detailed and some of the vendors may decline to participate altogether. The answers also need to be carefully evaluated, including going back to the vendors for clarifications, which again takes weeks.

- It is **expensive**. Tallying up the many hours that are required to create the RFP and to evaluate the answers may shock you. Price tags above $100k are not uncommon for the more complex proposals.

- It can be **misleading**. The accuracy and commitment implied by RFPs seem to guarantee that they will provide correct answers from vendors, but it's not that simple. First, much of the value of the RFP lies in the quality of the requirements. Since CRM systems are complex, it's difficult to word each requirement accurately, succinctly, and unambiguously, and you can't expect vendors' answers to be any more precise than the requirements themselves. Second, CRM systems are very customizable, so vendors may state that a particular functionality is included when in fact it would require some level of customization. The promise of a complete and completely accurate response is not often met.

- Many **vendors actively discourage RFPs**, especially those not at the high end of the market. It's always possible to insist on a response to an RFP, of course, but it requires some persistence and lots of time, which can be in short supply.

Because of the issues with the RFP process, it's often easier and better to use instead a streamlined process through which you actually walk through the requirements list and score each item yourself, based on your experience with each vendor's product. One way of thinking about the streamlined process is that it's very much like the RFP process except that you gather the responses yourself rather than having the vendor write them down before the evaluation. Using a streamlined process has many advantages.

- It can be **quite a bit faster** than the RFP process, since you don't have to prepare a formal document or wait for the vendors to respond (or decipher cryptic answers!)
- It is **likely to yield higher-quality information**. The probability that items will be completely misinterpreted by either the vendor or your RFP evaluation team is much less with a streamlined process. Also, the CRM team is more directly involved in the scoring and so will naturally focus on items of critical interest.
- It is **less resource-intensive**. Not having to create the RFP document is a savings. Although the scoring requires much more work since you need to do it yourself, it's usually easier than evaluating RFP responses. You should find that the streamlined process requires fewer resources, at least if you are shooting for a high-quality evaluation.
- It **allows you to flexibly revise the requirements list** during the evaluation process as you discover new information. Clearly you should strive to have a complete and accurate requirements list right from the start, but it's not unusual to make changes to the requirements list during the evaluation. Managing changes in an RFP process is difficult and confusing.

I very much believe in using a streamlined process but it does have a couple of drawbacks. One, the RFP process forces you to create a very clear and complete list of requirements. If you decide to use a streamlined process instead but you are not disciplined enough to create a strong requirements list, you may end up with a very poor fit because you never bothered to define what a good fit would be.

Another situation in which an RFP process might be preferable is if you need to attach the formal results of the evaluation to the contract. If you want to use your scoring sheet for that purpose you will need to get it approved by the vendor, which will pretty much negate the time savings of the streamlined process. However, you will still benefit from the higher quality of information you obtain by doing the scoring yourself.

Seriously consider using a streamlined process over a standard RFP.

## Setting Up Productive Vendor Meetings

Regardless of whether you use an RFP or a streamlined evaluation method, being able to orchestrate productive interactions with vendors will go a long way in shortening the evaluation cycle and, more importantly, in ensuring that you gather accurate and complete information. This important coordination work is usually performed by the project manager, although some delegation is appropriate, at least for larger projects.

To create the long list you might have used conference exhibits and webinars to get a feel for the various tools and vendors. During the evaluation you will want to switch to personal meetings that require coordination and preparation. For high-end tools, the meetings will most probably be handled face-to-face. For the lower-end tools some or all meetings may be held through web meetings and conference calls. The contents and attendance issues are very much the same regardless of the channel, however.

The number and the organization of the vendor meetings depend on the complexity of the project, the size of the team, and logistical considerations. A common approach is to start with an initial meeting of the whole team (perhaps preceded by a smaller-scope evaluation from a smaller group) followed by a series of in-depth meetings attended by only those team members who are interested in the specific area being discussed. For instance, the business users (business owners and super-users) will want to see detailed demos of the functionality. See Figure 6.1 for an overview of the meetings. The balance of this section describes recommended audiences and agendas and specifically describes how to get better demos.

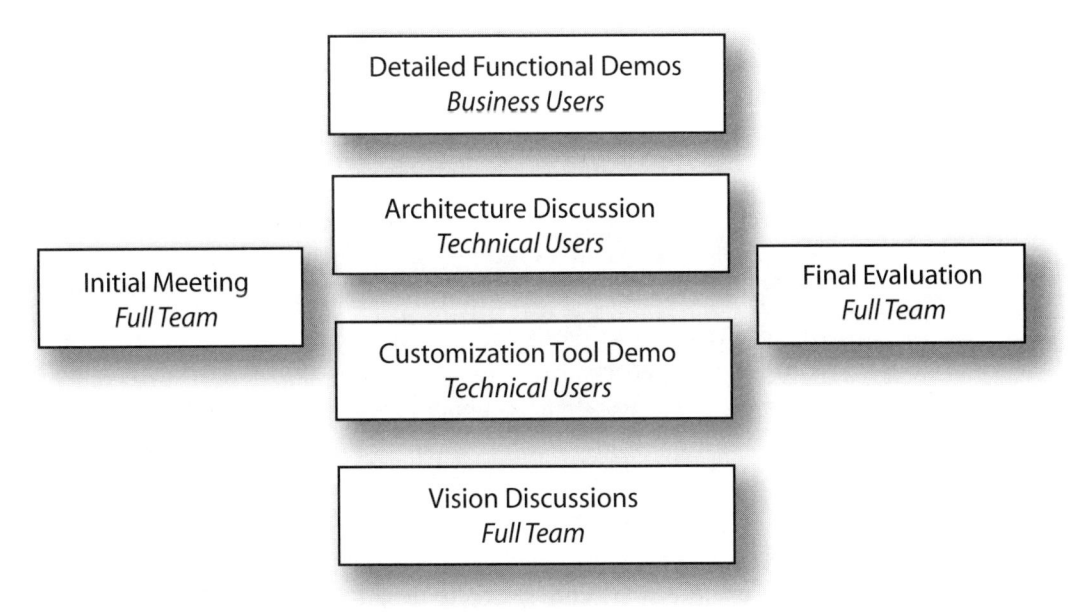

**FIGURE 6.1**
Vendor Meetings

**Who Should Participate?** It's very important to hold most vendor meetings with every team member in attendance. It's sometimes desirable or necessary to hold focused meetings for only a part of the team (for instance, an in-depth architectural discussion with only the technical staffers). However, holding separate meetings as a matter of course makes for a disjointed and longer evaluation process, and eventually a poorer decision as each component is evaluated independently of each other.

The project manager must orchestrate the various meetings. The process starts with the introductory meeting, a short meeting with the full team, branching off as needed into specialized meetings, and culminating in a longer group meeting for the final evaluation. The final meeting is almost always held face-to-face, often at the vendor's headquarter so all key staff members on the vendor's side can be present.

Although it's certainly possible to include some team members through teleconferencing while others are physically in the same room, I find that such meetings quickly focus on the participants who are in the room and ignore the remote participants. It's very difficult to stay involved when one cannot hear all the conversation, cannot see what's being demonstrated, or cannot participate easily in the conversation. If you must hold meetings with some but not all participants on a teleconference, take great pains to ensure active participation from the remote participants. Send them materials ahead of time so they can preparefor the meeting and follow along during the discussion. Test the web conferencing connections and other tools that will be used during the discussion. Make a point to include remote participants in the discussions.

If your project team is very large, it makes sense to have a core group do an initial evaluation of the vendors, bringing the entire team into the process only for vendors who pass the initial evaluation. If you choose to use a core group:

- **Make sure all functions are represented** in it. A core group composed entirely of super-users will miss technical architecture items, and a group of technical staffers will miss business functionality.
- **Include different hierarchical levels** in the core group. Don't use the core group idea to shield the business owners and the IT owner (or to shield the super-users and the technical staffers). To ensure the quality of the initial evaluation all levels must be included in the core group.
- Try to **use the same core group to do all the initial evaluations**. This means that it will have the same blind spots (bad) but it also means that it will get more efficient with each evaluation (good) while keeping a good level of consistency (also good).

- **Don't use the core group for the entire process**, only for the initial evaluation. If you feel the core group can indeed handle the whole thing, then perhaps your project team is too large, or not committed enough to the project.

You may think that there is a tremendous burden placed on the project team at this point. Multiple meetings with all the vendors on the long list? That's not often the case. Many vendors can be eliminated after the initial meeting, at least if you use the initial meeting to focus on the critical requirements. Especially with a large project team or a long list with many vendors, a suitable core group should be able to handle the initial evaluation so that the entire team only has to meet multiple times with a handful of vendors.

**What Should Be on the Agenda?** If you let the vendor set the agenda for the initial meeting, you can expect a rather lengthy presentation on the company, the CRM field, and the high-level product architecture, followed by a brief and slick demo highlighting the more clever features of the product. The demo is usually customized to your requirements to the extent that they are known by the sales rep. A "standard" initial meeting is slick and smooth. It also makes for a terrible way to evaluate the product.

Since standard vendor presentations don't work, you should always set the agenda for vendor meetings. Define both the topics you are interested in and how much time to devote to each. Remember the five categories of requirements?

- Vendor
- Technical architecture
- Functionality
- Implementation and maintenance
- Price

You should aim to cover all five categories in the initial meeting. Of course, you shouldn't bother to dig very much into implementation and maintenance topics until you are satisfied that the tool can deliver the functionality that you need, and you can't expect to get a final quote that early in the process. A typical first meeting can last an hour to an hour and a half (more is better if you want a meaningful demo) and can be structured as follows:

- Vendor introduction—no more than 10 minutes (cut off the vendor after 10 minutes to ensure that you have enough time for the rest).
- Functionality—5 minutes for a short presentation and 20 minutes for a demo. Since twenty minutes is not much for a demo, this is where to

invest additional time if you can stretch the meeting to the recommended 90 minutes. Otherwise, plan a follow-up meeting if you like what you see the first time around. We'll talk more about demos in the next section.

- Technical architecture—10 minutes. This topic will bore the business users and cannot be covered adequately in less than an hour anyway, so you will need a follow-up meeting for the technical staffers but address essential concerns to be able to determine whether it's worth proceeding to the next step.
- Implementation, maintenance, price—5 minutes.
- Q & A—10 minutes.

The project manager needs to spend time with the vendor to prepare for the meeting and to ensure that the vendor fully understands that deviations from the agenda are not acceptable. Otherwise you will find yourself veering back to the standard blend of 95% PowerPoint and 5% canned demo, a most unsatisfying use of the team's time. The project manager also needs to assertively redirect meetings that do not follow the requirements. Better set the stage in the first meeting than suffer through unproductive presentations.

The project manager should conduct a feedback session with the team shortly after the initial meeting. If the meeting is held at the vendor's site, it can be difficult to convene right after the presentation, but try to hold the debriefing very quickly afterwards. The goal of the debriefing is to decide whether to continue evaluating the vendor, as well as to improve future meetings and presentations. Short debriefings should be conducted after each meeting.

If only a core group participates in the initial meeting, assuming that they like what they see, repeat the meeting with the entire team in attendance. You can take advantage of the repeat to further refine the agenda to meet your needs.

After a successful initial meeting with the entire team, you will want to set up follow-up meetings to discuss specific areas. Plan on several follow-up meetings, targeting functionality, architecture, and implementation. The follow-up meetings can be attended by only a subset of the team members. However, it's always desirable to have at least one representative from a non-targeted group in attendance as it helps with information sharing and group decision-making. For instance, ask a super-user to attend the architecture discussion even though it's mostly for the technical staffers. A good format, if you can arrange it, is to schedule parallel meetings for the various subteams and to allow individuals to move from one track to the other for full coverage.

Regardless of how many meetings are scheduled and how they are arranged, they must be planned in advance by the project manager or a team member to ensure that the agenda and attendees are appropriate. One of the main complaints of CRM team members is that they waste time in unproductive meetings. There will be plenty of irritants down the road over which you have little control, so make sure meetings are well organized. Use the outcome of the debriefing sessions to make each meeting more productive than the last one.

**Getting a Meaningful Demo** Although demos are invaluable to share what the tool can and cannot do, many demos are poorly planned and end up being either divorced from (your) reality or excruciatingly dull as each field and each screen is visited and commented on without an overall vision of how real tasks can be performed. Here are practical ways to turn demos into useful selection tools.

- **Request a vanilla demo**. It's fine if the vendor wants to put your logo on the screen to personalize the tool, but stay away from extensive customizations that obscure the actual implementation requirements. Generally speaking, the more time you give the vendor to prepare the demo the more customizations may creep in, so push for a reasonably close date and make it clear that you do not expect customizations.
- **Define what you want to see** during the demo. An excellent strategy is to go through a normal workflow such as working a customer lead from inception to purchase, or working a customer service case from beginning to end. Stress that you are not interested in seeing each screen sequentially and in detail (you can always do that on the second pass if appropriate), but rather that you want to experience the flow of the product from one task to another.
- During the demo, **ask questions**. If the demo shows corporate customers and your customers are consumers, ask how they can be accommodated. If the routing of service calls is by product and you want to route by geography, ask how you can be able to change that. If your normal workflow requires a manager's approval before sending a quote, ask how that can be built in.
- As much as possible, **drive the demo yourself**. This may not be appropriate on the very first go-around, as you are still getting oriented to the product, but you should definitely do it later on in the process. If the tool is very new, driving the demo allows you to uncover what I politely call soft spots—plainly said, features that do not work yet. Regardless of the maturity of the tool, driving the demo gives you a

very real feel for how intuitive it is. Experienced demo givers make it look effortless to use the tool, and only when you are doing the typing do you realize that the screens are poorly laid out, or that the workflow is not what you need.

- If possible, **get an evaluation copy** of the software to have complete freedom for testing the software. This is now standard with ASPs, since they are all set up for that, but still pretty rare for the licensed package vendors. Vendors are often reluctant to set up evaluations because they fear, often rightly, that evaluations delay the sales cycle while requiring lots of effort on their part. If you decide to use a hands-on evaluation, set a reasonably short schedule and create a formal project plan. Hands-on evaluations are very time-consuming, so eliminate less promising candidates before embarking on them.

During a hands-on evaluation, ask the super-users to perform the tasks they would normally perform with the software, noting each area of discomfort as well as each hole in functionality. If you have a good workflow defined for the particular business function it should not be too hard to do. For instance, support reps should create cases, work cases, and close cases. Working in a customer role they should be able to use the support portal to open cases, check status, and add to existing cases.

Meanwhile, the technical staffers can put the software through its technical paces. Is it fast enough? Is it stable enough? Can customizations be accomplished easily?

Often the evaluation copy will be installed at your site by the vendor. Assign appropriate technical staff to be present during the installation to see how difficult it is. In addition, the vendor staffers that are doing the installation are quite open and much can be learned through informal conversations with them. The smart project manager may want to hang out in the data center on the day of the installation and chat them up.

## Tough Questions for CRM Vendors

Cleverly arranged demos are very powerful, and so are pointed questions to the vendor. I list here questions about the technical and functional aspects of the product. Pricing-specific questions are covered in Chapter 7, "Buying CRM Systems," and questions about integrators are covered in Chapter 8. For best effect, ask the tough questions several times during the evaluation from different individuals and compare the responses you get for consistency.

- Are you using your own tools in-house?

    All vendors have customers. If the vendor is not using its own tools in-house, something's very fishy.

    Ask for a demo of the way the application is used in-house. Does it look anything like what you saw in the demo? Usually the in-house version is kept pretty close to the vanilla version, both because it makes it easier for upgrades and also because the cobbler's children are poorly shod. Question any differences between the customer demo and the in-house demo. The demo giver is often a regular employee, not a sales rep, so you have another opportunity to get candid input.

    Is the version used the current version? If not, why not? Using older versions internally is a sign that upgrades are painful. Make a note of it.

    Is the tool integrated with any other tools within the organization? If not, it may be yet another manifestation of the cobbler's children getting poor footwear, or it could be that integrations are complex and difficult. Try to find out why.

    Ask how many people are responsible for administering the system and what their skills are. Also find out how many users the system supports and what problems they are encountering with it.

- Is it vanilla or is it custom?

    This question should be repeated for each and every feature of the product. A most useful question during demos, it can also be refined to "What work is required to create this particular customization?" Some tools have easy-to-use facilities to create minor customizations, so that minor changes are not an issue.

- What happens to customizations when you upgrade?

    Upgrades are often very difficult for CRM tools because customizations need to be examined one by one to decide whether they are still needed for the new version. Then, the ones that need to remain need to be re-implemented against the new version. Grill the vendor on this topic as much as possible and request recommendations for creating customizations that minimize the maintenance requirements in the future. Questions about how to handle customizations during upgrades should be on your list when you talk to references as well.

    Another good question about upgrades is to ask the percentage of customers who are running the latest release. Unfortunately, there's no way to audit the answer, but the number of customers running the new release is a good indication of how difficult it is to upgrade versus how compelling new features are.

- Do you have a user group?

  A vendor without a user group would be rather suspect to me. Ask whether the user group is driven by the vendor or is independent. Most user groups receive significant financial and operational assistance from the vendor, which is certainly a good investment in terms of customer satisfaction and marketing.

  If there is a user group, take time to talk to its representatives, keeping in mind that often the people who are active in the user group are great fans of the product.

- Can we talk to your support manager?

  Speaking as an ex-support manager, I know that all the dirty laundry eventually gets aired to that group. While the support manager will be restrained when talking with a prospect, much interesting information can be gleaned from seemingly innocent questions. Ask how many support staffers are in place today, what kind of profile they have, and what the current backlog of cases is compared to the incoming volume. (Remember that CRM systems are complex, so a backlog of about two weeks worth of cases is normal—but much more may mean that problems are hard to troubleshoot). You should also ask what percentage of cases are bug-related (ask this question of multiple individuals—more than 10% indicates that the product is overly buggy).

- What key features are you planning to release over the next year?

  While you must refrain from buying a system based on future features, which may or may not be released, and may or may not be released on schedule, it's very useful to understand the short-term product priorities. Do they fit with your priorities? If not, then perhaps another vendor would provide a better fit.

Another source of relevant questions is the RFP template at the end of this chapter. The questions are valid whether or not you are planning to use a formal RFP process.

## Creating the Short List

Having asked the right questions, having seen the right demos, you have the tools to create the short list. The short list should be really short, with only two or three vendors, and should consist only of tools that you are happy with from a technical and functional perspective. It is often the case, in my experience, that you are truly happy with only *one* vendor, but force the team to consider a backup so that you are not forced into an unhealthy financial surrender to one vendor. On the other hand, if you have lots of vendors that meet your needs at this point, look a little harder at which ones are the best fit from a functional perspective.

## It's a Gradual Process

Creating a short list is rarely a big-bang event. Gradually, as the evaluation unfolds, candidates may fall by the wayside, sometimes as early as the very first meeting when the key requirements are evaluated: too expensive, or not robust enough, and off they go.

Don't be afraid to disqualify candidates as you discover major issues with them so you can focus on more promising ones. You can always go back to them later if the front-runners fail to fulfill other requirements.

## Scoring the Requirements

Since there are so many factors to selecting a CRM tool, it's useful to have a logical process to analyze your findings. Whether you are using an RFP process or a streamlined process, it's very useful to create some kind of a rating matrix for the various candidates to organize the scoring.

**Use the Requirements List** If you did your homework for the requirements list, you have the essential elements for a rating matrix: the requirements list. It's fine to add, delete, and change some requirements as the evaluation progresses, but if you find yourself making significant changes you should go back to creating a long list again.

## Define Weights

Not all requirements are created equal, so it makes sense to give weights to the various elements in the requirements list. Rather than spending hours assigning very precise weights, I suggest you use a simple 1/2/3 weight selection, starting with assigning each element a weight of 1 (normal, lowest weight) and picking out the key requirements to have a higher weight. For instance, the must-have requirements can have a weight of 3 and all others a weight of 1.

Don't spend too much time fiddling with the weights. I've found that most evaluations end with remarkably few strong candidates so that the decision hinges on strategic considerations rather than a few points here and there, weights or no weights.

**Score Each Item**  Here's the fun part. Go through the entire requirements list and score each vendor still in competition for each requirement. This needs to be done whether or not you use an RFP (in other words, don't just take the vendor's word for meeting a requirement). It is useful here to compare vendors to develop a robust scoring method. For instance, if you are scoring scalability and you need the tool to support 500 distributed users, you may want to give 10 points to vendors who have multiple production installations with more than 500 distributed users, versus 5 to vendors that only have one such installation.

Scoring is often an iterative process. Taking the scalability example, you may realize as you are scoring that you did not confirm the exact number of users for each reference so would have to go back to the reference before completing the scoring. This is completely normal and should be planned for in the project schedule. I like to start the scoring process relatively early so I can spot and correct problems before the scheduled end of the selection phase.

**Add 'em Up**  Unless you are spreadsheet-challenged, adding up the scores should be pretty easy. Once it's done, compare the scores. Typically the candidates that the team thinks are best come out with the best scores (although not always in the order one would expect, as we will discuss below) and the others come out significantly behind.

If you find large surprises, such as an underdog coming up with great scores, go back and analyze the areas that made the difference. It could be that that the weights for the scoring system are not defined appropriately, in which case you can go back and fix them. Another reason for surprises is that the team's impression of a vendor is strongly colored positively or negatively by the relationship with the sales team. If that's the case, remember that the sales team will fade away as the purchase is completed. If the tool is poor you will be stuck with a poor tool anyway. If the tool is great but the sales team is difficult to deal with, make an effort to work with other individuals on the vendor's side, in particular the post-sales team: are they efficient and friendly? That's more important than the performance of the sales team in the long term.

## On or Off the Short List?

The whole business of scoring is to help you make a decision, but scores cannot and should not make the decision for you. Compare the scores but also trust your intuition: if a candidate is scoring higher but the team truly likes another one better, it may well be that the preferred candidate is the better one for you. The scoring sheet is only a tool and it may not be perfect, usually because of the choice of the weights. If a candidate truly feels better than another, it's probably the better choice.

Thank the vendors that did not make it to the short list (making sure that you have at least one backup to your preferred candidate). There's no need for them to expend more energy at this point, or for you to put effort into maintaining a relationship with them. As you say "no thanks" you may be surprised to receive some interesting financial proposals from the rejected vendors. If the only reason for rejecting a particular vendor was that the expected price tag widely exceeded your budget but you are now offered something reasonable, by all means reverse your decision.

# Sample RFP

This section contains a sample RFP structure that you can customize if you wish to use an RFP process. RFPs are massive documents because each and every item in the requirements list will need to be translated into an RFP question. This sample simply refers to the requirements list when appropriate to avoid needless repetitions, but shows the other sections in detail. Many companies have standards for RFPs so use the suggestions here to augment the process that already exists in your organization if there is one.

RFPs are organized as follows:

- A cover page
- A cover letter
- RFP instructions
- Company information
- Vendor qualifications
- Product overview
- Technical requirements
- Functional requirements
- Implementation and maintenance requirements
- Pricing information include configurations, often spreadsheet
- Appendices: vendor exhibits

Let's explore what each section contains.

## Cover Letter

The cover letter is simply a transmittal memo that summarizes the purpose of the RFP, orients the vendor to the way the RFP is packaged, and states the basic requirements for responding to the RFP.

Date

Vendor Contact
Vendor Name
Vendor Address

Dear Vendor

We have selected you as a candidate vendor to provide a proposal for a CRM application.

This package contains complete instructions for preparing and sending the completed proposal. Please follow the instructions exactly so we can easily evaluate your responses as well as the other vendors' in an objective manner. I am available to answer any questions that may arise. I can be reached by e-mail or by phone.

Please return your completed proposal by Date. We will be unable to consider proposals received after that date.

Sincerely,


Project Manager Name
Organization Name
Phone Number

## RFP Instructions

This section describes how the RFP process will work and gives specific instructions on how to respond to the proposal.

**Proposal Guidelines**  Start by giving a short summary of the context of the RFP: why are you interested in a CRM tool? What are you trying to achieve? What target dates do you have in mind? This is only a summary so the vendor can confirm its interest in preparing a response. A more detailed description is included in the next section. Then, give the following factual information about the process:

- Contacts and communications (on your side). Who will be able to help the vendors with questions?

- Evaluation and selection process: how will the RFP process be run and what criteria will be used to perform the evaluation?
- RFP and selection schedule. This is not a formal commitment to making a decision by a particular date, but it's useful for the vendor to understand your general timeframe. RFPs for CRM systems rarely exceed a couple of months for preparing the answer, and another month or two for reaching a decision.
- Effective dates of pricing: give yourself plenty of time in case the selection process is delayed.
- Legal considerations for the RFP. Ask your legal team to confirm what is best to include here. Almost always there is a so-called "right to reject" clause, stating that you are free to make a decision on any basis, including deciding not to make any purchase at all, with no recourse possible for the vendors.
- Confidentiality: it is customary to ask the vendors to keep the RFP confidential and to commit to keeping the answers confidential except as required to make a decision.
- Costs: vendors should bear all costs of responding to the RFP.

**Vendor Instructions**   Give instructions to the vendor on how to complete the RFPs, typically to provide clear and concise answers, to use the rating scorecards for the technical and functional requirement sections, and perhaps to provide pricing in a spreadsheet format. State that the RFP answer will become part of the contract.

Give detailed instructions on when to respond and how. Electronic responses are common and they are often preferred because they can be shared easily. State any format requirements.

## Company Information

This section gives the vendors information about your organization. It's important because it sets the tone for the proposal and it allows the vendors to tailor the RFP to your particular needs. The company information section should include the following subsections:

- A company profile including the market you serve and the goals of the business (one or two pages).
- Your existing technical environment including corporate standards, applications, database management systems, workstations, network topology, and vendors for all of the systems. Information about how

the systems are administered is not always given, but I find it very helpful to include it as well.
- A description of the business functions to be served by the CRM tool. For each business function, include its specific role within the organization ("Partner Sales" may be obvious to you, but maybe not to the vendor), its staffing level and reporting structure, the locations, goals, measurements, and anything else that pertains to how the system should work. Define whether the tool is replacing an existing tool, and if so why. Include your business goals for the new system. This section can be several pages long for a complex CRM project.

## Vendor Qualifications

This section asks the vendors to describe their corporate fitness to meet the requirements. Many of the questions are taken from the "Vendor Requirements" section of the requirements list. Many deserve the full written answers that are asked since they don't lend themselves to the scoring system we will see later for the technical and functional requirements.

**Vendor Profile** This section typically starts with a free-form statement from the vendor. I recommend limiting the length here for fear of getting back a very long and not very relevant expose. It is useful to get a feel for the history of the company, though, as it can indicate much about the vision and the executive team. After the overall statement, questions in this section include:

- Business vision
- Financial history (typically you want to request the financial statements for the last two or three years)
- An overview of the products offered (limit the length here again!)
- Industry experience: does the vendor have similar clients?
- R&D investment: how much is the vendor investing in developing new products and new technologies
- Geographical location of development, sales, and support offices
- Partnerships with relevant vendors
- User group
- ISO 9000 compliance
- Product awards

**Product strategy** Ask the vendors to explain their plans for new releases, new markets, and new customers. Place a limit on how many pages you will consider or ask specific questions to avoid getting massive amounts of information that's not directly useful. I recommend asking both for a long-term plan (say 3-5 years) and for the contents of the next major release, which should be firmer.

**References**   Specify type of customer, location, configuration, etc. We'll discuss references more fully in Chapter 7. Ask the vendor to provide contact information for each reference.

**Contractual Terms**   An RFP is not the place to negotiate detailed contract terms, so your goal is to gather information on standard terms so you can get ready to negotiate. If specific terms and conditions are important to you, by all means include them in the RFP.

Specifically request:

- The terms of a standard contract
- Acceptance criteria
- Warranty information
- Non-disclosure protections
- Payment terms
- If the vendor may provide implementation services, terms and conditions for the implementation, including a statement of work, ownership of the finished product, and warranties on the work and on the milestones.

## Product Overview

Provide an overview of the recommended system.

## Technical Requirements

The technical requirements section, like the Functionality Requirements section that follows it, is usually constructed to match exactly the requirements list you created. Both require the vendor to answer each question in detail as well as rate its ability to match the requirements in a scorecard similar to the one we showed in the last chapter when we discussed requirements.

Questions take time to create, which is one of the main reasons why the RFP process is resource-intensive—the other reason is the scoring—but they are often necessary to communicate the nuances of each requirement. Compare the following RFP question:

> Describe your technical architecture and how it supports scalable deployments. If several options are available, describe the ones that are better able to meet our requirements as discussed in the statement of work section.

with its corresponding, terse item from the requirements list:

> Scalable architecture

It's clear that you will get more information from the question than the item as is. And, at the same time, it will take you much longer to interpret and score the answer to the question than to look at the rating. Whenever possible, use short and precise questions to increase your chances of getting unbiased information.

Start the section with instructions on rating the items. It's usually very dangerous to use a simple yes/no rating system, since anything that's remotely possible will be rated with a "yes". Most RFPs use a system similar to this one with four categories:

- Features that are available today in the out-of-the-box product
- Features available in future releases (the vendor should specific both the release name and its targeted date)
- Features that require minor modifications (no coding)
- Features that require major modifications (coding)

## Functional Requirements

This section is by far the longest in the RFP, matching its length in the requirements list. Proceed as you would for the technical requirements section, asking vendors to provide both written answers and ratings.

## Implementation and Support Requirements

This section explores the implementation and support requirements per the requirements list you created. If you expect the vendor to provide implementation services, you will probably have to create a separate statement of work and negotiate it separately, but you can ask about high-level information in the product RFP. Even if you are completely certain that the vendor will not be the integrator, it's useful to get the vendor's high-level estimates of what an implementation would consist of so you can use it when selecting an integrator.

Here are items to request for the implementation:

- Overview of implementation project
- Technical requirements
- Sample project plan with schedule and deliverables
- Strategies for each major phase: planning, requirements gathering, testing, rollout
- Suggested staffing including qualifications and roles
- Recommended strategies for minimizing maintenance requirements of customized tools

For training, request the course list, complete course descriptions, pricing, end-user training options, and the availability of a train-the-trainer program. Request recommended backgrounds and custom curriculum suggested for system administrators and implementers. Request training schedules and course availability: if courses are always booked, your technical staffers may need to wait for a long time before they can be useful.

You may want to request sample user documentation in the RFP.

For support and maintenance, be sure to detail the requirements down to the SLA (service-level agreement) level.

## Pricing

Request firm pricing quotes for the configuration(s) you require. It's useful to request several quotes for different configurations, as it may be advantageous to purchase a license for slightly more users than you currently have. Quotes should include implementation (if provided by the vendor), maintenance, and other services such as training.

Request future pricing information as well. For instance, are maintenance price increases capped? How will maintenance be computed in the future?

# Buying CRM Systems

## Express Version

- Reference checking rounds off the evaluation process with critical insights on how other customers are using the system. Checking references is the only way to properly evaluate some requirements. Checking references should not be viewed as a substitute for a proper technical evaluation, however.

- Target reference accounts that have similar needs to yours in terms of size, type of business, and product use. You may need to check various aspects with different reference accounts to get a complete picture.

- Prepare reference checks using your requirements list. Ask specific, detailed questions rather than staying with "Are you happy with the tool?" For large decisions, make a site visit and include technical staffers and super-users.

- Negotiate each aspect of the contract, paying careful attention to the warranty and the terms and conditions for maintenance and support.

Maintenance and support last essentially "forever" so missteps there will cost you in the long term.

- You can expect significant discounts from list prices, especially for high-end tools, large purchases, and if you time the purchase to coincide with the end of the vendor's fiscal quarter. Don't focus blindly on the license price. Since you will keep the tool for many years, maintenance and support costs will exceed the purchase price and should be negotiated with the same level of attention.

- It's often a good idea to buy licenses for more users than you need today since you can get a much better price that way. Make sure you don't buy more licenses than you will need a year from now so you don't pay maintenance and support on unused licenses, which will negate your savings.

- Preparing an ROI analysis is part of any major purchase. Do not overstate the benefits in an effort to make the justification more attractive. Most CRM purchases require months after deployment to become profitable.

# The Home Stretch

Here comes the fun part. You have put together the project team, created the requirements list, evaluated the candidates, and narrowed down the vendors to one favorite and one or two backups. You are now ready to buy. But not so fast! There are some critical activities left to accomplish: checking references, negotiating the best terms, and getting a good price. They are covered in this chapter. Selecting an integrator should also be completed as you finalize the tool purchase, since it makes no sense to buy a tool only to find you have no one lined up to implement it. Integrator selection is covered in the next chapter.

The main obstacle to a successful purchase is over-enthusiasm. Once you get to the short list you've usually fallen in love with one of the candidates and it's hard to keep a cool head to complete the process. The reality is that the final steps, checking references and negotiating the best possible deal, make a big difference in both the quality of the decision and the long-term cost of ownership of the tool. Checking references, when well done, gives insights you cannot get through even an in-depth evaluation, and a good negotiator can save a bundle on long-term costs. Even if you can't wait to start the implementation, force yourself to be thorough for the rest of the buying process.

# Checking References

Checking references is a big part of business life. We check references when we hire someone and we check references when we make a large purchase. I'm a firm believer that reference checks can give you additional insight that you could not have gotten otherwise, helping you make a better decision. But reference checks only work if they are conducted properly, and that's what is discussed in this section.

Reference checks may be done to choose between two qualified vendors or to confirm that your favorite vendor is indeed solid. Often, extensive reference checks are done only for the favorite vendor.

A reference check is just a check. It's not a journey of discovery, and it cannot replace the evaluation process. In fact, you can only check what you already know, or at least what you know enough to ask about. You can discover new facts during a reference check, but only if you are asking the right questions from the right people, and that requires proper preparation.

## Why Do a Reference Check?

Reference checks take time and resources, especially if you want to get real information out of them. Why bother?

- **To confirm** that what you learned through the evaluation is indeed correct. You don't need to check each and every detail, and the individual providing the reference check probably won't want to spend hours with you confirming each and every detail anyway. However, you should check that the critical functionality for you is indeed working properly. If you suspect trouble, then ask more detailed questions.
- **To extend your evaluation.** CRM systems are complex beasts and there's simply no way that you can check everything yourself. For instance, the only practical way to check that it's possible to get the tool to talk to your accounting system is to ask someone who has done it successfully. Performance questions are also best answered through appropriate reference checking.
- **To get ideas**. Although I will once again warn against rampant customizations, the fact is that references may inspire you to try wonderful ways to use the tool.
- **To get implementation tips**. If you ask the right questions, of which we will see many examples shortly, you can and should find out plenty about what's required for a successful implementation including who

should be involved, what time lines are reasonable, and hidden "gotchas." This kind of information is particularly difficult to get through other means, so make sure you focus part of the reference-checking questions on the implementation process.

- **Because it's required** within your company process. Just because it's required doesn't mean it's useless bureaucracy. Gain from complying with the rules by making the most of your contact with the references.
- **To cover yourself.** This may be inglorious but it's a sad reality that the one who does not check references gets blamed. My view on covering yourself is the same as for following the process, discussed above: if you have to do it, you might as well do it right and improve the quality of the evaluation.

## When to Check References

Although this book, by necessity, presents the tool selection process as linear, there is no reason to keep reference checking for the very end of the evaluation. Indeed, if you are working with a fledgling vendor or if you need confirmation on a specific point during the evaluation, it's not a bad idea to start checking references early.

Don't expect to complete a reference check early in the process, however. The key to good reference checking is asking the right questions, as we will see later, so you can't be ready with all your questions until you have completed your own evaluation. It's fine to check references in stages, confirming some key points early on and coming back with a more detailed checklist later on. Always leave the door open for more questions if you need to.

## Picking a Good Reference

The traditional way to get references is to ask the vendor to provide a list. There's nothing wrong with that, but of course the vendor will only give you good references (if not, it's time to end the romance), and may or may not give you accounts that are good fits for your particular requirements. To improve the odds of a good fit, specifically request accounts that match your requirements.

- Accounts that have a similar **number of users**. This is about both scalability (can the tool support the user load) and, just as importantly, complexity (is the tool sophisticated enough to support the process complexity to match the number of users). If you have 500 users and you are interviewing a 40-user account, you simply won't get appropriate data on metrics or escalations, to name just two areas where complexity matter. Similarly, if you have 40 users but are talking to a 500-user reference, you may find that their elaborate customizations are completely inappropriate for your size.

Don't be obsessed by matching exactly the number or the distribution of users as long as you are in the same ballpark. You don't need perfect clones.

- Accounts that have **similar business models**. Look for organizations with similar customers rather than organizations in the same line of business. Actually, checking references with competitors is a nightmare since it creates competitive issues, so much so that the references may be unusable.

  Rather, concentrate on the reference account's relationship with their customers: are they selling to Fortune 500 companies or to consumers? Are they selling worldwide or only in the U.S.? Are they selling directly or through distributors? Do they sell standard goods or is each contract custom? Match the selling model rather than the specific field you are in.

- Accounts that are **in full production** with the tool. It's not completely useless to talk to accounts that are in the implementation phase, but the proof is in the pudding so you absolutely must have at least a couple of references in production. This can be hard if you are working with a fledgling vendor but be warned that being at the forefront can be painful when it comes to CRM.

  While you should talk to customers that are in production, it's good to talk to at least one reference that implemented within the past year so you can get meaningful feedback on the implementation process.

- Accounts that are **using the same products** or modules you are planning to use. There's no point to talk to a reference that's using the service-tracking module if you are planning to implement the sales-tracking module.

- Accounts that are **using the current release**. Following up on the previous point, talk to accounts that are using the release you are planning to use. This can also be a challenge, especially with traditional vendors, since the upgrade process is difficult and established customers are in no rush to move up. Talking with accounts that are running the current release allows you to check that the new features you need are indeed working properly. If you are not that interested in new features, and assuming that the latest release is not a complete rewrite of the tool, you may relax this rule (and probe for how arduous the upgrades are).

- Accounts that are **using a similar technical infrastructure**. If the vendor offers several choices of technical environments, or if you have specific architectural requirements, check that other customers are in production in similar environments. It's not absolutely crucial that the reference(s) with similar technical infrastructure also use the products in the way you will use them since this is more of a technical check. However, confirm that the user loads are similar.

- Ideally, account that are **close by** so you can visit in person. A site visit may seem to be a crazy extravagance both in time and resources but if you can afford one you will learn a lot more than you could through a regular phone conversation. Site visits almost always feature a hands-on demo, which may be harder to stage from afar and which almost invariably will give interesting information. Site visits also allow much more contact with various users, allowing you to ask more questions and to get a more balanced view of usability and issues.

If the vendor mentioned some established accounts during the sales process that you think would be a good fit for your requirements, don't hesitate to specifically request to talk to them. It's not necessarily a bad sign if a particular account is not available for reference checking (after all, there's such a thing as reference-giving fatigue) but you might as well probe on those names that were flung out to impress you early in the evaluation process.

There's nothing better than an unsolicited reference, so if you find people in your network who are using the tool, go talk to them even if they don't quite meet the criteria above. Unsolicited references are usually more open since they already have a relationship with you, even if it's slight, and unsolicited references are also more candid since they are not controlled by the vendor. Make allowances for the differences between the references' environments and yours when evaluating the answers.

How many references should you talk to? Two or three references from perfect-fit accounts would make me very happy, and more would get repetitive, not to mention very time-consuming. Since you are unlikely to find many perfect fits, you may need to talk to slightly more than three, but each discussion will be shorter than with a perfect-fit account since you can focus only on one aspect of the tool. For instance, you may talk to one account about the implementation, to another about performance, and to yet another about the SFA features. Don't overdose on references. Strive for quality rather than quantity and remember that you have unique needs and a unique approach so what worked for others may not work for you, and what didn't work for others may work for you.

## Whom to Ask

When checking references, you want to talk to at least two people, the business owner and the IT owner, so you can probe both the technical and the functional sides. Whenever possible, talk to end-users and system administrators for more details and, often, a more candid analysis of issues.

The vendor will typically give you only one contact, which could be either the IT owner or a business owner. Simply ask that individual to give you the other contact during the reference check. It's usually a pretty simple matter.

## Are References Impartial?

There's a great deal of appropriate concern about the level of impartiality of references. Vendors know very well, especially for enterprise applications, that positive references are a must for the vast majority of sales (in other words, most buyers aren't just dazzled by the cute demos). Vendors put a great deal of effort into cultivating references and the question is: do such efforts go too far?

It's true that vendors often offer enticements to customers who are willing to take the time to serve as references. Part of it is completely normal: after all, serving as a reference takes time and resources, and it's quite appropriate to thank customers who have done a favor with a small trinket or a nice meal. However, you need to be aware that, especially in the high end, vendors may offer a variety of very tangible rewards to reference customers, including:

- Product discounts
- Special pricing on maintenance and support
- Free training
- Free attendance at user group meetings
- The chance to participate in beta programs
- A seat on the customers' advisory board (The customer advisory board, not to be confused with the corporate board, of course, nor with the user group, is a vehicle that many vendors use to collect formal input from customers on new releases and other strategic decisions. The existence of a customer advisory board is actually a good thing as it shows interest in getting customers' input into the planning process. Depending on the influence of the advisory board, members can hold quite a bit of power in getting features implemented that benefit them. Therefore, it's always interesting to note the composition of the board and the way board members are chosen. )

- Access to top executives, either informally or formally. It's hard to put a value on this but it comes in handy when one needs to ask for a new feature or an expedited software fix.

Some larger vendors have a formal reference reward program in place that works very much like airline frequent-flier programs: participants get points as they give references and they can redeem the points as they wish. Is it a problem that references get rewarded? Not really, although you should find out what the rewards are, and weigh the feedback appropriately. While there is nothing wrong with a reward system, I feel that it should not be kept a secret. Ask the vendor and the references about a reward system even if it's not easy to get straight answers on this particular topic.

Regardless of the existence of a formal reference reward program, you should be aware that reference accounts are likely to get preferential treatment from the vendor in a variety of ways, and in particular for support services. This means that you may experience less responsive support than what they describe during the reference check.

Even if you have doubts about the impartiality of the references the vendor gives you, do check references! It's not unusual for buyers to simply rely on the long list of "big names" on the vendor's web site without ever checking further. This is a mistake. Listing a well-known Fortune 50 name as a satisfied customer may simply mean that some small subgroup in the company bought the product some time ago and may not be using it any longer. Check references and don't assume anything.

## Who Should Do the Reference Check?

Typically the project manager checks references, but it's wonderful if the business owner(s) and the IT owner can join in, either as a group or individually as required to check out particular aspects. In any case, it's best if the entire project team can help create and approve the list of questions to ask the references.

If an onsite visit is planned, take a cross-section of the team along, not just the business owners and the IT owner. Onsite visits create opportunities for end-users to talk to end-users and for technical staffers to talk to technical staffers in a much more open manner than standard reference checks. You will get much more out of the trip if you can prepare everyone to ask the right questions.

## What to Ask

A reference check is only as good as the questions you ask. Most reference checks used on mediocre questions such as "How's the tool working for you?" and "Are you happy with the support you are getting from the vendor?" Vague questions beget vague answers, so you must be specific.

The good news is that the questions are all ready for you, right in your requirements list. And as you work through the evaluation you should make a note of the points you want to confirm with the references, either because they are particularly crucial or because you can't quite pinpoint how the tool performs on them, so that by the time you check references you should already have a list of questions to ask.

Part of checking references is simply to confirm that the information you got from the vendor is correct. So if the vendor tells you that the pre-packaged CTI integration kit makes for easy integration with brand X, you'll want to talk to somebody who did that particular integration and was successful with it. If the vendor says that upgrades are easy because customizations are clearly differentiated from the base code, talk to a customer who upgraded recently and find out how it went. As discussed above, you may need to check multiple references to confirm all your requirements.

Reference checks must be prepared in advance. A thorough check (without a demo) may take a full hour and you should set aside a similar amount of time to prepare for it. After all, the person giving the reference is doing you a favor so you should minimize the interruption while ensuring your critical questions get answered. Customize the questions for each person you talk to: don't bother asking the long-term customer for detailed implementation stories, or asking the smaller account for scalability stories. However, it is very useful to ask some of the same questions from several references, as individual experiences vary.

Here are 20 good questions to ask references.

- How are you using the tool today?

    This is a general question to launch a discussion of the specific environment of the organization so you can check how well it matches your environment. In particular, you want to check: the user population including how many users there are, where they are located, and what their roles are; the business processes being managed through the tool; and the particular modules they are using.

All these questions allow you to align the reference's environment to yours. If differences are large, the reference check may not be very valuable.

- What is your technical environment?

  This question focuses on the technical architecture. Things to check include the exact products and versions they are using; the hardware and operating system for the hardware involved (servers, desktops, laptops, other devices you may require), the network setup, and the database management system.

  The IT owner should be able to answer these questions. Business owners usually don't have such a detailed view.

- How long have you been in production?

  As mentioned above, a reference that's not yet in production is not a real reference, in my opinion. Make sure they've rolled out all the users, not just some small sample.

- Were you a part of the team that decided to select this tool? What were the top reasons why you selected it? What other tools did you consider?

  If the reference is a long-term customer, which is not rare (and a good sign in and of itself!) it may be difficult to locate individuals who were on the original project team. Don't worry too much if you can't get to the original decision makers, especially for long-term customers, since the competitive landscape has probably changed a lot since the purchase. For more recent customers, however, it's always interesting to see what criteria they used and whether your findings match theirs.

- Do you use this particular feature [that you are interested in]? What makes it valuable to you? What do you wish was different?

  This is where your evaluation of the tool comes in handy, both to focus on the truly important questions (you can't check *all* the features in a reference check) and to be able to interpret what the reference is saying. And this is where a demo may be required to truly make sense of what's possible, what's easy, and what may not work.

  Don't forget to ask about features of the development environment, not just the end-user environment!

- What performance do you experience with the system? How quickly do screens repaint? How quickly do searches return results? Do you have performance concerns in any particular area? What if anything have you done to mitigate them?

  Performance can be a tricky area to discuss. First, there is the issue of comparable environments: don't bother asking performance questions of an account that's much smaller than you, for instance.

Even if the environments are similar, what's good enough for a reference may not meet your requirements at all. Exchanging benchmark numbers may be helpful, but also consider a site visit or online demo for a visual confirmation. Also try talking to an end-user.

- What customizations have you performed with the tool? Why?

  You are on the lookout for two things here: are there areas of the tool that require customizations you may need? And how painful are the customizations? Weigh the customizations that the reference account implemented against your own requirements. You may not need them.

  If a number of references tell you that they customized a particular area of the tool, it's likely that there is a weakness there and that you may need to also do work in that area. On the other hand, if none of the references touched a particular area that you feel needs work, pay attention. It can be a sign that either the references are not good matches for you, or that your process is outside the norm and should be changed rather than changing the tool.

- Do you have a list of customizations you'd like to do in the future? How long is it? How old is the top-priority item on the list?

  The list of enhancement requests gives you clues about 1) whether the tool is really used and 2) how difficult it is to create customizations. If you find a reference that has no requests for enhancements, it could be that the tool is not used very much (not a good sign), or that the tool is perfect. Please drop me a note if you ever encounter the latter situation; I want to know! If the top-priority item is very old, it's likely that customizations are difficult.

- Tell me about the implementation process for the tool. Were you a part of it? How long did it take? Who was on the team? How many technical resources worked on the implementation? What would you change in retrospect about the implementation?

  This set of questions is useful for accounts with reasonably recent implementations. Don't spend too much time talking about implementation with accounts that are long-standing, as the tool may have changed significantly since then and people forget details anyway. Talk to long-standing accounts about upgrades instead of implementation.

  Getting first-hand accounts of implementations is critical because it's virtually impossible to find out about the implementation process in any other way. (You could instigate a pilot project, but that's a lot of effort and time.) Probe for all details of the implementation, and especially listen for experience and advice on selecting implementation staff and planning for enough time. If the references say to hire an integrator and you're planning for an internal bare-bones project instead, you should rethink your approach.

- What systems, if any, are integrated with the tool? Why did you decide to integrate them? What effort was required for the integration? Who worked on it? How long did it take? What problems if any are you seeing with the integration today?

  Ideally you want to talk to accounts that have integrations to all the main systems you plan to integrate with. This may require multiple reference checks and they are absolutely worth it, so don't skimp on this.

  Listen carefully for the reasons why the systems are integrated. For one thing, your needs may be different, and some integrations may signal weaknesses in the tool. For instance, are references saying they integrated the tool with a knowledge base system because the one that comes with it is inferior?

- Who maintains the system today? How many people? What is their background? Is it difficult for you to recruit such individuals? Why? Do you feel that it's a difficult system to maintain? Why? What would you recommend we do when we build our maintenance team?

  The ongoing maintenance of the tool is another area where you need to check references to define your own long-term requirements. Don't bother with these questions with accounts that are very different from yours in terms of scale and technical environment.

  Pay particular attention to the skills required to maintain the system. Will it be difficult for you to attract and retain such individuals?

- Have you had to upgrade from one version to another? What was the process like? How long did it take? Who performed the upgrade? Did you migrate any customizations? What did you have to do to make it work? Were you forced to upgrade by the vendor? How?

  Upgrades are usually mandated by the vendor on a regular basis, so unless you are planning to use the tool for a very short time, you will simply have to go through the upgrade process. This is a key area when talking with established accounts, as CRM systems have a well-deserved reputation for being difficult to upgrade. Qualify the answers you are getting based on the configuration of the reference account and especially the customizations and integrations they are using.

  Upgrade questions, like implementation questions, are best handled by the IT owners on both sides.

- Do you have occasion to call the technical support group? How does that work? How quickly do you get a response? How quickly do you get a solution? What support package have you purchased? When was the last time you had to report a problem? What was it? What was the resolution?

   This is a key question for all reference accounts. Ideally, try to talk to the individuals who are involved in calling the support group, and check that they are working with the same support center as the one you will work with.

   Keep in mind that CRM systems are complex beasts, so problems may take days or weeks to resolve. On the other hand, CRM systems should also run very smoothly so any production failure is a red flag.

- Have you had occasion to attend training? Was it at the vendor's site or at your site? How long did it take to schedule the training? How would you rate the training? What was the top benefit of the training? The top improvement you would ask for?

   Make sure you make a distinction between end-user training and technical training. Many vendors provide training for technical staff only, leaving the end-user training to the integrator since it's almost always customized.

   Try to talk to the individuals who attended the training to ascertain the quality of it. If they attended training recently, ask them about waiting lists: if you can't train your staff promptly, the implementation schedule will suffer.

- Do you participate in the user group? In what way? What would you say is valuable about the user group? What would you like to see changed?

   An active user group is a great help in getting information flowing to and from the vendor. Try to figure out who controls the user group: is it pretty much the vendor? Integrators and consultants (this is not rare, nor is it necessarily a bad thing)?

   Is there more to the user group than a yearly meeting with a lot of marketing hoopla? Being able to keep in touch with users year-round is very handy.

- What do you like best about the tool?

   It's good if references identify items of interest to you in this category.

- In what areas do you feel the tool is weak? Why? What are the top 3 changes you would like to see made in the product?

   If any items here match key requirements for you, beware!

- What ROI did you get with the tool?

    Although it's difficult to get candid answers to this question since references consider, rightly, that financial matters are confidential, try to get enough information to evaluate your own ROI goals. If references cite longish periods to get to ROI and yours is optimistic, you should re-evaluate your plans unless your implementation is a lot simpler than theirs (and, if so, maybe they are not such good references for you).

- Have you ever asked for a new feature? What is the process to do that? Was the feature integrated into the system?

    References often have a much better experience with feature requests than regular accounts since they have a closer relationship with the vendor. Your mileage will vary here, and not for the better. It's a good sign if there is a process to request new features, typically through the technical support group.

- How do you find out about upcoming features? Do new features match your needs? In what way?

    This is about new features in general, not just the ones requested by the account. The more open the new feature process, the better.

## Seeing a Demo

You wouldn't buy a tool without seeing a demo, would you? Yet, many people check references without seeing their implementation of the tool. Demos are much harder to set up than a simple conference call and they take more time but they are invaluable to evaluate customizations and end-user performance.

Demos can be performed as a part of a site visit, but a simpler and cheaper alternative is to hold the demo through a web conferencing tool that supports application sharing.

Regardless of the medium, references may be reluctant to show what they consider to be confidential information—which they may consider to be both the application and the data, neither of which is a problem in a typical vendor demo. You may be asked to sign a non-disclosure agreement for the demo.

In part because of confidentiality concerns, you will most probably be limited to watching your contact work with the application rather than driving it yourself. However, you can and should make requests on what you will see and ask questions as you go. You can refer to the guidelines in the previous chapter about getting good vendor demos: the principles are the same.

If you want to see the customer portal piece of the application, you may be able to access it freely on the company's web site. If there is a password-protected area, however, you will need to specifically request access from the reference contact.

A final note about checking references. Your project is as unique as your requirements. The fact that a reference was successful or not with a particular area of the tool doesn't mean that the same will be true for you. Do the reference check seriously, but don't let your decision be made solely on the basis of it. You need to have a solid evaluation process independent of the reference check.

# Negotiating the Contract

Down to the nitty-gritty. You are satisfied with the product, the references checked out, and now you're ready to sign. Well, almost ready: you should pay careful attention to the terms and conditions you are agreeing to, especially since the contract is likely to tie you to the vendor for a long time.

Warning: I'm not a lawyer and if there is ever a time to get your legal department involved, it's when you negotiate the contract. Do not rely solely on the recommendations listed here.

## When Should You Negotiate the Contract?

It's impossible to complete contract negotiations before you complete the evaluation process, and it's also silly to spend time negotiating contract terms before you are fairly certain that you want to proceed with a particular vendor, so wait until you have a short list to negotiate the terms. However, request a standard contract from the vendor early in the evaluation process so you can get your legal department to start working on terms you want to change. Be ready to negotiate as soon as you are reasonably sure you want to select that particular vendor.

Negotiation is partly a game of patience, so it's important to strike a good balance between reaching an expeditious conclusion and getting what you want. Vendors are remarkably flexible at quarter-end, and even more at the end of their fiscal year, both on prices and on contract terms. Take advantage of these deadlines to facilitate a fruitful yet quick conclusion.

In brief:

- Get the standard terms during the evaluation phase.

- Get the legal team engaged as soon as you get to the short list stage.
- Don't let up on negotiations even if you are thrilled with a particular tool: you can get a bad deal on a great tool by failing to obtain favorable terms.
- Schedule the purchase for quarter-end.

## Who Should Negotiate the Contract?

Contract negotiations are usually dictated by your organization's rules and customs. Do accept the help of the purchasing and legal groups; they have plenty of practice and they often find angles you would not have thought about. If they need to formally approve the purchase, you'll be better off if you involve them early.

On the other hand, purchasing groups may not grasp the business requirements behind a particular vendor's selection, and legal teams are notorious for fostering complex contracts, so you can't simply abandon the process to them, unless you are comfortable waiting a few months for a signed contract. The best strategy is to create a small, focused negotiation team with representation from the legal and purchasing groups and the CRM project team (typically the project manager, although the IT owner is often a part of it too). It doesn't make sense to involve the entire CRM team in the negotiations, especially the super-users and the IT staffers, except perhaps as advisors on specific points, and even that is unlikely.

If you buy at quarter-end or fiscal year-end to get favorable terms, as discussed above, make sure that your legal department is indeed available to you at that time.

## Contract Points to Consider

Be careful with standard contracts, as they are always written to benefit the vendor. If you are making a small, straightforward purchase, a standard contract may be just fine, but most CRM purchases are neither small nor simple. Here's a list of points to consider.

- **Are all terms clearly defined**? One of the very critical items is the definition of a user, since it drives the price structure in most cases. Is the vendor using named users (you have to buy a license for anyone using the database, even if they only log in occasionally) or concurrent users (you buy licenses to cover as many users as will use the system at the same time)? The method doesn't matter as long as it's clearly defined—and of course you should expect to pay more for a single concurrent seat compared to a named seat.

Pricing may be based on all kinds of other parameters, and they should all be clearly defined. I've seen pricing based on sales volume, number of customers, and number of support issues. Be sure you understand how the pricing is computed and what it will mean for you in the short term and in the long term.

What is the effective date of the contract? The effective date often drives lots of other items such as the start of the warranty and the support contract.

What are acceptance tests? Who conducts them and who audits them?

- **Who is licensed to use the software**? Can the software be used anywhere in the world (it better be if you have or plan to have overseas offices)? By subcontractors? By a subsidiary or acquired company? What about an outsourcing partner if you use one for telesales or support? What if your company is acquired or reorganized?

- **What if something happens to the vendor**? Contracts are all about laying out what happens when things don't work out. Check what would happen if the vendor were acquired: the license should survive the event. Contracts sometimes call for some kind of code escrow arrangement as protection if the vendor disappears altogether, although it's not clear to me what you would reasonably be able to do with the code.

- **What products are included**? Vendors often combine their products in many different packages, so double-check that you are purchasing everything you need but no more (there's no need to pay for the CTI integration product if you are not interested in a link to the phone system). Vendors typically list the licensed product as an appendix to the contract, usually Appendix A.

- **How is compliance checked**? Try to avoid forced audits that can disrupt your business operations. It's entirely reasonable for the vendor to want to check that you remain within the constraints of the license, but it should not create big problems for you. Most software does not include automatic compliance checking mechanisms so audits may indeed be required.

- **What happens if usage goes up or down**? For traditional (licensed) software, you need to buy additional licenses (usually at list price) if usage exceeds what you have purchased, and you continue to pay maintenance for the number of licenses you purchased even if you are not using all of them. If you are pre-paying for users or products that will be deployed later, try to delay paying maintenance on them until they are deployed. If you anticipate needing more users or more products, you can try to get favorable terms in the contract. We'll come back to this point in the next section. What's important here is that the use of the product not be blocked because you are exceeding the licensed levels.

If you are using ASP software, you should be able to pay lower fees if your usage goes down. Make sure you understand the formula to adjust the payments up and down.

- **What exactly is included in the warranty**? Many standard contracts essentially include no warranty. The software is what it is when delivered, and the only remedy is some kind of best effort, such as delivering fixes or workarounds on reported issues. Try to get a money-back clause if serious problems are discovered during the first few weeks or months. This is very hard to get because it creates revenue recognition problems for the vendor.

- **What happens at the end of the license term**? If you are purchasing a limited-term license, try to get some commitment for what happens at the end of the term. If you are getting a so-called perpetual license, you should be able to use the software for the life of the product, but even products with perpetual licenses are sometimes sunsetted.

  If you are working with an ASP, are there any termination fees? How will you get your data back?

- **What is supported**? Vendors usually provide support for the latest release, including bug fixes, and the one preceding it, but usually excluding bug fixes. Make sure you understand how releases are numbered and what constitutes a new release.

  Is there a guarantee on how long releases will be supported? You don't want to be forced to upgrade at a time that's awkward for you.

  Check that the particular technical environment you want to work in (hardware, operating system, database, web servers, etc.) will be supported for the foreseeable future with adequate provisions as those vendors upgrade. The IT owner should be able to help define what's required in this area.

  Finally, check whether licenses may be transferred from one environment to another as required. For instance, you may want to change the operating system you are using but continue to use the tool. That should be possible at no cost to you.

- **What is included in the maintenance contract?** Many high-end vendors bundle maintenance releases and new releases with support, but only for the particular products that were purchased. Some particularly unique new features may be packaged as separate products, for which there will be a separate fee. Make sure you understand what is included in the maintenance fee because you will need to work with it for years.

  If you are using an ASP, what is the process and schedule for upgrades? Will you be forced to upgrade at a time that's convenient to the vendor or do you have some leeway?

- **What is included in the support contract?** This is just as important as the maintenance issues, and for the same reason: you will be living with the support terms and conditions for years. Many vendors put the support terms and conditions (Ts and Cs) in a separate appendix.

  When it comes to support, you typically will have a choice between several packages. It's usually easy to switch packages when needed so you can select the one that best matches your current needs, but confirm the pricing strategy for higher-level support packages to avoid unpleasant surprises. For instance, if you need business-day support during the implementation and 24x7 support when you go production, it should be possible to upgrade the support contract at the time of the rollout for a reasonable fee. It may be cheaper to purchase 24x7 support from the start if you can get a better overall discount that way. Ask.

  The support package determines support hours, the number of individuals allowed to contact support, how quickly your requests will be attended to, and whether any account management or proactive support will be available. You will notice that the support Ts and Cs are pretty vague about details and focus on just a few things, typically speed of response and bug fixing strategies. It's usually easy to attach the support datasheet to the contract and to refer to it for specific commitments.

  Speaking as a not-yet-reformed VP of Support, I would advise not pushing too hard to get basic support Ts and Cs changed, for the very simple reason that in most companies the systems and processes in place are unable to accommodate exceptions. If you absolutely need a 45-minute response time when the commitment is for 60 minutes, save your breath and ask for a bigger price discount instead, or whatever else would make you happy. While you may be able to get the 45-minute response time enshrined in the contract, chances are that it will not be honored in the long run. It's not that the vendor doesn't love you; it's just that support works best as a large, one-size-must-fit-all machine.

That being said, there are lots of interesting areas to check with support including:

- Online self-support: is it available? Is it mandatory as a substitute to having a live person available? Are all contacts with support constrained through electronic tools?

- Any limits in the number of issues you can get support for. For high-end systems, support is almost always unlimited, but mid-range vendors sometimes limit the number of issues you can log over the course of the contract. Try to get an exception at least for the first few months since you may have many questions at the start.

- Support contacts: many vendors restrict the number of individuals allowed to contact the support group in an effort to minimize the number of requests and to increase the knowledge level of the people allowed to contact support. Vendors sometimes require minimum training requirements for the technical contacts.

  The number of allowable contacts and their qualification requirements are highly negotiable, so go for it if that's important to you.

- The hours: if you are buying a round-the-clock contract, known as a 24x7 contract, does that include all issues, or just priority issues? Who answers the calls at nights? On weekends? On holidays?

- The priority-setting scheme: in this day and age, you should be able to set your own priorities, but old-style vendors still insist they know best. Note that the priority of a support issue determines the response time, but not the resolution time. In addition, it has a very loose relationship with the priority attached to any underlying bug (politely called product defect in contracts).

- The response time, that is the time it takes to "get through" to a human being capable of starting the troubleshooting process, either by phone or electronically. Modern support-tracking tools give the customer an immediate confirmation of electronic requests. This is very important, but does not count towards the response time since nothing of substance is accomplished through this acknowledgement. The response times are usually stated as targets (the vendor tries to meet them) rather than commitments (if the vendor doesn't meet them there is a penalty of some sort). Is the response time for emergencies good enough for you? Buying up (to a higher level of support, that is) may get you a better (shorter) response time.

As discussed earlier, it's not worth negotiating for better response times so stick with what's offered and get your jollies somewhere else.

- Resolution time commitments. Although vendors typically have response time targets, they usually do not have targets for resolution time. Resolution time is what really matters if you think about it, since you want your problems to be resolved as quickly as possible. The reality is that some problems may never be solved at all, and some may take days to work through. I would personally be wary of vendors that give absolute time commitments for resolution since it's simply impossible to guarantee such a thing with software.

  However, you can work on mitigating strategies, including an escalation path to the vendor's executives in case of a serious problem. Automatic escalations based on the age of the case are not bad, but you should try to get a list of individuals that you can call if issues are not resolved to your satisfaction.

- Access to a senior-level group. When you select a higher level of support you can sometimes get access to a dedicated support engineer or a group of such individuals. The benefit is that you get to talk to people who are more knowledgeable than the average support rep. If the group is small enough they get to know your particular environment, so the diagnostic process is faster. All great in theory. In practice, such high-level support groups may be quite "virtual," so don't fight too hard to get that special access unless you can validate, perhaps from the references, that there will be a tangible benefit to you.

- Proactive support. Standard support contracts are reactive: you call, they respond. If you want proactive technical account management through which you get regular briefings, case reviews, and proactive information on new releases, you typically have to pay for it. Proactive support is often bundled with dedicated support engineers, although it doesn't need to be. If you choose this option, be sure to specify the deliverables: are the briefings scheduled? How often do they occur? Are onsite visits included? Who pays for travel?

- ASP maintenance windows. If you are using an ASP, what is the scheduled downtime? Can it be tuned to better match your needs and your customers' needs?

- **What implementation services are included?** This is a key provision if the vendor is handling the implementation. We will discuss implementation-related choices in Chapter 8.

- **References**. Some standard contracts give the vendor the right to use your name as a reference by default (for instance, they may list your name on their web site). It may be wise to delay that listing until you are happily in production.
- **Dispute resolution**. Your lawyer will be able to help you review whether the dispute resolution terms are acceptable. The vendors' standard contracts often limit greatly what you can do if push comes to shove.

Some vendors do not modify their terms and conditions at all, and even the ones that do may not be open to changes for smaller contracts. Whether or not you want or can change the terms of the standard contract, make sure you understand exactly what is covered in the contract. You will have to live with the terms for a long time.

# Getting the Best Price

Part of negotiating a good contract is, of course, getting a good price. Price negotiations are presented here in a separate section because they are very important.

## Discounts are Meaningless

"Save 50%." Is that a good deal?

Yes, if the pre-discount price is reasonable and customary. No, if the pre-discount price is unknown or irrelevant. Since you typically don't have access to the vendor's price list (and if you think you do, it's time to remember the miracles of desktop publishing—anyone can create a price list these days), discount levels are meaningless. Forget the discounts: focus on the net price.

## Use Good Old Competition

If you are negotiating prices, you've fallen in love with a particular tool, right? I have yet to experience a CRM purchase where there is not a clear differentiator between candidate #1 and candidate #2. In other words, CRM decisions are rarely based purely on financial considerations.

Even if candidate #2 is a big step down from candidate #1, make sure you keep it alive enough to give you a firm quote. Share the interesting tidbits of that quote with your preferred vendor to activate some competition. For instance, if candidate #2 is throwing in the customer portal for free, inspire candidate #1 to do the same.

## Understand the Sales Rep's Compensation

Sales reps are always compensated on license sales, often on sales of implementation services (but sometimes at a lower rate) and sometimes on the first-year support fees (often at a lower rate). They always have a license sales quota, but that's not always true for services. Most will be flexible in proportion to their compensation.

## Play the Clock

CRM vendors, like other enterprise software vendors, are known to be much more flexible around the end of their fiscal quarters, and even more at the end of their fiscal year. While you may not be able to schedule your purchases so precisely, it doesn't hurt to try.

This is even more true for large purchases. If you are planning a large purchase, you really should schedule it for the end of a quarter. It could mean an additional 10% discount, or more.

## Negotiate Now, Buy Later

Does it make sense to purchase licenses before you need them? It might. It's a matter of balancing two opposite facts: larger purchases get bigger discounts, but maintenance is usually charged for all licenses from day one (we'll revisit the latter below).

If you anticipate needing licenses for additional products or additional users within a year to eighteen months, it's probably cheaper to purchase them right away to get a better price. But if future purchases are uncertain or may occur in more than eighteen months, it's usually better to make them when needed rather than incurring the maintenance fees.

You can go for the best of both worlds by negotiating the price of add-on purchases within the contract. It's best to agree on a specific price for add-on purchases, for instance to stay with an established per-user price for a given timeframe. For distant purchases, or purchases of future products that are not yet priced, the best you can do is to get some level of discount. Since price lists are not published you'll have to trust the vendor to apply the discount, but it's better than nothing.

## Site Licenses

For large purchases, or purchases that will grow large over time, you may want to negotiate a site license that gives you the right to use all the vendor's products for any number of users. There's typically no price list for site licenses so plan for a long (but usually fruitful) negotiation. Make sure you understand what products are covered under the agreement. The vendor is unlikely to give away all future products but should be able to offer reasonable guarantees if products are renamed or discontinued.

## Focus on Maintenance and Support

In the long run, support and maintenance fees can be higher than the cost of the licenses themselves. Just do the math: if the support fee is 20% of the license fee, in five years you will have paid more in support than in licenses. (If you must consider the time value of money, please whip out your spreadsheet and add some reasonable inflation number to the support fees—you will find that your sophisticated computations yield a result that is awfully close to five years).

Therefore, it pays to be very clear about support pricing. Ask the following questions:

- **What is the basis for computing support fees**? Support fees are typically computed as a percentage of the *list* license fee so you want to make sure you understand the exact computations for the first year as well as for future years.

  If you are getting a discount on the license fee, does it extend to the support fee? This is not automatic, so check. Some vendors have a policy of no discounts, or limited discounts only on support.

  Let's run through an example. Say that you are buying $200k of license (list price) with a 30% discount for a net price of $140k. The *list* price for support at 20% of the list license price would be $40k. If you can get the same discount on the support fee as you got on the license that would make it only $28k. Notice that a 30% discount on a $40k purchase is rather generous, much more generous than the same 30% discount on a $200k purchase, isn't it? The numbers are summarized in Table 7.1.

**TABLE 7.1** Example of Pricing of License and Support Fees

| License List Price | License Discount | License Net Price | Support List Price (20% of list license) | Support Net Price (20% of net license) | Support Net Price (15% of net license |
|---|---|---|---|---|---|
| 200k | 30% | 140k | 40k | 28k | 21k |

While you have a pretty good chance of getting the vendor to compute the support fee off the net license price, getting an even lower support price is going to be very difficult, although you may want to try it. For instance, you could request a 15% percentage of the net license fee rather than 20%, giving you 15% of $140k or $21k. This is the last column in Table 7.1.

That was fun, but it only works for the first-year support fees, and what really matters for support fees is the long run. So the next step is to define how the fees will be computed in subsequent years. A reasonable request is to apply the initial discount forever. So if you got 30% off the first year, as in the example above, you get the same 30% the following year. But 30% of what? If you make no additional purchase, then it should be pretty simple, yes? Not necessarily. Vendors make pricing changes from time to time and contracts typically read, "Support fees are computed from the then-current price list", so your support fees can change even if nothing changes in your configuration. Also, you may make follow-on purchases, so make sure that the contract defines how they are treated for the purposes of computing the support fees.

Finally, pay attention to support levels. Say that you picked "Silver" today (vendors love the so-called metal packages) and you negotiated a permanent 30% discount on it. What if you later decide to upgrade to "Gold"? Do you get the same 30% discount on Gold or does the discount go away? And what if the vendor decides to retire the old support packages, which is not uncommon? Ideally, your discount level should apply to *all* future support fees. You may need to settle for something more modest, however.

- **Can there be a cap on support fee increases**? You just have to ask (really!). Vendors readily agree to limit fees to the consumer price index, but you can ask for anything else that seems attractive to you. You should not get much pushback from the vendor on this as long as you are using a reasonable index. Make sure that caps apply yearly. In other words, if the vendor doesn't increase prices in a particular year, you can't get a double increase the year after.

You should be able to get a special deal if you prepay for several years of support, but you don't necessarily want to prepay that much ahead of time. You might be able to get a (smaller) discount if you commit to buying several years of support even if you don't pay for them upfront. The small savings associated with that strategy are not usually worth the trouble, to be honest.

- **When does the support contract start**? Standard contracts usually have support start on the effective date of the contract, which could be months before your implementation date. (To be fair, you will be using support services during the implementation, unless the vendor is handling it for you, so this is not completely irrational).

A relatively easy concession to get is to delay the start of the support contract to a reasonable date, roughly corresponding to a speedy implementation. (The vendor is unlikely to agree to start the support contract on your actual implementation date because that date is subject to change and is outside the control of the vendor, even if the vendor is involved in the implementation.) If you delay the start of the support contract by 3 months you just got yourself a 25% discount on the first-year support fee. Congratulations!

If you are buying licenses in advance of your needs, as discussed above, you may be able to negotiate a delayed start of the support fees for a reasonable portion of the licenses. Again, the vendor will probably insist on a firm schedule for the start date rather than a schedule tied to your actual deployment. For example, if you are planning to deploy half the licenses this year and half next year, you could argue to pay only half of the support fee for this year.

## Pay Late

No, I'm not suggesting you be late on your payments, but rather that you negotiate extended payment terms. For large purchases, you should be successful, although you should expect to pay at fixed dates rather than dates linked to your successful implementation or deployment of the tool, as discussed above.

## Odds and Ends

The big-ticket items are described above, but there are some areas where you can get some leverage, usually without much of a fight: training credits, membership to the user group, and executive sponsors.

Vendors, especially the smaller ones, often throw in some free training to sweeten the deal. Make sure that you can actually use the training. For instance if the free training is for vendor-site classes and requires extensive travel you may find that a fee-based class at your site is actually cheaper (and, unfortunately for you, the training credits won't transfer over to training at your site). Also check the waiting lists. Often free training is available only on a space-available basis, which may translates to not in this lifetime. Finally, check on expiration dates.

Complimentary user group memberships may be negotiable if the user group is controlled by the vendor. Check to see whether this includes registration to the meetings. You will most likely have to pay for travel expenses.

And then there are the executive sponsors. An executive sponsor is an executive who is assigned to maintain a good relationship with your organization. Beyond that no one really knows what an executive sponsor does (but it sounds good, doesn't it?). Ask for details. It's never a bad thing to have a good rolodex including someone you can call if you run into trouble. Take the executive sponsorship but don't expect much from it, and certainly don't give up on other important negotiation points because you have an executive sponsor. If you have a choice, I recommend selecting someone as high as possible in the hierarchy for the maximum amount of leverage. I would also pick someone based at headquarters since that's where the action is with escalated issues.

## Are Used-Car Buying Techniques Worthwhile?

Some people think that hardball negotiation is best. Ask for the world, they say, be ruthless, and you'll get the best deal. While such tactics work well when buying used cars, I'd stay away from them when buying a CRM system, especially for a large purchase.

For starters, an overly tough negotiation strategy may prod the vendor into a similar behavior, perhaps fostering unreasonably stringent terms in areas of the contract that you are not focusing on. More importantly, by squeezing out the last drop you may alienate the vendor when in fact you need a build a strong partnership for a long time. Don't destroy the goodwill that will get you responsive, cheerful help during the implementation and for the life of the support contract, in ways that cannot be regulated in a contract. And finally, vendors who are willing to give in to harsh demands may be desperate. If the vendor says yes to everything, will it stay in business for the long term?

## Preparing an ROI Justification

Many CRM purchases include the ritual of a Return On Investment (ROI) analysis. A ROI analysis contrasts the costs of the CRM project with the expected benefits, and among other things forecasts how long it will take before the benefits outweigh the costs. ROI analyses traditionally focus on the cost savings created by the increased productivity made possible by the tool, but it's also important to consider potential revenue increases the tool may bring about.

ROI are often required to get the purchase approved. While many companies used to take a leap of faith into CRM without making a quantitative justification, this is changing as top management is insisting on cost justification. Even if you don't have a corporate requirement to prepare a ROI analysis, it's very useful to map out what you will get for your investment. You may even find that you curb some of your desires for fancy customizations when you realize that the payback is not commensurate with the expense.

While a thorough ROI analysis is the domain of professional financial analysts, the impetus for the ROI and much of the benefits estimates must come from the business owners, so they need to be the ones driving and validating the ROI process.

This section contains checklists to help you organize the ROI analysis and some examples to get you started.

### Costs

It should not be difficult to define the costs (there's much less guessing involved compared to the benefits!) but you need to be disciplined and include all costs, even indirect ones:

- **License fee** for the tool.
- **Maintenance and support fees**. If you are doing a multi-year ROI analysis (and most CRM tools require several years to break even), be sure to take into account likely increases in the fees.
- **Purchase costs for ancillary items**, including hardware and software. It's not unusual to see ancillary costs approach the costs of the tool.
- **Maintenance and support fees for the ancillary items**.
- **Implementation costs**. They could run much higher than the license cost, depending on complexity.

- **Training.** Include end-user training and training for developers and the system administrator. Costs could be out-of-pocket (to the vendor or a third party) and/or internal costs, especially for end-user training.
- **Internal staff.** Internal costs are rarely included, and part of the reason is that they are difficult to compute, especially for staffers that only spend part of their time on the project. I feel it's important to capture at least the cost of resources that are spending a significant percentage of their time on the project including technical staffers, the project manager if that's an employee, and super-users.

Table 7.2 shows an example of a cost analysis for a modestly sized initiative that includes internal costs. Note that, although the implementation is farmed out to an integrator, there are significant IT costs to support and maintain the tool. Further note that, without the internal costs, the Year 1 costs would be only 65% of the total shown here, so internal costs are very significant.

**TABLE 7.2** Sample CRM Project Cost Analysis

| Item | Year 1 | Year 2 | Year 3 |
|---|---|---|---|
| License | 150 | 0[1] | 0 |
| Maintenance[2] | 30 | 32 | 35 |
| Hardware cost | 40 | 0 | 0 |
| Hardware maintenance[3] | 7 | 8 | 8 |
| Database system | 10 | 0 | 0 |
| Maintenance[4] | 2 | 2 | 2 |
| Implementation | 120 | 0 | 0 |
| Training/IT | 35 | 10 | 10 |
| Training/end-users[5] | 25 | 5 | 5 |
| IT staff cost | 120[6] | 100[7] | 108 |
| Super-users cost | 60 | 0 | 0 |
| Business owners cost | 40 | 0 | 0 |
| Total | 639 | 157 | 168 |

1. This assumes no additional purchases, which may or may not be realistic for you.
2. This uses a 20% of license price and a yearly increase of 8%.
3. This figure is based on an 18% price structure and a yearly increase of 8%.
4. This assumes a price structure of 20% of license and a yearly increase of 8%.
5. The training figures assume no travel. Training for years 2 and 3 is for updates (IT) and new-hire training (end-users) respectively.
6. This amount is for the selection and implementation project and the support and maintenance after the rollout.
7. This amount is for the support and maintenance of the tool.

## Benefits

Now that you have a big fat cost number, it's time to add up the benefits to see which side wins and how quickly.

**Baseline**   Before you can define savings, you need to establish a baseline for your current situation and costs. To that end, you need to establish the number of CRM users, broken down by categories, their compensation (averages by category are sufficient) and the key metrics for the tasks they accomplish. Key metrics for sales reps include the average deal size, the closing ratio, the number of appointments or proposals per month, etc. For service reps, this would be the number of issues resolved per month, the ratio of reps to customers, etc. Chapter 10 of this book explores the topic of metrics in depth, but at this point you're only looking at basic metrics that capture your cost of doing business. They should give you the current cost per sale and the cost per support case, as well as a structure to forecast the impact of the new tool.

It may be difficult to gather reliable data about the current situation, and indeed this may be the impetus for getting a new tool in the first place. Nevertheless, you must estimate the missing data as best you can in order to make progress on the ROI analysis.

**Cost Savings**   Once current costs are known or properly estimated, then you need to estimate the productivity improvements brought about by the new tool. If today service reps close 10 cases a day, will they be able to close 11? More? If sales reps close (win) 70% of the deals, can they win 80%?

Estimating productivity improvements is difficult. The best approach is to break down the tasks being automated by the project both by specific individuals and specific areas of their jobs, and to estimate the savings on each subtask rather than making a global estimate. If sales reps spend 25% of their time preparing for sales calls and the tool allows a productivity improvement of 20% on that activity, perhaps by making it easier to gather relevant materials or by improving collaboration amongst the sales team, then the overall improvement for sales reps' productivity is 5% for that particular activity. (Note that a 20% improvement is very large indeed, so you should question and revisit your assumptions if you should come across such large numbers).

Table 7.3 shows an example of how you can use a subtask analysis to forecast the efficiency improvements the tool will bring. Note that the end figure, 8%, is not so large as to be suspiciously over-optimistic.

**TABLE 7.3**  Example of Productivity Improvements for a Sales Group

| Activity | % Of time spent | Projected % Improvement by Activity | Overall Impact % |
|---|---|---|---|
| Making appointments | 5 | 2 | 0[1] |
| Pre-call planning | 25 | 20 | 5 |
| Sales call | 20 | 0[2] | 0 |
| Proposal creation | 5 | 10 | 1 |
| Contract negotiation | 10 | 0 | 0 |
| Travel | 10 | 5[3] | 1 |
| Follow-up work | 10 | 5 | 1 |
| Reporting | 5 | 15 | 1 |
| Administrative tasks | 10 | 5 | 1 |
| Total | 100% |  | 8% |

1. This is not really 0% (it's really .1%).
2. It's rare that a particular area would show no improvement whatsoever, but don't be afraid of admitting where the tool will not help.
3. Can a tool increase the effectiveness of travel? Yes, if it helps prevent unnecessary travel.

To give you another way to approach the same problem, Table 7.4 is an example for a support group that focuses on how the tool will expedite the resolution of an average support case. Here again, the forecasted efficiency gain (about 10%) is reasonably small and believable, although you would need to dig a lot deeper to validate each of the assumptions.

**TABLE 7.4**  Example of Productivity Improvements for a Support Group

| Activity | Minutes Spent Now | Projected % Improvement by Activity | Forecasted Minutes Spent |
|---|---|---|---|
| Check entitlement | 1 | 20 | 0.8 |
| Log case | 3 | 5 | 2.85 |
| Dispatch case | 1 | 0[1] | 1 |
| Resolve issue | 15 | 20 | 12 |
| Escalate to level 2[2] | 1 | 0 | 1 |
| Level 2 resolution | 10 | 10 | 9 |
| Wrap-up | 1 | 10 | 0.9 |
| Total | 32 |  | 28 |

1. Estimating improvements for tiny steps is usually not worth it, although if this were a very large support center with thousands of calls it would be worthwhile to do so since everything adds up. For instance, CTI typically shaves just a few seconds off a case's processing, but shows clear overall savings for heavy-volume centers.
2. Not all cases are escalated to Level 2 so the numbers here reflect the escalation effort for the *average* case, not the actual escalation effort for cases that are escalated.

## CHAPTER 7 ▸ BUYING CRM SYSTEMS

The business owners should be very careful about creating the list of tasks and their distribution since the entire analysis will be driven by the numbers. For instance, in the support example above, if the Level 1 resolution actually takes 30 minutes rather than 15, the overall efficiency improvement in case handling time would be a whopping 16%—from 47 to 40 minutes— compared to the already respectable 14% figure—from 32 minutes down to 28. So make sure you get the big pieces right rather than obsessing over the details.

Here are some suggestions for how a CRM tool can improve efficiency for a sales environment. Use them to jog your memory as you analyze the subtasks.

- Will the tool increase the productivity of telesales agents? Will they be able to handle more conversations during a given day? Think both of outgoing and incoming contacts, as appropriate. You may want to break out each step of contacting customers if you have a large group or are implementing specific technologies for that team.

- Will the tool help generate better quality leads, thereby improving the conversion ratio?

- Will the tool improve the distribution and routing of leads?

- Will the tool help sales reps prioritize and organize their work more effectively?

- How much time do sales reps spend locating information? How can the tool decrease that? You should get nice savings here.

- Will the tool help sales reps communicate with customers more effectively?

- How much time do sales reps spend locating information? How can the tool decrease that? You should get nice savings here.

- Will the tool decrease administrative chores for sales reps?

- Will the tool decrease the need for sales calls? Will it help decrease the length of sales calls? Expedite their preparation? What effect if any will it have on travel required?

- Will the tool speed up the generation and approval of proposals and quotes? This is particularly important if you are operating in a price-sensitive environment.

- Will the tool allow for more accurate sales orders? This is a key benefit if your product is complex and you are introducing a configurator. Inaccurate sales orders in turn could create costly returns and changes.

- Will the tool help increase deal size? This may be through decreased discounting (through better management control perhaps), or the ability to call higher into accounts (through better enforcement of sales methodology), or simply access to better information.
- Will the tool increase the win ratio?
- Will the sales cycles decrease? By how much?
- Will the tool allow sales reps to spend less time on post-sales activities such as checking on delivery or service?
- Will the tool allow sales managers to recruit, train, and manage sales reps?
- Will the tool help reps and mangers to create forecasts?

Here are some analysis questions for support centers.

- Will the new tool decrease the volume of incoming issues? Fewer issues coming in mean less work. This is a big deal for self-service initiatives.
- Will the new tool expedite customer entitlement and logging of issues? This may be significant if customers will now be logging their own issues electronically.
- Will the new tool save time in routing issues? For instance, a new CTI system can deliver questions to the right agent automatically. Even tiny savings here can add up if you have a lot of incoming calls.
- Will the tool save time during issue resolution? You may want to break down the tasks further here and consider easy, repetitive issues separately from complex issues. For easy issues, you should save big with a new knowledge base, especially if you can resolve issues in one interaction. For complex issues, you may save time with automatic escalations or collaboration features. Can the tool prevent escalations to Level 2 entirely?

    The tool should make it easier to communicate with customers, so you can shave some time there too, and especially for complex issues.

- Will the tool save time administering the user database? For instance, self-registration on the portal may be a big help.
- Will the tool save time in collecting and sharing information? A cumbersome document creation workflow may be cut down to size with a good system for writing, reviewing, and posting documents.
- Will the tool save training time and resources? This can be significant if you have high turnover, or lots of new products and systems to train on.

- Will the tool save time in obtaining appropriate metrics for the managers? And will the very existence of the metrics allow for savings or increased productivity? For instance, a workforce management tool will shine here.

- Will the tool make for easier revenue collection, whether you sell yearly contracts or incidents?

- You may be able to find additional inspiration in Chapter 10, which discusses metrics.

Once you have estimated the productivity improvements, combine them with the cost data to figure out cost savings. This can be a pretty complex operation, perhaps better suited to the talents of a financial analyst, but the idea is simple. If today you accomplish a given amount of work (sell a million dollars' worth of goods or support 1000 customers) with X resources costing Y, with the tool you would be able to accomplish the same amount of work with fewer than X resources at a cost that is less than Y.

**Revenue and Strategic Improvements**  Most ROI analyses stop right here with the productivity improvements, even though productivity improvements alone rarely launch a CRM project in the first place. Instead, CRM projects often arise from strategic needs to meet market demands, to respond better to existing customers, or to reach new markets. Although it's harder to forecast or even to quantify some of these benefits, I feel it's important to at least give it a try. Here are some questions to answer to identify and quantify top-line benefits.

- Will the tool allow you to deliver entirely new products, new services, or to reach new markets? For instance, you may be able to start an e-commerce channel, or to provide (and sell) proactive monitoring and alerts as a support option. Perhaps the tool will allow penetrating larger accounts. What is the size of the new market?

- Will you be able to cross-sell more effectively to your existing customers? For instance, you may be able to use marketing automation to identify products your existing customers may be interested in. Or you may increase your support contract renewal rate. What additional revenue can you expect from cross selling?

- What will be the impact on customer satisfaction? It may be negative, for instance if you are forcing customers to use self-service, but on the other hand customers may be clamoring for a level of service you cannot deliver without the tool. Transforming customer satisfaction improvements into dollars is an art in itself, so try something tangible such as increasing the retention rate.

- Will the tool increase employee satisfaction? If the tool decreases turnover, perhaps as employees are able to spend less time on boring issues, you may be able to identify a significant upside.
- What will be the impact of better analytics? This is a large area, starting with better revenue forecasting and pipeline analysis, useful to both the finance group and the manufacturing group. Better analytics also allow you to identify the top customers so they can get special treatment. They make it easier to cross-sell and up-sell existing customers, and to achieve better market penetration by replicating wins and avoiding repeated failures. Can you quantify the benefits of better analytics?

I like to be conservative in ROI analyses, keeping only tangible, measurable benefits and leaving the intangibles out of the numerical analysis altogether while listing them alongside the numbers. I feel that making sweeping assumptions about the intangibles suggests that the rest of the analysis may not be that realistic either and many CFOs agree with me. If you can't make your case without the intangibles, you may simply not have one.

As you prepare the benefits part of the ROI analysis you may find that, in order to gain some of the benefits afforded by the tool, you will need to make changes to your current business processes. To take a simple example, you may see that you need higher caliber sales reps in order to sustain the penetration of larger accounts that is made possible by the tool. If that's the case, you need to go back to the cost section and record the higher cost so you end up with a correct analysis, which is a good segue for the next point.

## Are ROI Analyses Realistic?

The honest answer is: not very. Most ROI analyses are slapped together to create an acceptable justification, and as such occasionally massage the truth to show a neat, short-term benefit.

If you want to be able to stand by your analysis for the long term, be realistic rather than optimistic. In particular, sweeping productivity increases are rare. If you are forecasting a 20% increase in sales rep productivity, double-check your numbers. They may be right, but I bet you will find opportunities to temper your optimism.

Another area of raging optimism is how quickly benefits will accrue. In my experience, most projects experience a temporary *decrease* in productivity when the tool is rolled out, as users need to learn their way around the tool (and, not infrequently, technical problems need to be sorted out). Productivity improvements may not appear for weeks or even months after the system is rolled out. The more complex the system, the longer it will take for the improvements to show up.

Finally, ROI analyses are most accurate and useful when they focus on reasonably short-term wins, not fuzzy long-term chimeras. Make sure that your short-term benefits are accurately researched and justified. Then you can present the long-term benefits as icing on the cake.

The next chapter focuses on selecting an integrator. Integrator selection should occur at the same time as the final selection of the tool, so be sure to advance both paths concurrently.

# Selecting an Integrator    8

## Express Version

- Implementing CRM systems is rarely a do-it-yourself task, except for very small projects. It's best to get help from a team who has done it many times before and therefore can be much more effective than you can.
- Start selecting the integrator when you determine that a tool will make it to the short list. The availability of a solid integrator is a part of the tool evaluation. If no experienced integrator is available, you should consider passing on that tool.
- Most tool vendors offer implementation services, but usually they target only the larger ones, and even for those they may not take on the entire project. Therefore it's very likely that you will work with a third party.
- Get integrator recommendations from the tool vendor and from your colleagues. Only consider integrators who have worked with the par-

ticular tool(s) before. Some tool vendors have certification programs and they are a good start, but do your own check as well.

- If you need help on the business side, especially with process definition and change management, look for an integrator that offers a complete package of services, not just technical implementation assistance.
- Check references with ultimate zeal. It's almost impossible to evaluate an integrator properly without checking references.
- Whenever possible, try to identify the specific individuals who will work on your project before you sign the contract.
- Integrators can work on a fixed-price basis or on a time-and-materials basis. Although fixed price contracts are attractive, they can become quite rigid so it may be better to go with successive fixed-price steps.

# What's An Integrator And Do I Need One?

Any tool you select will need to be installed, customized to your needs, perhaps integrated with other systems, and finally deployed. This is the technical side of the implementation, a big task in itself and one which you probably will need outside help to accomplish. In addition, you may need help with making changes and improvements in the business processes that are involved in the automation project, rolling out the process changes to the teams, and providing training. So while there is a technical side of CRM implementations, there is another set of business-oriented activities, at least some of which will be required for your project. They include:

- **Process analysis and definition**. Successful CRM implementation projects are built on a clear set of processes for interacting with customers. If your processes are already clearly defined, well documented, actually used by the organization, and deemed effective for the foreseeable future, you should be able to proceed to implementation with just a quick review and no more than some minor tweaking as required to adapt to the tool.

    In all other cases, you need to tackle some significant work with processes before the CRM tool can be implemented. This may be for a variety of reasons. It could be that the organization has been operating informally so far, and therefore processes need to be formalized so you can automate them into the tool. This may require harmonizing locally inconsistent processes. Or it could be that the existing processes are not working well. In that case, they should not be implemented in the tool as they currently stand; instead, they should be modified and improved before starting the implementation. In rare cases, it could be that the existing processes, although working well, cannot easily be automated in the tool (and despite the best efforts of the CRM team it has proved impossible to find a tool that would easily automate them). In this situation, review and adapt the business processes to the ones modeled by the tool to minimize customizations.

Whenever possible it's best if the process definition and implementation work can be done before the tool implementation starts (although that would be pretty much impossible in the situation that was just described). However, it's common to find that the review of the business processes is triggered by the tool implementation itself and therefore the technical and business efforts must proceed together. It's not such a bad thing actually because you can get inspired by the tool and avoid designing processes that the tool will not easily support.

- **Change management**. CRM projects, however modest, bring changes to the organization. If the changes are small and the organization is working well in general, the amount of so-called change management will be limited and the existing management structure should be able to handle it. Larger changes will require a more concerted approach, which may call for outside help from an experienced integrator.

- **Training**. End-user training is critical both to ensure proper use of the tool and to facilitate its acceptance. The background of the users and the amount of the process changes will determine the scope of the training required, from simple cheat sheets, to hands-on tutorials, to process training. But all projects require some amount of training.

The first question you must answer when making a decision about integrators is the scope of the project. How much process definition, change management, and training will be needed in addition to the technical component of the task?

The second question is whether you should tackle the implementation yourself, without outside help. If your project is very simple and doesn't require much more than a quick installation of an off-the-shelf product, then you can probably do it by yourself (and, if so, you can skip this chapter entirely). Otherwise, you should probably get some help, and here is why.

- **Specialized expertise**. Implementing a CRM system requires some specialized skills that you may not have in-house and which you may not have time to develop.

- **Short-term need.** CRM implementation projects require large numbers of resources. While you need to retain a certain amount of permanent resources to support and maintain the system for the long term, that level of resources is a lot smaller than what you need for the project itself. So it usually makes sense to contract out the manpower that is required only for the project.
- **Experience.** Practice makes perfect. It's much easier and faster to implement a tool if you have done it many times before. While you could theoretically train your own staff and use it for the implementation, an experienced team will not only get it done faster but will also avoid many of the pitfalls that an inexperienced team may encounter. In short, using an integrator will make for a faster and higher-quality implementation.

Of course, getting maximum benefits from working with an integrator requires you select a good one and that you properly manage it throughout the implementation, topics which are addressed in the rest of this chapter and in the next chapter, respectively.

## When Do I Start Looking for an Integrator?

Early is best. While it makes no sense to look for an integrator before you select the tool (since you want to choose an integrator that's experienced with the particular tool you are choosing to get the experience benefits described above), you don't want to get all the way to the tool purchase without having evaluated integrators in parallel. You don't want to find yourself in the very unpleasant situation of having spent good money on a tool that you cannot implement because you cannot find anyone good to do it for you, or, worse, having to go with a sub-optimal integrator so you get a sub-optimal solution.

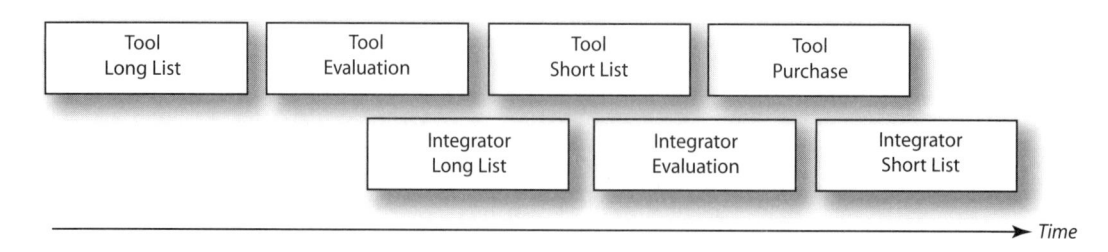

**FIGURE 8.1**
Scheduling Tool Selection and Integrator Selection in Parallel

As shown in Figure 8.1, start collecting suggestions for integrators as you get seriously interested in a tool during the tool evaluation phase. Your long list of integrator candidates should be ready as you finalize the short list for the tool vendors. Evaluate the integrator candidates while you negotiate the tool contract and aim to finalize the choice of the integrator as you are finalizing the tool purchase or shortly afterwards. This schedule will allow you to get going with the implementation quickly. Also, if your evaluation of the integrator candidates is not fruitful, you will know that before you complete the tool purchase so you can re-evaluate the tool selection itself and avoid ending up with expensive shelfware.

## Tool Vendor or Third Party?

Does it make sense to select a third party to do the implementation rather than to ask the tool vendor to do the job? Let's start by stating that this is not always a real dilemma since many tool vendors cannot or will not handle entire implementation projects. After all, vendors are in the software business, not the consulting business, and therefore prefer to spend their resources and energies on their core business rather than on services.

Don't get me wrong, vendors almost always offer implementation services, but they target the technical aspects of implementations, only rarely addressing either the process definition or the change management components. If your project requires a comprehensive scope you may not be able to get all the necessary resources from the tool vendor.

Moreover, tool vendors leave the smaller-size implementations to third-party integrators and choose to focus almost exclusively on the larger, more strategic implementations. They handle the larger implementations because the larger clients demand it. They also fear potential negative publicity for themselves if such projects were to fail, believing (correctly) that their involvement reduces the risk of failure. Even on the projects the tool vendors take on, they frequently contract out the tactical coding pieces and concentrate on the strategic areas of the project.

The ASP vendors are an exception to the rule, in that they always provide implementation services. ASP vendors also focus on the technical aspects of the job rather than on process definition. This may not be as large an issue in this case since ASPs limit the customization options so you pretty much have to follow a predefined business process.

Although you may not have the option of having the tool vendor perform the implementation, here are pros and cons of going with the vendor rather than with a third-party integrator:

- The big plus is to have **one responsible party** for the entire project, both software and implementation. It's certainly possible for a CRM project to fail while the tool vendor is handling the implementation, but it's a big relief to avoid the potential finger-pointing that can arise when multiple parties are involved. The simplicity of working with a single owner is often the main reason why customers choose to work with the tool vendor.

- The tool vendor should be able to provide **well-trained consultants**. This particular benefit may fail to manifest itself if you are working with a fast-growing or brand-new vendor, or a vendor that subcontracts carelessly. Ask plenty of questions about exactly who will work on your project and how much experience each individual brings to the project. I'll cover how to do this later in the chapter.

- On the other hand, tool vendors **may be biased**. Their direct objective is to get the software installed and working to meet any deliverable requirements in the contract, and they may cut corners in the process. A third-party integrator can be more objective in analyzing issues and may be more motivated and effective at getting problems addressed with the vendor, as upside-down as this may seem.

- As mentioned above, the tool vendors' capabilities are often **limited outside the technical arena per se**, whereas with a properly chosen integrator there is no limit to the variety of skills and services available.

- Tool vendors **may lack experience with specific integrations**. After all, they know their product best, not other vendors'. Here again, an integrator with the appropriate experience is preferable.

If you are considering asking the tool vendor to handle the implementation, put the vendor through the same evaluation process as you would a third party integrator. Do not assume that the vendor's implementation team has handled projects similar to yours before, or even that the team will be technically competent just because it's on the vendor's payroll. (If nothing else, a vendor with a lot of new consultants will have to put some inexperienced individuals on the project.) The other reason to perform the same evaluation is that vendors are often more pricey than third-party integrators, and cost should be an important component of your evaluation.

## Mix and Match?

A mix-and-match approach to staffing implementations is perfectly reasonable. Actually, leaving *all* the implementation work to the integrator would be a disaster, and we will come back to this point in the next chapter. Start by assessing the resources that you either already have in-house or are planning to acquire, perhaps to provide support for the tool. It makes no sense to hire a contractor to do a task for which you have appropriate talent already (assuming said talent is not fully consumed by other tasks.) Mixing your own team with hired guns is perfectly reasonable.

What about mixing and matching resources from multiple parties, and in particular getting some resources from the tool vendor and some from an integrator? When does it make sense to do that?

It's important to realize that mixing and matching is likely to occur in the background if the tool vendor is responsible for the implementation. Most tool vendors subcontract widely, especially the non-strategic, coding part of the job. In that situation, since the vendor is taking ownership for the job, you may not care too much about the subcontracting, but it is happening anyway. (By the way, third parties almost never subcontract back to the tool vendor.) That being said, because of the complexity of the coordination required when using multiple parties and because of the potential for finger pointing, it rarely makes sense to divide up the project between the vendor and a third-party integrator. Stick with just one player for the implementation.

However, if you are working with an integrator you should seriously consider getting two things from the vendor. One is a list of implementation guidelines that spells out how to minimize maintenance issues and that the integrator should follow. There should be no additional fee for this. The second thing is to request that the tool vendor come in for audits at crucial junctures in the project such as validating the project plan before the actual development starts, reviewing customizations before they are deployed, and confirming the deployment architecture before hardware is purchased. You will have to pay the vendor to get the audit services, but audits are short and therefore not that expensive. View them as insurance that the project is on the right track. If they should uncover a problem you have an opportunity to make changes before the consequences are too serious.

Purchasing audit services from the vendor should bring you guru-level technical expertise, which may not be available from a third-party integrator, however experienced. Providing audits also forces the tool vendor to put a larger stake in the game. Audits help decrease frustrating and fruitless finger-pointing between the integrator and the vendor and they provide a solid start for the long-term support that the tool vendor will be providing.

## Are Certified Partners Better?

Many tool vendors have a partner certification program through which third-party integrators can receive training and assistance and get a seal of approval in return. If the vendor has a certification program, it's best to seek out a certified partner, more because serious integrators seek out certification than because certification by itself is a badge of quality. In other words, serious integrators are certified, but not all certified integrators deliver quality.

Certification programs run the gamut from bare-bones programs focused on information delivery to sophisticated setups that include a serious testing component. Many certification programs are amateurish and do not include any testing component. Most programs do not include any hands-on testing. Your first concern should be to get a description of what the certification means from the vendor's Professional Services or Partnerships manager. Here's what to look for.

- Certification should include some **training** requirements so that the developers can maintain their technical edge. Certification programs that require neither training nor testing are simply marketing programs with no bearing on the technical capability of the integrators. Substituting on-the-job for classroom training is just fine since many useful skills can be picked up through working on implementation projects, sometimes above and beyond what classroom instruction can do.

- Certification should include some level of **testing**, and the testing should be hands-on as much as possible. Many smaller vendors do not have the resources to create formal testing programs, but an informal program can be very effective if based on real-life conditions. For instance, the vendor may award certification based on a certain number of successful implementations. That's just fine, and, provided the implementations are audited, should provide a more meaningful guarantee of success than a contrived classroom-based test.

- Certification should cover **all staffers** at the integrator. This is a tricky issue, since integrators need to hire new staffers over time and since they often use subcontractors. Most certification programs apply to the organization rather than to the individuals, so check how new employees or subcontractors are included in the certification. If only a few core individuals are certified and other people are living off that reputation, you may not get much for the certified label.

Even if you find that the certification program is rigorous and includes meaningful testing, you still need to evaluate the integrator to make sure it meets your standards. In particular, no certification program can tell you whether the integrator has been successful with implementations similar to yours.

If you find that the certification program is a bit of a joke, you may disregard the label when evaluating integrators. Serious integrators may not bother getting certified if they think the program is a waste of time. Also, with a weak certification program, you will need to perform a particularly thorough check of the candidates, including their technical abilities, since the certified label is meaningless.

## Implementation Scenarios

Let's consider some typical scenarios and the corresponding options for selecting integrators. (They match the examples given in Chapter 4, "The CRM Team.")

**Simple Tool, Simple Implementation**   A small support team (15 people) is implementing a new support-tracking system with an integrated knowledge base and customer portal. The new tool replaces an existing system that only provided case-tracking features. Little disruption to the existing case resolution process is planned. The tool that was selected is a mid-range tool with a particularly easy implementation, so much so that the vendor reports that many customers are able to do the installation themselves with the assistance of a couple of conference calls with support personnel.

This is a straightforward project, certainly from the technical side, since the customizations are minimal and no integration is planned at this point. The process definition side is potentially more complex since knowledge management processes can be intricate, but with an organization this size nothing should get too complicated. The choice of the integrator depends mostly on what technical resources are available.

- If appropriate technical resources are available in-house, the implementation may not require an integrator at all. The primary candidate would be the IT group, at least if it has properly qualified people available. If the tool is as simple as the vendor says it is, an individual from the technical support group (a super-user) may even be able to handle the implementation.
- If internal resources cannot be found, the tool vendor does offer a two-day, fixed-priced engagement to perform the implementation, although it is not pushing professional services and is actually recom-

mending that customers do their own implementations. (By the way, the mere existence of such a small-scope implementation offer is a sure sign that the product is really simple to configure.)

This vendor implementation package is technically focused and assumes that all business issues have been settled ahead of time. For instance, the consultant may ask how the customer wishes to route issues, but will not spend time advising on an appropriate routing scheme for the organization. In a situation like this one where processes are already established, it should work just fine.

- Even for a small project like this one, it's important to have a project manager in place. If no one from the support organization is available, a consultant that specializes in tool implementations from a business perspective is a great choice. That individual should be able to guide the organization through the business and process choices that also need to be made.

**New Tool, New Processes** This medium-size sales organization (120 people) is global and is implementing a sales-tracking system to replace manual processes, contact managers, and forecasting spreadsheets. The tool that is being selected is a traditional, client-server tool with significant implementation requirements, even for a relatively straightforward implementation like this one.

There is some amount of process definition to be done before implementing the tool, since nothing is automated at this point.

- The tool vendor maintains a roster of certified partners to do the implementations and generally does not provide comprehensive implementation services. A selection will be made among experienced, local candidates. To supplement the integrator and provide an additional level of confidence, the vendor will be asked to provide an audit of the code and of the deployment plans to ensure quality. (Vendors almost always provide audit services even when they do not provide complete implementation services.)

- The integrator will also be asked to drive the process definition effort so the ability to conduct such a project will be a critical piece of the selection requirements. The integrator will be asked to guide the process definition exercise towards processes that can be easily implemented with the tool.

- Participation from the organization itself is very important, both on the IT side (to ensure that the system is properly integrated and will be supportable for the long run) and on the business side (to ensure that the processes can and will be implemented). All members of the CRM project team will be participating in the implementation.

**Integrated System, Politically Charged Organization** This medium-sized organization is implementing a unified system for sales and support tracking to improve communications about customers throughout the company. There will be about 300 users altogether. The tool chosen is a mid-range suite that will minimize integrations, and indeed none are planned for the initial integration.

There is some skepticism and pushback from both the sales team and especially from the support team against implementing a new tool. The support team already has a tool in place that is functioning adequately, although providing only barebones functionality, so it's not an overwhelmingly attractive proposition to have to switch to a new one. The sales team has no unified tool in place so there's a clear benefit to the new system, but also concerns about having to follow a set, potentially rigid process.

- The tool vendor provides implementation services and is proposing to take on the implementation to ensure its success because it correctly senses the political tensions within the company and does not wish to be associated with a failure. However, the vendor's strength is mostly on the technical side and it's not clear that its consulting team will have the political savvy to navigate the expected pushback from the business owners.

- The other option, and the better one in my mind, is to engage a third-party integrator, and indeed a third-party integrator with a good record for managing politically charged implementations should be able to carry off the project very well. Also, a third-party project manager is often better accepted by the business owners than one internal to the organization when it comes to making process changes because that individual is seen as being unbiased. That could be very useful with the sales team.

- The tool vendor will be asked to provide audit services for the deployment part of the project. There will be synchronization required for the mostly field-based sales team and synchronization is always a tricky item, so it's worth getting the vendor involved for that piece. Audits for the project plan and the code review are always useful but they could be skipped here if the budget is tight since the project is quite straightforward from a technical perspective, with minimal customizations and no integrations.

- It's essential that the teams involved be kept well informed and optimistic about the project throughout its course because of the political concerns. The communication piece of the project is particularly critical and should be carefully considered in the project planning.

**Large System, Merger Situation**  After a merger, two support groups are merging to a combined size of 400 people dispersed around the world. Both teams have used traditional support-tracking systems that need to be replaced for various business reasons.

- The tool chosen is a high-end, complex tool with a long implementation period. However, the strategy is to keep customizations to a minimum. Only a handful of integrations are planned, the main one being with the bug-tracking system.
- The project is large enough to be of interest to the tool vendor so the organization has a choice to either use an integrator or work directly with the vendor. Beside price, the decision hinges on the tradeoff of the desirability of working with a single vendor versus the ability of the vendor to provide process definition assistance. Since most vendors focus on the technical side, a third-party would be a better choice if significant process definition assistance is required.

  If the tool vendor is under consideration to handle the implementation, it should be vetted through the same process as any other third party integrator would be.
- Because processes are being merged, the business owners will need to be involved intimately with the project at least at the beginning, to ensure the success of the process side.

# Finding Integrators

We already mentioned the tool vendor as a resource to find integrator candidates. Make sure that you get more than one suggestion from the vendor since you may not find a perfect match with the first candidate.

Colleagues are another good source of references. However, one of the main requirements for integrators is that they have worked with the tool before, so your network may or may not yield good results there. A great way to find integrators is to ask the reference accounts for the tool. At least the ones that had recent implementation projects should be able to give you particularly interesting suggestions.

Build the long list by keeping the following basic requirements in mind for the candidates:

- They should have **experience with the tool**. Even if your project is heavy on process definition or change management, look for an integrator with the appropriate technical expertise. You don't want to be the guinea pig on their first project with that particular tool.
- They should have successful **experience with similarly sized projects**. Asking an integrator with a history of small projects to take on a large one is clearly dangerous, but asking an integrator with large project experience to take on a small one can be just as frustrating to everyone involved, as complex, overly bureaucratic methods and approaches can overwhelm internal resources and enthusiasm.
- They should have appropriate **geographic coverage**. It's possible to work with a far-away integrator, but it's more difficult and always more expensive because of the travel costs. While the nitty-gritty code development could occur anywhere (and, increasingly, is done overseas), it's best to stick with local project managers and architects.

### Is Small Beautiful?

Many (good) integrators are boutique firms that are unknown outside the community of users of the particular tool you are considering. Don't be afraid to keep such smaller integrators on your list of candidates as long as they can meet your business requirements. Boutique firms that are focused on a particular tool provide an excellent level of technical expertise for a much better value than larger, better-known firms.

## Evaluating Integrators

Evaluating integrators is just as important as evaluating tools. Evaluating integrators is more difficult than evaluating tools because it's pretty much impossible to demo an implementation process. You will have to rely a lot more on references and other indirect checks. However, the evaluation process is basically the same as what was recommended to evaluate tools:

- You need a **requirements list**; that is, you need to define what you expect from the integrator versus what you will provide through your internal resources.
- You need an effective **reference checking strategy** to evaluate the various points on your requirements list.

- You need a **scoring mechanism** to evaluate the various points on your requirements list.

Your task is to confirm that the integrator has been successful with projects similar to yours in the past, and that the staff that will be assigned to your project will be the same or of the same caliber as staff that participated in past projects so that you can expect the same level of success. Therefore the first step is to be very clear about what your project requirements are so you can identify similar projects and benchmark against them.

## Integrator Requirements List

Building a requirements list for an integrator is very similar to building the requirements list for the tool: you need to define what you want and need, you need to capture it in reasonable detail, and you need to identify the high-priority items. The project team creates the requirement list for the integrator selection just like for the tool requirements list, although usually only a small subgroup is involved. The IT owner usually plays a key role in creating the integrator requirements, especially if the project is mostly focused on technical issues.

The integrator requirements include five categories: corporate fit, methodology, technical expertise, experience, and price. They are discussed here together with many suggestions on how to approach each area with the integrator candidates.

**Corporate Fit**  Although you don't need to be quite as demanding about the corporate fit with the integrator as you would about the fit with the tool vendor, you do need to check its financial health and strategic focus, especially for larger implementations. Make sure that the integrator will be able to sustain your implementation comfortably through the rollout stage and a little beyond, just to be sure. For instance, the integrator should have a long-term focus on the tool you have chosen.

**Methodology**  To be successful, integrators must have a system that is logical and repeatable and that encompasses your requirements, whether they are technical or business-based.

- Does the integrator use a proven methodology to drive projects to a successful conclusion?

    There should be identifiable stages for defining, executing, and testing with tangible milestones, together with an acknowledgement that the reality is not always as well structured as the theory. Many integrators incorporate at least some so-called Rapid Application Development (RAD) methods, whereby multiple prototypes are shared with the users and refined until a positive and complete outcome is achieved. Such methods accelerate development by making sure developers get feedback early on.

- How does the integrator minimize project risk?

  For any implementation project you want to identify the high-risk areas early on and get them working and tested first (or at least as soon as possible) so that a backup strategy can be defined and executed in case there is a problem. It's always interesting to contrast the points of view of several integrators on what they think the high-risk areas are. Ask the tool vendor, too!

  Ask many questions about testing. There should be both unit testing (does it work for one person) and load testing (does it work for bunches of people).

- How does the integrator elicit and maintain support from the business owners?

  There should be mechanisms in place to ensure good communication both on a regular basis and on an exception basis. Look for a mix of formal and informal communication techniques. Chapter 9 includes practical suggestions so you may want to read ahead for inspiration.

- Can the integrator handle process definition and implementation? Is the integrator familiar with best practices in the areas that you are considering? Can the integrator handle detailed task analysis if that's the level of detail you need?

  This is usually an easy item to evaluate. A short conversation with the integrator staffers should tell you whether they have heard about consultative selling, issue routing, or whatever other business process area you are concerned about. Make sure that the integrator is not blindly wedded to a particular way to approach the business process, unless you are yourself convinced it's the only way to go.

- Can the integrator help you with change management?

  Change management is a part of each CRM project since by definition the CRM tool will be a change. However you may have particularly high requirements in this area if there will be significant process changes, if there is internal opposition to the project, or if there are lots of other changes happening at the same time. Integrators that flatly state that you should be handling all change management issues have a purely technical approach to implementation and may not be right

for you. Thoroughly review this particular point when checking references if you have any concerns about it.
- How does the integrator measure success?

  Look for meaningful business metrics being defined at the start of each project and measured throughout. Metrics that start and stop with the project (for instance "deliver the project on time and on budget") are good but not sufficient.
- How does the integrator handle post-deployment issues?

  Most projects need tidying up after deployment, beyond the expected handholding required for the rollout, even if the project was successful overall. Experienced integrators plan for that so that required hardware adjustments or software changes can be handled properly. Beware abrupt departures on the day of the rollout.

  Will you need long-term support? Some, but not all integrators offer full-blown support services.
- Is documentation developed? What kind? How is knowledge transfer handled for system administrators?

  Since most integrators do not provide long-term support, it's essential to transfer knowledge to the IT staffers who will administer and support the system after implementation. Integrators usually create some written documentation, which ranges from sketchy to robust, but it's best if the integrator has some way of getting the system administrators meaningfully involved and briefed along the way rather than relying on a hasty discussion at the very end of the project.
- How does the integrator handle end-user training?

  Some integrators don't do it at all, which is fine, but in that case they need to build in time and a process to provide information to the curriculum developers.

**Technical Expertise** Methodology isn't everything; the integrators also need to have the technical resources that you need.
- What is the background of your project managers? How do they approach their work? What are typical items that the project manager handles and which items doesn't he or she handle?

  In many ways, good project management is the key to a successful project, so make time to understand what project managers do and who they are. Ideally, you want to meet the project manager that will be assigned to your project ahead of time. Sadly, project managers are usually assigned late in the game so you won't really know who the project manager will be until he or she starts. You should be able to make a pretty good assessment based on the project managers you meet during the evaluation, however. Make sure you understand whether project managers manage the entire project or just the technical side. Probe both their project management skills and their communication skills.

- What technical resources are available to the integrator? Are the resources employees or subcontractors? What skills and experience are present on the team?

If you find it difficult to determine who the project manager will be ahead of time, you will probably find it impossible to find out who any of the other individuals will be, so here again you will have to make do with overall impressions.

Integrators often use subcontractors so probe about the type and quality of subcontractors used. If an integrator subcontracts out all work of a particular type, question why they choose not to do that type of work in-house.

Specifically probe for the technical areas that are required for your project. If you are integrating with SAP, look for SAP expertise. If you are doing a wireless project, look for experience in that area. Don't assume *anything* and ask about network, database, operating system, etc. that match your configuration.

- How long have employees been with the integrator?

Skilled resources have many appealing choices when it comes to employment, and consulting is a tough way of life, in particular because of the travel requirements. If the integrator you are considering is managing to keep employees for a long time it's a good sign that things are going well there. Also, long-tenured employees have more experience and that should be good for your project, too!

**Experience** A good methodology and a good set of skills are critical ingredients, but can the integrator combine them into successful projects? Look for integrators who have recently completed projects using the same tool, with the same level of technical complexity (customizations and integrations). They should have worked with a comparable number of users and a similar distribution of those users. Consider whether they have done an implementation for an organization in a similar industry, that is, retail if you are doing retail, selling complex products to Fortune 500 companies if that's what you do, etc.

Ask the integrator for examples of similar projects. If the integrator suggests projects that are widely different from your requirements, this may be a sign that the integrator doesn't understand your business and you need to keep looking.

The next section, about checking references, goes into more details about how to gauge similarities between projects.

**Price**   Price is an important element of selecting an integrator. Because integrator pricing is less flexible than tool pricing, you should bring up pricing earlier in the evaluation process.

- What is your target price?

  There's no sense in evaluating an integrator that's way outside your price range. Although no serious integrator will give you a firm quote early in the game, you should be able to get ballpark estimates once you have defined the tool and a high-level strategy.

- How does the integrator determine pricing?

  Some integrators offer fixed-price but many do not. If you have a preference, better find out early on.

We'll talk about price negotiation strategies in the major section

## Evaluating the Integrator

The process for evaluating the integrator is similar to the process for evaluating the tool. In particular, you may choose to use an RFP. There are some differences, however. Many items on your requirements list will require checking references since they are not as tangible as the items on the tool requirement list. (You should be able to eliminate completely unsuitable candidates before the reference check.) Also, since the consulting business has a heavy communication component, trust your instincts when it comes to communicating and customer service. If a particular integrator candidate is not delivering in that area before the sale, you can be sure that things won't improve appreciably after the sale.

## Checking Integrators' References

**Selecting References**   Selecting references for the integrator is very similar to selecting references for the tool. Actually, it would be ideal to use the same references for both, since it would save you time and also make for stronger, all-around references. Ask the tool references who did the implementation for them: you may get good ideas, or at least interesting feedback. Look for references that have gone through similar projects reasonably recently. "Similar" means that the projects should be:

- For the **same tools.** The main reason to go outside to staff an implementation project (beyond the requirement for bodies) is to benefit from the expertise of the individuals you are bringing in. Therefore, for me, successful implementation experience with the very tool or tools you are selecting is not negotiable.

- For roughly the **same technical complexity.** It's not easy to gauge the technical complexity of a project before you start it, but as a rough estimate you can compare the level of customizations and the number and type of integrations. It's also very useful to consider projects for companies with similar business models since that has important consequences for CRM systems.

- With **equivalent business consulting requirements.** For instance, if you need process definition assistance, check that the integrator has successful experience there. If you want the integrator to handle end-user training, they should present you with a reference for whom they handled it.

- For about the **same number of users**, and, ideally a similar distribution of users. Deploying a system for 20 users is completely different than for 300, both in the infrastructure requirements and in the level of customizations that will be required. A mismatch is just as bad if the integrator usually works with much larger projects. I was once a part of a tool implementation for a smallish company that decided to work with what was then one of the "Big Five" consulting companies. The integrator had plenty of experience with similar projects, but all of it was gained while working with much larger organizations. Although the integrator deployed a very much scaled-down team for that particular project, their approach almost overwhelmed the company's staff with an overly formal and thorough methodology. The project was successful in the end, but it was much more painful than it could have been.

- **In production**. The proof is in the pudding. It can be useful to talk to references that are still in the implementation process, in particular to gauge how best to work with the integrator during the implementation, but you must talk to references that are in production to confirm that the process is indeed successful. Make sure that reference has been in production through business peaks such as quarter ends or the holiday season, depending on your business model. Reasonably recent implementations are best, since the tool won't have changed too much since them.

Integrators should be able to supply you with references. If the integrator cannot come up with production references for the same tool, complexity, and number of users, it's a red flag and you should select another integrator.

**Asking the Right Questions** When you talk to the references you will want to check the items from the requirements list that you could not confirm directly. You also want to confirm all aspects of the implementation projects they went through with the integrator. The questions below give you a structure for organizing the questions.

I like to ask the same questions to the integrator and to the reference and I compare their answers. If the integrator tells you that the project was on budget, but the reference disagrees, check what the size of the difference might have been. Perceptions are important for consulting work so any gaps between the answers are potential flags for you.

- Describe the project the integrator worked on for you.

    This is a calibrating question to make sure that the project characteristics are reasonable matches for yours in terms of technical complexity, user base, and the types of services the integrator provided. Was it a team effort with the internal team? Was the integrator asked to lead a process definition effort? If the project is significantly different from yours, thank the reference and check with someone else.

- When did the project take place?

    Check that the project is now in full production but still reasonably recent. Several months of successful production are ideal as long as they include a business peak. Don't waste time checking references with an account that is not in production yet.

- Did you participate in the implementation?

    You want to talk to someone who was on the implementation team, preferably the business owner or the IT owner—ideally both. If the reference no longer works for the organization where the implementation took place, go through the reference check but ask to talk to someone within the organization to confirm that the tool is still in place and functioning properly.

    Don't bother checking references with someone who did not participate actively in the implementation. Such an individual will not be able to respond to most of your questions anyway.

- Describe the overall implementation process.

  Listen carefully for signs of an orderly process that matches what the integrator described to you. If you hear something quite different from the integrator's description, go back to the integrator. It could be that it is now using a new process (which may be a good thing, although you should decide whether you want to be a guinea pig) or it could be that the neatly described process is for pre-sales use only. The latter is a potential red flag.

- Was the project on time?

  Accept that all projects are a little late, and the delays are not always caused by any problems on the side of the integrator. I would not worry about a small delay, say 10% of the total length, and I would not worry about even a large discrepancy if there is a "good" reason for it, such as the customer putting a temporary halt to the project for financial or other business reasons.

  On the other hand, delays caused by unforeseen, last minute technical issues are a red flag. Should the integrator have predicted the problem and tested that particular part of the project earlier? Also probe delays caused by political issues, since a good integrator should be able to skillfully manage the client and to anticipate when the business owners have not bought into the project, or the executive sponsor is flagging, both common causes of project delays.

  Probe how well the integrator handled the delay. Were efforts made to mitigate the delay? To work around issues? To communicate with the client to explain the delay and the action plan?

- Was the project within budget?

  Here again, expect some overage and remember that clients often choose to add features midway through projects. Find out whether the integrator pushed back on scope creep. It's usually better if large, newly discovered requirements are scheduled for a second phase. It shows that the integrator did a decent job of gathering requirements in the first place so that the last-minute candidates are not absolutely required for the initial rollout. It also demonstrates that the integrator has the skill and strength to manage to an orderly process.

- How was the communication process? What worked and what did not work?

  Most implementation projects are long and suffer at least one major problem, as we will see in the next chapter. Therefore, good communication is essential. If the report is particularly positive, find out who the project manager was and try to get the same individual to work on your project.

- What worked very well? Why did it work well?

   Note any characteristics that are meaningful to you. For instance, if the references are praising the benefits of a kickoff workshop while you don't think you can bring your team together for such an exercise, it may be the proof that you just have to make it happen. As another example, if the references liked a very hands-off approach but you feel you need close ties with the integrator, you may want to rethink your approach or find another integrator who would provide a more hands-on approach.

- What did not go so well? What would you do differently next time?

   Most references don't like to say anything negative, so gently probe until you get an answer. Pay attention to statements such as "The integrator wanted to do X but we did not, and in the end we should have followed their suggestion." Was the integrator clear enough in presenting arguments? Did the integrator simply fold under pressure? You want an integrator with a bit of a backbone. If an item is critical, a good integrator should know to push back even if the client is persistent. Figure out how much pushback the integrator managed.

   It's a red flag to hear something like "We wanted to do X, but the integrator refused and then we had to do it over."

- Anything you did not implement that you wish you had? What was the involvement of the integrator in this particular decision?

   Try to determine if the integrator should have foreseen the situation, and how the situation was handled if the gap was discovered prior to the end of the project.

- Anything you did do that you now think was useless? What was the involvement of the integrator in this particular decision?

   If anything pops up here that you are thinking of doing yourself, make a note of it. Although each implementation is unique, you may be able to take something off the list, especially if the reference is very similar to you. Again question whether the integrator should have provided better advice on the decision.

- Did you hit any problems during the implementation? What were they? What did you do to overcome them?

   Unless the project being referenced is extremely simple, insist on an answer to this question. I have yet to encounter a single implementation where there was no problem whatsoever. Most implementations encounter at least one large problem, so the question is not whether a problem occurred, but rather whether it should have been forecasted, and how well it was handled. Did the integrator take an active role in finding a solution, even if the problem was not something it created? Was the integrator creative?

- Anyone particularly good on the team? Anyone weaker than the rest?

  Take note of the individuals that are particularly recommended and try to get them assigned to your project. Be warned, it's a difficult task since the stronger people tend to be in great demand. If the stars have moved on, find out why, since the strong people tend to abandon ship first when there's trouble aboard.

  Specially request that weaker individuals not be assigned to your project, at least if their weaknesses are relevant to your project. Be sure to ask about subcontractors as well.

- Did you participate in selecting the integrator? What criteria did you use for the selection? Who were the other candidates?

  Perhaps you are considering the same candidates and, if so, you could learn much from how the references ended up selecting one over the other. You may even end up making the opposite decision they made because your requirements are different.

- Do you think you got good value from the integrator? Why or why not?

  Comparing prices with the references is not that useful since each project is different. Talking about value is more helpful since it focuses on the outcome. Explore where the value could have been greater and adapt your project accordingly.

- Would you use the integrator again on a new project? Why or why not?

  This is a classic reference-checking question, but always useful, especially when you hear the reasons for the choice.

# Negotiating With Integrators

Once you have chosen your preferred integrator, it's time to negotiate the best possible agreement. Much as in the case of the agreement with the tool vendor, it's very important to negotiate the contract carefully, even if you are thrilled with your choice. It's true that the span of the contract with the integrator is limited, unlike the contract with the vendor that has consequences for the very long term through the support terms. However, surprises during the implementation have very negative consequences on the quality, date, and cost of the rollout, so it pays to scrutinize the contract.

## Fixed Price or Time and Materials?

A fixed price contract promises to deliver a fixed scope for a given price. A time-and-materials (T&M) contract is a "pay as you go" arrangement, in which the final price is unknown and depends on what is required along the way, although T&M contracts often include a not-to-exceed price.

Many people believe that a fixed price contract is the only way to contain costs and is therefore the only way to go. Whereas fixed price contracts are indeed alluring, the concept of a fixed scope creates its own dilemmas.

- The critical issue is that they **require that the scope be known upfront**. This is not a trivial matter for larger CRM implementations, in which many issues need to be resolved prior to making any implementation-related decisions so that the scope is essentially unknown at the time the initial contract is negotiated.
- Partially because the scope is rarely crisp from the start, fixed priced contracts tend suffer from the **incredibly shrinking scope** syndrome. The integrator keeps pushing features to the phase two list in an attempt to keep the scope within the originally agreed upon mold. As a result, the initial rollout can be unattractively skimpy and potentially derail the project as users are turned off by it.

This is not to say that T&M contracts are perfect. They offer little incentive for the integrator to contain costs and they therefore require a very hands-on project manager with good cost-control procedures to avoid wild bills. So what to do?

If your project is small and relatively easy to scope, then go with a fixed-price project. You should be able to both define the scope properly and keep to it without problems.

If your project is larger, try using successive fixed scopes. Start with a fixed-price implementation requirements definition phase. Although the scope of the entire project is not known at this point, the integrator should be able to define how long it will take to figure out the scope (and it should not take months, either). The outcome of the requirements definition project is a detailed list of requirements, which outlines the scope of the project.

From the detailed implementation requirements list, the integrator may be able to define a fixed-price deliverable for the entire project. If you are still working out some of the details for the rollout, then perhaps a fixed-price bid can be created for the coding project only, with the rollout bid coming later. At the very least, even for the most complex projects, the integrator should be able to proceed to a fixed-price bid for the detailed coding requirements phase.

Each successive subproject should have a clearly identifiable deliverable, theoretically usable even if the integrator doesn't participate in the next phase. Switching integrators almost never happens since the ramp-up time for a new team is prohibitive, but it's good practice to require deliverables that can stand on their own at each step of the way.

In the end, don't worry too much about the way the payment is structured. As long as you have strong references and you are managing the project properly (we'll see how in the next chapter), you should be able to be just as successful—and just as thrifty—with a fixed price contract as you would be with a T&M arrangement.

## Contract Checklist

Involve your legal team in the contract negotiation so it can catch any issues that may not be captured or are not sufficiently detailed here. Use this checklist as inspiration, not a replacement for legal advice.

- **What is the scope**? It's often difficult to nail down the scope of the project right from the start, but attach the best requirement document that you have available to the contract. Assume that anything that's not specifically described in the scope is not included. Common areas of fuzziness include who will specify, purchase, and install the development, test, and production environments; who will provide training and documentation for the project, and what they may consist of; and how much rollout assistance will be provided, including fixing any bugs discovered during the rollout.

- **What are the milestones**? They should be described as concrete deliverables whenever possible, and they typically require some kind of signoff process. Payments should be associated with milestones rather than be made on a fixed schedule. A modest deposit of 10-20% is fine, however.

- **Who will work on the project**? Are any subcontractors used? The number and skills of at least the main players should be identified. It's best if the critical individuals are identified by name, including the project manager and the technical lead, although it's often impossible to get that kind of commitment in writing.

You may want to request prior approval of all the members of the integrator's team, but the integrator will usually push back on such a request. In any case, expect delays in starting up the project if you insist on screening the team members.

- **When does the project start**? You don't want to be kept waiting while the integrator lines up the team.
- **When does the project end**? Are there any penalties associated with a late delivery? Because a lot depends on your team's ability to handle specific items and to approve deliverables, contracts very rarely include late completion penalties. You can try for an early completion bonus, however.
- **Who owns the code**? It's crucial to check that code developed on the project actually belongs to you so you can use it and change it in any way that you see fit. If it's important to you that your code not be reused, specify that.
- **Are non-disclosure guarantees in place**? The nature of CRM projects means that some or a lot of confidential information will have to circulate to the project team. Typically, non-disclosure agreements are in place even before a delivery contract is in place to allow the detailed discussions required to establish scope. Make sure that non-disclosure agreements also apply to subcontractors.
- **Is there appropriate liability insurance**? Integrators typically decline responsibility for liability related to the project itself (that is, if the installed tool miscalculates commission payments, they won't be held liable for erroneous calculations) but make sure you are covered if an employee or a subcontractor slips and falls while at your site.
- **Who pays for travel costs**? The answer is easy—you do—so the real question is actually what the travel costs add up to. With larger integrators, some team members may travel from afar to participate in the project. You may want to define reasonable costs for travel, for instance by requesting that the integrator adhere to your travel policy. Note that travel costs are often added to fixed-price contracts, so you need to ask about them regardless of the pricing structure.

Make time for a thorough evaluation of and negotiation with the integrator. Picking a strong integrator is very much worth the effort, as it will determine the fate of the implementation, which is the topic of the next chapter.

# Implementing CRM Systems

## Express Version

- Implementation is just as critical to the success of your project as the initial tool selection.
- Start with a solid list of agreed upon objectives and requirements (these are detailed implementation requirements, not selection requirements). The best way to create the requirements list is to bring the entire implementation team together for a kickoff workshop. Having everyone in the room allows for fruitful brainstorming and immediate buy-in.
- Define the testing criteria at the start of the project. It helps clarify the requirements and contain scope creep.
- Plan for end-user training during the implementation and leverage the training development as a testing aid. Create self-paced training materials even if the initial training will be done face to face, for use as reinforcement and to train new hires.

- Make extra amounts of support available at rollout to ensure as smooth a start as possible.
- Frequent, short, face-to-face status checks during the implementation allow a better flow of information than standard written reports. Face-to-face status checks are particularly important when it comes to spotting emerging issues.
- To ensure that you get the most value out of the integration team, make sure you provide all contractors with the logistical support they need when they are onsite and maintain appropriate control on the project even if they work offsite.
- Super-users and other business users should be involved throughout the project to test that each milestone meets the requirements.
- All implementations go through problems, and some will be major issues. Schedule the high-risk work early on so you can spot problems early and therefore have more time to invent creative solutions.
- Promote the new tools to employees and to customers during the implementation. Be upbeat but conservative about what can be expected in the first phase of the implementation to avoid disappointments.
- Hold a post-mortem review after the project to identify high and low points, and especially opportunities for different approaches.

## Implementation Overview

This chapter describes how to manage a successful implementation once the tool and the integrator have been selected. It's true that the success of the overall project is very much correlated with the quality of the tool and of the integrator, so if you made careful selections you should be on your way to a successful implementation. However, CRM implementations are long and can be a little tricky, so well run implementations definitely make the difference between very successful projects and not so wonderful ones. A strong implementation will make a fair tool work well, while a poor implementation can make even a good tool perform poorly.

CRM implementations large and small include the following components:

- **Defining detailed implementation requirements**. This goes beyond the requirements that you created to frame the tool selection, although the tool selection requirements are a very good start. A good implementation requirements list is not only complete and detailed, it is also

understood and approved by all the stakeholders. We'll discuss how to get a quick and genuine buy-in in the next section.
- **Implementing the requirements** through coding and integration work. The coding piece is often the longest phase of the implementation. It's most effective when preceded by effective planning and when accompanied by frequent and focused communication within the project team.
- **Testing.** Testing needs to occur both for functionality and for load. We'll discuss how to leverage use tests to ensure that the business requirements are met and to improve the usability of the tool.
- **Training**. Although I firmly believe that CRM systems should be "intuitively obvious" to use, a short end-user training program that covers both the process and the tool is usually required. We'll see how to combine self-paced learning and instructor-led training to deliver effective training without breaking the bank.
- **Communicating with internal and external users** to ensure the acceptance of the system. This is an important and often neglected component of CRM projects. We will see that it's important to start early and to avoid an overly rah-rah approach that makes users suspicious and often sets expectations at an unrealistically high level, creating disappointment in the long run.

The two key principles for successful CRM implementations are to use rapid-development techniques that have proven to bring about high quality solutions faster than traditional techniques and to promote early customer acceptance throughout the development time. The techniques described below all relate to one or the other key principle.

Because this book is focused on the business side of CRM, this chapter discusses how to conduct the implementation and how to approach technical decisions from the business owners' perspective. The technical details of the implementation are only alluded to when they are relevant to the business owners.

# The Kickoff Workshop

There are many ways to define the implementation requirements. As long as they produce a complete set of requirements that users can agree on within a minimum amount of time, they are all valid. For me, the best way to define implementation requirements is to start by holding a team workshop focused on the requirements right at the start of the project. A team workshop is effective because having all the stakeholders in the room makes for excellent brainstorming, so you are less likely to neglect important aspects of the requirements. Moreover, since the workshop includes immediate discussions of any areas of disagreement between the interested parties, the team can identify, confront, and resolve issues so you can get to a group consensus quickly. I call this workshop the kickoff workshop.

## What Should It Cover?

The kickoff workshop is not a lightweight introduction to the implementation phase of the project, nor is it intended to create a detailed technical blueprint for the project. The workshop is meant to confirm measurable goals and a high-level project plan for the implementation. Specifically, the objectives of the workshop are to:

- Define measurable goals for the project.
- Identify gaps between the product and the desired result.
- Define a high-level project plan with schedule and owners.
- Identify large issues.

Let's examine each of them now.

**Define Measurable Goals**   Are you trying to increase revenue? Decrease costs? Increase customer satisfaction? Decrease lead turnaround time? The workshop is an opportunity not only to define the particular areas for improvement, but also to set measurable targets. Ideally, you should be able to measure your current level of performance and to forecast improvements from the baseline. If no baseline is available, define a target number that seems reasonable.

You must have all the stakeholders in the room to have a chance of defining goals for the project. The technical team members may have little say in setting the business objectives, and some of them don't have much exposure to the business side at all. Nevertheless it's important that everyone on the team understand the business goals since they will shape subsequent decisions. I like to start the workshop with the business goals since it gets the business owners emotionally engaged in the workshop (sometimes very much so!) and it sets the tone for the rest of the work.

You must end up with an agreed upon list of goals, not just discuss the goals at a general level or set tentative goals to be approved later. Since all the decision makers should be in the room you can press for firm decisions.

When you invite the business owners to the workshop, especially if the team is very large, tell them that the project goals will be set during the workshop so they can hold preliminary discussions with their teams if they wish and arrive at the workshop ready to commit to firm goals. The executive sponsor should attend at least the goal-setting portion of the workshop to reinforce and expedite the decision-making process.

**Identify Product Gaps**   Some teams like to start with a "blue sky" approach, where the business users are asked to model the ideal processes without thinking of the tool at all before the team attempts to reconcile the differences between the ideal processes and what the tool can do. I find that this approach takes a lot of time, since there may be many differences between the ideal process and the tool. It is also frustrating to the business users, who are asked to dream only to find out that their dreams cannot come true. Therefore, I prefer to start with a hands-on demo of the tool. I ask the business users to reflect on how they can use the tool to support the business processes and where changes will be required.

This particular part of the workshop can't get too far without having well-defined business processes in place. You need to include either a review of the current business processes if they are basically fine or a business process design session if the processes need work.

If you are creating processes from scratch, you can, in theory, follow the "blue-sky" method described above, and indeed some consultants recommend this approach as somehow more "pure" and likely to yield better efficiencies. I'm afraid that it often yields processes that require lots of customization work on the tool, hence causing delays and risks, while a more tool-centric approach is faster, cheaper, and safer. An experienced integrator should be able to facilitate the process definition phase of the workshop by suggesting common alternatives that can be implemented without too much trouble. The integrator may even go as far as starting with a quick demo of the tool to start on the right (low-customization) foot.

If large amounts of process definition work are required, it may be appropriate to dismiss most of the technical staffers from the workshop during that discussion since the value to them is small. However, all team members must be fully briefed on the outcome of the discussion.

It's very helpful to organize the process discussion around user roles, first defining what types of people (roles) will use the system and then what they will do with it. For instance, a telesales rep will perform certain tasks that are different from the tasks of a field rep, which are different from the tasks of the technical sales specialist. If you picked the super-users well all roles will be represented on the team so it will not be difficult to proceed.

The gap analysis should identify the critical changes and accommodations that are required to meet the business objectives defined earlier. The workshop leader (we'll come back to who this may be very soon) should gently question how each identified gap relates back to the objectives, especially if the team veers off into a mode of requiring extensive changes. As long as there is not a complete incompatibility between the tool and the process, it's easier, faster, and less risky to adapt the process to the tool rather than the other way round.

Especially if lots of process work is required, the executive sponsor should attend this portion of the workshop to guide the business users to reasonable compromises.

**Define A High-Level Project Plan**   No, I'm not crazy, at least not about the feasibility of creating a high-level plan during the workshop without having explored all the intricacies of the design. For starters, working from firm deadlines is a good discipline. That is, if you need a solution in six months, set a six-month goal and see what can and cannot be achieved within that timeframe, rather than building an ideal solution only to discover that it will take nine months. Second, with an experienced integrator and appropriate technical staff in the room, you should be able to make ballpark assessments of what is required for various implementation options (if not, the experience level in the room is insufficient). Third, with everyone in the room you can assign owners and get commitments that are witnessed by all, saving a lot of time compared to a more traditional process.

Attendees should understand that they will be expected to make commitments to a high-level project plan during the workshop so they can prepare appropriately prior to it and either consult with or bring along critical individuals as needed.

Kickoff workshops often identify functionality that cannot or should not be implemented in the first phase of the rollout. Start a list of such features right away, identifying specific phases whenever possible, so the business users can have an overview of when they will be rolled out.

**Identify Large Issues**   The last objective of the workshop is to catch large implementation issues, and ideally to resolve them. The point is not to find each and every issue that may exist, as that's not possible, but rather to identify significant challenges. For instance: the tool was purchased to serve

300 users, but another 120 also need to use it; the deployment environment was planned to reside in the main data center, but the data center has no room available; the target deployment date conflicts with the sales meeting; the tool is supposed to be integrated with the back-end accounting system but that system may change soon; etc.

Any large issue identified in the workshop and left without a resolution by the end of it must be assigned an owner who is responsible for resolving it and an early resolution target so it doesn't cause problems down the line. From the set of examples above, the deployment date can be adjusted not to conflict with the sales meeting right in the workshop. On the other hand, the issue of the changing accounting system will need to be settled with the owner of that system soon after the workshop and before integration work starts, probably by the IT owner on the team.

The end result and deliverable for the workshop is a high-level project plan that includes the desired, measurable goals for the project; high-level specifications for the customization, which will be fleshed out later; ownership of the various phases and aspects of the project; and a high-level schedule. For smaller projects, the deliverable can be the full specification set for the implementation.

To meet the objectives and create the deliverable, a typical agenda includes the following:

- An **introduction** to the project and to the workshop, including introductions of all the team members, a review of the schedule, logistics, and ground rules, led by the workshop leader.
- A session to define the **goals for the project**, introduced by the executive sponsor.
- A **review of the business processes** covered by the project, as well as critical business processes around it. For instance, for a sales automation project it would be useful to understand how orders are recorded and customers billed, even if it's done outside the system being deployed, since integration work may be required and in any case the order processing may require specific information from the system under construction. The project should not be allowed to go forward without a clear, agreed upon understanding of the underlying business processes.
- A **product demo and high-level gap analysis**. That is, the basic flow of the product should be demonstrated so that technical and business staffers can identify where the product supports the business processes and where it needs to be changed or added to. This is not the time to

worry about *how* the changes will be made, although it's very helpful if the integrator can gently challenge requirements that are known to be difficult and suggest easier alternatives.

This is the largest chunk of the workshop if business processes are reviewed rather than defined there and could take several days for complex projects. We'll come back to recommended workshop lengths a little later.

- Finally, a **review of the decisions** and requirements defined in the workshop and high-level plans for future steps. The review is more than a simple summary and includes a formal commitment from each team member to the decisions that were made during the workshop. The value of the workshop derives in great part from the strength of the commitments that are made in it and not just what the commitments contain.

## Who Should Be There?

Everyone! All project team members should participate in the workshop, including the business owners, the IT owner, the super-users, the technical staff, and of course the project manager. The executive sponsor should attend whenever possible, and in any case should introduce the session to reinforce the business goals and to inspire fruitful participation from all team members. If there is any possibility that political issues may mar the workshop, the executive sponsor should plan to attend it in its entirety.

One of the functions of the kickoff workshop is to define what additional talent may be required for the project, so it's possible and even likely that individuals who did not participate in the kickoff workshop will become part of the team later on. For instance, each and every programmer who will touch the tool doesn't participate in the workshop. Each and every IT function does not participate in the workshop. But the lead programmer (usually from the integrator) and the IT owner should attend and ensure that appropriate resources attend the workshop or are on call for any questions, especially the database administrator and the individuals responsible for any system that will be interfaced with the CRM tool.

## How Long Should It Be?

The length of the workshop is determined by the scope and complexity of the project. That being said, even a very simple project will require several hours to ensure that all aspects of the implementation are examined, while the law of diminishing returns dictates that the workshop not exceed a week even for a very large project. A good rule of thumb would be as follows:

- One day for simple projects, that is, point solutions for one business function with a small user base, and no more than a couple of integrations. Add half a day to a day to address process definition if processes are informal or are known to require changes.

- Two to three days for medium-complexity projects, that is, projects that target one or two business functions, for a moderately large user base, and with only a few integrations. Add another day to address significant process changes.

- Four to five days for high-complexity projects that address multiple business functions with lots of functionality, users, and integrations. It's simply not practical to keep the participants engaged and contributing for longer periods of time, so for the larger projects the best approach is to target only a high-level definition of the project for the kickoff, with follow-up work from various subgroups taking place afterwards to get to the level of detail required. Another feature of complex projects is that it's possible, necessary, and fruitful to run parallel sessions for each business function on some of the topics so even though you have only 4-5 days you should be able to multitask for 2-3 of those days.

Some groups work faster than others, and some groups work more harmoniously than others, which also makes for faster results, but it's very unlikely you will be able to compress the timelines significantly. Plan for a reasonable timeframe and reward fast-working groups with an early dismissal.

Although it's theoretically possible to hold the kickoff workshop in short segments spread over days or weeks, it's much more efficient to schedule it in one go. Much momentum is built by scheduling a single session and it's easier to get everyone together in one place if team members need to travel to the session.

Since many individuals on the team are involved in customer-facing operations, schedule breaks during the workshop so they can take care of urgent issues. It's best to schedule two or three longer breaks during the day rather than sprinkling short breaks here and there. Frequent short breaks are never long enough to accomplish anything significant and create challenges when trying to regroup. The breaks can be used profitably by the workshop leader and other key individuals to regroup, summarize, and get ready for the next session.

## Where Should It Be Held?

Standard wisdom is that kickoff workshops should be held in an offsite location to ensure that participants don't wander off to take care of other business. I find that offsite locations can be a hassle for participants to get to (and you want happy participants in the kickoff workshop, trust me on this!). More importantly, they make it difficult to include unplanned participants when needed, which is not unusual for the more obscure IT specialties. Sure, you can call people by phone, but since kickoff workshops are usually heavy on pictures and notes scattered about boards and flipchart paper, a phone conversation is usually not enough.

The decision between onsite and offsite mainly comes down to discipline. The issue is not so much the physical location but your ability to maintain the participants' attention on the topics at hand; although you could herd the bodies it's really a matter of herding the minds. If you are concerned that an onsite meeting will be poorly attended, by all means go offsite, but try to stay close enough to be able to include last-minute participants. Anticipate that you will encounter other problems that can crop up in an undisciplined environment.

The kickoff workshop is the one meeting that should be held with all the participants in the same room. Brainstorming sessions and complex decisions are best made with lots of notes and interactions, which no conference call can simulate. It's quite possible to use conference calls to discuss status during the project, but not for the kickoff.

Especially for multi-day workshops, select a location that offers a comfortable environment with room to move around, plenty of note-taking equipment (flipcharts work best since you can post sheets around the rooms and even take them back to the office to extract notes) and a number of smaller breakout rooms. Sometimes it's difficult to find a suitable environment onsite, and that's a good reason to seek an offsite venue. Try to find a place that is secure overnight so you can leave all the notes in place from day to day. Also, since you will need to do a demo of the product, and perhaps to access some of the in-house systems to check technical facts, an appropriate computer system with a dialup capability and a projection system is a must and is yet another reason why onsite venues are desirable.

Finally, kickoff workshops can get intense. Being able to indulge in recreational activities is a plus, even if it's nothing more than a walk in a park.

## Who Should Drive It?

It seems obvious that the project manager should drive the kickoff workshop, but it's sometimes the case that someone else would be better at it. Let's start by reviewing the characteristics of a good workshop leader.

- **Understanding of the business issues.** The workshop leader doesn't need to be intimately familiar with the way the organization does business (and actually it's often better if the workshop leader is somewhat detached from the issues) but the leader should be conversant with the business concepts and terminology and the technical issues at hand. The goal here is to be credible with all members of the team.
- **Disciplined but flexible**. The leader needs to make sure all topics get attended to within the time allotted, but without making the participants feel trapped into an inflexible agenda. Diverting from the stated schedule or goals is just fine if circumstances change, and a rigid approach is counterproductive.
- **Not a key decision-maker.** The workshop leader should not get dragged into the minutiae of the meeting, and should certainly not take sides in any particular discussion. It's usually best not to place a key business owner in that position for fear of squashing the debate.
- **A bit of a cheerleader**. Even short workshops have low points. The workshop leader should be able to sense when the participants are getting discouraged or frustrated and to offer appropriate comfort. A sense of humor is also very helpful.

If the project manager doesn't have the appropriate skills to lead the workshop, pick someone else from the team who does. The project manager, the workshop leader if it's not the project leader, and the other key players should carefully plan the workshop ahead of time to ensure that the attendees, agenda, and location are conducive to an effective meeting.

## Managing A Successful Workshop

**Breakout Sessions**   Much of the power of the workshop lies in having all the players exchanging ideas and creating agreements and commitments. However, there are good reasons to also include breakout sessions that focus on specific issues. Some of the topics are of marginal interest to some of the participants; a brief exposure can achieve the desired awareness and commitment while avoiding a long, boring, interest-sapping session.

Therefore, the typical agenda includes a mix of group and breakout sessions, at least for larger projects. Kickoff workshops for simple projects are usually short enough that breakout sessions are more trouble than they are worth (and, to be sure, with a small team breakout sessions don't make much sense). For longer workshops, breakout sessions are useful for two topics.

- **Defining business processes.** If all that's needed is a review of the existing processes and a small amount of tuning, then a group session is sufficient. But if you need a lengthy session it can be conducted with only the business users in attendance since the technical staffers would have little input anyway. Regardless of whether you have a breakout session to define process, hold a review of the processes for the entire team. The technical staffers should be exposed to the business processes since they will need to integrate those processes into the technical deliverable.

- **Performing the gap analysis.** Unless you have a small group, start the gap analysis with a reasonably short group session and then break out into subgroups to get to the next level of detail. Ask the business staffers to focus on process gaps while the technical staffers focus on technical issues. Organize the business staffers by business functions so sales employees look at sales issues, marketing employees look at marketing issues, etc., if multiple functions are represented. If you prefer, you can ask the managers to look at management processes while the support-users concentrate on individual contributors' issues. Meanwhile, the technical staffers should work in specialty groups so the database folks look at data model issues, the network people talk about the network issues, etc.

   Headcount permitting, it's very useful to do some mixing and matching for the gap analysis breakout sessions. For instance, invite some service folks and some technical folks to attend the sales gap analysis. They may not be able to provide much information but they should be able to contribute interesting questions since they are free from the idea that "we've always done things that way." Even if it's not possible to assign outsiders to the breakout sessions, encourage each subgroup to pull from other groups when they feel it would be beneficial to add cross-functional expertise.

While breakout sessions are useful for some topics, others should be strictly handled through group sessions because requiring the entire team to participate makes for a better informed and more committed team. For instance, defining the business goals can be viewed as the exclusive domain of the business users and indeed it is, to a great extent. But I would definitely hold it as a group session to ensure that the technical staff is fully briefed on this foundation topic.

Finally, even those topics that lend themselves to breakout sessions must be concluded with a group presentation where each team presents its work and others are encouraged to ask questions. Such group presentations facilitate cross-pollination and buy-in from the entire team. If the breakout sessions are particularly long, I also like to punctuate them with group sessions every few hours to exchange updates. It's good for teamwork and it's a good incentive for each team to avoid long and fruitless discussions in breakout sessions since they have a short-term goal of preparing a meaningful update.

**Records** The deliverable for the end of the workshop is a high-level project plan, including the objectives for the project, a high-level description of the customizations and integrations required, and an overall project plan including schedule and owner. Moreover, that project plan should be approved by all the stakeholders, who should be in the room if your project team is properly designed. Since you are going both for content and for decisions, I strongly suggest eschewing traditional minutes and concentrating instead on building the project plan document right during the workshop.

At least for larger meetings, it's best to designate an individual other than the workshop leader to do the recording so the leader can concentrate on the management task. (If the project manager is not leading the workshop, that individual is a good candidate.) Capture relevant notes and pictures drawn on boards and flipcharts.

Make time every day or every half-day to review the draft plan and to confirm the team's approval. Approval should not be difficult to get since you are recording facts and decisions that attendees have agreed to already.

Note that the project manager must keep detailed records on all agreements and decisions made at any time during the project. This is not a trivial requirement since CRM projects are long and complex. Some attention to how the records are kept and how they are made accessible to the team members is useful from the start of the project.

# A Few Technical Notes on the Implementation

Let's now consider two technical issues that have implications in business decisions starting early in the project: the issue of the development environment versus the production environment, and the issue of migrating data from existing tools to the new tool. Both should be addressed and a strategy developed in the kickoff workshop.

## Development/Test/Production Environments

It's good practice to maintain three distinct hardware and software environments for CRM systems (or any other systems for that matter): one for development, where any coding and changes are performed, one for testing, where development changes are checked before impacting any real work, and one for production, where the users do their work. The advantage of maintaining three different systems is that it's possible to experiment safely without impacting the production environment.

At the start of the CRM project you only need the development environment, of course. If you are using an integrator, it's likely that the development system will reside there, which allows the programmers to be more productive and which typically requires little setup work. At some point down the line you will need to create a development environment at your site so you can handle further development past the rollout date, if nothing else. Development environments are very small versions of the real thing and therefore easier to set up and much less expensive. Nevertheless, make sure that the setup of the development environment is planned and scheduled appropriately, down to who will be responsible for purchasing, installing, and configuring each piece.

The testing environment is required from the first series of tests, as we will see below, and even earlier if the development environment is set up at the integrator's site so you cannot use it to do demos or other work at your site. The testing environment should resemble the production environment as much as possible if you want to run realistic tests, although it's usually on a smaller scale. Here again, determine who will purchase, install, and configure the test systems.

One major concern about maintaining the development, testing, and production environments is devising a robust system for migrating code and data from one to the other. It's best to have an automated system to do that to avoid human errors. Sadly, many CRM tools are very weak in that area. Follow the suggestions of the integrators for how best to handle the migration to minimize effort and mishaps.

Many smaller companies cannot afford to maintain three different environments, and indeed some companies work with only one. It's clearly dangerous to make unproven changes right in the production environment, so try to maintain at least two environments, so you can develop and test on one without impacting production.

## Data Migration

If you are moving from an existing system to a new system, you will have to face the issue of migrating existing data to the new system. Existing data usually requires some amount of coaxing to match the new data structure, and sometimes quite a lot. Therefore, before you undertake what can be a very large effort indeed, you should think long and hard about whether the old data is worth transferring, and how you can make sure that the data you want to transfer is as "clean" as can be.

For instance, if the old system contains your customer database, you probably will want to move it to the new system. But is the data in the database correct? For instance, if you have scads of dormant customers, you probably don't need to bother transferring them. If you have duplicates, or other bad quality information, you should put in place a data-cleansing program rather than moving junk over. After you spend time and effort cleaning up the data for the migration, you'll want to keep it clean, so define an ongoing process for checking and cleansing data. This is not a part of the CRM project per se and may not have much impact for months, but it's one of those additional touches that make the difference between so-so and great CRM implementations.

As you analyze data to be migrated you may find that some is not worth moving at all. A common example is old knowledge base documents. In a fast-paced world, documents over a year old, or documents that are waiting for review are probably of little use and should simply be left behind. Make a backup if that makes you feel better, although I bet you will never use it. The same is true with old service calls or old sales records. Don't expand effort migrating data that will not be used.

# Testing

The technical team should be able to construct, set up, and perform appropriate testing for the project. The aim of this section is not to create a checklist for the technical team, but rather to describe how the business users can assist in creating test cases and performing some of the testing.

## Use Cases

An excellent technique for testing applications is the awkwardly named "use cases." A use case is, very simply, a short scenario for real-world functionality. For instance, Table 9.1 is a use case for identifying a customer who is calling for assistance from a help desk system.

**TABLE 9.1** Use Case Example for a Customer Assistance Call

| Use Case | Perform customer search |
| --- | --- |
| Actors | Help Desk rep |
| Purpose | Find a customer based on information provided to the support rep. |
| Overview | From the Main screen: Enter the search information in the customer area. Press "Search" button. Is all the information visible (name, building, etc.)? Repeat test after adding a new customer to the database. Is the new customer visible? Repeat test after removing a customer from the database. Is the customer no longer visible (deactivated)? Repeat test after changing a customer record in the customer database. Is the change reflected? |
| Cross References | Search for a customer case. |

The purpose of use cases is to define the required functionality of the system before it is implemented through tasks that need to be performed with specific outcomes. There should be a use case for each piece of functionality required, so you are looking at dozens of use cases for fairly simple systems and hundreds for larger systems. They should capture all the different tasks that end-users perform with the system. Going back to the idea of user roles discussed in the section about the kickoff meeting, each role will have a number of use cases specific to that role (and, to be sure, some use cases will be shared across roles).

Use cases are, of course, used for testing, but they are also very useful to the developers to confirm the exact functionality required. Defining use cases ahead of time makes it easier to resist scope creep and also to get user buy-in since testing occurs against the very tests that the users designed, not some mysterious technical requirements.

Use cases should be created as a part of the project specifications document, and they must be created and approved by the user community, not by the technical team. They are rarely created during the kickoff workshop since they are rather too detailed for it, and they cannot be finalized until the high-level technical design is completed anyway. They are usually the very first action item for the business users immediately following the kickoff workshop. During the kickoff workshop you should be able to list the titles of the use cases (since they match the various business processes that are discussed there) and for simple projects you may get all the way to a first draft at least.

## Functionality Testing

User testing should occur at each milestone, using the use cases that are appropriate for that portion of the tool being delivered at the milestone. Super-users should conduct the testing against the use cases, although other end-users may be recruited as well. The technical team should run through the use cases before the delivery, but the technical staffers, not knowing the business purpose behind the cases (and, to be sure, knowing entirely too much about the tool) often miss subtle and not so subtle issues with the use cases, issues that are spotted within seconds by the business users.

It's very useful to get multiple individuals to perform the tests. Untrained testers have inconsistent approaches to testing and may miss crucial misbehaviors, which is also true of trained testers but to a much smaller degree. Whenever possible, hold the testing in a central lab with some developers in attendance to observe the testers, answer questions as needed, take notes on testing outcomes, and even, whenever possible, to make immediate changes based on the feedback, allowing an immediate opportunity to retest. Testers should not be required to file copious reports, just demonstrate the problem behaviors to the developers. Make it easy for them!

Although testing should concentrate on whether or not the objective tests are successful, much interesting information about usability also emerges during the testing sessions. Therefore, the developers in attendance should observe the users and note any hesitation or confusion. Are users confused about what screen to use? Are they overwhelmed by a particular screen? This is where having testers who are not the super-users is helpful, since super-users know the tool "too well" to be objective by that point.

Usability testing is best done by simply observing the users performing their tasks rather than interviewing them afterwards about the experience. Users have their pride, so they may not admit that something was difficult. Or they may forget! In the same vein, an unobtrusive observer does better than videotaping or recording users, which makes them nervous and distorts the results. Stick to informal observations and invest the recording money somewhere else.

## Load Testing

Load testing is mostly a technical issue, however from the point of view of business users it's critical that the system be tested under adequate loads (numbers) of users and transactions. Much of that testing can be done through automated tools so you should not have to ask end-users to all bang on the system at the same time, as we did in the olden days. Just make sure that the load testing is done, that it's done as early as possible to give the team time to address issues, and that it be done with the actual customizations in the product. Experience shows that a product may perform well right out of the box, but crawl miserably under inadequate customizations. Integrations are another notorious cause of performance issues.

# Training

Training is often neglected in CRM projects, which is a shame since much of the user acceptance and productivity improvements rely on a good training program. Since training is a relatively minor part of the implementation in terms of the effort required to make it work, it's worth planning for it to make it successful.

## What Should the Training Cover?

The training should help the end-users accomplish their tasks using the tool. Therefore, it needs to present the business process being automated, matching each step in the process with the appropriate manipulation in the tool. If the process is changing, the training needs to present the new process, together with the benefits expected from it. The training should *always* be task-oriented. Don't waste the attendees' time with a tour of all the features of the tool: the vast majority does not care about them. Instead, demonstrate how to accomplish each task using the tool. How does one enter a new lead? How does one record an activity on a lead? How does one create a forecast? How does one create a new service call? Annotate it? Close it? If the tool includes a customer portal, make time for a short overview of how customers can use the portal, even though it's not a task for the end-users per se, since it's good for them to understand the customer's experience and how it ties into what they are doing.

Leverage the use cases to create the training. By definition, the use cases should cover all the various tasks the staffers would accomplish with the tool, so much so that, if you find that a particular task is missing from the use cases when you create the training you need to go back and add it to the list. Training is a great and underutilized testing ground.

CRM training must include hands-on work. You will probably want to start with a demo for each task, but it's critical that attendees have a chance to apply their new knowledge in a realistic environment. A CRM training class with no hands-on exercises is pretty much useless. Use the test system for the training, since cleaning up after the students on the production system is a pain (l learned this the hard way). It's fine to create training-only accounts so you don't have to create accounts for each and every user on the test system, but make sure that the permission scheme is set up properly so the students can practice *exactly* what they will be allowed to do in the production system and nothing more. Realistic hands-on practice is yet another way to improve the testing, especially in the tricky area of permissions.

I recommend testing attendees at the end of the training session, for instance by having them perform various tasks that culminate in an alert or a predefined result that the instructor can test. For instance, sales reps may be asked to march an account through the sales process. Don't be content with having the users play around the system; you need to check that they really know what to do.

When in doubt, make the training a little too basic rather than a little too complicated. If the attendees are using the tool every day, they will undoubtedly become curious about more advanced features, and they will discover them on their own. Keep the training reasonably short: each staffer should spend no more than a couple of hours, a half-day at the most, unless there is a significant process change.

## Who Should Create the Training

Training for end-users is best viewed as a part of the implementation work. Few tool vendors offer end-user training at all, and the ones that do only offer training for the vanilla product, which is unlikely to match what you are delivering and which does not include the process training you need.

Some integrators have staff in place that can create and deliver end-user training. Others, especially smaller ones, do not. Regardless, you can easily engage the services of a free-lancer to create the training if your own organization does not have the required talent on board. It's best to find someone who has experience creating process and tool training materials. In particular, if you have an internal training organization that specializes in product training you may find that the skills are inappropriate for developing task-oriented training.

Before rolling out the training, make sure that the training materials are carefully reviewed and critiqued by a representative sample of the users. The super-users are a logical group to conduct the review, and indeed their participation in the project makes them very well equipped to serve as subject-matter experts. However, by the time training comes along the super-users are typically too well educated. Consequently, they will recommend adding more and more material and advanced features to the training, making the training too advanced for the needs of the end-users. Therefore, it's very helpful to supplement the super-users with a small set of "fresh" end-users to make sure that the training materials are not too difficult and too advanced.

The delivery of the training can be handled by professional trainers or by internal staff. I like using internal staffers to deliver the training. In particular the super-users make good trainers because they have a lot of process knowledge and they are credible to the attendees. It's not always possible to tear internal staffers away from their normal tasks not only to do the teaching (that's the easy part really) but also to learn how to deliver the training. You may have to get creative and use a combination of internal and external resources.

Actually, because of scheduling constraints, it's not rare to have to have to rely on a rather large team of instructors with varying levels of ability, some of whom will need help answering tougher questions during the training. Set up a mechanism to get the questions handled by an expert either during the workshops themselves or very quickly afterwards. In addition, collect such Q&A information on a central web site for everyone to access.

## When Should It Be Delivered?

People learn best when they have a short-term need, and they retain best if they can practice. Therefore, the ideal time to deliver training is about a week before rollout. This is a hectic time for the project team, and the concentrated schedule makes it hard to assemble a proper team of instructors, but it's worth sticking to it because of the learning benefits. If you must schedule the training over a long period of time because of instructor shortages or other constraints, be prepared to deliver a quick review a few days before the rollout.

So far, the topic of training has been covered as if training is always delivered in a classroom setting. Now is the time to state emphatically that a classroom setting is not the only way to deliver training. Classroom settings are very effective for tool training, but they are also inflexible since you need to bring together students and instructor in one place, and to supply the required venue to boot. If classroom training is not possible, web conferencing is an effective alternative (you do need a visual component so regular phone conferencing falls short). If training will be delivered from afar make sure that it includes a solid test component.

Even with the flexibility of teleconferencing you can count on the fact that some of the end-users won't be able to attend for various reasons, and of course new hires will require training down the line. Therefore, I heartily recommend creating a self-paced training document. The self-training document can be used for the classroom training as a refreshing change from PowerPoint slides, or create a few PowerPoint slides if you can't live without them. After the training sessions, the document can be used as reinforcement for the attendees and also in stand-alone mode for users who cannot attend a training session. For self-paced students, ensure that that an appropriate online environment is available to complete the work.

I find that many students also use the self-paced training document as a reference, especially if it includes an index, since they are already familiar with its organization and therefore can navigate it well. In addition to it you may want to create a quick reference guide for the tool. A one-page summary of often-performed tasks is something many users appreciate and *use*.

# The Rollout

Rolling out the project (or "going production," as it's often called) is the culmination of the project and can be hectic.

Many companies like to use a gradual approach for rollouts. Stretching out the rollouts, it is felt, gives the team an opportunity to handle any problems on a small scale rather than running the risk of a major fiasco. The trouble is that it's often difficult to schedule meaningful gradual rollouts. For instance, if the project targets support centers around the world and the centers are providing Follow-The-Sun support, it's awfully difficult to roll out one center at a time. I've done it, and having to go back and forth between systems was confusing and burdensome. More importantly, the data never seemed to sync perfectly with each rollout wave.

Another rollout strategy is to run with both the old and the new systems in parallel for a while, until the business users are convinced that the new system is reliable and perhaps even better than the old one. I find using parallel systems to be an unbearable overhead, but your situation may warrant it.

Which brings us to rollout rule #1: plan for the rollout early so that you can make informed decisions about data synchronization and whether to maintain concurrent systems for a while. This is not a decision to be made only by the technical team for technical reasons; the business owners must be fully briefed about the feasibility and dangers of the various approaches so they can support the decision, whatever it is.

The second aspect of rollouts is that, even with great attention to training and even with a very well tested system, some things are bound to go wrong at deployment time. If nothing else, the staffers may get confused about some aspects of the system. On the disaster end of the scale, the system may just collapse. So rollout rule #2 is to plan for appropriate support at deployment time. This means, for the most part, that the entire project team should be on deck and that an emergency support process be in place. Don't dismiss the integrator the minute the system goes live! Yes, it will cost you money to keep the team engaged and yes, you may end up with a team that has little to do; that's called insurance and you will be very glad to have spent the money for nothing if that's indeed the outcome.

When possible, super-users can deliver roving support to staffers who need it while technical staffers are ready to help should there be the mere hint of a technical problem. It's a good discipline to log all the problems as they come in so you can track them to completion and also analyze (later!) where training could have been stronger. Almost all rollouts trigger the need for some immediate changes. Users are at their most vulnerable—and cynical—during the first few days of the rollout, so try to address their concerns quickly before they blame the system for all their problems. This means that the project team should remain engaged until the problems simmer down.

Then there is the issue of contingency planning: what if things go really badly? Is there some kind of fallback mechanism, such as going back to the old system? Rolling back strikes fear in the heart of technical teams because it's almost impossible to do, mostly because the data starts changing the minute you turn the switch. Sure, you *can* go back to the old system, but you will almost certainly lose some data in doing that. If you simply must have the security of a rollback option, build it into the plan and include criteria for when you may choose to exercise that option, and who is responsible to make the decision. Good luck!

That was rollout rule #3: decide in advance how you will handle rollback decisions. Rollout rule #4 is to keep everyone informed, both the project team and the user community, on what's happening during the rollout. Plan for how the communication will be handled long before the rollout, since rollouts are often chaotic and are not a good time to improvise. It's great to have a communication plan based on the tool itself, but prepare for the reality that the tool may fail; a good old phone tree may be a great tool to have as a backup.

A few more thoughts about rollouts. It's not unheard of that the initial day of the rollout is satisfactory but that problems creep up over time, either because usage was light initially or because problems only show up as more data is entered. Don't declare victory for at least a week after you experience a smooth day, and only if you can verify that the system is actually being used (the managers should be enlisted to check on that).

Unless you have chosen a strategy of parallel systems, turn off the old system as you roll out the new one. Otherwise, users may prefer to continue using the old, familiar system.

# Successfully Managing an Implementation

CRM implementations are challenging projects to manage because of their scope and complexity. This section focuses on two project management aspects, milestones and status reports, and a softer, but critical point: keeping in touch with the tool vendor.

## Milestones

A key principle of project management is to use milestones rather than a linear schedule to manage projects. Milestones should be associated with deliverables so there is no ambiguity about whether they were met or not. Ask the technical staffers to ensure that any particularly difficult or risky subtask gets done early so that any obstacles can be worked around.

Following the precepts of rapid development, make each milestone a self-contained, working system, so that it can be touched, experienced, and tested by the user community. Having a working system at each step is an effective morale booster. It also allows catching and correcting problems early rather than waiting weeks and months for the opportunity to perform any testing. This limits risk.

Using tangible milestones has two more positive consequences. One is that they make schedule slips obvious. The other is that, being self-contained, they make it much easier to modify the project plan when needed. So if you know that you will miss the target date for milestone #4, you have a choice of either extending the deadline or simply making do with milestone #3 as the "final" deliverable. In other words, you have a modular system that gives you more flexibility.

Many project managers choose to use formal signoffs from the business owners on each project milestone. I have mixed feelings about it, since for me signatures can never replace trust and commitment. However, signoffs do clarify when agreement is reached and if they are a part of the organizational culture they should be used. Just don't expect signoffs to take the place of good lobbying and communication by the project manager. We'll come back to this when we talk about involving users later in this chapter.

## Status Reports

Traditional weekly written status reports are helpful, but they usually fall short of presenting a complete and timely picture of what's really going on with the project. Putting it bluntly, a week is a very long time to wait if there is a problem (or a breakthrough). Written reports also tend to use non-committal language that obscures what's really going on while leaving out all the subtleties of face-to-face communication.

Therefore, I much prefer using short, daily status checks with representation from all the active teams (so the database guy doesn't need to attend if there's no database work being done at this moment, but the technical lead should attend and should know when to pull him in). Anyone who is able to attend in person should do so, and remote participants can participate on a conference call. Status checks are mandatory for all key team members. The project manager can prepare a short written summary for the team based on the daily check, but it's very important to keep that daily direct contact with the key team members. A regular time and venue for the meeting is best to ensure participation.

Short means that the status meetings should take less than an hour, and probably less than 30 minutes, at least if no large issue has emerged. Each team should present a quick highlight of what was accomplished today, an estimate of how they are doing compared to the planned schedule, and any significant issue encountered that day (or resolved that day!). It's critical that team members provide very frank reports on issues they encounter, as many failed projects are victims not so much of the technical and political issues that they encounter but rather of the lack of timely knowledge that decision makers have about the issues. By the time the decision makers realize what the problems are and have a chance to design a solution, so much time has passed that it's very difficult to avoid a negative outcome. Make sure that all news, especially bad news, travels fast.

The daily status checks are not designed to resolve all the issues they raise (although that's always nice if it's possible!) or even to get details on each subproject, but rather to spread information quickly and to keep everyone on their toes. In addition to the daily status meetings, the project manager must also proactively perform detailed status checks with each subteam and ensure that issues are appropriately handled.

There are "quiet" times in a project where daily meetings would be too much, for instance during the coding period. The project manager should feel free to decrease the frequency of status meetings during those times. But daily meetings are required as you get closer to deployment.

In addition to the daily checks, longer, more detailed status meetings should be held as each milestone is reached. Here again I prefer a meeting format to a written status report so you can get more information (and you can always write minutes if you like the formality of written reports). Face-to-face milestone meetings are much more effective than conference calls so try to get at least the key players to be physically present together.

### Keeping the Tool Vendor in the Loop

If the tool vendor is serving as the integrator, you will naturally keep in close touch with the vendor through the implementation team, so this is really an issue only if you are using a third-party integrator.

It's very wise to keep the vendor in the loop during the implementation. You may well need specific assistance to fix bugs, resolve problems that are beyond the scope of the integrator, or provide audit services when you want to double-check advice or an opinion given by the integrator. The project manager should provide regular status reports to the vendor regardless of what's happening, good or bad, on the project. In addition, invite the sales person (or the technical sales specialist) and the regional services director to milestone meetings.

It's also useful to start establishing good relationships with the support organization as bugs are reported. It's much easier to get prompt and cheerful assistance in a crisis if a solid relationship has been established in happier times.

## Care and Feeding of the Integrator

You're spending a lot of money with your integrator, so make sure you get the best value from it. It so happens that the suggestions below also bring you much better deliverables.

## Make the Staffers Productive Onsite

Make sure that the integrator staffers can be absolutely, 100% productive at all times when they are working on your project. If they are working at your site, make sure that they have everything they need the minute they walk in: keys, entry cards, security clearance, a place to work, office supplies, computers, network access, etc. I've seen expensive consultants twiddle their thumbs in frustration because they could not get a system login for days (just thinking of the bill for the thumb-twiddling makes me cringe). The project manager takes care of all these so-called details ahead of the need.

An important component of productivity is appropriate office space. No, consultants do not need a corner office, but they should be allocated space close to their contacts and close to each other. Ideally, arrange for a "war room" setup where the consultants can work either alone or in a group, can set up hardware when needed, and can hold meetings including the daily checks.

Consultants need in-house contacts for specific tasks. Make sure the contacts are available and easy to reach. Consultants should be able to show some initiative in getting a hold of contacts and scheduling meetings, but the introductions should be arranged for them in advance.

## Make the Staffers Productive Offsite

Many times consultants can be much more productive working at their site rather than yours. This is especially the case during the coding phase. Customers are often leery of letting consultants work offsite: what are they doing out there? Are they working on our project? The reality is that you don't need to hold consultants hostages to make progress. As long as you have well-defined milestones in place and regular contact with the project lead for status reports and issue resolution, you can safely agree to specific portions of the work to be accomplished at an alternate location.

One potentially significant advantage of offsite work is decreased costs. Offsite work saves on travel costs, which can be significant with larger integrators who assign people from a vast geographic area. If work is outsourced overseas you should also see significant savings on hourly rates. Finally, integrators usually have fully set-up systems, allowing the programmers to be immediately productive.

# Involving the Users

One view of implementation is to shelter the users from it: get all the work done within the technical team and then unveil the glorious finished product to the appropriately awed users. I don't buy it. Actually, I believe that having users involved throughout the implementation increases the quality of the final deliverable, increases the adoption rate of the new system, and is a good investment of the users' time.

As discussed in Chapter 4, "Selecting the CRM Team," the best way to involve the users is to select a team of so-called super-users to participate in the project (in addition to the business owners, that is). Other individuals should also be added at crucial junctures, as discussed throughout this chapter.

Since you want to attract top performers to be super-users, it's crucial to orchestrate their participation carefully so that it has minimal impact on their availability for other tasks, and, very important, that they never feel that their time is wasted. Throughout the entire project, but particularly throughout the implementation phase, a good project manager protects and leverages the time of the super-users, carefully balancing the need for low impact against the requirements for their participation. Don't dump work on the super-users! At the same time, the project manager should monitor the performance of the super-users and quickly move to resolve any issues, including replacing super-users who are not contributing. Strong ties with the business owners helps with all aspects of successfully managing super-users.

If the project manager for the implementation is the integrator, and especially if that individual is more on the technical side, it's helpful to put in place a business project manager responsible for coordinating the activities within the business function(s), both with super-users and with the business owners. That individual does not need to be on the integrator's team, but needs good ties with the technical project manager. On larger projects, it's a full-time job.

What should super-users be involved in?

- The **kickoff workshop**. The super-users bring a good dose of reality into the discussion. They also know how the job is really done on a daily basis, something that may not be completely clear to the business owners, at least in larger organizations.
- The **definition of the use cases**. The super-users know the crucial steps in their work and can translate them into solid use cases.

- **Each project milestone**. If you follow my recommendations to make each milestone a deliverable, as limited as it may need to be, then the super-users should be asked to review it as it is delivered, with the help of the use cases. If something's not quite right, as is most often the case, then back to the development team it goes.
- **Training**. The super-users' input to the training materials and delivery mechanisms is precious since they have actual hands-on experience. The training materials are a deliverable just like any other and should be reviewed by them as well. By the time training comes along, however, the super-users know too much about the project to be reliable reviewers for suitability (they are great reviewers for content, however). Super-users are not infrequently asked to deliver some of the training. This is a suitable use of their talent and knowledge, although they should not be overly burdened.

Should super-users be involved in the daily status checks? Probably not en masse, for two reasons. First, it's impractical to expect that they will be available daily. Second, there may be relatively little action from their point of view on a daily basis. I like to encourage super-users to attend the status checks when they can, for instance by making sure that there is a standing conference call set up for them to use at their convenience. For the most part, their presence should be required mostly for milestones and as determined necessary by the project manager.

## Internal Promotion

Because the success of CRM projects depends in great part on user adoption, it's a good idea to promote the system to its future users during the implementation. It doesn't need to be a sophisticated marketing campaign and it doesn't need to take a lot of time or resources, but it should be done.

There are two opposite mistakes to avoid when doing internal promotion. One is to do none, which, since no one likes surprises, won't do much for your adoption rate. The other is to hype the system to the moon, which creates an unpleasant backlash when the users discover that all is not as wonderful as was implied. Here are some guidelines for striking a successful middle ground:

- **Start relatively early and crank up** as you near deployment time. Internal users should be aware of the CRM project from the start (when the selection process starts, that is—don't wait until the start of the implementation period). Rather than creating special tool information meetings, which may not draw the crowds you would expect, schedule short tool briefings during normally scheduled staff meetings instead. Make the tool story a part of the normal set of business information. Publicize large milestones. By deployment time, users should welcome weekly updates.

- **Use informal promotion techniques**. There's no need to be flashy or complicated to achieve effective internal promotion. In addition to leveraging the communication channels that are already in place, remember that your best spokespeople are the project team members, especially the end-users. Give them tools to communicate information. In particular, set up a project web page to centralize all the information about the project, making sure that it contains information suitable for end-users as well as more detailed and technical information for core team members. Don't expect end-users to check it on a regular basis: make sure the information gets to them instead.

- **Don't aim too high**. Claiming amazing productivity gains will surely backfire when the new tool is deployed and, as is normal, productivity decreases while users get the hang of it. As pitiful as you think the existing system is, it's likely that users have developed efficient strategies for using it, which they will miss when the new tool comes around. You may not be able to deliver all the features you are planning, which may cause users to perceive the project as a failure even if the new system is good overall.

Remember that users are often skeptical. Anticipate their objections and address them. One objection you are almost certain to face is why a large investment is being made in a tool when other choices could be made, such as hiring more staff or making improvements in processes. Enlist the project team, from the executive sponsor to the super-users, to justify how the project will simplify certain procedures, or increase revenue, or whatever else the business objectives are. If they have doubts, the rest of the team will have more.

Make sure that internal promotion addresses issues that are important to the end-users: what's in it for *them*. They may not care much about working on the latest technology, while they would care that they will now have access to all customer purchases online. Collecting user questions and providing answers to them is a good way to catch what initial communication may have missed.

Although the end-users will not know as much about implementation issues as the project team members, don't shield them from the problems. Credibility is important.

Finally, be cautious with schedules. End-users are quick to conclude that projects are doomed if they are late. Better announce one larger delay than a bunch of small, successive delays.

# Customer Promotion

In most CRM implementations customers are users too, so they need some degree of information just like internal users. The schedule and depth of communication may not be quite as aggressive as for internal users but the principles remain the same.

### Focus on Benefits

Customers sometimes get the (true!) message that the CRM system will decrease costs. The more sophisticated and less cynical bunch may conclude that a decrease in cost is actually good for *them*, since in the end lower costs equal lower prices. However, many will conclude that service levels will decrease, so you need to provide some reassuring information.

Make a concerted effort to extract realistic and, ideally, measurable benefits for customers. That could include:

- Faster service, whether through self-service or by leveraging electronic channels.
- Instant information on products availability or service conditions.
- Online configuration for complex products avoids errors and speeds up ordering.
- The ability to subscribe to proactive alerts on user-defined topics.
- Free support for all users through the online knowledge base.

### Use Many Channels

Depending on your customer base and the type of information you have on your customers, use all the appropriate channels to deliver the CRM message.

If you're just starting out and your database of e-mail addresses is not entirely reliable, as is often the case, use a hard copy mailing, making sure to collect reliable e-mail addresses once the customers visit the portal. You may want to entice customers to visit with an appropriate reward. Simple raffles work very well (post the recipients of the award on the site for additional effect).

E-mail notices are perfect if you have a reliable set of e-mail addresses. Use them to announce major upgrades too.

Mention the portal in your on-hold messages. This works well for call centers. Don't expect customers who are calling in to hang up and go to the web instead (although some might, especially if the wait is long), but some customers will try the portal the next time around.

Add a mention of the portal to all e-mail messages sent through the new system. For added effect, add a URL that points to the specific issue or support case the e-mail is about, reinforcing the use of the web site as a status-checking tool.

Ask all staffers to reinforce the use of the customer portal. For instance, a telesales rep could e-mail a customer the online version of a datasheet they discussed, specifically highlighting the URL of the datasheet. Staffers will only reinforce the use of the portal if they are convinced of the value of the tool for their own work, which is another reason to work on internal promotion.

Tell new prospects and customers about the customer portal. If the portal functionality is particularly deep, offer an online orientation to ensure that customers experience all its features.

Finally, provide the same level of service to customers who choose to do business electronically and to customers who call in. Many companies respond 10-30 times *slower* to electronic requests and then wonder why customers keep calling. Customers who conduct business from the portal are also much more likely to use self-help, so reinforce their good habits.

## To Limit Access or Not?

To me, the whole point of customer portals is that they should be wide open. Granted, some information may need to be shielded from competitors, although much energy is expanded in that direction without much cause, in my mind. Determined competitors can usually access the information anyway through an alias of some kind, and little if any proprietary information is visible to customers in any case.

If you wish to restrict access to your customers, by all means define a registration process and assign logins and passwords (and create a process handling or overseeing the registration requests). Beyond that, it's counterproductive to limit online access to only certain segments of customers. The incremental cost of serving customers through electronic means is so much lower than through other channels that you should attempt to serve all customers through electronic channels whenever possible, reserving the more expensive channels for your better customers.

### Leverage Customer Usage

Once you attract customers to your portal, leverage their experience to improve it. I'll discuss ways to collect and measure what they do on the site to determine what's working or not in the next chapter, but don't neglect good old-fashioned feedback. Provide an easy way for customers to report problems and make suggestions for improvements. The traditional e-mail to the web master is fine if someone will indeed attend to the request, take appropriate action, and get back to the customer about it. If the tool you are implementing has a support component, it's a great idea to leverage it for such as purpose.

## Handling Implementation Problems

This section focuses on implementation problems. Problems are inevitable during a long project so proper expectations and a game plan are useful.

### You Can't Expect a Trouble-Free Implementation

I imagine that there have been a few truly trouble-free CRM implementations since the beginning of time, but I have never been a part of one. Even relatively small projects hit problems at some point, and larger projects, being so complex, are pretty much guaranteed to experience several significant problems. This is the case for all implementations, even those that follow thorough, well thought-out selections for both the product and the integrator and that enjoy good executive support. Implementations that don't enjoy a good start or good ongoing support do worse, of course.

Therefore, you should expect to encounter some amount of problems including at least one major problem, a showstopper that forces you to do without an important feature or that requires significant amounts of money for unforeseen additional hardware, software, or development work to address. Don't automatically conclude that the project is a failure just because you hit a snag, even a major one.

The good news is that many problems are, in fact, predictable. For instance, if your project includes such traditionally problematic features as a tricky integration to another system, a deployment to far-away offices with slow network connections, or plenty of customizations in the underlying data model, then chances are that large problems will crop up there, not when changing the color of the screens. What to do? Start by confirming that you absolutely need the problematic feature or functionality. If you do, schedule the associated technical work so that the more difficult areas are tackled first. Once the trickiest bits are in place and tested, it's an easier ride to the finish line. A big goal of the kickoff meeting should be to highlight those areas of technical (and, more rarely, business) risk and to schedule the work for them early on in the project.

## Resolving Issues

If you do run into a big issue, don't panic or make rash decisions. Problems may turn out to be less grave than anticipated, and in any case you need to investigate the issues thoroughly before you make a decision. Involve the entire team in the decision rather than looking at them strictly from the technical side. (A strictly business approach is no better, but usually the problems that are uncovered are of a technical nature and the usual, flawed impulse is to find a technical solution). For serious issues, convene a brainstorming session with the entire team to help you uncover novel solutions.

Now for some examples of problems and potential approaches for them. Let's say the problem is poor performance from remote offices. Perhaps it's just the nudge that you needed to upgrade the network despite the hefty cost. If you asked the references about that specific point and they did not report problems, perhaps the tool vendor could audit the situation to isolate configuration improvements. Both alternatives so far are technical solutions. Perhaps a combined business and technical solution would work: can you stage the deployment so that remote offices are last in line? If an upcoming release is targeted towards communication improvements, perhaps that could be the ticket for you. Notice the potential problem with this solution—it delays facing the problem until the very end, and it is completely dependent on the tool vendor to provide a timely and effective release.

The worse thing you can do when faced with a big problem is to hide it. Hiding problems is widespread because of the political attacks that are sure to follow the admission of a problem. I advocate the opposite strategy: go out of your way to seek out problems because a known problem is much easier to deal with than an unknown problem (although, of course, there's nothing as sweet as a resolved problem). Be very candid about problems, especially with the executive sponsor. What you are after is trust: if you are open about issues, the executive sponsor and the business owner will not spend their energies worrying about hidden issues and will be more cooperative about solving the problems that do occur.

## Should You Ever Give Up?

It could be, although it's very rare if you are careful during the selection process, that you will find a problem serious enough to scrap the project rather than patching it together. It's a very extreme measure and of course a costly one, since the tool investment is typically spent by that point, as is some amount of integrator effort and the effort of all the internal players. It's very painful to come to the conclusion that a project needs scrapping, not just because of the financial pain but because the main players have been so involved with it that they just can't contemplate terminating it. (By the way, I think getting attached to a project is, overall, a good thing since a good emotional bond helps you to stick with the project through difficult times). Consider scrapping the project if you are experiencing severe problems in the technical, business, or financial areas:

- Key functionality just is not functioning as advertised. This includes both usability items and performance.
- The business model has changed so drastically that the tool that was chosen no longer meets the need.
- The budget has changed or requirements have increased to the point that you cannot sustain the implementation.

If you have to scrap the project, do hold a post-mortem, however painful it is. It is extremely valuable to understand whether the issue should have been foreseen and avoided, especially since the project may need to be restarted in another form to adapt to the new conditions.

## Post-mortem Review

Regardless of the outcome of the project, hold a "post-mortem" review with the project team, with the goal of identifying both effective and ineffective practices, together with potential remedies where possible. Lessons from the review are useful to all team members for future projects. Since most CRM projects occur in phases it's quite likely that a similar team or subteam will get to work almost immediately on phase two, so the review will be immediately useful.

For large teams, conduct the review in stages, with each specialty team holding its own review before bringing it to the full project team, although you need to bring at least the key players together to complete a proper review. Schedule it for a few weeks after deployment so there's enough time to experience the production system, but not so far down the line that events are no longer fresh in people's memories.

Two opposite problems to avoid during a review are too much pussyfooting, where no one dares to be frank for fear of offending others and, on the other hand, aggressive attacks on other team members with a design to assign blame to others while shielding oneself. By this stage in the project, it should be easy for the project manager to anticipate which problem is more likely and to encourage everyone to approach the review with an open mind and a quiet temper. It's useful to reinforce the theme of making the next project run more smoothly, rather than either assigning fault or making everyone feel good about the current project.

The review should cover:

- What went well and why, in all areas of the project, whether on the business side (training, perhaps) or on the technical side (the performance tuning approach), and whether mundane (the location of the kickoff meeting) or critical (the executive sponsor stepping in to rescue the project after the technical setback on week 3).
- What did not go so well and why, and what could have been done to change that. If a large deployment issue was discovered the week before the rollout, forcing a postponement, could it have been predicted earlier? Why was that particular test not performed at the beginning of the project? Was it something that should have been checked with the references for the tool? Although the goal is not to rub people's noses in it, it's important to pin down the cause of the problem as well as to define alternative paths to avoid it in the future.

Serious reviews can take several hours. If you are using an integrator, as you probably are, hold a private, shorter, summary review afterwards to examine how well the integrator performed on the project, and whether it should be retained again and under what conditions. You may also use this time to examine any internal issues you do not want to air in front of the integrator staff.

Summarize the results of the review, focusing on any changes that should be made for future projects, and make sure the changes are taken into account. Don't bother with the review unless you can be reasonably certain that changes will be made as a result of it.

CRM implementations have a well-earned reputation to be challenging and not always meeting the lofty goals they started with. To be really successful, start with a kickoff workshop in which the whole team works together to create objectives and perform the gap analysis. Stay on top of the project by using meaningful milestones and frequent, face-to-face status checks. Finally, communicate without hype to the users. That should bring you to a pleasant and relaxed post-mortem.

# Measuring Success    10

## Express Version

- Metrics are used in two ways. First, metrics can be used to measure the success of the CRM project by using before/after comparisons. Second, they allow the managers to make better decisions about the business by providing accurate and timely information. Different metrics may be required for these two objectives.
- To measure the success of the CRM project, define measurable improvement goals, each with a baseline, at the start of the project.
- Metrics to run the business can be refined and improved in the long run, but plan for the key business metrics when creating requirements during the kickoff workshop. This will ensure that the relevant data is indeed available and can be reliably gathered over the normal course of using the system.
- Concentrate on a few key business metrics, including operational metrics and strategic metrics. Operational metrics are activity-based, for example, how many telesales calls were made and how quickly service

requests are attended. Strategic metrics are outcome-based, for example, win/loss analysis and customer satisfaction ratings. You can run additional, analysis-focused metrics as needed to supplement the handful of key metrics that are run regularly.

- In all but tiny organizations, slice and dice the metrics to show each manager the right level of detail of what's happening within his or her group without having to wade through the details of other groups.
- Look for graphics and trends to make metrics easier to understand and easier to act upon. Group the metrics in compact dashboards so all the critical information is available at one glance.
- Deliver metrics automatically and allow individuals to subscribe to the metrics they care about to maximize the value and use of metrics.

# Why Metrics Matter

Metrics (you may prefer to say statistics or reports) matter because good information about the business allows you to make good decisions. Getting better information about customers is often one of the reasons why companies are interested in implementing a CRM tool in the first place. This benefit can only be realized if you plan for metrics along the way so that the tool captures the right data and you can extract it in ways that are meaningful for managers and executives within the organization.

Metrics are also critical in measuring the success of the CRM project itself. As discussed earlier in the book, you want to define measurable goals for the project as you start it. For instance, you may decide to cut the average sales cycle from 3 months to 2.5 months. Or you may want to decrease the average effort time per support case from 30 minutes to 25.

A measurable goal has both a baseline measurement (the three-month average cycle or the 30-minute average effort time) and a target for improvement (cut .5 months off the sales cycle, or 5 minutes off the effort time per case). Sometime it is difficult to establish a baseline since the data required to create it is not tracked in the first place, and indeed the lack of tracking could be one of the main justifications for the CRM project as a whole. You can make an educated guess, or you may want to set up a short-term measurement project to get a good baseline. You could ask the sales reps to recall when they started working on deals they closed this month, or ask the support reps to track their time manually for a few days. A quick and dirty estimate is useful, even if you know it's not completely reliable.

Targeting ambitious but realistic improvements isn't easy either. It is best approached by breaking down each task into smaller components and estimating improvements for each component. For instance, you can break down the sales cycle into the initial assessment, planning, sales calls, creating proposals, etc., and define the impact of the new tool on each phase.

Despite the genuine difficulties of setting meaningful and reasonable quantitative objectives, it's essential to define measurable goals, for without them the success of the CRM project will always be open to questions and doubt.

### Didn't We Talk About ROI Already?

Yes, we did. We talked about creating an ROI analysis as part of making a CRM purchase in Chapter 7. ROI analyses include many of the same techniques used when creating metrics, in particular in the areas of cost containment and efficiency, and this chapter may be useful to you as you prepare the ROI analysis. However, metrics go well beyond ROI considerations as they include topics other than cost, revenue, and profit.

This chapter discusses both how to measure the success of the CRM project itself and how to use the CRM tools to measure the health of the business in the short term and the long term. It shows how to make reasonable choices in defining and implementing metrics so that you get the right information for a minimum amount of effort and cost. It concludes with many examples of metrics you can use to create your own set.

## Types of Metrics

One of the overwhelming discoveries of new CRM users is that the tool gathers so much data that you could literally spend all day looking at data about any aspect of the process, including minute details. Before you go data-happy, it's important to determine what metrics make sense for you.

Rather than starting with the data, start with your objectives. Consider both your business goals (for the business metrics) and your project goals (for the project metrics), although both sets can and do overlap for most implementations. Your metrics choices depend greatly on your industry, the types of functions being automated, and the specific business strategy you are following. Nevertheless, you can think of metrics as belonging to four categories: revenue, cost, efficiency, and customer satisfaction.

Table 10.1 gives examples of metrics for each of the four categories, grouped by logical subcategories. The examples are simply meant to illustrate what the four categories mean. Certain examples may not fit your requirements and you may have ideas that are not listed in the table.

**TABLE 10.1**  Sample Metrics by Category

| Category | Examples |
|---|---|
| Revenue | Sales volume, average sales size, revenue by customer, revenue per lead, revenue per campaign, number of new customers<br>Forecast volume, sales versus quota<br>Lifetime value of a customer, size and frequency of orders |
| Cost | Cost per lead<br>Average cost of sales<br>Customers per support staff, cost per service call<br>Order error rate, profit by customer or by segment number of service requests |
| Efficiency | Campaign response rate, leads per source, prospects per source<br>Daily calls per telemarketing rep, appointments per telesales rep, lead conversion rate, RFP response time, revenue per sales rep<br>Number of prospects in the pipeline (funnel analysis), lead to sales time by source, length of sales cycle, % close rate<br>Cases per support rep, case backlog, service call length, number of contacts to resolve a service issue, percentage of issues resolved through self-service, case by problem type<br>CRM tool usage<br>Cross-selling rate |
| Customer Satisfaction | Customer retention, customer churn, support renewals rates<br>Ratings on satisfaction surveys, ratings of knowledge base documents<br>Customer references |

## What Makes a Good Metric?

A good metric is easy to collect, easy to understand, and meaningful. Ease of collection means that it should not require excessive effort to gather the underlying data, which ideally should be collected as a normal part of the users doing their job. For instance, if you are looking to measure the length of the sales cycle and you can get the tool to automatically time-stamp leads as they are entered into the system, you've just set up an automatic data entry for the beginning of the sales cycle. Besides saving effort, an automatic record also means that the results will be unbiased, which may not be the case if the users are free to enter leads at their leisure (yes, users have been known to manipulate the system to meet stated goals).

The second criterion of good metrics is that they should be easy to understand, which means that they should be "blindingly obvious." For instance, a pie graph that shows the percentage of leads coming from different sources is a blindingly obvious illustration of your most effective lead-generation efforts, whereas the very same information presented in a long list of detailed numbers for each and every campaign would not be half as effective.

Blindingly obvious may also be blindingly misleading, which is where the third criterion, meaningfulness, comes into play. The example we just considered of the distribution of leads from various sources may be easy to understand, but it's not as meaningful as the average cost per lead for the various sources you used. For instance, cost per lead would tell you that, although webinars generated only 15% of your leads, their cost per lead is just 1% of the cost for trade-show leads and therefore you should expand your webinar program.

The three criteria—easy to collect, easy to understand, and meaningful—often require tradeoffs. In particular, meaningful metrics are likely to be harder to collect and generate, so much so that you may need to give up some of the meaning in favor of easier collection. A common example is the desire to track effort time for various tasks (acquiring a customer, resolving a support issue, etc.). For most tools and in most environments the burden on users to keep detailed records of their time is very large, and you may decide to forego detailed time metrics for fear of alienating them from the system entirely. We revisit the issue of data collection in the next section.

## Tangibles vs. Intangibles

Some metrics seem easy to quantify even without a CRM tool: how much revenue has been booked this quarter? How much are you spending on support? Others become a cinch with a proper CRM system: What's the average sales cycle? What's the size of the support backlog?

Some metrics are difficult to quantify, the most notorious being satisfaction for all the various users of the system. Are your customers happy? Are your employees happy? While it's very difficult to create an unbiased and meaningful measure of such soft benefits, it doesn't mean that you shouldn't try. Customer satisfaction is a critical component of business success, while employee satisfaction is an unrecognized but interesting objective to include in the CRM project goals. So what can you do with intangibles?

The direct approach is to create a concrete, yet artificial measurement, typically a survey. To maximize the reliability of the survey, keep it short and focus it on a specific event such as a sales transaction or a support case. We'll come back to customer satisfaction surveys when we discuss data collection later in this chapter.

Another useful approach is to rely on measurements of tangible events that are viewed as proxies for customer satisfaction. For instance, instead of asking employees how satisfied they are with the new tool you could track their usage of the tool, or go for a big-picture measurement such as employee turnover. Proxy measurements are valuable because they are easier to collect and they don't suffer from traditional survey biases (for instance, employees may fear retribution if they give negative ratings to the tool). On the other hand, proxies are just that and may be misleading. For instance, employees may be using the system but they are only entering stub information because it takes too much time to track everything. In this case, you would have a positive proxy measurement (usage) but in fact employees are not satisfied with the system. Or employees may be quitting because of a salary freeze even though they love the system, giving you a negative proxy measurement (turnover) while employees are very happy with the system. So choose the proxy wisely and, when possible, use more than one.

Do not avoid intangibles altogether but strive to apply reasonable measurements to them. It's usually very difficult to translate intangible benefits into hard dollars, although some brave souls have tried[1]. Therefore, intangible benefits usually don't belong in an ROI analysis.

## Strategic vs. Operational

You may find that the business functions involved in the CRM project focus too much on internal productivity metrics. This is often the case with call centers, which seem to be obsessed with such items as the average speed of answer (the time callers spend on hold) and the average handle time (the average time of a conversation). While both metrics are relevant and useful to managers, such internally focused, operational metrics completely fail to address the outcome of the activities in the call center. Did the callers get what they wanted? Did the company get value from the interactions?

Some call center managers even argue that the operational metrics they love are appropriate strategic metrics. For instance, they believe that the average speed of answer captures customer satisfaction. Their reasoning is that if a

---

1. See the work of Frederik Reichheld, for instance *Loyalty Rules*.

customer waited less than 30 seconds, then the customer is happy and the call center did its job. Wrong! While we can all agree that a customer who is forced to wait on hold is likely to be less satisfied than one whose call goes right through, a customer who stays on hold for a few minutes but then gets a complete answer will likely be more satisfied than the one who has no wait but also does not get a satisfactory answer within that first call. Beware of operational metrics pretending to be strategic metrics!

Why are operational (productivity) metrics overused? One reason is that call center supervisors and managers often have a limited view of the business strategy, hence a limited view of metrics. The other reason is that it's easy to get operational metrics, since all the data is nicely logged in the tracking tools. In fact, the vast majority of canned reports offered by the CRM vendors are operational metrics. I must admit that it's hard to tell whether this is because the vendors lack an understanding of strategic metrics or because customers only demand operational metrics.

Operational efficiency (making lots of sales calls, generating lots of proposals, answering lots of service requests) is an important component of effectiveness (closing lots of business, increasing customers' loyalty), but it's not enough. Think of effectiveness as efficiency combined with quality. Making lots of sales calls is efficient. Calling on the right prospects is quality. Capture both efficiency and effectiveness in your metrics, that is, include both operational and strategic metrics.

Operational metrics are often stuck within a particular business function. Measure results *across* business functions whenever possible. For instance, instead of counting the number of leads that the telemarketers deliver to the sales team, measure the value of the leads as they turn into bona fide customers. (It takes a while to work through the sales cycle so you may need to be patient.)

## Short-Term or Long-Term?

The metrics that measure success for the CRM project focus on the reasonably short term, while the metrics you need to manage the business will be with you for a long time. So it's a good investment to focus the requirements definition on the business metrics, and to do so early in the process (starting at the kickoff workshop) so that you can count on the data you are interested in to be collected and available in the tool.

Aside from the data collection issues, the other decisions about metrics are fairly easy to change based on changing needs so don't worry too much about getting them exactly right the first time around. This includes the specific mathematical analysis of the data and the formatting of the reports or graphs. In that sense, metrics are a work in process.

## Garbage In...

As just noted, you can't measure what you are not capturing. If you don't capture the sources of your leads, you won't be able to compute the response rate on your marketing campaigns. If you don't log each prospect, you won't be able to calculate an accurate win/loss ratio. If you don't log each and every support case, you cannot hope to know your support volume. If you don't track the authors of knowledge base documents, you won't be able to reward the top contributors. Thus, the first step is to make sure that the data you want to measure is indeed available in the system.

One obstacle may be the CRM tool itself. For instance, if the CRM system doesn't allow capturing the sources of your leads, you won't be able to track what promotions were most successful. If you want to calculate the effort time spent on each support case, you will find that most tools do not allow for easy tracking of effort time (at best, they let the reps enter effort time manually, which is neither user-friendly nor accurate).

The major obstacle to data collection, however, is not a matter of any limitations in the tool itself but rather poor compliance by users in logging data and events. This can be because the users don't see the value of logging everything, because logging is overly cumbersome, because it's not enforced, or because counter-productive targets make it advantageous for the users to be selective in their logging efforts.

The issue of counterproductive targets is particularly insidious. Let's say you decide to pay very careful attention to closing ratios and to give awards to reps with particularly high closing ratios. One of the likely consequences of such a system is that the more iffy deals will never get recorded in the first place, ensuring that close ratios remain very high. So you will get inflated, incorrect close ratios, but in addition, other analyses based on the data will be incorrect too. For instance, don't hope to perform any meaningful win/loss analysis based on a selected sample of deals. The cure here may be to ask the telesales reps to log the leads (assuming they are not measured on the close ratio).

The same is true in the service realm. Say you have an initiative to decrease the number of interactions required to resolve service requests, correctly sensing that customers prefer to have their issues resolved in as few turns as possible. You run the very real risk of reps "forgetting" to log interactions on complex issues, impacting not only a proper count of interactions required to resolve issues, but undermining the entire case logging accuracy to boot. To avoid problems, use another measurement of quality in tandem, for instance implement a customer satisfaction survey.

Be careful about setting goals and objectives that create incentives not to log events.

## Get the Logging Religion

Beyond avoiding obvious disincentives to logging specific events, educate the users about the wisdom of logging all transactions not only because it's the expected standard of behavior, but also because it has benefits to them and to the organization.

- It will help them keep track of where they are on each project, which is a great help in busy environments where users juggle many issues and many customers.
- It will help their co-workers if they have to help with or take over a project, especially if there's no time for a debriefing. This should be a no-brainer in environments with a team approach.
- It will help everyone figure out what happened if a win/loss or post-mortem analysis is required.
- It will help the entire team by building up a knowledge base of best practices.
- It will help the managers forecast resources and goals more accurately. Just think of what would happen if you forecast for a 2:3 close ratio when the real number is 2:10; or if you staff the support center for 30-minute cases but the average is really 45 minutes.

Logging compliance is an ongoing battle. Be prepared to monitor system usage and apply discipline accordingly if you want to ensure compliance.

## Make it Easy to Log

While responsible end-users are quite aware of the benefits of logging all transactions, they still chafe at having to jump through hoops to record basic stuff or spending time recording exotic data that seems to never be used down the line. If you want good, reliable data, you need to make it easy for the users. Here are some examples.

- Entering a new prospect should be done with one screen, with one click, and should allow for on-the-fly duplicate checking. Can your system do that? If not, why not?
- Logging a simple support case (question and answer within a single phone interaction) shouldn't take more than two clicks: one to find the customer in the database, and one to close the case.
- A recent (custom) system I worked with required support reps to enter no fewer than *four* categories to describe, respectively, the topic and sub-topic of the cause of the case, and the type and sub-subtype of the resolution of the case. That's too many! Simplify data entry to increase compliance.

Remember that the performance of the tool plays an important role in reinforcing the logging discipline. Slow tools automatically increase the likelihood of under-logging. If it takes an hour to download data to a laptop, sales reps will skip the synchronization and only use the system from the office, if at all. If the response time is bad in smaller offices, even desk-bound reps won't record all their activities. Make sure the system really works for everyone.

## Capture Customer Satisfaction

As discussed earlier, a special concern for metrics is to capture direct measures of customer (or employee) satisfaction, which are not typically logged as a by-product of logging cases. I will discuss customer satisfaction here since it's the one most people focus on, but the same principles and strategies would apply to measure employee satisfaction.

There are two ways to measure satisfaction, transactional surveys and overall surveys. Overall surveys are typically conducted once or twice a year, often include questions about many aspects of the relationship between the customer and the company, and gather feedback about many different interactions over a long period of time. A transactional survey, on the other hand, focuses on a particular interaction, be it a purchase or a support case, and is conducted soon after the fact, while memories are still fresh.

Overall surveys are useful to get a periodic temperature of the customer base and also to survey all customers, even the ones that have not recently placed an order or a support request. Because of their scope, they tend to be quite long, creating a challenge to get customers to actually complete them. If you choose to do an overall survey, it's probably best to conduct it by phone to pretty much ensure that each customer who starts the survey finishes it. You may also want to give a small thank you gift to each customer who participates. Be careful with your sampling technique so you reach enough customers at minimum cost, and do keep the survey as short as you can: anything above 30 minutes is far too long, in my mind! Many specialized organizations offer outsourcing services for customer surveys if you prefer not to do it alone.

While overall surveys have their place, my preference is for transactional surveys because they are specific, fast, and action-oriented.

Because they focus on a specific transaction, transactional surveys allow you to trace both positive and negative feedback to a particular rep or a particular organization. In fact, you can use the satisfaction ratings to evaluate the performance of the specific individuals that helped the customer.

Transactional surveys are fast. You get results the next day, not six or twelve months later. This is useful if you need to take action based on the feedback.

Transactional surveys are action-oriented. They are not a mere measurement. You can use them to circle back to the customer with a resolution or thanks as needed. And you can do it fast since the results come back fast.

The weakness of transactional surveys is that response rates can be low. What's even more worrisome is that customers who are particularly happy or particularly unhappy are more likely to respond than customers in the middle. This results in a biased sample. One of the best ways to combat it is to boost return rates. Here are three suggestions to do that.

- Make it very easy to respond to the survey. In particular limit yourself to a handful of questions, say four or five (so we are talking a few minutes for a transactional survey versus a minimum of 15 to 30 on an overall survey). Use e-mail surveys for an unobtrusive delivery mechanism that allows customers to respond at their leisure. This is particularly effective to survey transactions that were conducted electronically since the customers are already comfortable with the medium.
- Promptly get back to customers who are particularly happy or unhappy. Their likely response: "You guys actually *read* the surveys?!" Set thresholds for when to contact the customers and do so within 48 hours of the surveys for maximum impact.
- Publish the results of the surveys to customers. This can take guts if the ratings are not that great. As a compromise, highlight specific changes you are making based on the surveys.

Finally, don't be overly obsessed by the potential for biased results. Do what you can to boost the response rates and then just work to improve the results, whatever they are. It doesn't matter if they are a bit biased.

## Don't Be Average

Most managers are not expert statisticians so we let ourselves believe that averages are the way to go for metrics. Want to capture how long it takes to close a deal? Compute the average sales cycle. Want to see whether calls are answered promptly? Measure the average speed of answer. Want to check individual productivity? Calculate the average calls per rep per day. Want to know how long it takes to resolve support issues? Measure the average time to resolution.

The problem with averages is that they may meet the criteria of ease of collection and ease of understanding, but they may not be very meaningful. Let's take a simple example from an inbound call center (either telemarketing or support) that uses average speed of answer as its main metric.

The target response time is 30 seconds. On day one, the center gets 100 calls. Half the calls are handled within 5 seconds and the other half in 45 seconds (significantly over the target). The average speed of answer on day one is 25 seconds, which is under the target of 30 seconds. This is completely misleading since fully half of the customers experienced a significant delay compared to the target.

Contrast this situation with day two, where the opposite problem with averages surfaces. On day two, 100 calls are received again. All calls are responded to within 25 seconds except for one call that waits for 9 minutes (suggesting a very patient caller and most probably a snafu in the rep scheduling algorithm). The average speed of answer is just above 30 seconds, dragged there by the one slow response and signaling a problem even though only one customer was inconvenienced—and, more importantly, even though the day one average did not show a problem!

One can build similarly disturbing examples around customer satisfaction, cost of sales, or revenue by customer. So what's the alternative to averages?

The solution is to set targets and to measure against the target. In the call center example, measuring achievement against the 30-second hold time target would yield a score of 50% on day one and 99% on day two, a much better indication of customer experience. Measuring achievement against targets is fine even if the customer does not know what the targets may be. For instance, telemarketing call centers rarely tell their customers what their target hold time is. That's fine; you can still set a target and measure against it.

In some areas it doesn't make sense to set a single target, or you may not know enough to define a meaningful target yet. Try using several levels of target achievements and measuring against the multiple targets. For instance, if you are measuring the length of the sale cycle, try computing the percentage of deals that take less than a week, a month, and less than a quarter (or whatever time units fit your particular situation).

The rule is: be wary of averages. Use achievement against target instead whenever a target can be defined.

# Slicing and Dicing, Babushka-Style

Small functional teams with a single manager do well with just one set of metrics. Larger teams require a more sophisticated approach to metrics, whereby each geographical area, each manager, and each product line gets a customized view of the data, yielding more focused and therefore more useful reports.

One of the obstacles in the quest for detailed metrics is whether the system keeps track of the information you need to retrieve and arrange the data. For instance, many systems do a poor job of tracking reps' managers, making it virtually impossible to get a report for only manager X, while region Y (or product Z) may be an easier task. Do not assume that the tracking system will accommodate your reporting needs and always make sure that the variables you want to report by are indeed tracked. This should be surfaced during the kickoff workshop.

Assuming that your system can keep track of who reports to whom, you will end up with what I call babushka-style ("Russian doll" style) metrics through which:

- First-line managers see detailed information for all the staff members in their teams.
- Second-level managers see aggregate metrics for each of their teams, without having to wade through metrics at the individual level.
- Directors can see metrics by region, with details for each team within the region.
- The worldwide VP can see metrics by geographical area.

Babushka metrics allow managers to zero in on exactly the level of detail they care about, making them more productive and improving their opinion of the usefulness of the tool, which is a nice benefit in the early days of the rollout.

Besides the time savings for managers, babushka metrics make it easy to spot and remedy errors. Errors are often hard to find in high-level rollups, but first-level managers can usually spot errors immediately in their reports. Since it's to their obvious benefit to get the errors corrected they are likely to take appropriate action. For instance, if a sales rep left the company but was erroneously left as "active" in the system, his abysmal productivity will cause his team's productivity to dip, prompting his direct manager to resolve the problem on the spot. His (former) second-level manager may notice a problem, but would probably not be able to link it back to the cause as quickly. Using babushka metrics will improve the quality of the entire metrics set.

Make babushka metrics a part of the first phase of the rollout, even if you have to sacrifice some of the scope of the metrics set in exchange.

# More is Not Better

Most CRM tools come with dozens, even hundreds of canned metrics, with the possibility of creating ever more to fit your exact needs. Unfortunately, most of the canned reports are poorly thought out, and quantity certainly does not help here. Who has the time, not to mention the inclination, to study dozens of reports each day?

There are really two issues here. One, what metrics are worth looking at, and two, can multiple metrics be combined in a way that makes sense and that actually adds to the comprehension of the situation. Select a small set of metrics for your core set, combine them wherever possible, adding ad-hoc reports when needed to analyze a particular situation. Here are recommendations for the core set by business function. Annotated examples are presented at the end of the chapter.

## Marketing and Lead Generation

Marketing organizations focus on lead generation and therefore must determine the success of the various strategies they use. Metrics to be used on a regular basis by marketing organizations include:

- **Lead generation analysis**. This shows the number of leads per source, the cost per lead and per closed sale, the revenue per lead and per source, and the sales cycle time per source, contrasting the results across campaigns and other lead-generation mechanisms.
- **Telesales productivity**, including the volume of calls (inbound or outbound) and the number of leads and prospects generated, both by individual and for the group as a whole.

Marketing organizations also run many ad-hoc analyses, some of which may become enshrined in regular reports. In particular, metrics around the lifetime value of a customer, the buying patterns of customers over time, the percentage of new customers versus existing ones, and profit patterns by product or by customer are useful to both marketing and sales efforts.

## Sales

The foundation report in all sales organizations is a pipeline report. The details will vary based on your industry and your sales model but all pipeline reports show the current forecast versus target and where the deals are in sales cycle. The pipeline report is a good example of a report that should be carefully tuned for maximum productivity since it is used so much. The ability to navigate pipeline data from the summary level to the individual deal is also very important.

Beyond the pipeline report, sales organizations usually track sales productivity indicators, including:

- The sales cycle length
- The close ratio
- The average sale size and average cost of sale
- Order accuracy

It may be a good idea to also track the average time to collection as an indication of the quality of the sales.

## Support and Service

Here are the must-have metrics to all support organizations, even small ones.

- **Case productivity**, including the volume of inquiries, the promptness of their resolution (and in particular whether the case was a "first call close"), and the individual and group productivity of the reps.
- **Knowledge base productivity**. This metric focuses on knowledge base documents rather than cases.
- **Issue distribution**. This is a more analytical set of metrics that looks at the types of support cases with the goal of identifying the top causes (and, whenever possible, take preventive action) as well as staffing to match the needs.
- **Case aging**. A more tactical kind of metrics, case aging is a tool to manage the backlog. A case aging report lists the open cases that exceed predefined targets, such as having been open for more than 48 hours.

- **Customer satisfaction.** The most important metric in my mind for support organizations, but often overlooked, customer satisfaction should be based on a transactional survey delivered to an appropriate sample of customers as soon as their issue is closed.
- **Support renewals.** For fee-based support centers, metrics about the sales of support products and renewals of support contracts are required. The needs here are similar to sales and therefore the metrics are similar to sales metrics.

Larger support centers and ambitious small centers can add a few more metrics, including:

- **Financials.** Financial metrics are very important, of course, so you may wonder why they did not make it to the set of "must-haves." This is because the standard financial reports run by the finance group suffice for smaller centers.
- **Top 10 customers.** To identify the heavy-usage customers, who may be either struggling or abusing the system.
- **Knowledge base usage.** To analyze the health of the knowledge base and increase the usability of individual documents.
- **Metrics by manager** and by geography. Babushka reports become necessary in larger centers with multiple managers and product lines.

Annotated sample reports are presented later in this chapter.

# The Dashboard Concept

Even if you are careful about selecting only a core set of metrics as described above, it still takes time to wade through many different charts and graphs and it's difficult to synthesize all the information to make good decisions. If you are overwhelmed with data, the solution is to create a concise yet complete dashboard where all the important information is available at a glance, ready to inspire action.

What makes a good dashboard?

## It's Short

A good dashboard fits on one page, one side of one page, to be precise. And don't cheat by using minuscule 6-point type. Be serious about enforcing the discipline of minimal but key information. This is critical if executives are to use the metrics.

This means that only a few metrics can make it to the dashboard. If you must maintain metrics that are not on the dashboard to analyze detailed operational issues, fine, but don't bother creating detailed metrics unless you actually take the time to review them, interpret them, and take action based on the results.

## It Shows Key Metrics Against Targets

The dashboard should give you a complete picture. Would you drive a car that has a speedometer but no gas gauge? (It creates problems. I know because I used to own such a car and I ran out of gas more than once.) Gather metrics for all the key areas of the organization, selecting from all four categories of metrics: revenue, cost, efficiency, and customer satisfaction.

Not only should you strive for completeness but you must also show targets and achievements against the targets. (Think about the red zone on the gas gauge: useful, no?) Let's say that response time performance is on the dashboard. You should not only measure the percentage of calls responded to within the response target, but further compare that percentage to where you want to be (typically 90-95%). If you pick a 90% achievement target and you are performing at 85%, show that you are below the mark.

Targets may change over time to reflect improvements in performance (or declining standards, but that's less glorious). Targets are especially useful for outsiders to the functional team, who often find it difficult to gauge how well things are going from the metrics. How can one interpret a sales forecast if it doesn't show the sales quota?

## It Shows Trends

Experienced functional managers do well with snapshot data because they have completely internalized the workings of their team and they can tell immediately from a single number whether the trend is up or down, and how significant the change is. For everyone else, time progressions are very useful. It's positively uplifting to see that the forecasted revenue is inching up every week, even if you are still below the quota. And it's instructive to spot a downward trend in customer satisfaction, even if you're still above target.

Looking back four to six time units is usually enough (and should still fit in the one-page limit of the dashboard).

## It's Visual

A one-page format with targets and a time progression makes dashboards easy to read. To further improve readability, add visuals if possible. If a picture tells a thousand words, five pictures on your allotted one page tell a long story. For example, try a red light/green light format to show whether you are hitting targets. Or illustrate the time progressions with line charts that also show the targets.

Do you want more ideas and you are willing to invest a few dollars and hours? I recommend *The Visual Display of Quantitative Information* by Edward Tufte, a classic with many inspiring examples drawn from many different areas, although not a single CRM dashboard.

# Streamline Delivery

### Make Metrics Widely Available

What do you have to hide? Secret metrics generate only suspicion and bad feelings. If the selected metrics and the data they are run against are sound, then everyone should be able to see them. This means everyone inside and outside the functional team, within the limits of confidentiality concerns and permission levels, of course.

One word of caution: a well-informed individual can learn much from apparently "innocent" functional metrics, so label them as company confidential and make sure they do not leave the company.

### Use Subscriptions

Ever get an unsolicited letter? Did it go straight into the recycling box? That's what happens to metrics that are forcibly dumped in users' laps.

Instead, allow users to manage subscriptions to the metrics they choose to receive. A self-service approach removes most of the administrative overhead and, as long as permission levels are clearly defined, subscriptions should not interfere with the existing confidentiality requirements. Users should be able to request tailored metrics that way, metrics that show what's happening in their particular team.

### Make Them Timely

Metrics should be available promptly as the measurement period ends, so for instance weekly metrics should be available on Monday mornings. Old news is incredibly less valuable than new news: old news is no news.

You may need to do some manual processing to produce the more complex metrics, in particular the dashboards, but stay with the discipline of almost-instant delivery. I always vote for a basic but timely metrics over fancy but delayed reports.

### Make Them Automatic

Have the metrics run automatically. For one thing, that will help make them timely, and it will also ensure that they are generated even on busy days, which are the days they are most needed. The best arrangement is to deliver an e-mail to the subscribers containing the URL of the site where the metrics can be viewed—and printed if desired.

Ideally, all metrics run at a particular point in time should be presented in a single e-mail. (I have yet to see this apparently simple feature in any tracking tool, sigh!)

With complicated metrics such as dashboards it's worth automating the creation process once the structure of the dashboard is fixed.

### Make Tweaking Easy

Rather than trying to create perfect reports for everyone, especially for "what if" types of analyses, use so-called stub reports that allow users to enter parameters before running them so they can be tailored to the specific needs of the moment. For instance, if you have a detailed campaign success analysis report, allow the users to run it on the campaign of their choice.

### Make Spreadsheet Analysis Easy

One of the most useful analysis tools is a spreadsheet. Don't pretend you can meet every need even through stub reports and plan to offer a way to dump useful data into a spreadsheet. Complete dumps are often too granular to be useful to the users (no, users do not want to wade through every account note or every case note). Try using the more popular reports as a basis for the dumps.

## Suggested Metrics

There are many ways to arrange meaningful metrics. This section shows some practical samples that you can copy and adapt for your use. For each report, you will see:

- Its goal, a one-phrase description of what it's all about.
- A suggested frequency, since some reports are really meaningless if run against a very short period. Feel free to adapt this to your needs.
- A sample report to give you a clear visual impression of what it may look like.
- Comments about the contents or the usage of the report. In particular, I point out similarities across reports. The fact is that there are only a few different types of reports that can be used for a variety of purposes. For instance, a telesales productivity report is very similar to a support center productivity report (they are both about hitting volume targets), while a pipeline report is very similar to a knowledge base productivity report (they are both about moving through a process). After a while, you should be able to spot the similarities yourself.

Reports are listed roughly in the order in which they appear in the last section ("More is not Better"). Not all reports are shown, however, only the more interesting and complex ones.

## Lead Generation Analysis

**Goal** Track the outcome of various lead-generating initiatives so you can make decisions about what actions to take again and what actions to de-emphasize.

**Frequency** Weekly (and monthly, quarterly), depending on the size of the organization.

**Sample**

TABLE 10.2  Sample Lead Generation Analysis Metrics

| Lead Generation Analysis for Q1 2003 |||||||||
|---|---|---|---|---|---|---|---|
| Source | Total Cost ('000s) | # Leads | Cost Per Lead | Revenue per Lead[1] | Revenue per Source ('000s) | Cost per Sale | Sales Cycle (days) |
| Ad- BusWeek | $ 200 | 1025 | $ 195 | $ 5402 | $ 2700 | $ 390 | 35 |
| Direct mail—List A | $ X | X | $ X | X | $ X | $ X | X |
| Webinar—Best Practices | $ X | X | $ X | X | $ X | $ X | X |
| TradeShow—Boston | $ X | X | $ X | X | $ X | $ X | X |
| All | $ X | X | $ X | X | $ X | $ X | X |

1. This number will not be known until the end of the sales cycle, so be careful about interpreting early results. This is also true of all the columns to the right of this one.

**Comments**   It's best to show actual costs and revenue figures, but if it's difficult to do within the confines of the system, you can simply report on leads generated. Of course, having the financial information available right there is much better.

This productivity report is very similar to productivity reports for other functions.

## Telesales Productivity

**Goal**   Track volumes against targets per person and overall.

**Frequency**   Typically daily (and weekly, monthly, quarterly).

### Sample

**TABLE 10.3**   Sample Telesales Productivity Metrics

| Telesales Productivity for 21 March 2003 | | |
|---|---|---|
| Name | Calls (% Target) | Leads[1] |
| Anna | 45 (+50%) | 2 |
| Bert | 30 (+0%) | 1 |
| Carlos | 36 (+20%) | 1 |
| Denise | X | X |
| Ellen | X | X |
| … | | |
| Total (Target) | X (%) | X |

1. Your labels will vary depending on your terminology.

**Comments**   Note the combination of raw numbers and target achievement in the "leads" column. This is a simple example of how to make metrics richer and more meaningful.

This productivity report is very similar to productivity reports for other functions.

## Sales Pipeline

**Goal**  Track the progression of support deals through the sales cycle by sales rep and overall.

**Frequency**  Typically weekly but could be daily at quarter end and other sensitive periods.

### Sample

**TABLE 10.4**  Sample Sales Pipeline Metrics

| Sales Pipeline for 20 March 2003 |||||||||
|---|---|---|---|---|---|---|---|
| Name | Prospect Stage[1] | Needs Analysis | Proposal | Negotiation | Committed | Closed | Q1 Forecast $ (% target) |
| Anna | 1,000 | 1,300 | 750 | 200 | 300 | 330 | 1,095 (50%) |
| Bert | X | X | X | X | X | X | X |
| Carlos | X | X | X | X | X | X | X |
| Denise | X | X | X | X | X | X | X |
| Ellen | X | X | X | X | X | X | X |
| ... | | | | | | | |
| Total | X | X | X | X | X | X | X (%) |

1. Your labels will vary depending on your sales methodology and reporting requirements.

**Comments**  This report computes the forecast based on a weighed formula rather than a straight addition of the amounts in the pipeline. In this example, "prospects" and "needs analysis" are not included in the forecast dollars at all, and others are included as a percentage only, except for closed accounts. Use the formula that works for your particular environment.

It's clear that detailed information related to the report is critical to fully comprehend the forecast. For instance, what are the deals that are close to being closed? A great reporting environment would allow the manager to click on, say the committed number for Anna and to see the detailed list.

This report lends itself well to slicing and dicing by region or industry.

Some tool vendors propose inventive, graphic interpretation of this report, for instance in a radar screen configuration. The data, however, is always the same: what is in the pipeline and where is it?

The structure of the report is comparable to that of the knowledge base productivity report, in that it follows items (deals here, documents there) from one state to the next.

## Sales Productivity

**Goal** Track sales productivity, indicators.

**Frequency** Probably monthly, depending on sales volumes.

### Sample

**TABLE 10.5** Sample Sales Productivity Metrics

| Sales Productivity for March 2003 | | | | | |
|---|---|---|---|---|---|
| Name | Sales Cycle (days) | Close Ratio (%) | Avg Deal Size ('000) | Avg Cost of Sale ('000) | Order Accuracy (%) |
| Anna | 42 | 40 (%) | $2345 | $54 | 89 |
| Bert | 21 | 30 (%) | $1234 | $23 | 78 |
| Carlos | X | X (%) | X | X | X |
| Denise | X | X (%) | X | X | X |
| Ellen | X | X (%) | X | X | X |
| ... | | | | | |
| Total | X | X (%) | X | X | X |

**Comments** Add targets and accomplishments against targets where they exist.

This productivity report is very similar to productivity reports for other functions.

## Support Productivity

**Goal** Track volumes and how quickly issues are traveling through the system.

**Frequency** Typically daily (and weekly, monthly, quarterly). Very busy centers will want to analyze volume in shorter chunks, down to each hour or even half-hour.

## Sample

**TABLE 10.6** Sample Support Productivity Metrics

| Case Productivity for 22 March 2003 ||||||||||
|---|---|---|---|---|---|---|---|---|
| Name | Incoming Cases | Closed Cases | Reopened Cases | Backlog | Met Response Goal | Met Resolution Goal | Once & Done[1] | Escalated |
| Anna | 2 | 2 | 0 | 1 | 9 (x%) | 1 (50%) | 1 (50%) | 1 (x%) |
| Bert | 2 | 0 | 0 | 5 | 12 (100%) | X (%) | X (%) | 0 (0%) |
| Carlos | 0 | 0 | 0 | 4 | X (%) | X (%) | X (%) | X (%) |
| Denise | X | X | X | X | X (%) | X (%) | X (%) | X (%) |
| Ellen | X | X | X | X | X (%) | X (%) | X (%) | X (%) |
| ... | | | | | | | | |
| Total | 43 | 42 | 5 | 6 | X (%) | X (%) | X (%) | X (%) |

1. This is also called "first call close" and represents issues that were resolved within just one interaction.

**Comments** This is a good example of a "meaty" report. There's a lot of information in this table, but it's easy to read and to understand. Note how raw numbers and percentages are presented side by side. After a couple of weeks, managers should be able to tell at a glance whether anything extraordinary happened during the measurement period and whether any corrective action is required.

The sample shown here is best for high-complexity support centers (ones where cases take lots of time and effort to resolve). In low-complexity support and service centers drop the columns for backlog and reopened cases and replace them with handle time and abandoned call rate.

This would be the output for the report of a first-level manager. Higher-level managers would see results for subgroups rather than for individuals.

This productivity report is very similar to other productivity reports for other functions.

## Support Issue Distribution

**Goal** Track the type of issues that are coming into the support center so you can staff properly and/or invest in preventive measures.

**Frequency** Typically weekly or even monthly, except for very busy, dynamic centers, that may want to run it daily.

## Sample

**TABLE 10.7** Sample Support Issue Distribution Metrics

| Issue Distribution for Week Ending 22 March 2003 ||||
|---|---|---|---|
| Installation[1] | Configuration | Usage | Other |
| 2 (4%) | 12 (21%) | 34 (61%) | 8 (14%) |

1. Categories are illustrative only.

**Comments** The usefulness of this report is directly related to how meaningful the categories are, so pick them carefully. Typically this is done through hard-coded categories in the case-tracking system. It's best to use a relatively small number of categories (say around 7, and no more than 10) and subdivide them as required rather than allowing a large list of categories. Beware of over-detailed categorizations. Anything over 50 categories is pretty much useless: who can tell what is what with so many choices?

The sample is geared towards case topics but you could run something similar for root causes (say, bug/documentation error/user error/product usability, etc.) A root cause report is key for proactive efforts.

This report is similar to the lead generation analysis report, although it's much simpler.

## Support Case Aging

**Goal** Ensure that no case falls through the cracks.

**Frequency** To match to your target resolution time (daily if it's a day, weekly if it's a week or more).

### Sample

**TABLE 10.8** Sample Support Case Aging Metrics

| Case Aging on 22 March 2003 |||||||
|---|---|---|---|---|---|---|
| Case | Customer | Priority | Status[1] | Owner | Opened | Last Touched |
| 123 | XYZ | 2 | Engineering | Anna | 2/1/02 | 3/1/02 |
| 126 | XXX | 1 | Engineering | Bert | 2/22/02 | 3/22/02 |
| 367 | XXX | 1 | Customer | Bert | 2/2/02 | 3/2/00 |
| 404 | XXX | 3 | Research | Bert | 3/15/02 | 3/22/00 |
| ... | ... | ... | | | | ... |

1. Your labels will vary to match the case statuses you use.

**Comments**  You need to define what an "aging" case is. Here, it's any case older than a week. Some centers instead focus on the last update to the case. I think it's a lot safer to scrutinize *all* cases older than a particular target.

Another approach is to limit the aging list to "really important" cases, say only P1 cases.

Properly speaking, this is not a true "metric," but simply a list of cases. It is, however, very handy!

You could run a very similar report on deal aging for sales, showing all deals that have lingered a bit too much at each stage in the process. This is a good template for any kind of aging report.

## Knowledge Base Productivity

**Goal**  Track the progress of new documents through the knowledge base creation system, both by individual and overall.

**Frequency**  Typically weekly is enough, but busy centers require daily metrics.

### Sample

TABLE 10.9  Sample Knowledge Base Productivity Metrics

| KB Productivity for Week Ending 22 March 2003 ||||||||
| Name | New[1] | Waiting for Review | Reviewed | Published/ internal | Published/ customer | Waiting for Fix |
|---|---|---|---|---|---|---|
| Anna | 3 | 2 | 0 | 1 | 1 | 1 |
| Bert | 2 | 0 | 0 | 0 | 0 | 0 |
| Carlos | 0 | 0 | 0 | X | 0 | 0 |
| Denise | X | X | X | X | X | X |
| Ellen | X | X | X | X | X | X |
| ... | | | | | | |
| Total | 8 | 3 | 5 | 3 | 2 | X |

1. Your labels will vary to match the document statuses you use.

**Comments** An interesting improvement would be to track the timeliness of the reviews by setting targets for each level and reporting achievement against target in this report. See the case productivity report for an example of reporting achievement against response time targets.

This productivity report is very similar to other productivity reports for other functions.

## Customer Satisfaction

**Goal** Track the level of customer satisfaction.

**Frequency** Typically weekly is enough, but if you do a lot of surveys each day you may want to go for daily reports. You need to also have an alert mechanism in place to handle particularly good or bad surveys within a business day.

### Sample

**TABLE 10.10** Sample Customer Satisfaction Metrics

| Customer Satisfaction for March 2003 |||||||
|---|---|---|---|---|---|---|
| Name | Response[1] | Resolution | Professionalism | Overall | Number Sent | Number Received |
| Anna | 8.1 | 7.8 | 9.4 | 8.5 | 120 | 40 (30%) |
| Bert | 8.3 | 6.5 | 9.2 | 8.2 | 125 | 42 (33 %) |
| Carlos | X | X | X | X | X | X (%) |
| Denise | X | X | X | X | X | X (%) |
| Ellen | X | X | X | X | X | X (%) |
| ... | | | | | | |
| Total | 8.0 | 7.7 | 9.2 | 8.6 | X | X (%) |

1. Your labels will vary to match the questions in your survey. Response time, resolution time, professionalism, and overall impression are typical topics for support-based surveys.

**Comments** Track response rates because slow response rates decrease the reliability of the survey results.

Note that, despite earlier rants in favor of target achievement percentages, I'm using averages on this report because I find averages work reasonably well for survey ratings. If you prefer, you can use a target average rating (say 8/10) and report achievement against it.

Some support managers hesitate to run individual metrics for customer satisfaction. Don't be shy! Individual measurement and targets are essential for customer satisfaction, as differences between individuals can be literally startling. However, be cautious about using results if individuals receive few surveys (this example would be ok, with 40+ surveys returned per individual). With a handful of surveys, one particularly bad—or good—result could skew the result, whether you compute averages or achievement against target.

## Support Financials Summary

**Goal**  Get a snapshot of the financial data so you can make business decisions.

**Frequency**  Monthly (unless you get more frequent financial reports).

**Sample**

**TABLE 10.11**  Sample Support Financials Summary Metrics

| Support Financials Summary for March 2003 ||||||
|---|---|---|---|---|---|
| Revenue (over/under) | Expenses (over/under) | Profits (over/under) | Renewal Rate | Cost per Case (up/down) | Cost per Customer |
| $ (%) | $ (%) | $ (%) | X% | $ (%) | $ (%) |

**Comments**  This report would be ideal for a fee-based support center. Cost-based centers do not need the revenue-based columns, obviously.

I like to see financial figures using a rolling three-month average to smooth out monthly spikes, which are often meaningless.

A great improvement to the report would be to add trending information. And graphs would be good too.

Finally, the numbers should be broken down by geography or product family for larger centers

A similar report could be created for a sales team to track margins and cost of sales.

# Top 10 Customers

**Goal**   Track the heavy-usage customers so you can identify both customers who are struggling and customers who may be abusing the system.

**Frequency**   Weekly.

## Sample

**TABLE 10.12**   Sample Top 10 Customers Metrics

| Top Support Customers for March 2003 | | | | | |
|---|---|---|---|---|---|
| Customer | New Cases | New P1 Cases (%) | Closed Cases | Backlog | Rank Last Period |
| Customer X | 25 | 10 (40%) | 20 | 10 | 5 |
| Customer Y | 15 | X (%) | 10 | 6 | - |
| Customer Z | 5 | 0 (0%) | 20 | 3 | 1 |
| ... | | | | | |

**Comments**   Depending on the size of the center, show the top 10 or 20 or 40 customers. I chose to concentrate on new cases opened during the period, but it would also make sense to look for customers with the largest backlogs.

This report is particularly useful in centers that serve customers with support contracts.

If you have corporate customers, you may want to run this both by contact (individual) and by customer.

This would be an interesting report to run on customer sales rather than support usage to show the most important recent customers.

# Knowledge Base Usage

**Goal**   Track the documents with the heaviest and lowest usage and ratings so you can identify key issues and documents that need to be reworked. You can also use this to reward the authors of particularly successful documents.

**Frequency**   A weekly run should suffice, although a daily run may make sense in busy environments.

## Sample

**TABLE 10.13**  Sample Knowledge Base Usage Metrics

| Top KB Documents for March 2003 | | | | | |
|---|---|---|---|---|---|
| Category | Number | Title | Hits | Read (%) | Usefulness Rating |
| Installation | 125 | Installation Troubleshooting Guide | 320 | 300 (94%) | 27 (9%) |
| Configuration | 111 | Adding a Frame | 1004 | 280 (29%) | 279 (100%) |
| Configuration | 502 | API Guide | X | X (%) | X (%) |
| ... | | | | | |

**Comments**  This shows the top documents, but you should also run the report on the lowest-performing documents.

This shows ranking by reading scores, but you can also rank by user rating (or do both).

In this example, the first document (#125) is read in almost every search it is found, so the indexing seems to be working well. However, the very low usefulness rating (9%) points to serious flaws in the document.

On the other hand, the second document (#111) is showing up in a lot of searches in which it is not read, so its indexing should be improved.

# Where do I Go From Here?

Metrics can be overwhelming because there are so many choices, but you can do well with a reasonably small effort as long as you adhere to the following four steps:

- Define measurable objectives both for the project and for running the business long-term, starting at the implementation kickoff meeting. Limit yourself to a handful of the most meaningful metrics, preferably outcome-related metrics.

- Make sure that the tool will track the data required to create the metrics you need. To ensure that the data is indeed logged, make it very

easy for the users to log the information as part of their daily work, without requiring special efforts.
- Invest in "slice and dice" or babushka reports so that each manager has immediately useful data at his or her disposal from the start. This is more important than creating fancy or pretty reports, and even creating as many reports as you would like.

Keep working on metrics. As long as you are tracking the right data, you can always make improvements to the reports to fit the changing needs of the business.

# Rescuing a Failing CRM Project

## Express Version

- Whether you have inherited a failing CRM project or it's your own project that's failing, start by conducting a candid assessment of the situation to determine if the project is worth saving. The assessment process is similar to a post-mortem for a completed project. Carefully evaluate the three P's (people, process, and politics) that are usually the causes of project problems, as well as the tool, which is almost always blamed but is only infrequently the root cause of the problem.
- To be salvageable, a project needs a credible and engaged executive sponsor, even more so than other CRM projects, and a tool with a reasonable fit. Everything else can be overcome, but don't bother with a salvage effort if you don't have those two prerequisites.
- Make changes in people, processes, and politics as required and define a new project plan and budget for the project, simplifying the project as much as you can. When you gain approval for the new plan and budget, restart the project at a logical starting point following the same implementation process you would use for any other CRM process.

- With a salvaged project, pay particular attention to morale and communication within the project team and with the users, as well as careful project management.

## Project Failures

Although the techniques described in this book should yield reasonably smooth and successful projects, you may be reading it specifically because you have been handed a failing project and the responsibility to fix it. This chapter is for you.

This chapter is also for you if you suspect that your project is failing, although no one, not even yourself perhaps, has openly admitted yet. Generally speaking, if the project manager or a business owner thinks that the project is failing, even if other project team members deny it, then the project is indeed failing. Team members may refuse to accept that the project is not going well because they have so much invested in it.

The fact is that it's usually pretty clear when a project is failing, at least from an outsider's point of view: users have lost interest, the project team is struggling, the business requirements have changed drastically, or serious technical issues have been encountered. Frequently the project faces not just one but a combination of problems. And we are talking big problems, serious problems that the team is unable to address or sometimes even to face.

This is not to suggest that CRM projects fail in spectacular ways. More often it's a matter of losing momentum over time as problems pile up, unaddressed, until the project comes to an unceremonious halt. By then, it's usually too late to do anything, so always be thankful that you are intervening before the project slips from failing to failed status.

If you are faced with a failing project, use a three-step recovery process: assess the situation, restructure the project, and restart it.

## Step 1: Assess

### Why Projects Fail

CRM projects fail because of the so-called "three P's": people, process, and politics. Some CRM projects fail because of a poor tool choice, but it's actually quite rare that the tool itself is the root cause for the failure. True, the tool is a convenient scapegoat and is almost always blamed for project failures, and even branded as the *only* cause for the failure. The reality is that a properly run project should be able to conduct a successful tool evaluation that yields a solid, well-suited tool. If that selection should turn out to have been ill advised, a solid project team should be able to recover the project without going through a "failed" phase, although certainly there would be some unpleasant moments.

You need to determine how people, process, politics, or the tool contributed to the failure without automatically blaming the tool.

## The Assessment Session

Whether you believe your own project is failing or you were brought in to rescue a failing project, start by holding an assessment session. This is very similar to the post-mortem analysis described in Chapter 9, although post-mortem analyses follow projects that went to completion. Bring the entire project team together for the assessment, and as much as possible organize a face-to-face meeting since there are many emotional topics to be discussed. Make sure the executive sponsor attends the assessment.

The assessment should be conducted with the full team, just like a post-mortem, although the key internal players usually reconvene afterwards without the integrator and without the individual contributors to review the results of the assessment and to make the business decision on whether to proceed or halt the project.

It's somewhat easier for an outsider to conduct the assessment session because an outsider has a more objective view and is better able to explore unpleasant areas. If you are managing the assessment session for your own project, keep your emotions in check and make every effort to be objective and thorough, while leveraging the knowledge you have gained from working on the project to probe the issues.

In any case, expect the team's morale to be low by the time a project is in failing mode. Failing projects are depressing for all team members, regardless of their individual levels of responsibilities for the failure. Maintain a tone of reasonable optimism for the assessment session: after all, the project is failing, but it's not dead yet, and recovery can only occur after an appropriately balanced assessment session. This is not the time to despair, but don't allow fake optimism either: the team is in a serious situation that should be acknowledged as such.

**The Good**   Start the assessment by reviewing what went well with the project. It may seem crazy to start with the positives since there won't be many (after all, the project is *failing*) but it's critical to figure out the pieces that can be rescued if the project will be restarted, which is a very likely outcome. Also, starting on the positive side helps everyone's morale, which can be a big help at this difficult juncture.

Take a look at the three Ps, people, process, and politics. About people: are there key individuals that are contributing to the success of the project despite the challenges? Identify both technical team members and business team members.

About the process: although it has failed to produce a winning result, are there aspects of it that are working? For instance, is the communication process working? Is the testing producing good results? Are end-users appropriately engaged in the project? Is the coordination between the technical team and the business team working properly?

For the political aspect, the very critical question to ask is: is the executive sponsor active in the project and providing tangible support? If the answer is yes, then it's almost always worthwhile to press forward with the project, even if difficult choices must be made.

There may be other positive political aspects, in particular if the business functions are behind the project. Can end-users perceive benefits from the tool, even if only in a few areas based on the functionality released so far? If the end-users are demonstrating any level of enthusiasm during an assessment session, the future of the project is very positive even if the future looks dim right now.

Finally, look at the tool. Tools typically get blamed for any and all problems, and certainly CRM tools are far from perfect, but try hard to isolate the features of the tool that are working well. After all, the team selected it in the first place, so there must have been something attractive about it.

Especially at the beginning of the session, conduct the assessment in brainstorming mode, accepting all suggestions and delaying discussions until everyone has had a chance to participate. If you allow participants to discuss the suggestions as they are made, you run the real risk of shutting off the dialog.

**The Bad**   Once you have a list of positives, go to the negatives, looking again at the three Ps, people, process, and politics, and also at the tool.

Are the right people on the project? Are there any areas of weakness? Consider weaknesses at all levels, from the project manager to the business owners and super-users, to the technical team, and to the integrator. People issues are difficult to confront in a group setting, so expect roundabout answers, for example, a suggestion to add someone with a specialized skill rather than a condemnation of a particular individual. Carefully note the nuances. On the other hand, if the level of interaction gets aggressive, you will know that the team is not communicating well and that problem needs to go on your list of issues.

People problems can also arise within the user community. Are the business owners or the super-users not participating appropriately? Are end-users refusing to use the tool? Can you determine whether the reasons behind the refusal are based on (lack of) functionality? Communication issues? Motivational issues?

Moving on to process issues, it's common to find problems with the way the project itself is being conducted. Assessments often uncover that the requirements definition was done too hastily, that the project plan was overly ambitious, that the users have not been involved enough throughout the project, or were not involved early enough, and that testing and QA are insufficient. Besides determining what processes have been weak, probe carefully on *when* the project went wrong, not just how. This is because, if the project will be restarted you need to know at what point to restart it. If it's just a problem of buggy programming, then you can restart the programming phase (perhaps with different programmers!). But if the problem occurred at the requirements definition phase, you need to go back to that point, which means a great deal of additional time and resources will be needed.

Process issues can also come from the business side. Are the processes that are to be modeled in the tool inefficient, ineffective, or simply the wrong ones? If the project included formalizing processes for the first time it's quite common to find that the newly formalized processes are "wrong" and cannot be used as they are. They looked fine on paper, but once they got automated in the tool the users realized that they were simply not the right processes. If that's the case, go back to the process definition phase and use more effective validation techniques.

The tool is often blamed when the wrong process was automated, so make sure that users can distinguish between a bad automation of a good process (which is a tool or a customization problem) and a correct automation of a bad process (which is a process problem).

Process issues can also arise if the business model is changing, prompting process changes that are incompatible with the tool. If that's the case, the current configuration of the tool (assuming you have started customizing it) may not work any more, but this doesn't automatically mean that a new tool is required. What you need to do is to re-evaluate the tool against the new business model and processes before proceeding with a decision. You may be pleasantly surprised to see that the tool can be adapted to the changes, although it will take time and resources to perform the re-evaluation.

It's always tricky to probe political issues in a group meeting so you can limit yourself to one simple test: is the executive sponsor attending? If not, then you can politely thank everyone and go spend your energy on something else, since the project cannot succeed without the sponsor.

Political problems often take the form of active or passive resistance to the project from the business functions or from the IT group. What is the basis for the resistance? A strong executive sponsor should be able to help resolve the problems, but only if he or she is aware of them in the first place. An out-of-touch executive sponsor points to either a weak project manager or a power-challenged sponsor, both issues that would need to be addressed if a rebirth is to be successful.

Politics often get blamed for the lack of availability of an appropriate budget, and indeed negative politics can derail well-planned budget. However, do not allow politics—or the executive sponsor—to be blamed for failing to get large cost overruns approved. If the project costs are out of control, it's the performance of the project team that must be scrutinized, both at a process level and at the individual level. Likely you have problems with people or processes (or both) rather than political opposition.

Also include careful consideration of tool weaknesses in the assessment. Almost all projects run into some kind of tool problem, so the issue is not so much to make a list of the tool problems you encountered, or even to consider its length, but rather to qualify the impact of the tool issues on the project. Tool issues need not be an automatic death sentence for the project.

In my experience, tool issues that can completely derail a project are either disastrous performance issues or critical functionality failures that are in the way of meeting the basic project goals. If a tool just won't scale in your environment and the vendor cannot deliver or suggest appropriate fixes, the future is very grim for the tool. Chances are that users just won't use it consistently. And if you are faced with functionality gaps that make it impossible to achieve critical project goals, continuing the project will be throwing good money after bad.

I find it very helpful to invite the tool vendor to confirm the critical failures identified by the project team. Vendors tend to be very optimistic when it comes to fixing even large problems, so if the vendor tells you something cannot be overcome you can be sure that there is no hope. Evaluate carefully their recommendations for fixes.

The assessment session will last several hours. Consider it a good investment whether or not you conclude that the project can be saved. If the project can be saved, you should be able to use each and every suggestion made in the assessment to make the second half less painful and more successful. If the decision is to halt the project, the assessment brings certainty that it's the right decision, and the lessons can be carried over to future projects.

## Can the Project be Saved?

Many so-called failing projects are failing just a little bit: they were a little too ambitious perhaps, or the team lacked some discipline, or some technical problems were not properly anticipated. Such projects should be saved and require only small amounts of tweaking to turn into successes. But even a seriously failing CRM project can be saved as long as it has just two—admittedly demanding—characteristics:

- A committed, appropriately powerful executive sponsor.
- A tool that offers a reasonable fit with no critical gaps. This means that the tool can support the business processes as they are currently defined (which could be different from the ones that were used at the beginning of the project), that critical features are functioning as needed, and that the performance meets your requirements.

You should be able to confirm both items right in the assessment session, although making a final decision on the tool side may require some additional detective work with the technical team and with the vendor. As mentioned earlier, vendors are known to be optimistic about their assessments of the likelihood and the speed of repairs or alleviations of problems, so when they recommend fixes you must insist on a firm schedule. Table any further work on your part until the tool issues are resolved to your satisfaction and maintain assertive and frequent communication with the vendor to ensure your issues are given priority.

If the vendor says the issues cannot be fixed, agree with it immediately and negotiate a reasonable settlement. Contracts rarely have escape clauses for technical failures, but you should be able to get some concessions even though litigation is not likely to bring any positive outcomes. Vendors are very concerned about bad press so exert some appropriate pressure.

If the tool turns out to be a poor fit, the only alternative is to go back to square one: tool selection. You may be able to proceed a bit faster since you can reuse your requirements list, but it would be essential to understand why a poor tool choice was made using that list in the first place. Use the assessment to probe that point.

Assuming that you have both an executive sponsor and a reasonably fit tool, you can proceed to step 2.

## Step 2: Restructure

If the project is worth salvaging, you must create a revised project plan, making changes as suggested in the assessment. You may have identified multiple problems during the assessment, and if so you will need a multi-prong approach. For simplicity's sake, I'll comment on each type of problem and its recommended approach individually.

If you identified problems with people on the project team, you need to decide whether to replace individuals or to apply some motivational pressure. Replacing team members creates significant delays, as new members need to get up to speed on the project itself and also in terms of teamwork. Therefore, replacements are only worthwhile if performance management efforts are unlikely to be successful, but it's sometimes necessary.

If the problem lies within the integrator's team, consider switching integrators altogether, even if the problems exist only with certain individuals on the team. This is because the integrator should have an experienced team leader on the job, someone who should have caught and corrected the issue before it got to the point of declaring the project a failure. Having gotten to a failure point, you need to consider that the team leader is not doing his or her job. Moreover, if you made the appropriate amount of noise with the integrator's management before declaring failure, the situation should have been handled through normal processes much earlier. Professional services managers for tool vendors can all cite instances of badly-failing projects that were dumped in their lap after the original (third-party) integrator was found to be lacking and that went on to be deployed successfully and fairly uneventfully.

You may have to replace individuals on your own team, although you can and probably will want to exercise more flexibility with internal players. If the people problems are with the super-users, find replacements. The business owners cannot normally be replaced so instead see whether the executive sponsor can exercise some muscle until appropriate cooperation is shown.

If you identified process problems for the project itself, first consider whether the issues are related to people weaknesses, and in particular to the project manager. This is because a good project manager should identify process issues quickly and get them resolved before the project comes to a halt. The project manager is not the only target, however; the issues may lie with the users if they are changing the requirements mid-way through the project. Only after identifying and resolving any people issues masquerading as process problems can you have a clear picture of the pure project process issues, and you can then restart the project at the appropriate point with a new strategy. This may require going all the way back to the requirements definition if the problems started there, but going back to the last solid code deliverable should suffice if process problems affect only the latest slice of work.

If the project issues are business process issues, not project process issues, then you need to rethink the entire project. Because most of the decisions for the project are determined by the business processes being automated, you need to go all the way back to the project requirements and to revalidate the tool choice based on the new processes. There's a pretty good chance that the tool will be able to support the new processes, but if not you will have to go all the way back to selecting a new tool. Assuming that you get lucky and the tool can support the new processes, hold a new kickoff workshop. It won't be as long and involved as the initial one since the technical environment of the project should not have changed much, so only the business side needs significant work.

Address any critical tool problems with the vendor, making sure to establish clear deadlines and milestones. Put the project on hold while the issues are resolved, but keep in very close contact with the vendor to ensure that the schedule is indeed being met. I remember a project that had to wait for two *months* for a fix to address a critical performance issue (it was a memory leak) and that proceeded to a successful rollout, albeit significantly delayed.

As you craft a new project plan, seriously consider simplifying the project down to its critical components. Few CRM projects fail because their scope is too restricted (I can think of only one such project I worked with, and even then the failure was due more to under-involving the end-users rather than to a too-simple scope). But many CRM projects struggle because they try to do too much, too soon. Go for the essential and consider the bells and whistles for a second or third phase. If your project is in the "mildly failing" category, simply moving non-critical features to a later phase may be all it needs to be restarted and completed successfully.

You may have to deploy some inventiveness to put in place the changes that are required to continue—or restart—the project. Whatever you do, don't expect to successfully restart a project without making some major changes. If the project was failing, it will take some real changes, not just good intentions or just "working harder," to turn it around.

# Step 3: Restart

## Budget and Schedule

Successful projects have solid, approved budgets and schedules. A salvaged project invariably starts out over budget and over schedule, so both must be reworked and approved before you get going.

Because of the added stresses on a restarted project, be cautious rather than aggressive when planning the new budget and schedule. While it's always a good idea to underpromise for any CRM project, it's particularly important not to make claims that cannot be met in a salvaged project.

Almost all the successful salvaged projects I have worked with ended up being considerably over schedule (*months* late) and over budget (50% of more). The organizations chose to salvage them because it was faster and cheaper than starting over. Compare the costs of a salvaged project to the cost of starting over. Since restarted projects are expensive, proceed in small, incremental steps to reduce risk and show success faster than with a more ambitious project.

## The Process

The process for a salvaged project is very much the same as a regular project, so you can use Chapter 9 as your guide. However, after a major problem extra care is required to ensure that the project is on track and stays on track. The project manager must perform particularly careful, frequent, and detailed status checks. And the status checks require more skill in a salvaged project than in a regular project since team members are more cautious and may display many self-protective behaviors. It's essential that the project manager be able to encourage the team members to be open with bad news as well as with good news. It's also a good idea for the executive sponsor to be more involved in the project, for instance by holding periodic formal reviews in addition to the informal daily checks.

Keep the project team engaged and committed to the project. The team members, whether new or not, are likely to approach the project with caution and to hold back a bit. Judicious amounts of optimism and rallying the troops are recommended.

Also pay particular attention to the morale of the end-users. After an unsuccessful attempt, people tend to harbor suspicion and distrust, so open, candid, and frequent communications are particularly important. Brief the business owners and the super-users regularly and do not shield them from bad news, even for non-critical problems, since they may interpret any unshared news as yet another failure lurking about. A frank approach is more important than an optimistic approach in a salvaged project. Get the executive sponsor to use and reinforce a candid communication style.

There's no reason why a salvaged project cannot be successful, as long as it has strong executive sponsorship and as long as the root causes for the original failure are understood and dealt with, however difficult, delicate, resource-intensive, or unpleasant that might be. Salvaged projects particularly benefit from a small-step approach, strong project leadership, and clear communication. In the long run, salvaged projects can be as successful as ones that did not go through a failure phase.

# CRM Resources 12

The CRM world is very dynamic, so it's very important to keep up with current information through web sites, magazines, books, and conferences. Below is a list of useful resources, organized by type of resource and annotated so you can pick exactly the type of information you are looking for.

The information in this section is, by necessity, static. Up-to-date lists are available from www.ftworks.com/JustEnoughCRM.htm. You can also post additional suggestions there that will be shared with all readers.

## Web Sites

The web is a great place to look for CRM information and since almost all magazines have a web presence, I will comment here about the magazines that have web sites rather than in the next section. Since there are so many relevant web sites, they are organized by focus, starting with CRM-specific sites, then sites the focus on business functions, which all contain CRM information that's nicely tailored to that business function.

## Sites for CRM Information

- www.computerworld.com/softwaretopics/crm/resources. A set of links to recent CRM articles in ComputerWorld and other media, including some of the ones listed here.
- www.crmcommunity.com. Contains industry news as well as CRM-related classes and resources. Many articles are press releases or pointers to articles on other sites. Free registration.
- www.CRMDaily.com. A site that provides short, focused articles, often written by analysts about CRM vendors and CRM implementations. Includes links to *CRM Buyer Magazine*. Free e-mail news alerts.
- www.CRMguru.com. An online community focused on CRM, containing in particular Q&As on various CRM topics by and for business users. There is a weekly newsletter you can subscribe to called *CustomerThink*, focused on the business aspects of CRM. Free membership.
- www.destinationCRM.com. The site of the monthly *CRM Magazine*. Contains a variety of short industry articles that mixes vendor interviews, case studies, and interesting editorials.
- www.fierceenterprise.com. Provides a short daily bulletin of industry news, with an emphasis on CRM. Many articles are pointers to articles on other sites and tend to be limited to news, not analysis. Great if you want to keep up-to-the-minute on CRM topics. (Was FierceCRM.)

## Sites for Sales and Marketing

The sites listed here target the business functions rather than CRM per se, but all have occasional coverage of CRM topics from the point of view of the business owners.

- www.salesandmarketing.com. This is the web site for the *Sales and Marketing Management* magazine. The content is mostly focused on business processes, and mostly on sales rather than marketing per se. Sponsors the "Chief Sales Executive Forum," a yearly conference for sales VPs. To read most articles you will need to purchase a subscription.
- www.saleslobby.com. This is the site for the *SLC Insider*, a newsletter. It includes information about tools with an annotated list.
- www.sammag.com. This is the web site of *SAM Magazine* (Sales, Advertising, and Marketing). More marketing coverage here than in *Sales and Marketing Management*. Some articles are for subscribers only.
- www.sellingpower.com. This is the web site for *Selling Power* magazine, a magazine for sales managers. Includes a dedicated CRM section with short articles about various aspects of CRM, often focused on one particular solution.

## Sites for Support And Service

The sites listed here focus more on support processes than CRM topics, but all have occasional coverage of CRM topics from the point of view of the support and service functions.

- www.afsmi.org. The site of the Association for Services Management International and their newsletter, *Members' Newsline*. Focused on processes more than tools.
- www.callcentermagazine.com. The web site for *Call Center Magazine*, a monthly publication geared towards both incoming and outgoing call centers, and very much focused on the telephone as a communication channel. Includes many articles about technology, usually in the form of contrasting case studies. Also includes links to many different vendors.
- www.helpdeskinst.com. The web site of the Help Desk Institute, the association of help desk and other support professionals, and its electronic magazine.
- www.softletter.com. The online presence of the *Softletter* newsletter, focused on personal computer software publisher. Only selected articles are available on the web site, otherwise you need to subscribe. Well-researched, very practical articles, with some CRM commentary.
- www.supportgate.com. The web site of SSPA, the Service and Support Professionals Association and its electronic newsletter, *SupportWeek*. Contains lots of CRM coverage as well as information about processes. Has many (paid-for) links to CRM vendors and integrators.
- www.the-resource-center.com. An online retailer of all kinds of resources for support and service professionals, including books and tapes.

## Sites for IT

These sites are targeted at IT owners, but may be interesting to technically minded business owners as well.

- www.openitx.com/g/ITtoolbox/CRM-SELECT.asp. An open forum for IT staffers to discuss CRM topics. The counterpart of the CRMGuru forum, but from a technical perspective.
- www.cio.com. The site of *CIO Magazine*, a general-purpose magazine for IT executives with good-quality articles, including some about CRM. Free e-mail subscription.

- www.informationweek.com. The site of *Information Week*, a weekly general-purpose IT magazine. Free subscription.
- www.SearchCRM.com. A complete site for information about CRM from an IT perspective.

# Magazines and Trade Publications

Only printed magazines are covered here. Electronic newsletters are noted in the section above, under their sponsoring site. Only specialized publications are covered here, as they are less likely to be known or available in general bookstores; however the general business press (such as Business Week, Fortune, Forbes, etc.) regularly includes articles about CRM.

## Magazines for Sales and Marketing

- *Sales and Marketing Management*. See www.salesandmarketing.com above.
- *Selling Power*. See www.sellingpower.com above.
- *SAM Magazine*. See www.sammag.com above.

## Magazines for Support And Service

- *Call Center Magazine*. See www.callcentermagazine.com above.
- *Softletter*. See www.softletter.com above.

## Magazines for CRM

- *CRM Magazine*. See www.destinationCRM.com.

## Magazines for IT

- *CIO Magazine*. See www.cio.com above.
- *Information Week*. See www.informationweek.com.

# Books

*CRM at the Speed of Light* by Paul Greenberg (McGraw Hill 2001). This book is a good introduction to the various technologies CRM can bring to the business. Recommended for business owners who want to learn more about the available tools and technological buzzwords.

*CRM Automation* by Barton Goldenberg (Prentice Hall 2002). A good overview of the process and guidelines on tool selection. For the business owner.

*Essentials of CRM* by Bryan Bergeron. Wiley, 2002. An easy-to-read book for business owners that navigates when and how CRM technology can help a small to medium business. A good read to understand when to use technology.

*The CRM Handbook* by Jill Dyche (Addison Wesley 2001). A good coverage of CRM from the business owner's perspective, and mostly from a consumer-business angle. Nice "checklists for success" in most chapters.

*The Customer Relationship Management Survival Guide* by Dick Lee (High-Yield Marketing Press 2000). Starting by debunking CRM myths, discusses common misconceptions with CRM projects. A very direct, refreshing approach.

*The Loyalty Effect!* by Frederick Reichheld (Harvard Business School Press 1996). The classic book on the tangible benefits of customer loyalty.

*The Visual Display of Quantitative Information* by Edward Tufte (Graphics Press 2001, $2^{nd}$ edition). A classic treatise on making data "blindingly obvious" through clever graphing techniques. No CRM examples there, but lots of good inspiration.

# Analysts

Almost all analysts have a special study group for CRM, clearly accessible from their web site. Most web sites let you browse at will, including using more or less powerful search functions, but only short articles and press releases are readable at will; others require (pricey) purchase or membership.

- Aberdeen (www.aberdeen.com). Some reports are free, some require membership. There is a dedicated CRM area, as is the case for most analysts' sites.
- Forrester (www.forrester.com) Forrester uses the "wave" rather than Gartner's quadrants to classify vendors in categories. Only sketchy summaries are available for the fee-based reports.
- Gartner (www.gartner.com) An IT-influenced approach and their famous quadrants put vendors in neat categories that are useful to orient yourself to the field, although not necessarily to make your own

selection. Provides useful short articles to orient the user to the fee-based reports.

- Giga (www.gigaweb.com; don't use giga.com!) Fee-based articles only include a short summary so it's hard to decide what's in them on occasion.
- IDC (www.idc.com). Provides lots of information about market sizes and adoption rates.
- Meta Group (www.metagroup.com). Many articles are fee-based, although the abstracts are pretty clear and should help you decide which ones you are interested in. Free daily newsletter focused on CRM.

# Conferences

If you are a business user, most conferences focused on your business function include some CRM content, so check them first. The advantage of going to a functional conference is that the contents should be tailored to your specific functional needs. There are also CRM-specific events listed below. When selecting a conference, see whether it will include the type of information that you need, specifically:

- Presentations and demos from vendors, including the ones you are specifically interested in if you've already started looking.
- Information about business best practices, if they are of interest.
- Presentations by potential integrators.
- Case studies from similar businesses (so if you are a medium-size company, examples from very large organizations may not be as useful to you, and vice-versa; if you sell to consumers a B2B example is not as relevant, etc.).
- Networking with peers (business or IT owners) that have gone through or are going through similar decisions.

Here is a list of regular CRM-focused events. To find the current schedule, use your web search function to locate the appropriate web site:

- CRM Conference
- CRM Leadership Summit (DCI). Held in various venues throughout the U.S. and Europe. Targeted towards both business and IT owners.
- Gartner CRM Summit

# Glossary

**3-tier architecture**: an application architecture that separates user, business, and data services into three separate tiers to achieve better scalability and flexibility. The middle tier is the so-called application server, which handles the business logic and communicates with the database server. See client/server application.

**ACD**: see automatic call distributor.

**API**: see application programming interface.

**Application programming interface (API)**: a set of interfaces meant to facilitate the integration of a tool with other tools.

**Application software provider**: a vendor who provides business applications under a rental arrangement. The application could be developed specifically by the ASP to be available under a rental arrangement or could be available in a standard license package either from the same vendor or from another vendor who allows the ASP to run the application on its behalf (and who probably has similar arrangements with other ASPs). If the vendor functions as both an ASP and a traditional software vendor you may be able to migrate from a hosted model to a package model over time.

**ASP**: see application software provider.

**Automatic Call Distributor**: a piece of telephone equipment that handles incoming calls and distributes them among a set of agents. More sophisticated units allow the caller to route the call through a series of menus to the appropriate set of agents. ACDs can also report on the calls received, where they came from, and how many were abandoned (i.e., callers hung up).

**Availability**: a characteristic of a tool that makes it resilient to failures in the underlying systems. Although high availability is always desirable, it's also very expensive so that's a tradeoff that must be resolved by weighing the additional costs against the cost of a down system.

**Back-office application:** an application that handles "behind the scenes" work such as accounting, HR, or manufacturing. See front-office application.

**Breakeven**: in a ROI analysis, the point in time when the benefits from the investment balance out the cost.

**Business owner**: a manager or executive responsible for one of the business functions that is participating in the project. Business owners' acceptance and assistance is critical in the success of a CRM project. See executive sponsor.

**Campaign management**: the set of tools that are used to automate marketing campaigns.

**Case:** a single support or service issue, which may require several interactions to resolve. The basic unit in support-tracking systems.

**Case-based reasoning**: a way to resolve issues by reusing or adapting solutions created for similar issues in the past.

**CBR**: see case-based reasoning.

**Change management**: the set of activities required to implement successful change within an organization, in particular as it relates to people. Change management is often required for a CRM project.

**Chat**: a communication channel that allows instant messaging. In a CRM context, this occurs between a customer and a sales or support rep. It is typically initiated by the customer as an alternative to a phone call or an e-mail interaction.

**Client/server application**: an application that includes a back-end server that runs on a shared machine and a front-end client that lives on the user's computer. Older CRM tools perform as a client/server application.

**Computer-telephony integration**: a piece of software that allows the CRM system (or any other system) to exchange data and to coordinate with telephone equipment, typically an ACD. With CTI, you can route calls based on caller ID or menu choices chosen by the customer through the IVR interface. CTI allows you to do screen pops, painting the screen of the rep with the information gathered over the phone. CTI also allows you to dial phone numbers based on contact information in the database.

**Configuration**: the work required to transform an application from the out-of-the-box version to one that is tailored to the particular requirements of the organization. Also see personalization.

**CRM**: see customer relationship management.

**CTI**: see computer-telephony integration.

**Customer relationship management (CRM):** the set of processes and functions that surrounds the customer-oriented functions within the organization such as sales, marketing, and support. Also used to designate specifically the tools used for those functions.

**Customization:** the work required to transform an application from a vanilla application (pretty much as delivered, but with personalized data) to one that matches the processes and requirements of the organization. Customization usually requires skilled programming and results in changes that are readily apparent when compared to the vanilla version, whereas personalization is much easier and quicker. Customization can be extensive to the point that the finished product bears little resemblance to the vanilla application both in looks and in functionality. Also used to refer to the customized application itself. See personalization.

**Data migration**: the process of moving data in a meaningful manner from an old system to a new one. Data migration involves matching old fields to new fields, occasionally aggregating data from several systems, and processing information so it matches the new data model.

**Data model**: the kind of data stored in a database and the way the data is arranged. For instance, does the database think of customers as individuals or as organizations to which individuals belong? Does the database have a concept of one customer having different sites? Although most CRM systems allow changes to the data model, some changes may be difficult. For instance, if you wish to collect cell phone numbers for customers and the base data model doesn't allow it, it should be easy to add that field. On the other hand, if the CRM system thinks of customers as individuals and you think of them as organizations, the change may be difficult to impossible.

**Deployment**: the set of activities required to get the tool into the hands of the users in production mode. Deployment can occur over time if larger groups of users are involved. See rollout.

**Development environment**: the set of machines and systems where customizations and integrations are created. It's best to have a development environment that's separate from the testing environment, which itself is separate from the production environment. Smaller companies often make do with just one, but of course it means that any mistakes made in development will immediately have an effect on the production environment. See testing environment, production environment.

**Disconnected user:** a user such as a field sales or service rep who downloads information from the CRM system to a PC or other portable device, updates it while away from the office, and then uploads it back into the shared system. Disconnected usage calls for robust synchronization capabilities so the downloads and uploads can happen quickly and maintain data consistency even if multiple updates occurred.

**EAI:** see enterprise application integration.

**E-commerce:** a system that allows customers to conduct business transactions over the Internet in self-service mode. See e-sales.

**eCRM**: Electronic Customer Relationship Management. Used to designate systems that provide CRM functionality to the customer via a portal. See e-sales.

**E-mail response management**: functionality sometimes integrated into CRM tools that intelligently respond to customer e-mails by sending automatic replies and/or creating service requests within the CRM tool.

**Enterprise application integration (EAI)**: a technology that allows different applications to work with each other.

**Enterprise resource planning (ERP)**: a methodology and tools that automate procurement, manufacturing, and distribution functions. Typically seen as a back-office function.

**ERP:** see enterprise resource planning.

**E-marketing:** an application that allows organizations to reach customers online for marketing purposes. See e-commerce.

**E-sales:** an application that allows customers to make purchases in self-service mode. See e-commerce.

**Escalation:** used in support and service functions to mean either a case going from a level-1 rep to a more senior rep or a situation in which a customer, especially a corporate customer, requires dedicated management attention.

**Executive sponsor**: the individual who supports a project at the executive level, including "selling" it to the appropriate stakeholders, making sure that momentum is preserved, and helping to remove obstacles as they occur. The executive sponsor is usually not the project leader, except in smaller organizations. See project leader.

**Fixed price:** a way of pricing any project, but in particular a CRM implementation project, with a predetermined price based on a particular scope of work. See time and materials.

**Front-office application:** an application that automates the management of a function that relates to customers such as sales or service. See back-office application.

**High-end tool**: a tool with very rich functionality, extensive customization capabilities, and excellent scaling ability. High-end tools are costly and require significant time and resources to implement, but they afford the highest levels of functionality. See mid-range tool.

**History trail**: a feature that allows a tool to record all actions on a particular object, for instance, any changes of any kind to a knowledge base document.

**Implementation**: the process through which an application, including a CRM application, is installed, configured, customized, integrated with other applications, and then rolled out to the end-users. See customization, integration.

**Integration**: the work required to make data or screens that belong to one application accessible to another. Integration can be as simple as a recurring data download, or as slick as a real-time access from one application to the next, typically using data from the initial application (for instance, with a customer service issue on the screen, obtain the current status of the product defects reported by the customer and add comments to that entry). Also used to refer to the finished product of two or more applications functioning as a single application in some ways.

**Integrator**: an individual or company that focuses on implementing software solutions, either adapting packaged software licenses (most of the time) or creating them from scratch. Services delivered typically include project management as well as technical work (programming, system administration), and, very often, additional services such as change management, training, etc.

**Interactive voice response (IVR)**: a part of the telephone system that allows the caller to interact with data by making choices and entering data through their touch pad. Examples of uses of IVR include bank-by-phone systems, schedule-checking applications, and gathering routing input for an ACD system. IVRs were very popular before web portals came into being since they can perform similar functions, although in a much more limited manner since the information transferred needs to be short and the input device is limited.

**Internal rate of return:** the percentage of profits brought about by a new initiative, from an ROI analysis perspective.

**IRR**: see internal rate of return.

**IT owner**: the individual that represents IT management on the project. The IT owner is the counterpart of the business owners. See business owner.

**IVR**: see interactive voice response.

**Kickoff workshop:** a meeting of the entire project team that is used to create, validate, and approve the implementation requirements for a CRM project. This book advocates holding such a meeting to create requirements swiftly.

**Knowledge base:** a set of documents that relates to a particular topic. A good knowledge base is complete, accurate, easily searchable, and contains as few overlaps as possible. A knowledge base in and of itself is not necessarily automated or supported by a purpose-built tool, although these days most are.

**Knowledge management**: the set of processes used to maintain and augment the knowledge base. This includes creating and reviewing documents as well as ensuring that older or incorrect documents are removed or revised.

**Layered implementation**: an approach through which deliverables are carefully defined and scheduled so that functionality is delivered in stages that include complete solutions and add on to the previous ones. Layered implementations typically work with fairly short-term deliverables, 60 to 90 days each.

**Lead:** a potential customer, identified through a marketing program, who is not yet qualified to have real potential. See prospect.

**Logging:** the act of entering activities into a tracking system. Accurate logging of all activities is essential to get the full benefits of a CRM tool, in particular in the area of accurate metrics.

**Long list:** a list of potential CRM tools (or whatever else you're purchasing) that may fit the requirements you have for the project. See short list.

**Marketing automation**: the set of tools that automates marketing functions such as lead management and campaign management.

**Marketing encyclopedia**: the set of documents used by sales reps to work and close deals.

**Metric:** a set of quantitative measurements to report back on a business process.

**Mid-range tool:** a tool designed to deliver a solid but limited set of functionality, with limited customization capabilities and fairly good scaling capabilities. Mid-range tools are easier and faster to implement than high-end tools and are a good choice if you can live with the limits on functionality they come with. See high-end tool.

**Milestone:** a point in a project plan where something special happens, usually when a deliverable is met. The more tangible the milestones, the easier it is to monitor progress.

**Multichannel:** a characteristic of a system or a process that enables it to handle communications through more than one channel (a channel being the phone, e-mail, chat, etc.) in a way that integrates all the channels together. A system that processes e-mail in a totally different way from phone conversation, with the result that it's not possible to link a customer's phone interaction with the same customer's e-mail interaction would not be a good multi-channel system.

**New-wave CRM tool**: a newer CRM tool that offers a relatively small set of functionality, including key items and often some unique ones as well and that can be customized more easily than a traditional tool, although not as extensively. See traditional CRM tool for a different approach.

**OOB:** see out of the box.

**Out of the box**: a feature that comes with the tool, as opposed to a custom feature. Also called vanilla.

**Partner relationship management (PRM)**: similar to Customer Relationship Management, the set of processes and function to work with partners including sales, marketing, and support. Often used to designate exclusively the tools used for those functions.

**Payback period:** in an ROI analysis, the time it takes to recover your investment. The payback period always occurs after deployment and depends on how quickly benefits accrue compared to cost.

**Personalization**: the work required to transform an application from the out-of-the-box version to one that is usable including personalized values for drop-down lists, personalized messages, e-mail links, etc. Personalization is distinguished from customization in that it requires little work and no complex programming tasks. CRM applications are often unusable without the personalization work. Also used to refer to the finished product (the personalized application), which can be the finished product for the rollout. Most implementations use both personalization and customization. Also see configuration.

**Point solution**: a CRM tool that delivers functionality for one particular business function, or just one particular business problem. Point solutions need to be integrated with others for a complete system, but they have the potential to deliver much better functionality in the area they target compared to suites. See suite.

**Portal**: a web site that allows customers (who can be internal or external) to interact with the organization, and in particular with the CRM system.

**Post-mortem review**: a review of the entire project to determine what went well and what did not go well, with the goal of improving future similar efforts. Post-mortems are useful in CRM projects because they often have many phases so the outcome of the post-mortem can be immediately useful for the next phase.

**PRM**: see partner relationship management.

**Production environment**: the set of machines and systems that supports the end-users. It's best to have three separate environments for development, testing, and production, respectively, so the production environment is protected from any mishaps that can occur when making changes to the system. See development environment, testing environment.

**Production**: the state of the project where the end-users are using the system to do their daily work. In other words, production occurs at the end of the rollout period. See rollout.

**Project manager**: the individual who heads the project, including creating the project plan, managing day-to-day activities, and addressing issues as needed. See executive sponsor.

**Prospect**: a potential customer, who has passed some minimal qualification process. See lead.

**RAD**: see rapid application development.

**Rapid Application Development**: a methodology whereby multiple prototypes are created and tested immediately with the users until the desired goal is reached. RAD accelerates development projects by making sure developers get feedback early on.

**Request for Proposal**: a formal process to describe requirements (here, for a CRM tool, but that can be used for any other purchase) to a vendor and obtain a formal, written description of features together with a bid. Also used to designate the document itself. Chapter 6 gives an alternative method to the standard RFP process.

**Requirements**: a set of conditions that a tool must meet. The book refers to two different (but related) sets of requirements. One is the tool requirements, that are rather high level (aiming at functionality rather than specific screens) and are used to make tool selection. The other set are the implementation requirements, which are much more detailed and are used to customize the tool.

It's important to rank both sets of requirements to distinguish the key requirements from the others and to be able to prioritize various phases of the project.

**Return on investment (ROI)**: a financial analysis that gauges how the benefits created by a particular tool (or new plant, or whatever) surpass the initial investment. ROI is defined as the profits generated through the tool divided by the cost of the tool.

**RFP**: see request for proposal.

**ROI**: see return on investment.

**Rollout**: the period of time and the set of activities between the time the application is ready (complete and tested) and the time all users are actually using it. Typical rollout activities include setting up hardware, configuring the network, transferring data from the old system to the new system, and training the users. Depending on the scope of the project and the business environment, the rollout may occur within a brief window or over a long period of time if groups are brought to the project in a sequence.

**Sales force automation (SFA)**: the field of tools that are used to support the sales process.

**Scalability**: the ability of a tool to function with lots of users, and moreover to be extensible to more users through a simple mechanisms (e.g., adding more servers) as opposed to requiring a rearchitecture of the entire system. All systems hit a scalability barrier eventually, so it's really a matter of choosing one that will serve you for the present and the foreseeable future.

**Scope creep**: the phenomenon through which additional features and requirements are added to a project after initial requirements are defined and agreed upon. Scope creep can be dangerous since there's rarely an opportunity to do a complete review and replan of the project as features are added. It's also expensive.

**Self-learning knowledge base**: a knowledge base system that includes features that leverage usage into improving the knowledge base. Examples of self-learning features include simple things such as counting the number of hits against a particular document, all the way to clever analyses of unsuccessful searches.

**Service level agreement**: a set of commitments from one organization to another. Support groups typically have SLAs for their customers that define how issues should be reported and how quickly they will get a response.

**SFA**: see sales rorce automation.

**Short list**: a list of CRM tools that have been verified to meet your requirements, at least to a fairly good degree. You get a short list by analyzing the strengths and weaknesses of the candidates on the long list. See long list.

**SLA**: see service level agreement.

**Suite**: a set of integrated tools that support several different business functions (sales, marketing, service and support). Suite products have the advantage of being pre-integrated, but may not provide so-called best-of-breed functionality for each business function. See point solution.

**Super-user**: an end-user for the project that has the special role of advising the project team, including defining the detailed business processes, creating use cases, and participating in the testing and training. See use case.

**TCO**: see total cost of ownership.

**Terms and conditions** (Ts and Cs): the legal description of how a particular service will be rendered.

**Testing environment**: the set of machines and systems where testing is performed. It's best to have three separate environments for development, testing, and production, respectively. If you must, you can collapse the development and testing environments. See development environment, production environment.

**Thick client**: in a client/server model, the piece of software that resides on the client machine. Contrast with a thin client of 3-tier architectures.

**Thin client:** a client, usually web-based, that accesses both data and the application code through an application server in a three-tier architecture. Contrast with standard client/server applications.

**Third party**: in a CRM project, a vendor that is not the tool vendor. Integrators are almost always third parties.

**Three Ps**: the three Ps, people, process, and politics, are the most common causes of failure in CRM projects. The tool itself, although often blamed, is usually no more than a contributing factor, if it is a factor at all.

**Time and materials:** a way of pricing any project, but in particular a CRM implementation project, based on hourly fees for each of the participants. See fixed price.

**Total cost of ownership (TCO)**: the sum of all the costs associated to a tool, including not only out-of-pocket expenses such as the cost of the software, but also the costs related to supporting and maintaining the tool.

**Traditional CRM tool**: an older CRM tool that has lots of features, offers many customization and integration opportunities, but is harder to use and to customize. See new-wave CRM tool for a different approach.

**Ts and Cs**: see terms and conditions.

**Usability:** the quality of a tool that makes it easy to use, efficient, and effective for the end-user. Usability greatly increases user adoption, hence the overall success of a CRM project.

**Use cases**: a set of test cases to test functionality in a tool. A single use case describes one particular task that would be taken by an end-user to accomplish a specific business goal.

**Vanilla**: a feature that comes with the tool, as opposed to a custom feature. Also called OOB (out of the box).

**Vertical**: a tool that specifically targets a particular industry segment such as health care, financial services, government, etc., as opposed to a general-purpose tool.

**Voice over IP (VoIP)**: a technology through which conversations can be carried through computers (equipped with microphones and speakers) as if over the phone.

**VoIP**: see voice over IP.

**Warranty:** a legally binding agreement to remedy issues for a set period after the sale. For CRM systems, warranties last a few months and typically include a commitment to fix problems (bugs) rather than provide a money-back arrangement.

**Workflow-based system:** a system that takes work items through a multi-step process, typically through predefined groups of users that each handle a particular step in the process.

**Workforce management**: a tool that facilitates scheduling and forecasting staffing in a contact center.

# Index

## Numerics
3 Ps 358
3-tier architecture 127, 349

## A
Account management
    By tool vendor 219
    CRM functionality 145
ACD 132, 349
Alert
    As support deliverable 234
    For knowledge creation 139
    In sales cycle 144
    Proactive for customers 142, 292
    To handle customer surveys 325
    Use for training 281
    Wireless 135
Analysts 168
Analytics 6, 142, 235
    Integration with analytics system 128
API 18, 128, 349
Application programming interface 349
Application software provider 349
ASP
    And evaluations 188
    As a cost-cutting strategy 76
    Benefits 176
    Cons 177
    Cost 40
    Definition 349
    Dual model 124
    Examples 179
    Implementation 241
    Maintenance 221
    Pricing adjustments 218
    Termination fee 218
    Upgrades 219
    Vs. package 176
Audit
    During implementation 243
    Of CRM tool 21
    Performance 45
Automatic call distributor 349
Availability 127, 142, 350

## B
Babushka metrics 311
Back-office application
    Definition 350
    Integrating with 10, 174
Benefits of CRM
    Business intelligence 6, 8, 300
    Cost savings 6
    Customer loyalty 6
    Customer satisfaction 6, 303
    Employee satisfaction 7, 303
    For customers 292
    Internal accountability 7
    Profits 7

Breakeven 350
Budget
    As part of the requirements 149
    For a restarted project 340
Business intelligence 8
Business owner
    As part of the team 79
    Definition 350
    Level laddering 90
    Requirements 89
    Resources for 344, 345, 346
    Role 88
    Time requirements 89

### C

Campaign management 4, 144, 350
Case
    Aging 323
    Attribute 146
    Creation 146
    Definition 350
Case-based reasoning 141, 350
CBR 350
Change management 239, 251, 350
Chat 5, 43, 135, 350
Checklist
    Creating an ROI analysis 228
    Integrator reference check 256
    Integrator requirements 250
    Integrator Ts and Cs 261
    Metrics 317
    Tool reference check 209
    Tool requirements 150
    Tool RFP 193
    Tool Ts and Cs 216
Client/server 350
Collaboration 145, 147, 171, 179, 233
Complexity
    And cost 74
    And integrator requirements 64, 66, 68
    And kickoff workshop 271
    And time requirements 61
    And vendor meetings 183
    Factors 61
    High 67
    Low 63
    Medium 66
    Minimizing 75
    Project management 50
Computer-telephony integration 351
Configuration 351
Configurator 4, 292
Contact management 144
Cost
    Adjusting with usage 217
    And project complexity 74
    As a decision factor 149
    Discounts 222
    Fixed price 260
    For ROI 228
    Integrator 254
    License 73
    Maintenance 40
    Support and maintenance 73
    Training 74
    Travel 262
CRM
    Definition 2, 351
    Failures 12
    Process 27
CRM resources
    Books 346
    Conferences 348
    Magazines 346
    Market analysts 347
    Web sites 343
CRM suite 16, 174, 358
CRM tool
    And project failures 334
    ASP 176
    Categories 170

Index    363

CRM suite 16, 174, 358
Discounts 222
Evaluating 180
Evaluation copy 188
High-end 353
Homegrown 44
Mid-range 75, 355
Names 178
New wave 172, 355
Point solution 175, 355
Traditional 170, 359
Vertical 175, 359
CTI 4, 132, 351
Customer
    Benefits 292
    Loyalty 6
    Promoting the tool 292
Customer database 5, 17, 62, 137, 277
Customer portal 5, 31, 44, 133, 356
Customer satisfaction
    As a benefit of CRM 303
    Metrics 325
    Surveys 147, 307, 308, 326
Customization 351
    And ASPs 176
    And new-wave tools 173
    And traditional tools 171
    And upgrades 121
    And vertical tools 175
    Cost 41
    Definition 17, 351
    Minimizing 56, 67
    Vendor guidelines 243

### D
Data availability 142, 306
Data migration 276, 351
Data model 17, 137, 351
Defect tracking 147

Demo
    Cool 42
    In conferences 120
    In webinars 120
    Requesting a meaningful demo 187
    With references 206, 214
Deployment 351
Development environment 129, 275, 352
Disconnected usage 3, 135, 145, 352

### E
EAI 352
E-commerce 134, 352
eCRM 5, 352
Email integration 133
Email management 352
Email processing 36, 50, 133
Email utilities 133
E-marketing 5, 352
Employee satisfaction 7, 303, 308
End-user 358
    Involvement 56, 289
    Training 74, 199, 239, 252, 265, 281
Enterprise Application Integration 352
Enterprise resource planning 352
ERP 352
E-sales 5, 352
Escalation 130, 147, 205, 233, 352
E-support 5
Evaluation
    Checking integrator references 256
    Checking tool references 203
    Hard questions for vendors 188
    Integrator 249
    Integrator vs. tool 241
    ROI 228
    Scoring 191
    Tool checklist 150
    Tool vendors 180

Executive sponsor
  And failing projects 337
  As part of the team 79
  Definition 353
  Delegating 83
  Requirements 81
  Role 80
  Time requirements 83
  Transition 83

▶ **F**
Failures
  And availability 127
  And large projects 49
  And tool vendors 241
  Handling 332
  Minimizing 72
  Vs. problems 294
Field service 5, 147
Fixed price 260, 353
Forecasting tools 145
Front-office application 353

▶ **G**
Gap analysis 267
Goals
  Counterproductive 306
  Defining 58, 266, 300
  Using to set priorities 118

▶ **H**
History trail 147, 353

▶ **I**
Implementation
  And tool vendor 148, 287
  Complex project 248
  Cost 73

Data migration 276
Definition 353
Development environment 275
Gap analysis 274
Handling problems 294
Kickoff workshop 265
Layered model 50, 72, 75, 354
Medium project 247
Milestone 285
Non-technical activities 238
Overview 264
Post-mortem 296
Project plan 268
Rapid application development 356
Requirements 147
Rollout 283
Schedule 61, 148
Simple project 245, 246
Status report 286
Success factors 49
Test environment 275
Testing 277
Training 280
Integration
  As vision 10
  CRM suite 16
  Definition 353
  Effort required 15
  Politics 16
  Requirements 128, 137
  Time required 15
Integrator
  Care and feeding 287
  Certified 244
  Cost 254
  Definition 353
  Evaluating 254
  Experience 253
  Finding 248
  Fixed price 260
  Liability insurance 262

Methodology 250
Mixing and matching 243
Negotiating 259
References 254
Small 249
Switching 338
Technical expertise 252
Third party 358
Ts and Cs 261
Vendor vs. third party 241
When to start selection 240
Why you need one 239
Integrator selection 249
Checking references 256
Long list 249
Negotiating 259
Requirements 250
Interactive voice response 353
Internal rate of return 354
Internationalization 143
IRR 354
IT
Relationship with integrator 101
Role in CRM projects 19, 101
IT owner
As part of the team 79
Definition 354
Requirements 97
Resources for 345, 346
Role 96
Time requirements 98
IVR 353

### K
Kickoff workshop
Agenda 269
Attendance 270
Breakout sessions 273
Define project goals 266
Definition 354
Gap analysis 267
Keeping records 275
Leader 272
Length 270
Objectives 266
Project plan 268
Start with a demo 267
Venue 272
Knowledge base 5, 29, 37, 134, 354
Permissions 141
Productivity 324
Searching 37, 140
Self-learning 139, 357
Usage metrics 327
Knowledge management 29, 37, 138, 354

### L
Lead 354
Liability insurance 262
Logging 354
Encouraging 307
Long list 354
Integrator 249
Tool 166, 167
Using analysts 168

### M
Maintenance
Cost 224
Customizations vs. upgrades 67, 189, 199, 243
Vendor policy 148, 219
Market analysts 168, 347
Marketing
Encyclopedia 145, 354
Metrics 312
Requirements 144
Marketing automation
Definition 4, 354

Requirements 144
Resources 344
Meetings
    Productive 85
    Vendor demos 187
    With tool vendors 182
Metrics
    As success factor 29, 39, 58
    Babushka-style 311
    Categories 301
    Characteristics of good metrics 302
    Customer satisfaction 308, 325
    Dangers of averages 310
    Dashboard 314
    Data availability 142, 306
    Definition 355
    Delivery 316
    Distribution 143
    For intangibles 303
    Knowledge base productivity 324
    Knowledge base usage 327
    Lead-generation analysis 318
    Logging 307
    Marketing 312
    Operational 304
    Proxies 304
    Requirements 142
    Sales 313
    Sales pipeline 320
    Sales productivity 321
    Slice and dice 311
    Strategic 304
    Strategy 328
    Subscriptions 316
    Support 313
    Support case aging 323
    Support financials 326
    Support issue distribution 322
    Support productivity 321
    Telesales productivity 319
    Templates 142
    Top 10 support customers 327
    Why they matter 300
Milestone
    Definition 355
    In integrator contract 261
    Signoff 286
    Using 285
Monitoring tools 6
Morale
    At kickoff workshop 273
    In failing projects 333
    Maintaining 50, 85
Multichannel
    Definition 355
    Support 136

▸ **N**

Negotiating
    Hardball techniques 227
    Tool contract 215
    Tool price 222
    With integrators 259
Nondisclosure 195, 262

▸ **O**

OOB 355
Opportunity management 144
Out of the box 355

▸ **P**

Partner relationship management 355
Payback period 355
People
    And project failures 335
    As success factor 13
    Business owner 88
    Executive sponsor 80
    IT owner 96

Project manager 84
Super-user 91
Technical staffer 99
Performance
　And ASPs 177
　And tool adoption 45
　Audit 34
　Load testing 280
　Requirements 127
　Using references to check 203
Personalization 5, 17, 355
Phone integration 132
Point solution 175, 355
Politics 13, 80, 247, 332
Portal 356
Post-mortem 86, 296, 356
PRM 355
Process
　Analysis 130, 238, 274
　As success factor 14
　For a restarted project 340
Production 356
Production environment 129, 275, 356
Productivity
　Knowledge base 324
　Sales 321
　Support 321
　Telesales 319
Project issues
　And executive sponsor 337
　And people 335
　And processes 335
　And tool 335
　Assessing 333
　Changing requirements 49
　Complexity 50, 61
　Failure 332
　Integrator 338
　Morale 333
　Politics 49
　Root cause 332
　Salvaging 337
　Scope creep 357
　When to give up 296
Project manager
　And project failures 339
　And the kickoff workshop 272
　As part of the team 79
　Assessing failures 333
　Checking tool references 208
　Debriefing after vendor meetings 186
　Definition 356
　Keeping records 180
　Preparing vendor meetings 186
　Record keeping 275
　Requirements 86
　Role 84
　Status report 286
　Time requirements 87
Project team 78
Prospect 356

## R

RAD 356
Rapid application development 251, 356
Record keeping 180, 275
Request for Proposal 356
Requirements
　Account management 145
　Budget 149, 164
　Business rules 146
　Case Creation 146
　Collaboration 147
　Contact management 144
　Cross-functional 132
　Customer satisfaction survey 147
　Defect tracking 147
　Disconnected usage 145
　Escalation 147
　Field service 147

## INDEX

Forecasting tools 145
Functional 129, 152
Gathering 116
History trail 147
How detailed? 115
Implementation 147, 163, 250, 356
Maintenance 147, 163
Marketing automation 144
Opportunity management 144
Ranking 117
SFA 144
Support tracking 146
Technical 124, 151
Tool 113, 150, 356
Vendor 122, 151
Why create them? 114
Workflow support 146
Resources
    Large project 110
    Medium project 107
    Simple project 103, 105
    Team 77
RFP
    Alternative 181
    Benefits 180
    Definition 356
    Sample 193
    Streamlined process 181
    Weaknesses 180
ROI
    Benefits 230
    For customer portals 31
    In reference checks 214
    Internal rate of return 354
    Payback period 355
    Preparing a ROI analysis 228
    Realistic? 235
Rollout
    Definition 357
    Strategies 283
    Success factors 284

Routing 146
Rule 146

### S

Sales
    Metrics 313
    Requirements 144
    Resources 344
Sales force automation 3, 357
Scalability 127, 357
Schedule 61
    For a restarted project 340
    Typical 61
Scope creep 49, 52, 357
Security 133
Service level agreement 357
SFA
    Definition 3, 357
    requirements 144
    Resources 344
Short list 358
    Creating 167, 190
    Definition 358
Signoff 286
Site license 224
SLA
    Definition 357
    Enforced by CRM tool 7
    Metrics 321
    With tool vendor 148
Standards
    In tools 174
    IT 96, 126
    UI 173
Status report 286
Success factors
    Availability of technical resources 101
    Executive sponsor 80
    For rollout 284

Get users involved 56
Measure success 58
Stay in the box 52
Think small, dream big 49
Super-user
   As part of the team 79
   Definition 358
   Handling dissenters 94
   Requirements 92
   Role 91, 289
   Time requirements 95
   Top performer 57
Support
   From tool vendor 219
   Metrics 313
   Requirements 146
   Resources 345
Synchronization
   Data 137, 284
   Disconnected usage 145, 247, 308

### T

TCO 358
Team 78
Technical staffer
   As part of the team 79
   Requirements 101
   Role 99
   Time requirements 102
Terms and conditions 358
Test environment 275
Testing
   Functionality 279
   Load testing 280
   Strategy 277
   Use case 277
Testing environment 129, 358
Thick client 6, 126, 358
Thin client 5, 126, 358

Third party
   Definition 358
   Vs. vendor 241
Three Ps 12, 334
Time and materials 358
Timeline
   Complex project 67
   Compressing 69
   Medium project 66
   Simple project 63
   Vendor estimates 70
Tool kit 16, 171
Tool selection
   Checking references 203
   Hard questions for vendors 188
   Long list 166, 167
   Negotiating the contract 215
   RFP 180
   Short list 167, 190
Tool vendor
   Account management 219
   Business vision 124
   Discounts 222
   During implementation 287
   Geographical presence 124
   Hard questions 188
   Implementation assistance 221
   Implementation audit 243
   Implementation estimates 70
   Maintenance 148
   Mergers 45, 122
   Names 178
   Pricing model 224
   Product demos 187
   References 123, 203
   Salvaging a project 339
   Setting productive meetings 182
   Site license 224
   Support 148, 219
   Technical vision 124
   User group 190, 227

Viability 123
Training
    Audit 36
    Contents 280
    Cost 74
    Creating 281
    Delivering 282
    End-user 74, 239, 265
    Self-paced 36, 283
Ts and Cs
    Checklist 216
    Definition 358
    Integrator 261
    Negotiating 215
    Site license 224

### U
Universal queue 136
Usability 31, 33, 359
Use case
    Creating 91, 278
    Definition 359
    Example 277
User adoption 33, 290
User group 41, 190, 196, 207, 213, 227

### V
Vertical 359
Voice over IP 359
VoIP 136, 359

### W
Warranty 148, 218, 359
Wireless support 135
Workflow
    Definition 359
    For case management 146
    For contact management 144
    For knowledge creation 138
    For support 146
    Modifying 18, 53, 129
Workforce management 6, 359

# informIT

www.informit.com

## YOUR GUIDE TO IT REFERENCE

### Articles

Keep your edge with thousands of free articles, in-depth features, interviews, and IT reference recommendations – all written by experts you know and trust.

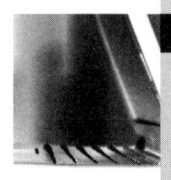

### Online Books

Answers in an instant from **InformIT Online Book's** 600+ fully searchable on line books. Sign up now and get your first 14 days **free**.

POWERED BY
Safari

### Catalog

Review online sample chapters, author biographies and customer rankings and choose exactly the right book from a selection of over 5,000 titles.

# Wouldn't it be great

if the world's leading technical publishers joined forces to deliver their best tech books in a common digital reference platform?

They have. Introducing **InformIT Online Books powered by Safari.**

- **Specific answers to specific questions.**
InformIT Online Books' powerful search engine gives you relevance-ranked results in a matter of seconds.

- **Immediate results.**
With InformIt Online Books, you can select the book you want and view the chapter or section you need immediately.

- **Cut, paste and annotate.**
Paste code to save time and eliminate typographical errors. Make notes on the material you find useful and choose whether or not to share them with your work group.

- **Customized for your enterprise.**
Customize a library for you, your department or your entire organization. You only pay for what you need.

## Get your first 14 days FREE!

InformIT Online Books is offering its members a 10 book subscription risk-free for 14 days. Visit **http://www.informit.com/onlinebooks** for details.

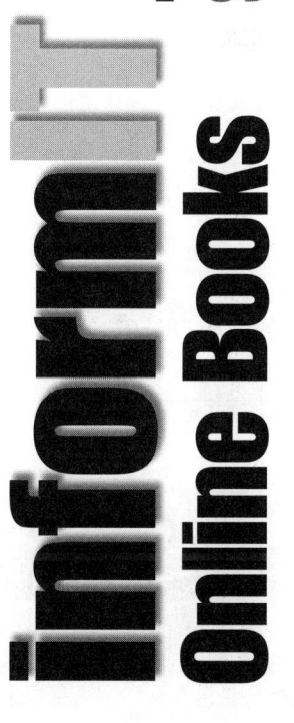

POWERED BY Safari

informit.com/onlinebooks

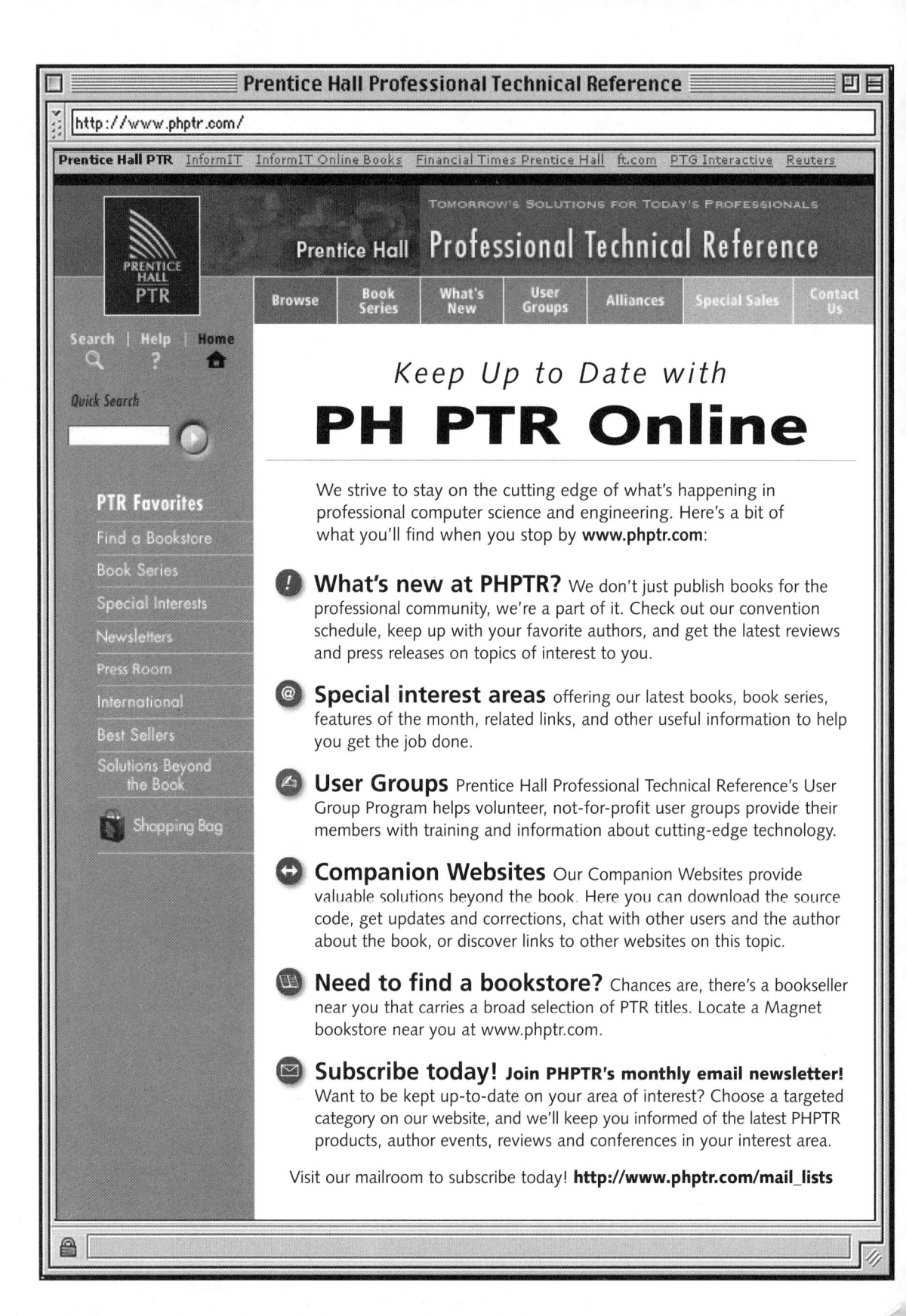

**Prentice Hall PTR** InformIT InformIT Online Books Financial Times Prentice Hall ft.com PTG Interactive Reuters

TOMORROW'S SOLUTIONS FOR TODAY'S PROFESSIONALS

**Prentice Hall Professional Technical Reference**

Browse | Book Series | What's New | User Groups | Alliances | Special Sales | Contact Us

Search | Help | Home

*Quick Search*

**PTR Favorites**
Find a Bookstore
Book Series
Special Interests
Newsletters
Press Room
International
Best Sellers
Solutions Beyond the Book
Shopping Bag

*Keep Up to Date with*

# PH PTR Online

We strive to stay on the cutting edge of what's happening in professional computer science and engineering. Here's a bit of what you'll find when you stop by **www.phptr.com**:

**What's new at PHPTR?** We don't just publish books for the professional community, we're a part of it. Check out our convention schedule, keep up with your favorite authors, and get the latest reviews and press releases on topics of interest to you.

**Special interest areas** offering our latest books, book series, features of the month, related links, and other useful information to help you get the job done.

**User Groups** Prentice Hall Professional Technical Reference's User Group Program helps volunteer, not-for-profit user groups provide their members with training and information about cutting-edge technology.

**Companion Websites** Our Companion Websites provide valuable solutions beyond the book. Here you can download the source code, get updates and corrections, chat with other users and the author about the book, or discover links to other websites on this topic.

**Need to find a bookstore?** Chances are, there's a bookseller near you that carries a broad selection of PTR titles. Locate a Magnet bookstore near you at www.phptr.com.

**Subscribe today! Join PHPTR's monthly email newsletter!** Want to be kept up-to-date on your area of interest? Choose a targeted category on our website, and we'll keep you informed of the latest PHPTR products, author events, reviews and conferences in your interest area.

Visit our mailroom to subscribe today! **http://www.phptr.com/mail_lists**